NORTH AMERICA'S GALAPAGOS

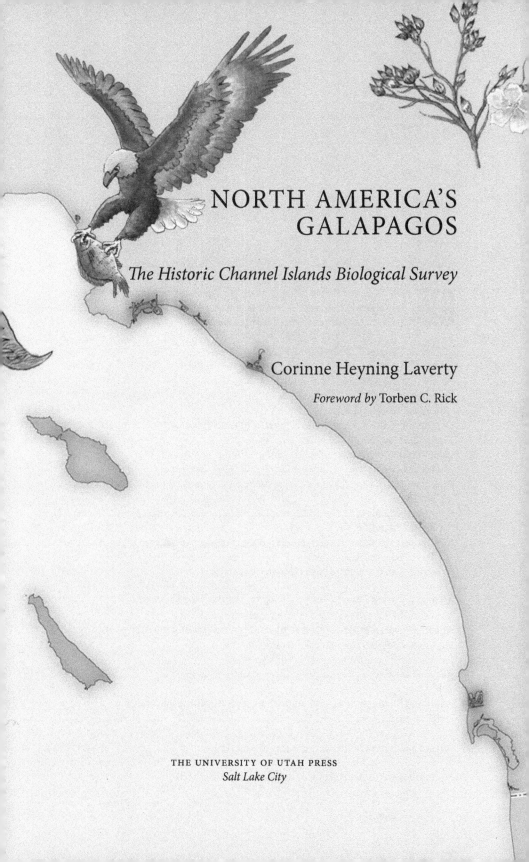

NORTH AMERICA'S GALAPAGOS

The Historic Channel Islands Biological Survey

Corinne Heyning Laverty

Foreword by Torben C. Rick

THE UNIVERSITY OF UTAH PRESS
Salt Lake City

The Defiance House Man colophon is a registered trademark of The University of Utah Press. It is based on a four-foot-tall Ancient Puebloan pictograph (late PIII) near Glen Canyon, Utah.

Library of Congress Cataloging-in-Publication Data

Names: Laverty, Corinne Heyning, author.
Title: North America's Galapagos : the historic Channel Islands biological survey / Corinne Heyning Laverty.
Description: Salt Lake City : The University of Utah Press, [2019] | Includes bibliographical references and index.
Identifiers: LCCN 2019013315 (print) | LCCN 2019014063 (ebook) | ISBN 9781607817307 () | ISBN 9781607817291 (pbk. : alk. paper)
Subjects: LCSH: Channel Islands Biological Survey (1939-1941) | Ecological surveys—California—Channel Islands. | Natural resources—California—Channel Islands. | Channel Islands (Calif.)—Antiquities. | Excavations (Archaeology)—California—Channel Islands.
Classification: LCC QH541.15.S95 (ebook) | LCC QH541.15.S95 L39 2019 (print) | DDC 577.072309794/91—dc23
LC record available at https://lccn.loc.gov/2019013315

All drawings created by Cypress Hansen, Tree by the Sea Design, https://treebytheseadesign.wixsite.com/treebytheseadesign
All calligraphy created by Alfredo Chiappini, Odyssey Maps and Calligraphy, http://www.odysseymapsandcalligraphy.com/
Portrait of the Lone Woman, oil by Holli Harmon.
All maps created by Chelsea Feeney, www.cmcfeeney.com

Errata and further information on this and other titles available online at UofUpress.com

Printed and bound in the United States of America.

Frontispiece: Artistic depiction of the eight Channel Islands

For Marlene and Nico. You stood by me through every-thing—even this. I am humbled by your faith in me and cherish our love.

Boileau said that Kings, Gods and Heroes only were fit sub-jects for literature. The writer can only write about what he admires. Present-day kings aren't very inspiring, the gods are on vacation and about the only heroes left are the scientists and the poor.

—John Steinbeck, 1939

CONTENTS

ACKNOWLEDGMENTS

A project like this is made possible because of the records maintained within institutions that believe the past has a place in the present. This preservation is vital because our understanding of history is affected by experience and tainted by fading memories, stereotypes, and ideologies. Collections such as those I used in writing this book allow each of us the opportunity to interpret and reinterpret the past and to collectively develop a shared understanding of it. Likewise, in significant ways, the collections the Channel Islands Biological Survey participants made over eighty years ago are helping to demystify history while contributing to a better understanding of the present and our future.

John Heyning did not know of this book, but his joyous embracement of life and his love of science was the inspiration for it. My gratitude starts with him.

I'm often asked why I wrote this book. To answer that, I have to thank Cathy McNassor, former archivist for the Natural History Museum of Los Angeles County (NHM). It was Cathy who steered me toward a set of dusty boxes labeled "Channel Islands Biological Survey 1939–1941," and said, "You should write that book. It's important." I am grateful to Cathy for her suggestion and wish she were alive to see this book in print.

It is important that I acknowledge the First People of North America. The account of how their ancestors arrived at this wonderful country and thrived on the Channel Islands constitutes an integral part of this story. The deeper my investigation went, the more my admiration for them grew. I hope my efforts honor them and their descendants.

During my years of research, I grew very fond of all the individuals who participated in the Channel Islands Biological Survey. I am happy to have gotten to know Jack Couffer, who breathed life into this story, and to have met Ken Stager numerous times. The others? I so I wish I could have met them personally. I strove to faithfully portray them as best I could, and if I erred, I am sorry.

While searching for a Channel Islands archaeologist to review my manuscript, Jenn Perry suggested I reach out to Mike Glassow. I had never met Mike and felt nervous about approaching a highly regarded researcher and complete stranger with my time-consuming request, but Mike put me at ease by immediately agreeing to help. His generosity will come as no surprise to those who know him. I have come to think of Mike as the godfather of Channel Islands archaeological research—not only because many of his students have gone on to become respected archaeologists themselves, but also because over the last few decades he has made steady and important progress in our understanding of the habitation of the Channel Islands. Mike was my compass, my mattock, my trowel, brush, and sieve. He generously read and reread my manuscript, supplied me with information and scientific articles, and corrected and gently directed me. His unwavering help gave me the confidence to explore concepts and ideas about which I knew nothing. I am indebted to Mike for his critiques and thoughtful guidance.

Along with Mike, Barbara Peterson carefully read and edited my manuscript. She also rolled up her sleeves and helped me dig into those dusty archives. More important, her eager anticipation of each new chapter kept me focused and working. I am thankful to Barbara for sticking this out with me.

To the staff at NHM, my appreciation goes beyond a mutual history grounded in shared friendships. Chris Coleman held the key to what became one of the most important parts of this book. He introduced me to Art Woodward's journals and generously shared them with me. Kim Walters helped me navigate through uncharted research endeavors, as did Richard Hulser, Yolanda Bustos, and Vicky Brown. Jim Dines reviewed large parts of my manuscript and patiently walked me through taxonomy—more than once, I'm afraid. Kimball Garrett also provided feedback on portions of this book and welcomed my participation in a bird skinning session. Kirk Fitzhugh invited me to give a talk to the museum's scientists, the most intimidating audience I will ever face, and Greg Pauley befriended me at overwhelming scientific conferences. Always ready to help were Dave Janiger, Brian Brown, and Xiaoming Wang. I would like to thank Grace Cabrera, Martha Garcia, Lindsey Groves,

Margaret Hardin, Tom Jacobson, Maria Ponce, and Tom Sitton for their assistance. I extend my special appreciation to Jane Pisano, Lori Bettison-Varga, Dick Volpert, Jim Gilson, and Luis Chiappe.

Torrey Rick of the Smithsonian patiently and regularly answered my emails and fed me research papers. He also allowed me to barge into his office for a good long chat one day and then sent me straight to Reba Rauch and the University of Utah Press. Much later, he and Amy Gusick from the NHM reviewed my manuscript for that same press, providing critiques, thought provoking commentary, and insights that helped better develop the larger story this book tells. Amy also donated big chunks of her time, shared her contacts, and helped me navigate some sticky wickets. She proved a sharp and able editor with a big-picture vision of what this book is and could be. I thank Amy and Torrey for their contributions and able direction.

During the research phase of this book (which never really ended), I depended on the kindness and cooperation of a great many professionals to cover so much ground. With no idea who I was, they showed remarkable willingness to answer my phone calls and emails. These conversations usually started with a single question, but quickly grew to many. More than that, their interest and enthusiasm for my project spurred me onward. I extend a very special debt of gratitude to Paul Collins and John Johnson of the Santa Barbara Museum of Natural History for their ongoing support covering a wide range of topics. They never let me down. In large and small ways, others who provided guidance include Rich Bark, Lisa Thomas, Todd Braje, Jon Erlandson, Kate Faulkner, Kristina Gill, Helen Haase, Ann Houston, Robert Hunt Jr., Ray Ingersoll, Steve Junak, Joe Kane, Annie Little, David Mazurkiewicz, Jim I. Mead, Don Morris, Jim Patton, Jennifer Perry, Jerry Powell, Steve Schwartz, Sara Schwebel, Robert Timm, Dirk van Vuren, Andy Yatsko, an anonymous reviewer, and all of the researchers whose papers I read. Despite the manuscript undergoing several rigorous scientific reviews, if there are factual errors herein, I accept them as being entirely my own.

I thank Jack Couffer for contributing his photographs and firsthand account of the survey. His youthful participation breathed life into this book, as did Holli Harmon's lovely and historically accurate portrait of the Lone Woman. Cypress Hansen's and Fredo Chiappini's creativity enlivened the maps in this book, turning them into treasures. The fun we had collaborating was an unexpected joy.

Among the institutions I accessed and wish to thank for their material stewardship are the Autry Museum of the American West, Los Angeles County Kenneth Hall of Administration, Manhattan Beach Branch Library, Museum of Vertebrate Zoology, National Archives Art Archives of American Art Smithsonian Institution, Natural History Museum of Los Angeles County, Santa Barbara Museum of Natural History, Santa Cruz Island Foundation, Tucson Arizona Historical Society, University of California Irvine, Special Collections and Archives, University of Hawaii at Manoa Library, Hawaiian Collection, University of Southern California Libraries Special Collections, and Western Foundation of Vertebrate Zoology. To make the most of these records, I am grateful for the help of Jennifer Albin, Bruce Crouchet, Mimi Damwyk, Christina Fidler, Jessica Gambling, Linnea S. Hall, Lisa Josephs, Myka Kielbon, Julia Kim, Steve MacLeod, Dore Minatodani, Claire Moore, Suzanne Noruschat, Derek Quezada, Terri Sheridan, Jim Turner, and others.

Early on, Judy Perlstein read my fledgling draft and hosted NHM fellows in her home to hear about the Channel Islands Biological Survey. The interest I felt from this group fed my efforts. I received feedback and encouragement from Ann Hood, Helen Schulman, and Les Standiford. Rand Cooper inspired me to dig where I was afraid to dig and helped me organize the theme of this book, namely the peopling of North America. Practically every day, I consulted either directly with Marla Daily of the Santa Cruz Island Foundation or *Islapedia*, the website she created. Marla's accessibility helped me enormously during the writing of this book, and her lifelong devotion to historical research inspires me. The interest and encouragement of many friends, family members, and others whose hopes for my finished project made we want to live up to their expectations include: Sonja Adams, Lisa Brown, the California Historical Society and Heyday Press, Cheryl Gage, Janet Hurley, Kristine King, Rory and Jess Laverty, Nancy and Jim Miller, Bonnie Rowan, Katherine Schipper, Gayle Wattawa, Carla Sprang, and Drew Webb. Gloria and Hugo Henriquez provided special help in making this book a reality, and Bari Brandwynne, Robert Matt, and George Morales kept me sane and maintained. I am grateful to Daniel Buchmeier for jumping in to help me develop the WWII story within the epigraphs, and to Molly Laverty for assisting with the Spanish language. Additionally, I am indebted to Deborah Burghardt, whose early close reading and critique of this manuscript helped it come to fruition. In memoriam, I wish to acknowledge Emmanuel Rosales's wholehearted encouragement.

Reba Rauch believed in this project long before it reached its final form, and calmly and ably guided me toward the finish line. I am also grateful for the efforts of Hannah Katherine New, Dianne Lee Van Dien, Jessica Booth, Kelly Neumann, and others at University of Utah Press for their guidance and assistance in making this book the best it could be.

I am forever indebted to my mother, who instilled in me a lifelong love for nature.

Finally, my husband, Rocky, who not only gave me permission to follow my dreams, but said I must. He hiked island trails; accompanied me to museums, meetings, and lectures; listened intently to my musings; and never once allowed any outcome other than this a place at our table. I thank him for his unwavering confidence and tender devotion. I thank you, my love, for nearly everything.

FOREWORD

The nineteenth to mid-twentieth centuries saw an increase in new natural history museums and heightened public awareness of their importance around the world. A hallmark of these early museums was global collecting expeditions to obtain specimens for research and exhibition and ultimately build the core collections of the world's museums. Although often rooted in colonialism and not without considerable social baggage, these expeditions resulted in collections of great benefit to science and society. Many of these early collections continue to form the basis for research today and contain significant natural history and cultural objects from important time periods of earth's history.

A driver of museum collecting expeditions was the fact that many museum professionals and collectors viewed themselves in a race against time. During the eighteenth and nineteenth centuries, the planet was changing quickly, scores of species had never been described, and charismatic organisms were being pushed to the brink of extinction, including bison, whales, seals, passenger pigeons, and many more. Similarly, globalization, the westward expansion, and colonialism were transforming many indigenous peoples as introduced disease, forced land claims, and other factors pushed their lifeways to the brink. Fast-forward to the twenty-first century and our planet again finds itself in peril as we confront the accelerating challenges of climate change, widespread extinction, and affronts to human cultural diversity around the world. All of these factors are components of the Anthropocene or "age of humans" that we are now living in.

Despite the importance of collecting expeditions for natural history museums, relatively few books have explored the history of museum collecting expeditions in order to evaluate their outcomes, benefits, and problems (e.g., cultural appropriation). Enter Corinne Heyning Laverty's excellent book on the 1939–1941 Los Angeles County Museum's Channel

Islands Biological Survey (CIBS). Conducted immediately before the United States entered World War II, the CIBS was an ambitious collecting expedition that focused on the eight California Channel Islands, a chain often called North America's Galapagos. This book provides context for those expeditions and highlights their value to science and society.

The CIBS is an expedition that is well known to those of us who work on the Channel Islands—for its ambitions, the interesting discoveries it made, its eight-island scope, and its short life due to the war. Still, the true extent of the expedition, the role of its major players, and just how important it was for the growing museum—now the Natural History Museum of Los Angeles County and one of the largest natural history museums in the world—are not mainstream knowledge.

The CIBS focused on biology, archaeology, botany, and at times geology. As noted within the book, there are aspects of these sciences as well as museum practices that have changed over time. Archaeological research is a good example of this, as North American archaeologists today rarely excavate human remains. Instead, they work in close consultation with—and approval from—local tribes. Moreover, museums like the NHM and the Smithsonian's National Museum of Natural History (where I work) continue to invest in and focus on repatriating Native American remains and sacred objects to tribes throughout the United States. Repatriation is a crucial part of modern museums, and the work between museum professionals and indigenous communities in North America and around the world continues to enhance museum research, collections, education, and outreach. Revisiting past collecting expeditions, like the CIBS, is an important reminder of how far we have come and where we can go in the future.

North America's Galapagos: The Historic Channel Islands Biological Survey captures the CIBS expedition in an exciting account that weaves together a personal and compelling narrative and covers all of the challenges—such as logistics, financial issues, and interpersonal disputes—as well as the successes, including exciting new species identifications and archaeological discoveries. Far more than just a book about the Channel Islands and an important collecting expedition, this text paints a diverse picture of early museum collecting expeditions and natural history museums more broadly. Readers of this book are challenged to assess all of the positives and negatives of this early expedition and how these lessons of museum history can help build more inclusive and diverse museums of the future.

Torben Rick
Smithsonian Institution

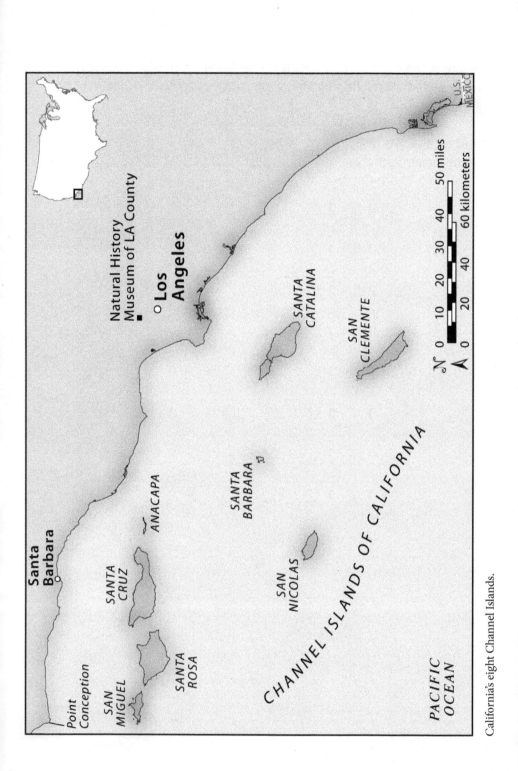

California's eight Channel Islands.

INTRODUCTION

North America's Galapagos

Resting in what resembles a megalodon-sized shark bite out of the California mainland, the Channel Islands lie within the Southern California Bight, a curvaceous expanse of water abutting three hundred miles of coastline that diverges from the characteristic north-south trending direction of the continental United States. Because these semi-wild islands first rose from the sea two million years ago, there evolved eight unique ecosystems, each surrounded by the Pacific Ocean. One hundred forty-five plants and animals that have made their home on the Channel Islands are found nowhere else on the planet—hence the islands' nickname: North America's Galapagos.[1]

Over eighty years ago, propelled by island allure grounded in smatterings of scientific findings, an assemblage of researchers, naturalists, adventurers, cooks, immigrants, and science-hungry teenagers came together under the aegis of the Los Angeles County Museum Channel Islands Biological Survey (CIBS) to explore California's eight Channel Islands. Their mission: to gather together the islands' broken shards of history and evolution like a bait ball. Thirty-three men and women raked, dug, set traps, skinned, collected, mapped, and traced the footsteps of those who came before them. They commenced this undertaking in the name of science, not only because the islands offered the unprecedented chance for them to make numerous noteworthy discoveries, but because these discoveries stood to go down in history, along with their names and institutions. Their exploration of North America's Galapagos Islands presented them with the chance to achieve scientific immortality in the way of Charles Darwin, Joseph Grinnell, and John Muir.

Before settling into the story of the CIBS, however, it is important to understand the Channel Islands' evolutionary past, their uniqueness, and certain adaptations of island-dwelling animals. Hopefully, this background will contribute to a better appreciation of the Channel Islands and their allure to humans whether in modern times or eighty, two hundred, or thirteen thousand years ago.

Surrounded by one of the world's richest marine environments, the Channel Islands dot a 160-mile swath of ocean stretching from Point Conception to San Diego, California, like paint splatters on a Google Earth-sized Jackson Pollock canvas. Akin to giant rock traffic pylons, the Anacapa, Santa Cruz, Santa Rosa, San Miguel, Santa Barbara, Santa Catalina, San Nicholas, and San Clemente islands emerge jagged, windswept, and largely uninhabited from the Pacific Ocean. At once remote and yet accessible, these eight islands hover tantalizingly close to Southern California's western horizon. They are not what they appear to be—tame little splotches of land floating within Southern California's urban, often bathtub-like ocean, each only a few hour boat ride or short plane trip from shore. Yes, they are lovely. Yes, they contain beautiful places to kayak, coves to anchor within, shorelines to snorkel and dive, and mesas and cliffs to hike. They are beautiful paradises seldom visited by the twenty million people living in the counties that populate their adjacent mainland shoreline, but they are so much more.

The Channel Islands are wild, harsh, thrilling, and spoiled. Spoiled, in terms of humankind's careless use of them through the introduction of exotic species that eradicated native ones, yet resilient in their unruly ability to resist domestication no matter how forcefully we enslaved them for use as ranchlands, movie sets, big game hunting parks, bombing ranges, and recreational venues. These islands have heart. They persevere, remaining wild in their essence and spirit. And each, certainly, was not created equally.

Distances vary, but most islands are visible from shore during at least parts of the year, if not always in the imagination. San Nicolas, at sixty-one miles from the mainland, is the most remote of the Channel

Islands, while Anacapa's three rocky islets are a mere eleven miles from Oxnard, California. With only one square mile to its name, Santa Barbara Island is the smallest in the archipelago, whereas Santa Cruz's ninety-six square miles of varied terrain—once the largest privately owned island in the continental United States—make it the mammoth in the chain. San Miguel, known for being windswept and desolate, is often cloaked in fog, while Santa Catalina's salubrious weather and Mediterranean-style casino hosted the likes of Clarke Gable, Charlie Chaplin, and Marilyn Monroe during Hollywood's heydays. Despite their differences, each island shares much in common with its neighbors yet has its own unique history and distinctive inhabitants, both plant, animal, and human.

On a map, the Channel Islands appear almost celestial, grouped as they are into two loose constellations of islands. The first noticeable difference among them is that the southern group—San Clemente, Santa Catalina, San Nicolas, and Santa Barbara—are oriented in a north-south direction and lie far from the mainland and each other. In contrast, the northern group—Anacapa, Santa Cruz, Santa Rosa, and San Miguel— sit like ducks in a row, tightly packed together in an orderly east-west direction.

When driving north on the Pacific Coast Highway through Malibu, California, tourists and locals clear Point Dume—the Santa Monica Mountains' exquisite terminal mainland outcropping—and may spot Anacapa Island's craggy silhouette lying not far from the coastline. In the language of the Chumash people who first visited the island's shores sometime between four and ten thousand years ago, the word "Anacapa," or *Anayapax* in Chumash, means "illusion," "mirage," or "deception." This is a fitting name because most people, upon seeing the isle's cleaved, sheer sides and the scoliosis curve of its three-islet spine reaching for Hawaii, assume that it, along with all the northern islands, are but an extension of the Santa Monica Mountain Range—a finger of mainland California, only the knuckles of which now rise above sea level to stretch westward. Further corroborating this assumption are the many similar characteristics the northern Channel Islands share with the mainland coastal environment. The National Park Service promulgated this misperception in a 1940 press release that described the Anacapa and Santa Barbara Islands as "once connected with the mainland . . . peaks of mountain masses now submerged beneath the sea."[2]

But just as Anacapa means "illusion," so too is this thinking a trickery that obscures the facts. Millions of years ago, the rocks that would become the Channel Islands lay on the seafloor near present-day San Diego as part of the continental margin of the North American plate. When this plate began shearing against the Pacific plate eighteen million years ago, parts of the continental margin were dragged as much as 150 miles northward and rotated as much as ninety degrees clockwise. The distinct landscapes known today as California's Channel Islands were conceived two million years ago when upward thrusting of the seafloor brought these portions of the continental crust to the ocean's surface.[3] This is an oversimplification of the complex geology that created the Channel Islands, of course, but it is crucial to understand that the islands were never part of any terra firma that could have colonized their flora and fauna.

Twenty thousand years ago, when the world was colder and much of it sheathed beneath an icy blanket, five large islands surrounded by a constellation of nine smaller islets floated off what is now the Southern California Bight like rough-cut diamonds strewn across the ocean's surface. By about nine thousand years ago, glacial ice melts had swallowed most of the little isles, leaving only eight to provide clues and evidence of their magnificent, complicated past. But before this happened, the now-submerged islands lay closer to one another and to the mainland and were much, much larger. The biggest were fat with forested valleys and mountainsides of Douglas fir, cypress, and pine, flush with rolling hills covered in springtime flowers, and crisscrossed by flowing freshwater rivers and streams that tumbled down from tall peaks, cutting canyons and gorges into their host island and creating marshy habitats that were attractive to insects, amphibians, spiders, reptiles, and bats. At last, the sweet island water plunged or trickled into the Pacific to mix with the cold, salty brine. Here, not far from shore, mussels, abalone, lobster, and other shellfish clogged the intertidal zone. Anchored in depths of 175 feet or more, thick kelp forests grew as much as 2 feet per day and attracted marine animals to the small fish that sought safe harbor within their canopy of long, rubbery leaves undulating in the currents as they reached toward the sun.

The most resplendent and largest of the islands at this time was Santarosae. At its zenith 20,000 years ago, this super island was 828 square miles, about the size of Houston and New York City put together, and parts of its shoreline lay only 5 miles from the mainland. Over the course of the next 11,000 years, Santarosae rapidly shrank as ocean waters submerged flatlands and crawled nearly 300 feet up steep sea cliff faces, eventually transforming this one island into the four Northern Channel Islands. Anacapa separated first from the mother island, followed by Santa Cruz, and then Santa Rosa and San Miguel, which became distinct landmasses around 9,300 years ago.[4] But the "new" islands' comeuppance came at a price: 76 percent of Santarosae's landmass disappeared beneath as much as 360 feet of water. Today, the combined acreage of the four Northern Channel Islands represents only 24 percent of Santarosae's vast former self.[5]

The Channel Islands have relatively little species diversity compared to the mainland. Only ten species of mammals, excluding bats, are indigenous to the islands. The island fox, spotted skunk, Santa Catalina ornate shrew, deer mouse, harvest mouse, and Beechey ground squirrel exist today, while the giant island deer mouse, San Miguel Island vole, Anacapa mouse, and both the Columbian and pygmy mammoth are extinct. The Channel Islands' mammoths are a monstrous example of island magic, deserving much more attention than a cursory mention amongst a list of extinct animals. Pygmy mammoths, together with the likes of the island fox and the Santa Cruz Island scrub-jay, demonstrate an ingenious attribute of island evolution that contributes to the allure of island life and lore.

For over fifty-eight million years, ten species of mammoths roamed widely across Europe, Asia, and North America. Some grew into massive beasts weighing up to ten tons and standing fourteen feet high at the shoulder. In North America, one grew in miniature. Two mammoths inhabited what is now the western United States: the Columbian mammoth and the oxymoronic pygmy mammoth, the most diminutive of proboscideans in North America.

Pygmy mammoths, also called the Channel Islands mammoth or *Mammuthus exilis* (in Latin "exilis" means thin, small, or poor), lived on the super island Santarosae, and their remains have been found on San Miguel, Santa Rosa, and Santa Cruz Islands but nowhere else in North America. They were a lightly furred little beast, though little only applies within the mammoth family—the pygmy was gigantic compared to the rest of the Channel Islands wildlife. In adulthood, this extinct relative of the Asian elephant could weigh as much as a baby grey whale at birth—2,100 pounds—and stand a little over six feet at the shoulder, though the average pygmy mammoth kept its five foot seven frame to a svelte 1,700 pounds or less.

Like elephants, pygmy mammoths were grazers, feeding on small shrubs and tree bark. Artists' renditions of this beast—rearward, downsloping back; solid, tree trunk-like legs; and broad, heavy head laden with two long tusks similar to the modern elephant—closely resemble those of the Columbian mammoth, and for good reason. Pygmy mammoths evolved from their much larger (twelve- to fourteen-foot shoulder height), heavier (nearly ten ton) cousin, which is remarkable considering the Channel Islands had no predators and less food. But how did such a massive beast get to the Channel Islands? And then, how—and why—did some of them become more than 50 percent smaller?

These are questions scientists have been discussing for decades and on which there now appears to be growing consensus. Beginning at least forty-seven thousand years ago[6]—and perhaps as long ago as two hundred thousand or more years ago,[7] when Santarosae was closer to the mainland than the northern islands are today—some Columbian mammoths swam across the Santa Barbara Channel. Scientists actually think that Columbian mammoths probably colonized the Channel Island multiple times, but evidence of the animal that they evolved into, the pygmy mammoth (undertaking the reverse commute), has never been found on the mainland.

Conjure up the improbable image of a huge mammoth stepping into the cold Pacific surf, waves crashing before it, salty foam swirling under its belly, sand slithering out from beneath heavy, pylon-like legs. Imagine the creature raising its head to bellow at the annoying ocean, then lifting its feet up and out of the foam, wet sand sloping back into the water. With a wild upward flick of its tusks, the animal moves into the swash, trumpeting loudly as the swells break over its back. Suddenly, the salty brine lifts the beast off the sand bottom and, with its buoyant mass suspended, the mammoth paddles like a wind-up toy, wildly swimming and trumpeting through its upheld trunk, now more snorkel than grass-grasper. Shortly, the beast makes for the break, the open ocean beyond and the promise of sweet-smelling grasses several miles distant.

Incredible? Impossible? Not at all. Elephants are good swimmers, and mammoth fossils have been found on islands across the globe. Why not the Columbian mammoth along the shoreline of what is now California?

There's a principal in biology known variously as Foster's Rule, the island rule, insular dwarfism or island gigantism, and, more colloquially, the breadbox rule. No matter its name, this theory explains how Columbian mammoths morphed into significantly smaller versions of themselves on the Channel Islands. J. Bristol Foster came up with the idea in 1964 after performing fieldwork on the Queen Charlotte Islands, now known as Haida Gwaii, in Canada. Based on his comparison of the physical size of 116 island-dwelling animals to their mainland kin, he succinctly published his idea in the well-regarded journal, *Nature*. Foster found that large mammal island colonizers, both herbivores and carnivores, tended to shrink in size relative to their mainland ancestors, whereas small animal colonizers, such as rodents, grew as they evolved in island habitats.

Three years after Foster published this theory, mathematical ecologist Robert MacArthur and E. O. Wilson (Harvard professor and prolific author who is one of this century's most well-known scientific names) published a book entitled *The Theory of Island Biogeography*. This book expanded upon Foster's work and helped launch a new field of study called insular biogeography, which propelled a fresh generation of scientists into the field to examine isolated communities and the factors involved with species richness—i.e., diversity—and island gigantism and dwarfism.

The basic tenant of Foster's Rule, or the breadbox theory, is that animals larger than a breadbox generally shrink when they inhabit islands and those smaller than a breadbox grow. Sure enough, after arriving on the Channel Islands, Columbian mammoths, unequivocally larger than a breadbox, dwindled in size to become pygmy mammoths. However, the exact opposite happened to the mainland scrub-jay, which colonized Santa Cruz Island and grew into the Channel Islands' only endemic bird species, the vibrantly colored, much larger Santa Cruz Island scrub-jay. Since the publication of MacArthur and Wilson's book, the theory has expanded to include any isolated habitat, not just islands, as the understanding of other ecosystems—such as mountain peaks, oases, fragmented forests, and habitats isolated by land development—still benefit from the application of this theory. Admittedly, the breadbox theory is an oversimplification of Foster's Rule, which subsequent theories have expanded upon and addressed.[8]

What evolutionary benefit do animals gain from growing or shrinking in comparison to their pre-island arrival size? A large size, it turns out, better prepares an animal for taking advantage of a wide range of resources—e.g., they can eat both large and small prey, or they can access flora found in trees or on the ground. Large size is a benefit in territorial battles as well as mate selection, the latter of which, when combined with relatively abundant food resources, allows them to give birth more frequently or to larger clutches or litters[9] and thus more successfully procreate. Larger animals can also more efficiently store energy and water, and therefore better survive famine or drought than smaller animals. Conversely, small animals don't need as much food or water, and thus may have adequate resources even when the environment is highly stressed. This requirement for fewer resources as well as their small size, which allows them to better hide from predators, uniquely adapts them to living on islands where resources are usually limited.

In the case of the Columbian mammoths, their natural predators were absent from the Channel Islands. This meant that maintaining a dauntingly large size was no longer necessary for the animal to forage nearly continuously while still keeping itself off the carnivore menu. This also allowed the herds of mammoths on Santarosae to grow large, but at some point the confines of island living stifled the populations' continual growth. This was exacerbated when rising sea levels flooded the mother island's prime low-level pastures, thereby making food resources even scarcer. These types of pressures conspired to favor smaller sized mammoths that could more easily survive during periods of scarcity. As a result, these animals were the successful progenitors who passed their smaller "genes" onto their offspring and contributed to the Columbian mammoth's trajectory into a Lilliputian world.

But Columbian mammoths didn't simply turn into smaller versions of themselves. In the process of becoming the pygmy mammoth, *M. columbi*'s anatomy strategically changed in response to the environment in which it lived. Case in point, 50 percent of Santa Rosa's terrain today includes uplands with slopes of thirty degrees or more,[10] locations that *M. columbi* could not reach due to their steep angle. To put this into perspective, the ten steepest roads in the United States have grades that range between

31.5 to 45 percent. The steepest, Waipo Road on the Big Island of Hawaii, leads to the beautiful, lushly vegetated Waipo Valley and is only accessible by four-wheel-drive vehicle or foot. Since scientists began collecting mammoth bones on the Channel Islands in 1857, no Columbian mammoth remains have ever been found in upland areas, only on lower marine terraces. Remains of pygmy mammoths, however, have been found in many different habitats, including riparian and steppe-tundra ecosystems, dunes, and both low and high elevation grassland plateaus.

The reason for this disparity is because Pygmy mammoths evolved in ways that let them conquer steep island slopes, but Columbian mammoths did not. For example, the pygmy mammoth's femur became rounder, causing muscles to attach differently than their ancestor, the Columbian mammoth, while also significantly lengthening it (relative to body size) at the same time their lower limb bones shortened. These three adaptations allowed low-gear upward ambulation akin to four-wheel-drive vehicles and added a breaking function for going downhill. Together, these adjustments permitted the species to take full advantage of all of the islands' food supplies and are the reason that pygmy mammoth bones are found all over the islands, while the larger mammoths were limited to the flat-terraced landscapes.[11]

When mammoths roamed on Santarosae, the island was heavily timbered by conifer trees that thrived in the cool island temperatures. Columbian mammoths primarily ate grasses and shrubs that, due to the island's size and the existence of shady pine tree forests inhospitable to grasses, were limited in supply. Because of this, the smaller island Proboscidea evolved to exploit an untapped food resource that became the pygmy mammoth's primary food: the leaves, twigs, and bark of fir and conifer trees. In short (pun intended), not only did the little-mammoth-that-could evolve in ways that allowed it to physically access island locations that the big Columbian Mammoths could not reach, but it also took advantage of a food niche that the larger mammoths did not want. Given these adaptations, the pygmy mammoth could coexist with the Columbian mammoth, and perhaps even "out-exist" its larger brethren.

As wonderful as these adaptations are, the possibility that pygmy mammoths and humans lived together on Santa Rosa Island for at least two hundred years is perhaps the most intriguing aspect of their life history. But because this time span is based on radiocarbon dating of charcoal that may or may not be associated with the time of a single mammoth's death, and because it was compared to that of a single human, some scientists remain skeptical about an overlap.[12] Giving into the possibility, however, is thrilling, as it allows the imagination to wonder what the first Channel Islanders might have thought about the dwarf mammoths as well as to consider whether island people were familiar with the pachyderm through oral histories and recounted stories of much larger mammoths living in Siberia, Asia, or North America. If they did overlap, what did life look like for the island mammoths when humans came along? Did they coexist peacefully with early Channel Islanders? Were they worshiped and given spiritual powers, harnessed into seagrass leads and ridden up steep hillsides, or treated as pets, as were some foxes and dogs? Alternatively, it's conceivable that with spear points advanced enough to kill a mammoth, the Channel Islanders might have hunted and eaten them as the Plains Indians ate buffalo.[13] While this latter thought is a technical possibility, no mammoth bones—either Columbian or pygmy—have been found that prove they were hunted, butchered, eaten, or cooked. Based on what scientists know today, no one can tell how, or if, humans and mammoths interacted on the Channel Islands—at this point, it's all fanciful speculation. Still, to dream of these possibilities with the curiosity of a child makes the pygmy mammoth's demise more real and harder to endure. Imagine the thrill of seeing pygmy mammoths plodding up and down steep island hillsides like the descendants of William Randolph Hearst's dazzle of zebras, who still graze on the golden grasses of the central California coastal town of San Simeon.

Assuming that humans and mammoths did live together on the Channel Islands for about two hundred years, it is curious that the overlap was so short—a mere blip in the mammoth's multi-million-year evolutionary history. However, the timing of the mammoth's extinction coincides with a global die-off of large mammals that occurred in what is known as the Quaternary extinction event. Several theories attempt to explain this larger die-off, such as over hunting by humans, climate change, or vegetation/food source changes, any of which could apply to the pygmy mammoth's demise.

In truth, no one really knows why the pygmy mammoth became extinct, but during much of the twentieth century the most popular theory focused on overhunting by humans. Scientists from all disciplines participated in the debate, dredging up archaeological, paleontological, and geological evidence, but because no charred mammoth bones have been found in middens (ancient trash sites) on the Channel Islands, no spear points have been unearthed next to fossil mammoth remains, and no evidence has emerged of projectile damage, butchery, or cut marks to fossil bones, most researchers no longer support this theory as being central to the little North American mammoth's demise.

This leaves climate and food source changes as possible—and probable—causes of the pygmy mammoth's extinction. As the Ice Age came to an end and the world began to warm, the Douglas firs and cypress forests that once covered Santarosae retreated. Where once great forests stood, only small patches of trees remained, and in their place grasslands and coastal sage scrub appeared. By this time, Channel Island mammoths had evolved to take their nourishment from fir forest leaves, twigs, and bark, not grasses. With the quickly dwindling supply of fir trees, pygmy mammoths had nothing to eat and may have starved to death. Thus, the rate of climate change and the accompanying ecosystem disruption that outstripped the animal's ability to evolve to accommodate new conditions, not human intervention, likely wrought the little giant's extinction.[14] Their demise casts a spotlight on the heightened danger that island species face due to the limitations of island living.

One defining resource that differentiates today's northern and southern Channel Islands is fresh water availability. Except for Anacapa, which has no perennial running water on any of its three islets and only isolated freshwater springs,[15] the northern islands are relatively well watered by freshwater seeps, springs, and streams that feed the oak woodlands, pine forests, and ironwood stands commonly found on the largest of the northern Channel Islands, Santa Cruz and Santa Rosa. The southern islands, in contrast, are drier. Santa Barbara has no fresh water at all, and Santa Catalina and San Clemente have little. Thus, the southern islands' vegetation is dominated by cactus, grassland, and coastal sage.

The availability of water affects animal populations, too. With the exception of Santa Catalina Island, the wetter northern islands support a larger variety of animals than the southern islands. The relative paucity of animals on the southern group is exacerbated because they are located further out to sea, making initial animal migration to them more difficult.

Water, along with landmass, also affected human population size and length of habitation. It has long been believed that the availability of freshwater sources affected Native Americans' village site selections, both permanent (San Nicolas, Santa Cruz, Santa Rosa, San Miguel, San Clemente, and Santa Catalina) and seasonal (Anacapa and Santa Barbara, which were only used during periods of rain and as stopover islands). Researchers are now learning that the availability of water had other affects on Channel Islanders. For example, 800 to 1,300 years ago, during the medieval climate anomaly (a period of severe drought that lasted decades and possibly as long as a century), native San Clemente Island people responded to this environmental stress by seeking new village sites where limited water sources could still be found, as well as reducing overall population size.[16]

Another important natural feature that plays into the differences between the northern and southern islands is that the northern islands were once one island, Santarosae, and its former, longer shoreline was only six miles from the mainland. This close proximity made it easier for plants, animals, and humans to reach it. Some species may have been blown by the wind onto Santarosae's plains (the Santa Cruz Island gooseberry flowering shrub), flown to its cliff sides (the Santa Cruz Island scrub-jay), swum or paddled to its shores (the Columbian mammoth and humans), hitched a ride on a floating log (the Channel Islands slender salamander or gopher snake), or were brought to the islands by Native Americans (the Channel Island fox). But regardless of the mode of transportation, Santarosae's former proximity to the mainland is key to understanding and explaining the similarities that exist between the plants and animals that inhabit the northern islands and the California mainland. The southern islands, in contrast, were never one landmass, and since they are spread further apart they do not share as much biota as the northern islands.

When Santarosae was a single landmass, animals freely wandered across it and plants dispersed seeds over the entire island—through either wind locomotion, being ingested by animals and then left in a new spot as scat, or snagging a ride on the fur coat of a skunk, mouse, or fox and later being shed. Humans have been on the Channel Islands for at least the last thirteen thousand years, and the large, water-rich island of Santarosae would certainly have been attractive to them. Because the super island did not begin breaking up until near the end of the Ice Age, about eleven thousand years ago,[17] early inhabitants would have witnessed the rapid changes occurring around them, including the loss of intertidal shell fishing areas, shrinking forests, and perhaps the extinction of the Channel Islands mammoth.

Understanding the impact of rising sea levels is vital to accurately interpreting the Channel Islands' current clues, some of which may no longer be available in a meaningful way. This is because fossils or other artifacts that today are found close to the waters' edge may once have been located in the interior of Santarosae. Likewise, items that were once coastal are now lost underwater, buried under sediments, or dispersed in such a way that their new provenance is no longer relevant, or leads to an inaccurate interpretation. Many archaeologists believe that artifacts from coastal peoples living near the shoreline when Santarosae was a large island may now be underwater, and that this is why evidence of human occupation potentially dating between thirteen and twenty thousand years ago has not been found.[18]

In recognition of the Channel Islands' biodiversity, in 1938 Franklin D. Roosevelt designated Anacapa and Santa Barbara as the Channel Islands National Monument. Forty-two years later, Congress added Santa Cruz, Santa Rosa, and San Miguel to create Channel Islands National Park. Today, this park is one of the Unites States' least visited national parks, in large part because it is difficult to access—the ocean passage can be rough and the boat landing areas potentially dangerous. On Anacapa Island, the ferry transporting passengers must back into a sheer cliff face that is on the outer curve of a very small embayment. When seas are rolling, the captain must time the stern's connection to the dock within the few moments of relative calm that exist between swell sets. Even so, the boat is never fully berthed and passengers must quickly climb a vertical ladder to reach the landing before the boat pulls away. From the wooden dock, the arriving passenger must then climb 157 metal stairs that switchback up the cliff face to the top of the little island.

European ownership of the eight Channel Islands began in 1542, when Juan Rodríguez Cabrillo claimed them as part of Alta California for Spain. In 1821, dominion of these lands moved to Mexico, and during its reign the Mexican government granted ownership of Santa Cruz, Santa Rosa, and Santa Catalina to private citizens. With the signing of the 1848 Treaty of Guadalupe Hidalgo, which concluded the Mexican-American War,[19] 525,000 square miles of what today comprises large portions of the American Southwest—including the Channel Islands—were ceded to the U.S. government. Although all eight Channel Islands became part of the United States, the three privately owned islands remained that way while the other five fell under federal jurisdiction.

Today, Santa Catalina is 88 percent owned by the Santa Catalina Island Conservancy (the environmental legacy of the island's former owners, the Wrigley family) and the Santa Catalina Island Company (in turn owned by William Wrigley's descendants); Santa Cruz is owned jointly by the U.S. National Park Service (NPS) (24 percent) and the Nature Conservancy (TNC) (76 percent); Anacapa, Santa Barbara, and Santa Rosa are owned and operated by the NPS; and San Miguel, though managed and operated by the NPS, remains under the jurisdiction of the United States Navy, as do San Nicolas and San Clemente Islands. Channel Islands National Park consists of San Miguel, Santa Rosa, Santa Cruz, Anacapa, and Santa Barbara Islands. Understanding the dominion of the islands is further complicated by the mishmash of counties in which they reside: Anacapa and San Nicolas Islands lie within Ventura County; San Miguel, Santa Cruz, Santa Rosa, and Santa Barbara Islands belong to Santa Barbara County; and San Clemente and Santa Catalina Islands reside in Los Angeles County.

Santa Catalina is by far the best known and most visited of the eight islands, and this is by no means an accident. Beginning in 1887, a series of Santa Catalina owners, each of whom envisioned the island as a tourist resort, began its transformation. Over the next thirty-odd years, in fits and starts—and through defaulted loans, fires, and bankruptcies—these owners converted the island from a rugged cattle ranch to the tourist attraction it is today.

William Wrigley, the Chicago chewing-gum magnate who purchased the island in 1919, succeeded admirably in this endeavor. Not only did he invest millions into the infrastructure of the island and its largest city, Avalon, but he sent his beloved Cubs baseball team to the resort for spring training. From 1921–1951, save for the World War II years, the Chicago Cubs trained on a baseball diamond in Avalon Canyon that locals dubbed "Wrigley Field," a christening that occurred prior to Weeghman Park's 1927 official name change to that very moniker. Hollywood arrived in Catalina in 1912 for the filming of the first Channel Islands-located movie, and soon thereafter the industry expanded filming activities, bringing stars, starlets, and the American buffalo to Santa Catalina Island. Notable island residents include Zane Grey, who built a home above Avalon Harbor; Marilyn Monroe, who lived with her first husband in Avalon; and General George S. Patton Jr., who met his future wife on the island when both were children.

Forgotten is the role Santa Catalina Island played in initiating a series of scientific expeditions undertaken in the late 1930s that were designed to secure a place in history, not only for the charismatic scientists who participated in them, but also for the Los Angeles County Museum of History, Science, and Art (LACM), today known as the Natural History Museum of Los Angeles County (NHM). One of these scientists, Donald C. Meadows, taught middle school biology in Avalon, Catalina's largest town, and achieved a small amount of recognition for his island butterfly research and peer-reviewed publications. His scientific aspirations propelled him to seek a sponsor for a series of larger expeditions that he envisioned. The factors involved in launching such an ambitious endeavor requires consideration not only of this one man's drive, but also those of his fellow participants and the institution that backed him—the LACM. Beyond these factors, the nature of the times and the mood of the people living in Los Angeles all played a part in the realization of the Channel Islands Biological Survey.

The Channel Islands Biological Survey

Los Angeles, California, is a city of dreamers. It is a place that spawned a talking mouse capable of charming the world for generations, a desert basin whose citizenry dared to encase its rogue river within a solid channel of concrete, and a city of opportunity where a germophobe college dropout made millions in film and went on to develop one of the world's most powerful aerospace companies. Little wonder, then, that in early 1938, as the country struggled to rise above the Great Depression and Los Angeles grappled with police racketeering and the aftermath of a flood

that buried one-third of the city under a foot of muddy water, two butterfly scientists began concocting a plan to survey eight Pacific islands,
the magnitude of which had never before—or since—been attempted.

The CIBS was not the first expedition ever mounted to study North
America's Galapagos. The California Academy of Sciences' work covering
birds, insects, and reptiles in 1918 and 1919 holds that distinction. Nor was
it the last. The Pacific Ocean Biological Survey Program, initiated in 1963
by the Smithsonian in conjunction with the Department of Defense, was
the most recent attempt to study all eight Channel Islands, but it focused
primarily on the banding of pelagic seabirds. There were others, too, but
none with the broad scope of the CIBS.

Today, it is doubtful that an expedition such as the CIBS could be
undertaken—the scope is just too big, and the cost too great. Additionally, it's not easy to access all eight Channel Islands, and relatively few
people have done it. Those who have are part of an exclusive group of
explorers known as the All Eight Club, administered by the Santa Cruz
Island Foundation. Only people who can prove they have set foot on each
of the Channel Islands are eligible to join. Research shows posthumously
eligible members include George Davidson, born in 1825, as well as seven
participants of the CIBS, though not all of them visited all eight islands
while on the survey: Jack von Bloeker Jr., George Kanakoff, George Willett, Lloyd Martin, Donald C. Meadows, M. B. Dunkle, and Reid Moran.
The All Eight Club is probably the most exclusive geographic club on the
planet. Compare its 2019 membership of 220 people[20] to the more than
800 members in the Seven Summits Club, the prestigious mountaineer-
ing club for those who have climbed the highest peaks on each of the
world's seven continents. The reasons for this are numerous, including
personal interest, the necessity of making many difficult channel crossings over often rough seas (hundreds of ships have sunk on or near the
islands), lack of fame surrounding the All Eight Club compared to the
Seven Summits Club, and the difficulties involved with convincing
the U.S. military to grant civilians access to two of their secretive bases
on San Clemente and San Nicolas Islands. Thus, the thirteen expeditions
of the CIBS were, and still are, the most focused, highly coordinated, and
multidisciplinary survey to ever study all eight Channel Islands.

Because of the explorations that came before them, the CIBS scientists understood the uniqueness of the Channel Islands, yet it was more

than their biodiversity that drew the researchers into their midst. Indeed, it was a magical time in science, a time when the world's great museums mounted extravagant scientific expeditions of discovery, an era known as the "golden age of exploration." Science was about to change—moving away from a collection, specimen-based discipline and toward genetics and experimental biology—but in 1938 there was still time and opportunity for a twenty-five-year-young museum to conduct a grand exploration, one that floated like a mirage in its own backyard.

Over the years since the CIBS launched, changes in technology, scientific methods, and ethics have transformed the way researchers conduct their work. It is no longer as easy for scientists to pick up a rifle, head into the field, and bring specimens back to their laboratories. Researchers must now obtain very specific permits that restrict their collecting activities in terms of the species, location, and number of specimens collected. They need permits to pick up roadkill or accept dead animals from citizens who find them on the beach, at the park, or on hiking trails. Archaeologists also operate within government regulations and ethical considerations that in the 1930s had not advanced far beyond the Victorian desire to collect interesting artifacts for museum and personal exhibition. This was particularly—and sometimes painfully—true with regard to human remains, which were not always treated with the sanctity and respect that we now understand they deserve. In contrast, many of today's archaeologists are inspired by native peoples and work closely with tribal members to help reconstruct the past in ways that might influence the lifeways of the living. Native American histories, knowledge, stories, and interests inform archaeological endeavors more than ever before. It might be easy for today's reader to scorn the methods used in the past under the name of science, but rather than condemn those scientists, perhaps we can seek to understand the world within which they operated, accept the inroads they made, and appreciate the changes in attitude and action their work affected.

Technologies that were just beginning to reshape science in 1938 have advanced exponentially, allowing researchers to collect and analyze data in ways never dreamed of in the early twentieth century. Telemetry, GPS, DNA sequencing, radiocarbon dating, high-resolution digital photography, satellite photographs, genome sequencing, X-ray guns that identify the chemical formula of an artifact, and magnetometry that measures the earth's magnetic field and aids in locating archaeological features such as buried buildings are just a few examples of the tools and technologies at scientists' fingertips today.

During the 1939–1941 CIBS, researchers created a Channel Islands floral and faunal library filled with artifacts, specimens, maps, charts, and notes. Their records reveal the extent of invasive species, the locations of archaeological sites, and the abundance or dearth of plant and animal life. They recorded the state of the islands, including the presence of native plants and both native and feral animals, the damage cattle and sheep hooves exerted on the environment, and environmental characteristics that may have played a role in the selection of locations humans utilized. They even mapped building sites, some of which no longer stand, and named canyons, hilltops, and water seeps.

After World War II, biological and archaeological studies on the Channel Islands diminished. Though some researchers from a few institutions continued to perform fieldwork on the islands, they did so largely without the regularity and breadth attempted by the CIBS. This began to change in the late 1970s, and by the 1990s the Channel Islands welcomed an array of scientists to its shores. Archaeologists have found the islands particularly rewarding due to both the quantity and quality of archaeological resources available there.

The National Park Service manages five islands—Anacapa, Santa Barbara, Santa Cruz (in collaboration with the Nature Conservancy), San Miguel, and Santa Rosa—that comprise Channel Islands National Park. The park service deems the archaeological sites located on these islands "among the most valuable in North America, if not the world . . . [because they] have the potential to inform on aspects of prehistory and history that cannot be adequately revealed through archaeological research on the mainland."[21] This point of view is shared by any number of preeminent scholars who are making groundbreaking discoveries on the Channel Islands. During the past twenty-five years alone, the oldest human remains in North America were documented from Santa Rosa Island, and San Miguel Island contains the oldest North American shell midden, both of which provide information about maritime peoples and the populating of the Americas. Moreover, "the Channel Islands contain an archaeological record capable of playing a role in research issues and questions of global significance."[22] And just what are those questions of global significance? An important one is the centuries-long pursuit of evidence that proves the manner in which, and when, the Americas were populated. This quest has increasingly drawn researchers to the Pacific Coast of North America—and especially to the Channel Islands, which are uniquely poised to help answer this and many other interesting questions.

No place in North America rivals the Channel Islands for the abundance of prehistoric sites dated to more than nine thousand years ago. Not only do these sites exist on the Channel Islands, but the semi-arid, salted sea air fosters a high degree of artifact preservation, including items such as baskets or clothing that normally deteriorate quickly. Additionally, the stratification of archaeological deposits has remained mostly intact because burrowing animals, whose activities tend to mix items between strata that date to different time periods, do not exist on the islands. Equally as important, with the exception of parts of Santa Catalina, San Clemente, and San Nicolas, the islands are largely undeveloped (other than some buildings and fencing erected for ranching operations), and therefore offer archaeologists the unparalleled ability—especially compared to mainland sites—to study whole communities and even multiple villages within a single island ecosystem. The one drawback to studying the peopling of the Americas based on the Channel Islands, though it applies equally to mainland sites, is that rising sea levels over the past fifteen thousand years have subsumed many early coastal sites. But given the importance of the archaeological information that might be found underwater, even this monumental barrier is sinking. In 2016, San Diego State University and its partners—including the NHM—launched a four-year, $900,000 federally funded program to explore underwater northern Channel Island sites.

John Adams Comstock, director of science at the LACM and the CIBS's champion, realized the importance of archaeology to the success of the survey. He placed the responsibility for this field in the hands of Arthur "Art" Woodward, director of history and archaeology at the LACM. Luckily, Woodward's journals are accessible, readable, and almost perfectly intact for the six expeditions on which he participated. As a historical archaeologist, Woodward's journals offer tantalizing clues into life on the Channel Islands in the 1930s and early 1940s that are likely

George Kanakoff sitting in front of the rock cut on San Clemente Island commemorating the initiation of the Los Angeles Channel Islands Biological Survey in 1939. Courtesy of the Department of Anthropology, Natural History Museum of Los Angeles County (NHM).

unrivaled by any others. Additionally, his journals are filled with interesting (and mundane) facts, speculations, site maps, details on artifact locations, conditions, soil composition, and the like.

Archaeology isn't the only discipline that has taken note of North America's Galapagos. Virtually every science has commented on the Channel Islands, and this increased interest—whether it be studying the islands, returning them to their "natural" state (though determining what that is, since humans have changed the islands so much throughout history, is not easy), or using them as laboratories of evolution to help predict what humans can expect to occur as a result of global warming and other ecological changes—has multiplied the value of the repository the CIBS created. The work done by the CIBS in the late 1930s and early 1940s can help the modern-day explorer better understand the Channel Islands' environment and the changes that have occurred since then. The information collected in the past can assist conservation managers striving to maintain North America's Galapagos as the worldwide resource and place of solitude and beauty that it is increasingly recognized to be.

When Japanese bombs struck U.S. shores on December 7, 1941, stranding the explorers on Santa Rosa Island and then subsequently scattering them like dandelion seeds in a windstorm, the CIBS's explorations and fieldwork abruptly ended. Thus, the accomplishments that were made (albeit not all adequately published) and the journey the explorers took have hung like a chad off the world's scientific ballot of significance— until now. This book aims to illuminate, for the first time, the journeys they undertook, the discoveries they made, the challenges they faced, the footprints they created, and the legacy they left for others on North America's Galapagos Islands. While this book focuses on the thirteen expeditions of the CIBS and the individual researchers' quests for scientific immortality, it is larger than this. Modern-day researchers are still doing much of what Comstock, Meadows, Woodward, and von Bloeker did in the late 1930s. Science may have changed technologically, but at its core it remains exacting, detailed, and, more often than not, backbreaking and mind-bending work. In these ways, the CIBS is a microcosm of other scientific endeavors. Ultimately, the survey's results—or lack thereof—are examples of the capriciousness of life and the continuity of the scientific process.

The *LA Times* referred to the Channel Islands Biological Survey participants as savants. Others called them Professor, Doc, husband, or daddy, but in their own hearts they were scientists. This is their story.

Chapter One

BIG DOG CAVE

"Europe Steps Up Preparations For War: Hitler and Mussolini in Huddle." Europe's new "peace front" bristled with guns
today as both democracies and dictatorships stepped up war
preparations.

—Joe Alex Morris, *Daily Times*
(New Philadelphia, Ohio), April 5, 1939

They saw it the moment they crested the bluff: the perfect bat habitat,
an eighty-foot wide, twenty-foot high dark slash across the cliff face,
a toothless grin leering at the Pacific Ocean. Thirty feet below, seawater
surged against volcanic rocks, launching saltwater rockets of froth and
foam to guard the cave's yawning mouth. Ignoring the threat, the men
stepped inside, entering a blackness that stretched hundreds of feet into
the island's guts. They were searching for bats, but instead of finding a
cave floor soft with guano and a ceiling squirming with warm-winged
creatures hanging by their toes, their boots dug into dry sand and their
fingers retrieved bits of grass rope, "debris, bones and abalone shell,"[1]—
the detritus of a Native American site.

On April 5, 1939, under cloudy skies, three men—Don Meadows,
expedition leader and lepidopterist; Lloyd Martin, staff entomologist; and
Jack von Bloeker Jr., staff mammalogist and bat expert, all representatives
of the second expedition of the Los Angeles County Museum's Channel
Islands Biological Survey (CIBS)—led by a U.S. Marine, trudged up a hill

Big Dog Cave, San Clemente Island, 1939. Courtesy of Don Meadows Papers (MS-R001), University of California, Irvine (hereafter UC Irvine), Special Collections & Archives.

located near the southwest tip of San Clemente Island, California. Their inspection of the interior walls revealed a narrow opening through which von Bloeker—unafraid of caves, dark belfries, or the underside of rattling bridges frequented by bats—crawled. When the stocky, darkly handsome mammalogist reemerged, he reported the vastness of the cave and its side rooms filled with "grass—bones, shell and bits of wood."[2]

For five days, they had searched this desolate strip of land for something of significance, and now Don Meadows, keen as mustard to seize the opportunity, formulated a plan. While von Bloeker and Martin began excavations, he would be the one to hike the two miles of rough terrain back to camp to deliver the exciting news to the one man able to interpret the clues they found: Arthur Albert Woodward, who once explained, "My name is really Albert Arthur, but I hated the name Albert, so in high school I changed it to Arthur Albert and no one cared."[3]

At forty-one years old, Art Woodward was a mustachioed, blue-eyed man of average height, cleft chin, and deeply receded hairline. Given to taking risks and seizing opportunities, he was a man who believed in himself. He liked what he liked, and let you know if he didn't. He bore himself with an air of confidence that some might call unearned. He left Berkeley two years shy of completing undergraduate degrees in history and anthropology, though that didn't matter to Woodward, who put little stock in such formalities, relying instead on common sense and a unique combination of skills few in his field had yet to employ. Apparently, his particular brand of bravado sufficed, since even without those degrees—and prior to obtaining the esteemed title of director of history and anthropology of the Los Angeles County Museum of History, Science, and Art—he succeeded in conducting groundbreaking archaeological work in Arizona, Utah, and California. Equally impressive, he unearthed funding from as far away as New York during the early years of the Great Depression.

When Woodward finally scrambled down that sea cliff's face carrying a notebook and writing instrument, von Bloeker and Martin would have greeted him with great enthusiasm. They had found something remarkable during the time that had passed since Meadows left them to fetch the expedition's archaeologist. If they had hesitated after coming upon it, it would have been a logical pause, for they were not archaeologists themselves and might not have known how best to proceed. However, they did know Art, and they knew better than to damage any of his artifacts, the penalty for which would be a vociferous dressing-down, one they'd just as soon avoid. So, instead of driving their shovels straight into the soil to attempt to lift their find out, they dug around it and near it. They gently smoothed their hands over it, blowing dirt and dust off it with their mouths. They worked carefully so as not to disturb its provenance, nor that of any other artifacts that might be lying nearby. They wanted only to surface as much of their find as possible for Art to examine.

Of course, immediately upon arrival, Woodward would likely have gone to look at the find, studying the way the bones lay partially exposed on the dry cave floor, noting that they appeared to have been disturbed. Perhaps he stood quietly in front of them for a moment, uttering, *que Dios le bendiga* ("may God bless you") under his breath, wondering about the cause of this death. No one can know exactly what he did or thought in the moments after first seeing the find, but one thing he most certainly would have done is assay the evidence: a ceremonial burial of large bones—canine bones, species type unknown—wrapped in coarse, burlap-like grey fabric made from hair. Later that day, in honor of the dead mutt, he named the site Big Dog Cave. By that afternoon,

Woodward's journals show him piecing together evidence that told the story of the cave's Indian occupation. Based on the quantity of debris they found, he could already speculate that San Clemente Island's caves had been inhabited, and "not merely for a short period."[4]

As that day wore on, more finds came to light: a human skeleton, several bits of textile, and a bird wrapped in cordage (later determined to be a chicken). Fueled by their discoveries, the researchers worked inside the cave until darkness made further excavations futile. No one complained when a marine from the base nearby offered the crew a ride back to camp.

A cool nighttime fog settled over the scientists as they repeated their evening routine: dinner and more work. At nine o'clock, the moonrise over Pyramid Head goaded the entomologists into stringing up moth sheets, simple white sheets backlit with lanterns—the perfect low-tech devices for attracting nighttime winged insects. Meadows enthused over the "fine results"[5] that ensued and must have been nearly giddy as he plucked the various large and small brown, grey, black, and white moths off the sheet and placed them into his collecting bag while the others busied themselves with preserving, skinning, pressing, and completing other scientific chores. At midnight, Meadows declared, "Lights out."[6]

It was Wednesday and the CIBS would be leaving the island on Saturday. Undoubtedly this compressed timeframe played into the conversations swirling about the campfire that night as they worked. Imagine the whispers, the gleeful shouts, the congratulatory slaps upon one another's backs; think what the intonation of their voices must have revealed about the gravity of their speculations. Who was the human? From what tribe? When did he or she die? Why were the dog and bird ceremonially buried? What else would they find in Big Dog Cave or on any of the other islands they would explore? Surely, the embers that flew from the fire that night sparked no more brightly than the scientists' imaginations, stoked by their great dreams.

When Woodward finally crawled into the sack at midnight, joints creaking and body aching from a long, hot day spent digging, his head was likely spinning with questions and thoughts. He and his contemporaries had their opinions about which tribes once lived on which islands, how many people lived on them, and when and how they got there in the first place, but proving it was another matter. All anyone could say for certain was that the padres (i.e., Christian priests) had removed most of the Indians[7] from the islands some 120 years ago. He knew this story and could recite it in his sleep: "Juana Maria was the last Indian to live on any of the Channel Islands before she got shipped off San Nicolas Island in 1853, eighty-six years ago. She couldn't speak a recognizable word, and she died seven weeks after stepping foot in Santa Barbara, apparently from dysentery. Hell, perhaps she would have been better off staying on that island."

"Amigo mio," he might have thought to himself as he lay in his sleeping bag. "I will figure this out if it's the last thing I do. I'm going to find out who lived on these blessed islands, and then I'm going to tell all those government guys, the shiny boys in their ivory towers, and those god-damned grave robbers, too. Thank goodness they didn't find the dog before I did; otherwise I'd have nothing left to work with."

Woodward's quest to "figure it out" seems a straightforward enough goal, but when viewed through a longer lens his objective was but a subset of the larger archaeological questions still puzzling scientists today: how, and when, did humans populate the Americas? Woodward had no reason to doubt the Bering land bridge theory of America's population. It was an old theory, proposed as long ago as 1590, and by 1939 it was widely accepted by anthropologists, archaeologists, and the public alike. Per the theory, the human remains lying in Big Dog Cave were the ancestors of the people who walked from Siberia across the Bering land bridge into present-day Alaska. From there, they migrated southward through an ice-free corridor into Canada and then to areas near Clovis, New Mexico, where they became known as the Clovis people, the first to inhabit the Americas. Having almost certainly studied this theory while at Berkeley, Woodward would have assumed that the people buried in Big Dog Cave descended from the Clovis people, who later migrated to the east and west coasts of what is now the United States, eventually developing a maritime culture that allowed them to reach San Clemente Island. Inherent in this theory is the admonition that the Pacific coast of North America, including California and the Channel Islands, was not inhabited until thousands of years after the Clovis culture established itself and that maritime capabilities were a relatively new invention.

Unfortunately for Woodward, rabble-rouser that he was, he died before a whole new generation of archaeologists made a sport out of poking holes in this stalwart theory. Had he been alive, he most certainly would have enjoyed knowing that his work as part of the CIBS—and that of his many colleagues to follow—would one day sink the land bridge theory as the only explanation of North American population beneath a sea of innovative archaeological thinking.

But that first night after discovering Big Dog Cave, as he lay listening to the sound of ocean surf hammering an ancient drumbeat against the shoreline, his thoughts probably did not wander to the future. No, they must have gone to the past, to the people (and dog) who used that cave many years ago.

When preparing himself for fieldwork, Woodward always read voraciously. For a trip like this, his reading list might have included the ships' logs of the first European explorers to visit the Channel Islands. The Spaniard Juan Rodríguez Cabrillo, who arrived in 1542, documented both the existence of the Channel Islands and the native people's interactions with him and his crew, the first white men the Channel Islanders had ever seen. According to Cabrillo, the islanders wore no clothes, were poor and dirty, and ate only fish. Sebastián Vizcaíno followed Cabrillo to the Channel Islands in 1602, mapping and naming the places his countryman had claimed for Spain sixty years prior. Woodward also partially translated Fray Juan Vizcaíno's diary, in which the Spaniard recounted both his 1769 voyage from lower (Baja) California to the Channel Islands of upper (Alta) California and his visit to the San Clemente and Santa Catalina Islands. Because Woodward spoke Spanish fluently, he read the diary in Vizcaíno's native Spanish, likely paying particular attention to Vizcaíno's description of his time on San Clemente Island and a seemingly friendly interaction with the island natives who brought him a waterproof basket made of reeds and tar. Vizcaíno wrote that he drank from this basket and that it was good. At some point, Woodward also read Captain George Nidever's account of the "rescue" of the Lone Woman of San Nicolas Island, who was baptized Juana Maria in 1853, and possibly the California mission padres' records of the natives, whose births, marriages, and baptismal dates gave proof of their conversion to Christianity. The CIBS archaeologist would have used these documents, as do modern scholars, to get a better idea of how the people who inhabited the Channel Islands lived.

Even armed with this information, Woodward would have had precious little insight into the lives of the estimated four thousand people who lived on the Channel Islands when the Europeans first made contact with them. All he knew for sure was that two different tribes occupied the mainland closest to the islands: the Chumash, who still inhabit today's Ventura and Santa Barbara Counties, and the Gabrielino/Tongva, who continue to live in the Los Angeles Basin.[8] Knowing this, however, didn't help Woodward determine whether one group claimed all the islands or if they split the isles between themselves, a damnable question no one seemed to have an answer for.

Perhaps tired from this endless puzzle, Woodward may have turned his attention to some things he did know about, like burials. He knew, for instance, that both the Gabrielino/Tongva and Chumash tribes buried animals, sometimes in association with humans, and sometimes purely as part of ritualistic ceremonies. The canine bones in the cave had certainly been carefully laid to rest. Perhaps he belonged to a shaman or village chief? Or, perhaps he killed a basking sea lion for the people to eat? Was he a great worker or a protector, warning the tribe of the approach of other people?

And, what about the chicken bones they had found? Indians believed birds could carry messages to the spirit worlds, and raptors, eagles, and ravens were commonly used in ceremonial burials, but Woodward had never heard of a chicken used in this way. The inhabitants of Big Dog Cave became acquainted with domestic fowl through the Europeans. To them, these birds were exotic and therefore to be treated with respect, even in death. After European contact, the people of Big Dog Cave may very well have substituted chickens for eagles.

Before the archaeologist fell asleep, he likely composed a mental checklist of things to look for the next day: whistles, pipes, crystals, eagle talons, etc.—things a shaman would have. If he could locate some of these, he could build a case around a ritualistic burial. If not, other questions would be raised.

The marines rumbled into camp early the next morning, offering Woodward and Meadows rides to Big Dog Cave. When they got there, the archaeologist resurveyed the site, creating a clean new grid within which to work. Every four-foot dirt square equaled two squares on the graph

U.S. Marines help with the excavation of Big Dog Cave. Courtesy of Department of Anthropology, NHM.

paper "map" he used to draw in the items they found. Next, the hard work of excavating a test trench that eventually measured thirteen feet long, three feet deep, and eight feet wide began with the grateful assistance of the United States Marine Corps.

Quickly they accumulated ecofacts: fish bones, abalone shells, cactus leaves, and other natural items unaltered by the human hand. Extracted from within a thick pile of debris in the middle of the cave, these items indicated that the Indians' diet included several different kinds of seafood as well as plant food. When they moved over toward the northern edge of this midden, its top layer yielded more pieces of dog-hair cloth—one bit a yellowish grey with reddish brown stripes, and another grey with blue stripes. These clues led Woodward to date the last—or top—layer of occupation to the Spanish mission era spanning 1780 through the early 1800s. Romantically, though he had no proof, he speculated that the Indians who discarded the items fled the missions where they were no more than indentured servants. Additionally, the existence of scraps of clothing made from otter fur, leather thongs, and olivella shells (known commonly as purple olive shells, which were used to make shell bead money) provided an indication of the relative wealth of the people buried in the cave.

Before the day's end, the explorers extracted a second ceremonial bird burial, this one "a Sp. [Spanish] rooster wrapped in a piece of beige cloth and tied with coarse 2 ply fiber cord."[9] The interment of the cock and the hen found the day before were the first such burials to be documented by archaeologists in California. And, as Woodward surmised, today it is believed that the domesticated fowls were a substitute for raptors, birds revered for their strength and ability to soar close to—to enter, even—the upper spiritual realm.

As the marines and the researchers worked inside the cave that offered up fragments of lives no longer lived, the air temperature outside rose to 81°F. The day's weather log read, "Feels warm." Although Woodward made frequent mention of weather conditions in his field journals, he did not mention anything about it during the week's excavation of Big Dog Cave. He did keep detailed records about the three human burials found, however, one of which he described thusly:

> [The skeleton] was flexed—with face down. The body ... tied with cords then a thin piece of skin wrapped around the corpse. Fragments of woven cloth around the pelvic regions indicated that a breech clout might have been worn. The body was then enveloped in another skin robe and tied with cord. Finally a net—probably a fish net of wild hemp—with 1" meshes was wrapped around the entire body.... No artifact was found with either body.[10]

On their last day in the field, the researchers discovered the week's final burial, this one an elaborate reburial of bones originally buried elsewhere. This reburial consisted of a flexed skeleton enfolded in a deerskin robe and then wrapped in a coarse netted cloth. The head, except for the lower jaw (which remained in place) had been removed and set on the back near the pelvis. Strands of olivella shell necklaces measuring eleven feet in combined length graced the neck, and a small abalone shell with red paint on it lay near the right hip. Two burned baskets, one of which Woodward identified as being of "mainland type"—meaning it was probably made out of juncus, a rush commonly used to make basketry on the mainland—were also colocated with the reburial.

Woodward does not speculate in writing who this person might have been, but he almost certainly wondered about it. Did the clothing and olivella necklace indicate that he, or she, had been someone of importance? Perhaps a chief or shaman? The presence of the deerskin robe is noteworthy, since no deer live on San Clemente Island. Thus, someone must have either traded for it on the mainland or hunted it himself and then skinned it before bringing it over. Either way, its presence both provides information and raises questions. The fact that they had deerskin (a nonnative species to San Clemente Island) proves they were a maritime people capable of getting back and forth to the mainland, but did the people who buried their friends or relatives in Big Dog Cave live on the island, or did they come to the island for the express purpose of burying them? Perhaps Woodward was correct when he poetically suggested that the people had escaped from the Spanish missions, though that is unlikely.

As he and his colleagues excavated the cave, Woodward took note of the details. He gave each artifact a number. He sketched the weave of the mission cloth. He counted the quantity of abalone shells and beads unearthed. He jotted down the type of soil, or ash, within which the artifacts lay and he kept records of the depth at which an item was discovered. He recorded it all in his journals, journals he wielded to ponder questions and postulate answers the way his fellow archaeologists use trowels to uncover treasure. Consider the amount of information found in this passage dated April 6, 1939:

> One thing was particularly noticeable—entire absence of any odor—although the integuments and even some of the hair remained. This held true of all of the animal remains—fur minus the hide is soft and recognizable. The excellent preservation is probably due to the salt in the ground and the constant dampness of the ocean air. Fragments of kelp were as tough and leathery as if put in yesterday. Pieces of leather thong—probably seal or sea lion were stiff and dry when found but left exposed overnight they became pliable.[11]

In addition to being rich in detail, this journal entry is significant because it documents the presence of infrequently found soft materials near the deceased. In both mainland and more exposed island sites, organic materials such as the woven cloth or fur robes found in Big Dog Cave biodegrade, leaving nothing behind. Thus, the comparative lack of such materials in most burials gives the impression that an individual buried in Big Dog Cave may have possessed more status than other people. In the passage above, however, Woodward speculates that the salty air and soil preserved these items, an assumption that researchers find reasonable today, and which obviates any special considerations—barring any additional finds that might confer a ritualistic burial—that would necessarily attach special societal status to the humans buried in Big Dog Cave.

Woodward's journals also demonstrate his self-confidence. Clearly unafraid of drawing conclusions, he hypothesized hunches and unabashedly made determinations, committing all of it in writing. He freely speculated that the bits of fur robe found in the debris represented remnants of sleeping garments and that the weave of the cloth indicated they dated to the Spanish mission period, circa 1770–1830. Just one day after the discovery of Big Dog Cave, he theorized that there were two Indian occupations of the site, one for "a considerable period of time,"[12] while the other, which followed a period of vacancy, was more temporary. Research over the last twenty-five years corroborates his opinions.

Another speculation he authoritatively makes is that Horse Cove, the bay lying between Pyramid Head and China Point, would have made a good landing and living spot for the Indians because "the level bench land offers fine camping facilities—very little cactus grows in this sandy area" and "the canoes could land easily." Furthermore, "the rocky points north of this site and south of the site were fine for shell fishing and in the kelp off shore were sea lions, seals and sea otter."[13] Presumably, Woodward mentions these marine mammals because they present potential high protein meals for the islanders. His recordkeeping included hand-drawn maps on which he noted the locations of significant sites, the types of ground coverings surrounding them, and nearby environmental features, as well as sketches of mortars, metates, tarred basketry, shell beads, and worked stone. He also photographed midden sites and the landscape.

As Woodward walked across the island, he wrote and mused about how the land may have affected its use: "The terrain is rocky . . . and covered with thick growth of cactus—this may be the reason for absence of permanent sites."[14] These observations indicated that Woodward not only looked for artifacts, but also thought about the way the people lived, where they lived, and what they ate and hunted. Given the manner in which he meticulously took notes, he had more than enough information to make him a recognized and influential name in Channel Islands' archaeology. All that was required of him was to publish.

History tells us that Woodward's kind of notetaking, including his attention to detail and interest in environmental and cultural cues, set his work apart from his contemporaries, who were mostly interested in developing chronologies of the time period in which artifacts belonged. Woodward was not the first to embrace the grid system that he employed in Big Dog Cave, nor was he a pioneer in utilizing stratigraphy or provenience in his work, but he was much more than an artifact collector. One important factor that distinguishes Woodward's work from that of the generation before him is that it was characterized "more by scientific inquiry than the acquisition of specimens for museum display."[15] Importantly, his work at Big Dog Cave began a "series of increasingly systematic and research-oriented archaeological investigations,"[16] an accomplishment that further differentiated him from his contemporaries. Moreover, he "practiced an early version of Historical Archaeology long before it was an accepted discipline."[17]

Historical archaeology is a branch within archaeology that uses written records (or oral traditions) to augment the study of objects and places during historical times. This field utilizes the knowledge of a diverse group of experts—including anthropologists, historians, geographers, folklorists, and ancestors' recollections—when examining archaeological sites. When Woodward read old ships' logs, perused accounts of past San Clemente Island archaeological digs, or chatted up the marines in an attempt to learn from their experiences, he actively conducted historical archaeology, which, in this case, documented European settlement and its effects on Native Americans.[18] In Woodward's own words, historical archaeology came "after Columbus" and consisted of "the residue of European materials found at Indian sites, everything from bottles to tin cans."[19]

Woodward's work practices were clearly influenced by his thoughtful and curious nature, as well as the coaching he received early in his career. This coaching came from none other than Alfred Kroeber, under whom he studied history and anthropology while at the University of

California, Berkeley, during the late 1910s and early 1920s.[20] Kroeber, director of Berkeley's anthropological museum, taught at Berkeley from 1901 to 1946 and famously befriended and studied Ishi, the last living member of the Yahi tribe. Kroeber is known as an early and influential anthropologist who played a major role in developing the field professionally. His writings and teachings changed the course of anthropology, shifting it away from amateurs, artifact collectors, and antiquarians and toward a rigorous scientific and academic discipline. He believed and taught the principle of cultural relativism, which holds that the morality, laws, and practices of any one culture are valid and must be evaluated in terms of the culture being explored and not from within the context of the researcher's own values. His views further shaped archaeology through his emphasis on material culture (tools, pottery, and dwellings) and the ways in which these items help reveal the symbols, social roles, and moral beliefs at play in the culture being studied. Today, as a result of Kroeber's—and others'—teachings and writings, most modern anthropologists consider all cultures to be equally legitimate and worthy of studying from a purely neutral perspective.

Woodward appears to have picked up much from his association with Kroeber, including his ability to refrain from passing judgment. Woodward's nephew recalls that his uncle told him, "you have to understand the history of the time and you can't make judgments based on what you would do."[21] In his journals, Woodward noted the length of bead necklaces interred with the deceased and the type of fur in which a chicken was wrapped upon its burial. These details infer a curiosity and interest in the social aspects and thought processes of the people who conducted the burial, but not judgment.

Later in life, Art began to mockingly refer to his style of historical archaeology as "tin-can" archaeology. In retrospect, this small joke may be more than a self-deprecating comment, but a reference to Berkeley's Phoebe A. Hearst Museum of Anthropology, which Hearst founded together with Woodward's mentor, Kroeber, in 1901. Over the years, the museum earned the sobriquets the "tin can" or "tin shack" because of the flimsy corrugated iron building that housed the museum's collection of anthropological artifacts. Given this history, it seems plausible that even though Woodward seemingly eschewed political and social hierarchies, his own self-label may have not only poked fun at himself and his profession but also ironically nodded at his academic and intellectual roots.

The nature of Woodward's notetaking alludes to another well-known scientist at Berkeley: Joseph Grinnell, director of the Berkeley Museum of Vertebrate Zoology (MVZ). Among Grinnell's many accomplishments was his vision for documenting natural history. He developed what is known as the Grinnell Method of notetaking, a protocol requiring naturalists and collectors to not only take detailed notes while in the field, but also to speculate and muse over the observed behaviors. Grinnell believed that "you can't tell in advance which observations will prove valuable,"[22] and he urged his students to make detailed fieldnotes that included species behaviors, vocalizations, weather, vegetation, time of day, or anything else that could prove useful to future investigators. Additionally, he instructed naturalists to both take photos as well as draw topographical maps annotated with the locations where specimens were taken. The purpose of these details ensured that "after the lapse of many years, possibly a century, the student of the future will have access to the original record of faunal conditions in California."[23] What sage advice this was.

While there is no direct evidence that Woodward studied under Grinnell, it would make sense that the directors of two of Berkeley's museums, MVZ and anthropology, would know one another and share philosophical points of view. Thus, it is completely within the realm of possibility that Grinnell's methods trickled down into the developing field of anthropology without the famous naturalist ever stepping foot into one of Kroeber's or Woodward's classrooms. Alternatively, Woodward may have been exposed to Grinnell's beliefs by attending a lecture given by the famous Berkeley biologist or befriending one of Grinnell's students. Certainly, the LACM archaeologist's fieldnotes and journals conform in spirit to the Grinnell Method of notetaking—there is no lack of details or musings in Woodward's journals.

Although Woodward came to believe that the Chumash exclusively inhabited the Channel Islands, modern researchers determined otherwise. The Island Gabrielino, who were related to mainland Gabrielino/Tongva, actually lived on and used the southern islands of San Clemente, San Nicolas, Santa Catalina, and Santa Barbara, whereas the Island

Chumash claimed the northern islands of Anacapa, Santa Cruz, Santa Rosa, and San Miguel. That Woodward would eventually be proved wrong about this does not detract from the records he made of Big Dog Cave. His work in this location provides scholars with an unassailable account not only of Island Gabrielino life on San Clemente Island, but also potentially of life on the mainland. This is because the items found in Big Dog Cave were well-preserved by salt spray, including fragile artifacts such as rope, clothing, and basketry that are only rarely found on the mainland—and nowhere in California in such abundance as the Channel Islands. Additionally, while there were once thousands upon thousands of middens and other archaeological sites on mainland California, over the years these have been exposed to the elements and "overwhelmed" by development. Many are no longer available for study and others are poorly preserved.

As a result, Big Dog Cave contributes greatly to archaeologists' understanding of Island Gabrielino lifestyles. Indeed, Woodward's fastidious notetaking aids ongoing research and sets him apart from earlier comparative archaeological investigations on the Channel Islands that "were lacking in field documentation and provenience" and thus "diminished the value of their results."[24] Finally, the mere fact that Woodward recorded so many archaeological sites, many of which have eroded out of hillsides, is important for archaeologists and historians because understanding the quantity of sites leads to a better understanding of San Clemente Island's role in Gabrielino/Tongva culture. This, in turn, provides the descendants of those buried in Big Dog Cave—the Gabrielino/Tongva and Island Gabrielino people, some of whom are eager to understand forgotten lifeways—a semblance of knowledge about rituals they may want to incorporate into their modern lives.

Over the next days, as Woodward directed the marines where to dig and what not to disturb, as he picked up a bone or turned a bead about in his fingers, it is conceivable—but unlikely—that he questioned the efficacy of his actions. As one of the original members of the Southwestern Anthropological Association, founded in 1928, Woodward served on the committee formed to protect archaeological remains from pothunters[25] and make recommendations for ethics and standards.[26] The year before the CIBS began, Woodward expressed his views on archaeological research,

Art Woodward with duffel. Photo taken on San Miguel Island, August 4, 1939. Courtesy of NHM Archives.

which were "published in August 1938 in the National Park Service's *Regional Review*, titled 'Archaeology—The Scrap Book of History.'"[27] In that article, Woodward makes clear his belief that archaeologists and historians are qualified to examine and interpret artifacts. Woodward saw nobility in his work and felt it his duty to conduct himself professionally, and even reverently, as he considered the smallest pieces of evidence. To him, each item represented an important clue to understanding the lives of those who lived before him. It is evident from the article that Woodward felt it was completely appropriate for scholars such as himself to touch, collect, and examine archaeological materials.

This was also the sensibility of Woodward's boss, John Adams Comstock, director of science at LACM. As an advocate of Indian rights in the 1920s and former director of the Southwest Museum of the American Indian in Los Angeles, Comstock served on a national advisory board on Indian affairs and later organized and became executive chairman of the Indian Welfare League, a group that worked to enact legislation to benefit Indians. But even with this background, Comstock did not consider collecting Indian artifacts for scholarly use immoral; rather, he accepted it as an appropriate research protocol practiced by accredited public and government agencies around the world. Furthermore, Comstock considered the archaeological aspects of the CIBS vital not only for the scientific information it yielded scholars, but because the interested public connected with this field of study. As an astute leader, he recognized the potential archaeology held for building community support for the LACM and winning benefactors for future projects.

For the CIBS, Big Dog Cave—which came so early in the survey—was a breakthrough, a jumping-off point for the explorers, its import much bigger than its physical size or the number of artifacts collected. It portended to the future, when the next five years of fieldwork would hopefully yield other equally exciting findings on the rest of the Channel Islands. For Woodward, it would be something on which he frequently corresponded, spoke about, and surely pondered over the course of his career.

Yet Big Dog Cave's importance to archaeologists in the early twentieth century pales in comparison to its importance today. The records the CIBS made of Big Dog Cave's contents are now priceless. In the twenty-first century, no one is allowed to enter this site—it is closed to the public, researchers, scientists, and government officials alike. The U.S. military cordoned it off. Unexploded ordinances litter the paths and entrance points to the cave's yawning maw, making it too dangerous to enter. Detonating them would damage the cave structure, almost certainly destroying anything still inside.

In order for Woodward, Meadows, von Bloeker, and Martin to stumble into a dark cave on a remote island in the Pacific Ocean during the second expedition of the CIBS, someone had to come up with the bright idea. Next, that someone—or someone else—had to agree to be in charge. After that, a detailed plan had to be formulated that could be "sold" internally to the scientific staff and the sponsoring organization's genteel and conservative board of governors. A big part of winning the board's approval for this ambitious and potentially exceedingly costly undertaking was not only finding a team willing to sleep on the ground, work in howling winds, and break their backs for little to no money, but also securing, *free of charge*, a few large boats for the survey's use. Acquiring permits from a labyrinth of unknown government and private ranch owners and lessees further complicated an already difficult series of tasks.

Most men, even of great ambition, might think better of such an undertaking—most did, in fact. Only two in the entire world had enough gumption to try it. Those two butterfly scientists, Dr. John Adams Comstock and Donald C. Meadows, embarked upon a journey to do what no one else before, or since, had done: completely survey North America's Galapagos—California's eight Channel Islands.

Chapter Two

BEFORE BIG DOG CAVE

"Nazi's Start Campaign of Revenge on Jews." Berlin—Germany tonight engaged in sweeping anti-Semitic vengeance for the shooting of a young Nazi diplomat in the Paris Embassy by a 17-year-old Polish Jew.

—*Los Angeles Times*, November 9, 1938

During the last two days of February 1938, rain splattered nearly nonstop against the stained-glass cupola of the Los Angeles County Museum of History, Science, and Art's Beaux Arts building. Seventy-five feet below the dome, three eleven-feet tall bronze goddesses stood dry and statuesque. The *Three Muses*, Los Angeles County's first commissioned piece of artwork, are stunning. Their gowns drape seductively off their shoulders, their shapely arms stretch upwards, their expressions exquisite as they survey the marble-colonnaded room with a dignity befitting their role as stewards of history, science, and art. Yet what captures visitors' attentions more than their fine feminine forms is what the muses hold above their heads in the palm of their hands: an oversized golden globe, a glowing symbol of possibility and of mysteries waiting to be unraveled.

Down one wing of the museum's traditionally T-shaped Beaux Arts building—not far from where sunrays pierced the museum's stained-glass copula and scattered dazzling patterns of yellow, red, blue, and green to the mosaic floor around the *Three Muses*—a solemn black microscope sat on a hefty oak desk in a one-windowed, third-story office, waiting to be put to use. Alongside it lay a number of trays, a few pads of paper, stacks of notecards, and books opened to pages of colorfully illustrated butterflies. Each tray held a rich cache of seemingly identical Lepidoptera, forever poised for flight with wings spread and pinned. Beneath every deceased insect, small paper tags indicated in tiny, perfect script the creature's scientific name, specimen number, sex, date of its collection, and collector's name. Bookcases lined the walls behind the desk, their shelves jammed with hardcover books jostling for space with paperwork, drawings, and butterfly and moth rearing cages. At the desk sat a middle-aged man, one hand resting on an open book, the other quiet, successfully resisting the urge to fiddle with the microscope's fine and coarse focus knobs.

The man was Dr. John Adams Comstock, director of science at the LACM. He was capable and competent, kind and generous, and skilled in art, business, medicine, and science. In museum photos he favored starched white shirts and ties, but in the field his attire was pure Roy Chapman Andrews (i.e., the director of the American Museum of Natural History in New York City from 1934–1941 and purportedly the inspiration for the Hollywood character Indiana Jones). Like Andrews, who became famous for leading large expeditions into Mongolia, Comstock's field attire consisted of jodhpurs or khakis, boots, a belted flak jacket, and a fedora with turned-down brim. A handsome man, the director wore small, round eyeglasses and a neatly trimmed mustache that gave him a gentleman-scientist-meets-Hollywood-star look. As he aged, his hair silvered and his hairline receded, but his light eyes never ceased to sparkle with mirth whenever his off-handed puns cajoled his audience to laughter. Warm and witty, Comstock formed close bonds with his staff that went far beyond the collegial. Letters to him frequently began with the endearing salutation of "Dear Doc," and his return letters often ended with sentiments such as, "Best wishes to the gang."

Of English descent, Comstock was one of seven children born into the wealthy enclave of Evanston, Illinois, in 1883 to the daughter of Judge Harvey B. Hurd, one of Northwestern University's founders and, for many years, its dean. Beginning in high school and continuing through his college years, Judge Hurd insisted that Comstock be privately tutored. He also saw to it that the Chicago Art Institute and the Laflin and Field Museums of Chicago supplemented the lad's fine arts and natural history

John Adams Comstock in his LACM office. Courtesy of NHM Archives.

coursework. "It was the wish of our family that I should follow art as a vocation, but my tastes were more inclined toward natural history. My insect collection was begun at the age of twelve," Comstock said.[1]

Aiming to please himself as well as his family, young Comstock deftly combined his interests in science and art. He became secretary of the Chicago Entomological Society at age fifteen, published his first scientific paper at nineteen, and at age twenty-two moved to East Aurora, New York, to work as an artist designing furniture, metalwork, book illustrations, and jewelry for Roycroft, the arts and crafts community founded by Elbert Hubbard.

His years in arts and crafts shops—both in New York and later in Santa Rosa, California—greatly informed his life, for he was both a sci- entist with a keen mind and an artist with heart. In 1927 he published *Butterflies of California*, which he researched, wrote, and self-illustrated with stylized, hand-colored butterflies. The book quickly became a classic in its field and its contributions were acknowledged in 1979 at the 26th Annual Meeting of the Pacific Slope Section of the Lepidopterists' Society, where Comstock was posthumously recognized as the name bearer for the society's first student award and became its first honoree. The society declared that *Butterflies of California* influenced the "popularity of butterfly collecting, and ultimately ... the study of natural history generally."[2]

Also in 1927, at age forty-four, Comstock came to the LACM having completed successful careers as a medical doctor, owner of an arts and crafts business, and director of the Southwest Museum in Los Angeles. He had also married, fathered three children, divorced, remarried, and become widowed (in 1926). In March 1928, he was married a third and final time, to Ruth Mary Gard, the woman with whom he happily lived until his death thirty-two years later.

During his lifetime, Comstock published over 230 scholarly articles[3] and accumulated dozens of professional affiliations and accomplishments to his name, yet what he is remembered most for is his concern for his fellow men. While director of the Southwest Museum, he founded the Indian Welfare League and also served on the U.S. National Advisory Committee on Indian Affairs. As a doctor he had a gentle bedside manner, and he frequently demonstrated concern for his staff at the LACM, even giving them money without expecting repayment during the hard years of the Great Depression.

Comstock didn't conceive of the Channel Islands Biological Survey himself, but his involvement ensured its approval by the museum's board of governors and his logistical gymnastics, administrative juggling, prolific letter writing, and considerable abilities as a purser made it a reality. Moreover, Comstock's innate good sense prompted him to pay attention when Donald (Don) C. Meadows, a high school biology teacher in Long Beach, California, came to him with an idea, and idea that eventually lead him to name Meadows "The Father of the Channel Islands Biological Survey."[4]

A chameleon in life, Meadows's varied interests led to a number of avocations, if not careers. An amateur lepidopterist since childhood, he had an experienced eye and a piercing gaze that could distinguish subtle variations in butterfly wing colors that differentiated one species from the next. He was a man of slight build and average height with an elfin countenance wholly at odds with the stylish way he wore his hair—longish and slicked back, just like Errol Flynn. When he smiled his upper lip disappeared beneath a thin, caterpillar-like mustache and his cheeks rose into little balls that squeezed his eyes into narrow crescents.

An enthusiastically ambitious man, Meadows much desired to make a name for himself. When the Long Beach School District absorbed Santa Catalina Island's school system, he saw his chance. He conceived of a plan to transfer to Avalon, Santa Catalina's largest town and home to the island's single schoolhouse, from whence he would embark on a complete survey of Catalina's Lepidoptera, an undertaking never before attempted. Meadows moved with his wife, a school librarian, to teach middle school at Avalon K–12 School in 1927 and began his island butterfly collection.

Because no one had ever collected micro moths (small moths) on the Channel Islands, his large collection—begat from Avalon's streetlights—inspired the *Los Angeles Times* to dub him "the Moth Man of Catalina." This notoriety, together with his published findings, made him the undisputed expert on Catalina's Lepidoptera. Though it seems consistent with his ambition, it's unknown whether Meadows also dreamed that several new species would one day bear his name, but three small moths do: *Arachnis picta meadowsi* Comstock, *Feralia meadowsi* Buckett, and *Sericosema wilsonensis meadowsaria* Sperry.

In 1930, after only three years on Catalina, Meadows became restless and challenged himself with yet another new endeavor. At the height of the Great Depression, he took a leave of absence from his teaching job to attend the University of California, Berkeley, his goal to earn his master's degree in science, which would lead to a zoology teaching position at Santa Ana Junior College. After completing the degree, he returned to Avalon for another three years, never attaining the teaching position to which he aspired. By the time he resumed permanent residence on the mainland in 1934, the seed of yet another ambitious undertaking—conducting an eight-island survey of the Channel Islands—had germinated together with another goal: to use the survey results to earn a doctorate in philosophy.

In most of Meadows's CIBS correspondence as well as newspaper interviews, the high school biology teacher refers to himself as "expedition leader." Indeed, his take-charge attitude and admirable focus lend support to this vision of himself. It's possible, too, that the notoriety he garnered from his Catalina moth work may have fueled this image of himself as a leader of men—replete with hat, pegged pant legs, and boots—a man equipped with the qualifications necessary to lead an expedition into the annals of history. It may also have prompted him to accept the nickname "Professor," a moniker more befitting a college instructor than a high school teacher, but which, if he did not coin for himself, he certainly did nothing to dissuade others from using.

It is uncertain exactly how Comstock and Meadows knew each other, but even today science is a relatively small field, one in which practitioners circulate amongst the same similarly minded people, all of whom know each other or know someone who knows someone. In January 1938, when Meadows approached his fellow lepidopterist and member of the Southern California Academy of Science, John Adams Comstock, with the idea of a Channel Islands biological survey, Meadows was a forty-year-old high school biology teacher, husband, and father with a personal collection of twenty thousand butterfly specimens. While Meadows proposed an expedition to a single island, Santa Cruz, he hinted at a more ambitious project, writing "that the present expedition can lead to several others sponsored by the museum. If there is enough . . . interest . . . there is a good possibility that the other islands off the coast may be explored."[5] Thus originated the idea of a complete Channel Islands survey, emerging like a butterfly from its cocoon, gently testing its wings and readying for flight.

The next mention of a survey comes in March 1938: "The museum is extremely anxious to make a general scientific survey of all the channel islands; a task never before attempted,"[6] Meadows told Edwin Stanton, the owner of Santa Cruz Island. Months passed without any further mention of the survey in either NHM's or UC Irvine's files, but Comstock had

Don Meadows hard at work spreading the wings of butterfly specimens. Notice his pack of Chesterfields, White Owl cigars, and pipe sitting near his pins, scissors, tape, and other useful entomological items. Photo taken in 1947. Courtesy of Don Meadows Papers (MS-Roo1), UC Irvine, Special Collections & Archives.

been busy during this time. The museum had undergone a major shift in management that affected him, his direct reports, and his department. When the museum opened to the public in 1913, its management rested with a nine-member board of governors reporting to the County of Los Angeles Board of Supervisors. The board of governors was composed of one representative each from the County of Los Angeles Board of Supervisors, the Cooper Ornithological Society, an at-large representative, plus two representatives each from the Los Angeles City Historical Society, the Southern California Academy of Sciences, and the Fine Arts League. This arrangement appealed to the board of supervisors, who were inexperienced in running a museum and believed that the representatives on the board of governors would serve the county best.

This structure remained in place until June 3, 1938, when the County of Los Angeles Board of Supervisors, besieged by the art-loving community of Los Angeles, bowed to pressure and made dramatic changes to the management of the LACM. First and foremost, the county created a new department responsible for all matters relating to the museum entitled the Department of History, Science, and Art. It then placed this department under the management of a board of governors selected by the board of supervisors and added six additional, more art-minded, individuals. In these ways, the museum's management, strategy, and—most importantly—vision were largely ceded to art.

Secondly, staff members at the museum were reorganized under five equal directors, one each for finance and operations, science, history, art, and art instruction, the latter being the Otis Art Institute. Collectively, the five directors constituted the administrative council, responsible for managing all interdepartmental issues, the use of exhibition and storage space, and making policy recommendations to the board of governors. At this time, Woodward's title changed from curator of history and anthropology to director of history and anthropology, and Comstock's changed from associate director to director of science.

For Comstock, this represented a demotion, his sphere of management drastically cut. A 1932 museum organization chart[7] shows that only Comstock and E. Roscoe Shrader—then the dean of the Otis Art Institute—reported to Director William A. Bryan, and that most of the museum reported up through Comstock. At that time, and presumably up until the June 1938 reorganization, Comstock's responsibilities spanned Hancock Park, the LACM curatorial staff—including the art department, museum collections, and administration—as well as the library, the cafeteria, taxidermy, photography, and others. While the reorganization was quite a change, Comstock, being both a level-headed leader and a scientist who didn't let his ego get in the way of progress, may have found some benefits in this new arrangement, such as the removal of his cafeteria responsibilities. In addition to these changes, the reorganization mandated the establishment of five standing board committees representing the five directorships. Committees consisted of a chairman from the board of governors, the appropriate museum director, and additional board of governors members. These committees were to meet and report regularly to the greater board.

At the first meeting of the new board of governors in July 1938, Rufus B. von KleinSmid was elected president. Von KleinSmid began his career teaching education at DePauw University. While there, he became

Indiana's state psychologist, oversaw the establishment of laboratories within Indiana's penal institutions that were tasked with studying criminal psychology, and founded the American Association of Criminal Psychology. Before leaving DePauw, von KleinSmid wrote *Eugenics and the State*, in which he referred to sterilization procedures as "the science of good birth."[8] He then spent seven years as president of the University of Arizona prior to accepting a post as president of the University of Southern California (USC) in 1921. In 1928, while president of USC, he became a founding member of the Human Betterment Foundation, a Pasadena-based leading eugenics organization. Fellow founding members included *Los Angeles Times* publisher Harry Chandler, Stanford University's first president David Starr Jordan, and Nobel Prize-winning physicist and Caltech head Robert A. Millikan, among others. While eugenics today is widely abhorred, in the 1920s and 1930s it was a popular social movement and did not affect the regard in which Los Angelinos held von KleinSmid, who was well known in the city and credited with transforming USC into an influential university of higher learning. In more current times, however, allegations of anti-Semitism and racism—particularly surrounding Japanese enrollment at USC in the aftermath of World War II—have been leveled against von KleinSmid, causing some USC students to question the appropriateness of naming a campus building after this former president.

The reorganization of the museum made it clear to Comstock and others that the LACM's focus was shifting away from science and history and toward art. As an astute manager, Comstock probably surmised that, beginning immediately, science and history would be more closely scrutinized and evaluated. Thus, the notion of a complete Channel Islands survey may have taken on greater importance because a successful series of expeditions had the potential for not only garnering national scientific recognition, but also increased local publicity. The outcome of these twin benefits could boost the science and history departments' visibility and, in turn, directly increase funding opportunities and long-term viability.

During the months leading up to and following the reorganization, Comstock would have had his hands full, and thus any lapse in attention he gave to the survey is understandable. However, he didn't let too much time go by before resurfacing the project. In a late November 1938 administrative council meeting of the LACM's five directors, he supported a letter authored by Meadows that suggested organizing a "scientific research party" on San Clemente Island. Interestingly, not only does this letter not mention Santa Cruz (as originally proposed to Comstock), but it remains silent on an eight-island survey as well. Why this change in scope is unclear, but the fact that the proposal stipulates the museum would incur no expense other than museum staff salaries might be a clue. The effects of the Great Depression were not yet over, and the dust from the reorganization still clouded the museum's air. It could be that the two butterfly scientists felt a less ambitious proposal might be better received than the longer, larger, and more expansive original idea. Regardless, the science committee approved the proposal—subject to the board of governors' further approval—and over the next twenty-one days Comstock and Meadows refined their plan, which, in its final form, once again encompassed all eight islands.

These few details are all that is known about the development of the Channel Islands Biological Survey. And though they are not extensive, it is clear given the span of time from inception to final proposal that much thought went into its creation.

On December 21, 1938, Comstock delivered a two-page letter addressed to the "Honorable Board of Governors." "Respectfully sub-mitted" by Don C. Meadows, it outlined the goals of the survey: most importantly, that it would be multidisciplinary, including archaeology, botany, geology, paleontology, ornithology, mammalogy, entomology, herpetology, and other scientific fields; and that its scope, as the name implies, would include all eight of California's Channel Islands. Though Comstock purposefully kept the proposal brief, Meadows wrote a sub-sequent progress report covering the first two expeditions that provides considerably more detail—namely that, in addition to the stated goals, the survey would seek to determine relationships between the islands them-selves and with the mainland, to study man's influence on the islands, and to publish the findings. Comstock envisioned the fieldwork portion of the survey to begin in 1939 and run for five years, through the fall of 1944. He further expected that another two years would be needed to assemble data, complete taxonomic work, and write the reports, includ-ing a comprehensive document covering the entire survey. Throughout this period, and especially afterwards, Comstock expected staff to publish for academic and public markets, and develop museum exhibits and displays based on their Channel Islands research.

The CIBS was a massive undertaking that required many steps and participants, including: input from the museum's most experienced scientists; tedious planning and coordination with numerous island owners (both private and the U.S. military) and lessees; transportation of equipment and personnel across treacherous ocean channels; and a commitment from the board of governors to publicly support the museum in its attempt to do something that had never been done before. Today, a survey of the breath and magnitude of the CIBS would likely never materialize. It would require too many people, too many disciplines, and too much money. Ironically, the clever way Comstock and Meadows addressed the topic of financing or, more accurately, the lack of funds needed to launch the survey, may have been a key component of the board's approval. The proposal as presented stipulated that all survey costs—camping gear, food, a cook, transportation, etc.—be borne by the survey participants themselves.[9]

There were only two exceptions to these costs. First, the museum would supply "all scientific supplies, materials and equipment ... needed for the proper collection and preservation of specimens destined for the Museum,"[10] a concession clearly in the museum's own self-interest. Second, museum employees would continue to receive their regular staff salaries while participating in the survey, though non-staffers, such as Don Meadows, would receive no monetary remuneration whatsoever. In dispensation, however, non-staffers would be given an agreed upon allotment of specimens that they could personally collect for their own use, as long as the items were not "type specimen" that would be used to define new species or the sole specimen of the species collected.

The proposal concluded with the suggestion that San Clemente Island be the first island surveyed, since "ecological modifications going on there incident to the occupancy by the United States Naval Authorities may result in very rapid biotic changes."[11] In other words, Comstock and Meadows were concerned that military exercises and training operations might destroy San Clemente's fragile environment before it could even be catalogued.

On Christmas Eve 1938, the LACM's board of governors approved the five-year Channel Islands Biological Survey.

Unbeknownst to anyone in Los Angeles, on December 22, 1938, the day after Comstock submitted his ambitious proposal, on a continent halfway around the world, a fisherman pulled a fifty-four-inch steely blue fish covered with hard bony scales and weighing 127 pounds out of the Indian Ocean. The fisherman made port in East London, South Africa, where he deposited the strange fish amongst a pile of sharks and rays that would soon be thrown away as unsalable. A few months later, a scientist from the British Museum would write about the capture of this homely specimen, a creature that defied categorization as either cartilaginous or bony in an article entitled, "One of the Most Amazing Events in the Realm of Natural History in the Twentieth Century."[12] This fish, the one that almost got away, was a member of the extinct order Coelacanthini— a lobe-finned fish related to fishes that once lived more than three hundred million years ago, and which scientists thought had died off with the dinosaurs.[13]

Yet here the coelacanth lay, very much alive only a mere few hours before Marjorie Courtenay-Latimer, curator of the small East London Museum in South Africa, spotted its odd, bright blue fin amongst the heap of castoffs she regularly inspected in search of unusual species. Her curiosity, insight, and persistence—first in hauling the fish out of the pile, and second in persuading a taxi driver to drive her and her smelly cargo back to the museum where she quickly photographed it, had it taxidermized before it rotted too much, and then persuaded the only ichthyologist in South Africa to help her identify it—gave the world this living fossil.

In March 1939, the esteemed journal *Nature* ran an article about this extant fossil entitled, "A Living Fish of Mesozoic Type." The *London Illustrated News* published another piece, as did the *East London Daily Dispatch* and the *Times* of London.[14] Scientists throughout the world debated this startling discovery, international newspapers reported on it, and the public ached to see the evidence. Courtenay-Latimer reported that twenty thousand people visited the fish at the East London Museum in South Africa.[15] The next years saw the publication of scientific works describing the specimen and increased public interest in locating another one.

The fervor surrounding the coelacanth's discovery was emblematic of the times: people were interested in the world around them and science captivated imaginations. Once news of this fish reached the West

Coast of the United States, its significance would not have been lost on John Adams Comstock, Don Meadows, or any of the scientists at the LACM. Moreover, the late nineteenth and early twentieth century is known as the "golden age of exploration," a time when the world's largest and most prestigious natural history museums—the British Museum in London, the American Museum of Natural History in New York City, the Field Museum in Chicago, the National Museum of Natural History in Paris, and the Smithsonian National Museum of Natural History in Washington, DC, among others—stretched their boundaries, both physical and scientific, to explore the world: Antarctica, Africa, South and Central America, Mongolia, or the Badlands of North Dakota. Every exploration was part of the great race to understand our world and provide the institutions that mounted them with a means to make an unforgettable name for themselves. The LACM's Channel Islands Biological Survey fit perfectly into this pack.

This golden age of exploration represented a time of possibility, one that the LACM embraced in the form of the *Three Muses*, the statues that offered Los Angelinos the universe, and one in which the LACM's scientists sought dearly to partake. Once news of the coelacanth's discovery reached California, it is easy to imagine it buoying Meadows's own hopes of achieving scientific immortality through the CIBS—and if not that, at least a doctoral degree and a job in higher education where he could rightfully claim the moniker, Professor.

As for Comstock, once the survey was approved he turned toward more practical concerns. How would the members of the first expedition to San Clemente Island get there, much less to any of the other islands? Who in that day and age would agree to transport them for free?

Chapter Three

JUAN RODRÍGUEZ CABRILLO SPOILED IT ALL

"US, Britain and France Warn 'Wanton' Hitler." The world's three great democracies—the United States, Great Britain and France—united yesterday in condemning Germany's "wanton lawlessness" and "attempt to dominate the world by force" in the absorption of Czecho-Slovakia.

—*Daily News* (New York), March 18, 1939

In 1542, when Juan Rodríguez Cabrillo sailed the *San Salvador* and two other galleons northward along the west coast of California, he claimed the mainland and the Channel Islands for Spain. When the galleons anchored in what is known today as Avalon Harbor on Santa Catalina Island, he and his crew became the first Europeans to encounter native Channel Islanders. Upon anchoring in Avalon Harbor, Cabrillo's logs note that between eight and ten Indians paddled toward the Spaniards in a single, sewn-plank canoe. While this initial meeting proved peaceful, a fight ensued sometime during the visit that left Cabrillo with a broken shinbone. When the wound became gangrenous in the winter of 1542–43, he died and was buried, legend has it, on San Miguel Island, but recent analysis of historical records suggests he was actually buried on Santa Catalina Island.[1] Sadly, the circumstances surrounding the explorer's death would set the tone for the future brutal clashes in which these two cultures would engage.

At the time of initial contact, no one realized that two diverse populations—the Chumash and the Gabrielino/Tongva—occupied distinct territories on the adjacent mainland and the Channel Islands, or that they spoke completely different languages. Additionally, scholars today can only estimate how many people occupied the mainland and island homes of the Chumash and Gabrielino/Tongva people. It is believed that approximately twenty-five thousand Chumash lived in what today are the counties of Ventura, Santa Barbara, and San Luis Obispo, with another three thousand on the northern Channel Islands.[2] In contrast, an estimated ten to fifteen thousand Gabrielino/Tongva are thought to have lived throughout the Los Angeles basin and the southern Channel Islands. Though it is unknown how many Gabrielino/Tongva islanders lived in permanent villages on the southern Channel Islands, far fewer lived on these drier isles than on the wetter northern islands. To get a sense of this population disparity, consider that Santa Catalina Island, the most densely inhabited of the southern Channel Islands, had only around five hundred people living on it.[3]

On the mainland, the Chumash and Gabrielino/Tongva tribes maintained separate, complex cultures that shared many traits. Both were hunters, fishermen, and gatherers living in established, separate villages across their territories with chieftains who ruled them. They ate similar foods and dressed alike. Both built large, domed homes, some as large as fifty feet across, in which three to four family groups of up to sixty people could live, and both used sturdy canoes to fish and travel between the mainland and the Channel Islands. Additionally, both tribes organized politically within their villages in terms of social and economic structure[4] and utilized money to facilitate trade with other tribes. Each also believed in the lower, middle, and upper worlds, with humans occupying the middle realm and the other realms accessed by animal spirits and shamans. Both held winter and summer solstice ceremonies and both achieved similar levels of technological advancement, evidenced by their crafting of circular shell fishhooks and plank canoes. They were in every regard complex and evolved societies. Modern researchers believe that the similarities between these two tribes developed over thousands of years as a result of occupying similar environments.

Yet even with so much in common, the Chumash and the Gabrielino/Tongva were distinct tribes defined by different language and kinship systems.[5] Woodward believed that the Gabrielino/Tongva spoke a Shoshonean language that hailed from the Great Basin area of the United

States, but today's scholars assign the Takic language to the Gabrielino/ Tongva. Takic is one of several languages included in the Uto-Aztecan language family spoken by native people all across the western United States and parts of Mexico. While Shoshonean is also a Uto-Aztecan language, it is in a different branch. Chumashan, on the other hand, is an isolate language family with no connection to any language spoken throughout the world. Woodward would have been fascinated to know this and could have used this information to rightly conclude that the Chumash have existed for a very long time.[6]

With respect to kinship systems and postmarital residence, the two tribes differed greatly. The Chumash were matrilocal, meaning that upon marriage the husband moved to his wife's community, whereas the Gabrielino/Tongva were patrilineal and patrilocal.[7] Additionally, mainland Chumash typically buried their dead together with animals, food, jewelry or special coverings, or other possessions that accompanied the spirit into the next world. The mainland Gabrielino/Tongva, however, cremated their dead to release their spirits to the upper realm.

By the time Woodward began visiting the Channel Islands in 1939, some of his contemporaries had come to believe that Shoshonean people—today's Gabrielino/Tongva and, more specifically, island Gabrielino—occupied the southern islands, whereas Chumash islanders occupied the northern islands. Confirming or disproving this assumption became one of Woodward's primary research goals for the survey. He noted to his colleague, Phil Orr, an archaeologist with the Santa Barbara Museum of Natural History, that "cremation burial[,] while occurring on San Clemente and San Nicolas[,] do not seem to be general for all of the Islands."[8] That is, he found cremation on some islands, burial on others, and, to his further consternation, both types of burials on others (Santa Rosa and San Clemente Islands, for instance). This mixture of burial practices is something he would not have expected to find in the mainland territories of the Chumash and Gabrielino/Tongva.

As Woodward puzzled over the question of which tribes occupied which islands, the complication in burial systems he encountered prevented him from applying the simple algorithm—Chumash bury, Gabrielino/Tongva cremate—in solving the islands' cultural affiliations. Setting aside the burial practices, Woodward focused on the many other commonalities linking the Channel Islanders with mainland people. Among

the similarities he observed were their canoes, fishhooks, steatite and abalone ornaments, extensive use of sea mammal bone and tarred pebbles
for waterproofing, seagrass basketry, and beadmaking techniques.[9] These
parallels led him to believe that the islanders' "material cultures were
more Chumashan than anything else."[10] Researchers today concur with
Woodward's observations regarding the commonality of material items
found on the Channel Islands, but they do not attribute this to the existence of a single tribe living on all the islands. Rather, they ascribe the
development of these similarities to shared, maritime living conditions.

The similarities between the various Channel Islanders did not lessen
when the California Mission fathers removed the Indians from their
island homes and placed them in missions to live with people from various mainland and island locations. Though they were converted to Christianity and forced into labor, observations of what happened with the
northern Channel Islanders demonstrate the strength of the island culture. In the unnatural mission setting, despite having their daily rhythms
and life cues stripped away from them, the island people established
"island" communities that allowed them to maintain subsistence and
ritual practices distinct from their mainland kin living alongside them.

Though Woodward was ultimately incorrect regarding his assumption about island cultural affiliations, the fact that he picked up on burial
practice differences, as well as various cultural similarities, demonstrates
his keen interest in the social and ethnological behaviors of the people he
studied. This characteristic is in stark contrast to the antiquity hunters of
the prior century and more closely aligns him with modern archaeologists, who primarily focus on investigating similarities and differences
in cultural practices that were influenced by the environment.[11]

Religious beliefs constituted another cultural difference between
the island Gabrielino and island Chumash. Within the island Chumash,
an elite group of political and religious leaders led their 'antap religion.
These individuals were charged with maintaining cosmic balance: "heal-
ing, rain making, predicting the future, making astronomical obser-
vances, and organizing feasts and ceremonies, such as those related to
winter solstice ceremonies."[12]

Beginning sometime after European contact, the island Gabrielino
religion, Chinigchinich, drew from a combination of ancient beliefs and
ceremonies while also paying homage to Chinigchinich, the supreme god.

This god gave life to all things, watched over the people, and protected and punished them as a means to enforce moral order. The Chinigchinich belief system shares characteristics with Christian styles of religion and perhaps even developed in response to European and mission-era cultural pressures. As a result, some scholars consider Chinigchinich a "crisis" religion that absorbed some European and Christian belief systems into their existing "pre-European shamanistic practices."[13] Examples include the Gabrielino/Tongva ceremonies and ritualistic practices associated with harvests as well as the belief that effigies had special powers capable of protecting people from danger. These practices are loosely akin to the Christian holiday of the Feast of Saint Martin that celebrated the completion of the autumn wheat seeding, or wearing St. Sebastian medals as a symbol of physical strength and endurance in athletic competitions.

The southern Channel Island Gabrielino carved steatite, or soapstone, effigies. While the two most common figures resembled pelicans and orcas (killer whales), ravens, cormorants, and other creatures were also carved out of stone. Each effigy held a special meaning and were believed to possess supernatural powers of protection. Pelicans and cormorants were thought of as "crewmen" on boats and were frequently taken along on voyages, a practice strikingly similar to the Christian tradition of wearing Saint Christopher medallions while traveling. Not unsurprisingly, pelican effigies are still found on San Clemente Island, which is one of the most remote of the Channel Islands.

Significantly, on the Channel Islands steatite can only be found in a single quarry on Santa Catalina, which allows researchers to draw conclusions about trade and the relative cultural importance of effigies. For instance, because only four steatite animal effigies[14]—and these having little provenience—have been found on any of the northern Channel Islands, researchers believe that the northern island Chumash's 'antap belief system had little need for effigies. In other words, the 'antap religion may not have believed in saints in the same way the Chinigchinich did. Additionally, this line of thinking holds that the few effigies found on the northern islands could either have been trade items or were mistakenly left by southern island visitors.

Cabrillo's arrival on the West Coast in 1542 was part of an intense European expansion known as the age of exploration that lasted from the early fifteen century until the early seventeenth century. In the two hundred years following Cabrillo's arrival, only a handful of explorers and trading ships encountered the Channel Island people and few records detail these interactions, a fact that speaks to the relative banality of these contacts. Thus, this period of relative quiet left the island Chumash and island Gabrielino people to thrive. They developed new technologies and their cultures grew more complex. But Cabrillo's fateful voyage begat the demise of these cultures as it ushered in increasingly destructive exchanges of New World plants, animals, and communicable diseases.

Spain, Great Britain, and Russia were all in a race to claim North America's West Coast. The rulers of these countries, hungry for new economic opportunities, greater personal wealth, fame wrought from discovery, and the expansion of Christianity, drove explosive growth along the West Coast during the age of exploration. To ward off competition, beginning in 1769 Spain embarked upon an aggressive fifty-three-year campaign to settle California and at the same time convert the native people to Christianity. To this end, twenty-one missions—plus one contemplated, but never constructed, mission on Santa Cruz Island—were built throughout California during what is known as the mission era.

At about this same time, the Russian Empire's expansion into Alaska and the Pacific Northwest grew more intense as Russian merchants realized the enormous potential of the maritime fur trade. By the early 1800s, Russian fur traders had expanded their sea otter hunting range into Southern California's productive waters. They brought with them native Kodiak (or Aleut) men, fierce and capable hunters, who, armed with Russian weapons, were no match for the island people. The hunting that ensued drove scores of sea mammals—sea otters, sea lions, elephant seals, and others—to virtual, or possibly total, extinction.

The peak of island Gabrielino/Tongva and island Chumash culture coincided with the first European contact, but waned rapidly until the early 1800s, their cultures' darkest years. During this time, their populations declined due to introduced influenza, typhoid, measles, and syphilis. Some died at the hands of the otter hunters, while others lost their land to the mission fathers and Spanish soldiers who seized it for themselves. In the end, the Channel Islands people were made to work and live in the missions, their culture and way of life dismissed.

Though at times the natives revolted, they were out-gunned, out-manned, and left with few options, causing them to eventually submit to servitude and Christianity. In 1835, the last Channel Islanders, save one woman and, new scholarship suggests, her son, were removed from their island homes.

Archaeological excavations of the Channel Islands began a few decades after the last native people left and continue today. Early explorers included representatives from the U.S. government performing geographic surveys, the Smithsonian, the Musée de l'Homme in France, as well as other institutions worldwide. Much of the archaeology of this time took the form of artifact hunting, an old Victorian notion of curio collection and display. In the early 1900s, increased civilian and institutional interest in southwestern Native American culture brought the Phoebe Hearst Museum of Anthropology (at the University of California, Berkeley), the Heye Museum of New York, and others to the Channel Islands.

Much of the archaeology of these times focused on burial sites where the most complete and beautiful artifacts could be found alongside or near human remains. Because museums and private collectors were willing to pay for artifacts, gravesites were often picked apart and taken at will by "professional"—usually amateur—collectors, often derisively referred to as "pothunters." Concerned citizenry increasingly took notice of these atrocities and began efforts to better control archaeologically significant sites. The topic of pothunting crops up throughout the CIBS archival record, as do the museum's attempts to stop it. Woodward photographed looted sites to document the desecration and damage, and Comstock wrote government officials requesting their help in controlling unauthorized and unscrupulous collecting activities.

The Antiquities Act of 1906 was the first U.S. law that provided protections to natural and cultural resources—which include human remains and associated funerary materials. It was put in place as the result of twenty-five years of work by a group of concerned citizens and scientists who, in the late 1880s, realized that historically valuable archaeological sites were being plundered by for-profit pothunters and other relic-hungry collectors. Concern over Native American archaeological sites in the southwestern United States provided much of the impetus for passage of this act.

The Antiquities Act gave the president of the United States the authority to protect "historic landmarks, historic and prehistoric structures, and other objects of historic or scientific interest that are situated upon the lands owned or controlled by the Government of the United States."[15] It also required anyone interested in examining these monuments to procure a permit from the secretaries of the interior, agriculture, or war, depending upon which department had jurisdiction over the land on which the remains were located.

Detractors of the Antiquities Act had several issues with this piece of legislation. First, the act, by way of inference, defined Indian remains interred on government land as "objects of historic or scientific interest" that can be "controlled" (a word some detractors say is akin to "owned") by the federal government. Some Native American groups found this offensive, not only because the act allowed the disinterment of Indian remains so long as permits are obtained, but more importantly because it implied that human Indian remains could be—and were—owned by the U.S. government. In addition, the act did not address tribal interests, laws, customs, or beliefs,[16] thus reducing Indian people to objects subject to examination by permitted professionals "unimpeded by amateur pot hunters and looters."[17] Moreover, because it treated Indian burials and other sacred objects differently than non-Indian remains, it was a form of racial discrimination.

In 1979, the Archaeological Resources Protection Act replaced the Antiquities Act. Though it provided additional safeguards to Indian artifacts and remains, it did not alter the offensive federal "ownership" aspect of "resources" found on U.S. property. In 1990, the Native American Graves Protection and Repatriation Act (NAGPRA) finally addressed the treatment of Native American remains within the perspective of human rights. NAGPRA not only gave the "ownership" of Native American (including Hawaiian) human remains to lineal descendants, but it also required museums or other institutions receiving federal funds to return remains or items of ritualistic or religious significance—such as funerary objects—within their collections to the appropriate descendants if lineage could be determined. In addition, NAGRPA provides that collaboration and consent of lineal descendants must be attained with regard to any actions taken on future discoveries. While NAGPRA made great strides, it does not apply to privately funded excavations on both private and state lands, nor to private collections legally obtained, and therefore some Native Americans feel that additional, broader protections are still needed.

Some people, including many Native Americans, believe that the only difference between an archaeologist and a pothunter is that one is sanctioned, the other is not. Artifacts and human remains are disturbed or taken in either case, with the larger injustice being that Native American remains are not treated with the sanctity their buried Christian brethren receive—a disparity that illuminates ongoing civil rights issues.

On the other hand, many archaeologists believe their work advances our collective knowledge of a shared past and leads to a better understanding of each other's cultures. Archaeology today often does not include the excavation of human remains, but does stress the development of a close working relationship with indigenous communities. Certainly, scholars working on the Channel Islands today believe in, and conscientiously follow, these protocols.

In 1939, the potential collection of Indian artifacts and remains constituted an important goal of the Channel Islands Biological Survey. LACM and CIBS participants adhered to established laws and reported instances of pothunting. They believed they were doing important work, and they were eager to get back to San Clemente Island.

Chapter Four

THE ISLAND OF CAVES: SAN CLEMENTE ISLAND

"Albania Masses for Italian War as Mussolini's Battleships Arrive; Poland Scorns Hitler Demand: Nazis Spurned in Attempt to Grab Danizg." Berlin—Nazi officials disclosed today that Poland had rejected a German proposal for settlement of Eastern European controversies, including cession of Danzig to the Reich.

—*Oakland Tribune* (Oakland, California), April 6, 1939

Almost immediately upon the approval of the CIBS by the board of governors in 1938, Comstock contacted the Secretary of the Navy requesting permission to begin work on San Clemente Island. Next, to solve his transportation problem, he turned his attention across Exposition Boulevard to the University of Southern California's (USC) red-brick campus and the Allan Hancock Foundation for Scientific Research. Earlier that year, Hancock donated seven million dollars to USC for the institute to further marine studies, house his large collection of specimens, and provide him with an academic platform from which to continue

---

*The title of this chapter comes from Don Meadows, who, in unpublished notes he put together for a talk of unknown date and audience, uses nicknames for the Channel Islands. They are: San Clemente, Island of Caves; Catalina, the Magic Isle; San Nicolas, the Lost Island; Santa Barbara, the Rock Island; Santa Cruz, the Forested Island; Santa Rosa, the Mysterious; and San Miguel, the Lonely Island (Anacapa was not given a nickname). Don Meadows Papers (MS-Roo1), UC Irvine, Special Collections & Archives.

his ambitious personal research expeditions. Today, the foundation is renowned for its library, modern laboratories, and unique collection of Pacific Ocean plants and animals, many of which Hancock personally collected during his far-ranging voyages.

In 1938, the oil magnate's interest in scientific exploration and his famously outfitted, ultra-modern research vessel, the *Velero III*, were familiar to Comstock, just about any seaman worth his salt, and most Los Angelinos, too. The Los Angeles press found endless opportunities to write about the oilman, wrangling invitations to board his yacht and rub elbows with Los Angeles's rich and famous. Designed to perform much like the newest U.S. Coast Guard cutters, the *Velero III* was 193 feet of oceangoing majesty. She could travel 9,500 nautical miles (almost 11,000 miles) without refueling while carrying a pair of 24-foot steel motor whaleboats and two 24-foot wooden shore boats. In an era when the newest luxury ocean liners were still powered by steam turbines, the *Velero III*'s twin six-cylinder Winton diesel engines propelled it to a top speed of 15.75 knots (18 mph) and a cruising speed of 14 knots. The ship's technologically advanced wheelhouse included a Sperry gyrocompass autopilot (a navigational device superior to typical magnetic compasses), a radio beam direction finder, and a fathometer (sonar depth finder). She had a fully equipped photography room and armamentarium (medical office) where the ship's doctor could perform surgeries. Additionally, she carried special research equipment such as heavy-duty winches, microscopes, tanks for holding dry and wet specimens, sorting tables, and 7,000 feet of marine cable for dredging.

Lest passengers find the ship all work and no play, guests dressed for dinner (served nightly at six o'clock) and were later regaled with concerts courtesy of the *Velero III*'s on-board orchestra—including a baby grand piano, flute, violin, and cello played by Hancock, who mastered the instrument while a member of the Los Angeles Symphony Orchestra. Staterooms outfitted with electric heat, forced ventilation, ceiling fans, and both hot, cold, freshwater, and saltwater private showers were anything but basic and were separated from the captain's quarters by a grand interior staircase. While the *Velero III*'s navy-like double hulls kept all within as safe as possible, its cork-lined interiors maintained cool quarters in hot climes. Hancock forbade the use of the word "yacht" to describe his research vessel, yet the definition fits.

The *Velero III* at sea. Courtesy of NHM Archives.

Luckily for the CIBS, Comstock's request for Hancock's services suited the oilman's liking. As a result, the pilot, sea captain, and adventurer agreed to provide the CIBS staff and their significant baggage with transportation aboard his research vessel whenever convenient for both parties. Thus, when in late January the navy gave the museum permission to conduct survey work on San Clemente Island, the two biggest obstacles—permits and transportation—were satisfied. On February 18, 1939, the CIBS reconnaissance team—Comstock, Meadows, and George Willett, senior curator of ornithology—boarded the *Velero III*, officially launching the first expedition of the Channel Islands Biological Survey.

San Clemente Island, situated in Los Angeles County, is the southernmost of the Channel Islands. Although visible from both Orange and San Diego County coastlines and less than a three-hour boat ride from shore, most Americans have never heard of it, much less know anything about it. Rather, the island is recognized because of its namesake, the seaside community of San Clemente, California, where Richard Nixon had his western White House. It was exactly this obscurity that probably attracted the U.S. Navy to San Clemente Island in 1934 for use as a fleet training base. Consequently, as spelled out in the survey's proposal, it was the military's use of the island that prompted the CIBS to initiate expeditions to it.

From the air, San Clemente's twenty-one-mile length and narrow girth—four and a half miles at its maximum, one and a half at its narrowest—give it the appearance of a dismembered elephant trunk floating in the Pacific Ocean. It lies in a north-south direction parallel to mainland California and is forty-five miles from the nearest point of land, the Palos Verdes Peninsula. Its highest point, Mount Thirst, looms 1,965 feet above sea level.

Primarily formed during the Middle Miocene era about fifteen million years ago, San Clemente Island's bedrock is volcanic in origin. A series of ancient beaches, or marine terraces, along its western shoreline give it a spectacularly distinctive stair-step silhouette that dramatically depicts how the island has been rising—and continues to rise, at a rate of approximately eight to sixteen inches per thousand years—out of the sea. Despite a rugged topography characterized by steeply eroded slopes, few freshwater sources, numerous caves pockmarking the landscape, and

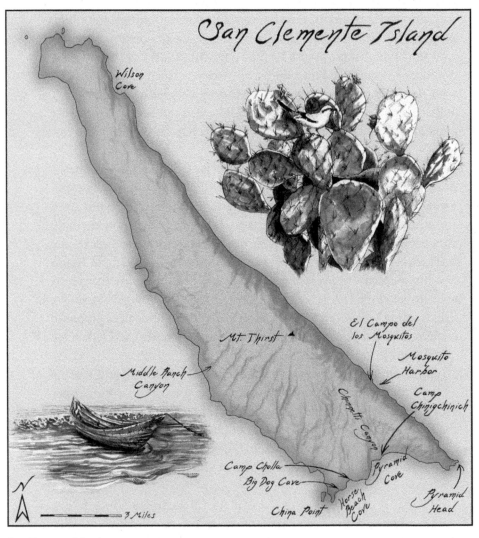

San Clemente Island.

towering cliffs fencing off the coastline, the island Gabrielino used the island beginning eight to nine thousand years ago.

By 1820, the island Gabrielino had departed or died out, leaving no written records of their time on the island as either a permanent living site, a resting place between channel crossings, a fishing spot, or a sacred place to conduct ritualistic ceremonies such as those that may have been performed in Big Dog Cave. San Clemente Island became federal land in 1850, though private sheep and cattle grazing businesses still leased it.

Around 1875, the first goats were introduced to the island and these ungulates, together with the sheep and cattle, greatly damaged the land and its indigenous plants and animals. Ranching occurred on all of the Channel Islands, with the result that nonnative plant and animal species took over native habitats and, in some cases, decimated indigenous flora and fauna populations. The Channel Islands' ranching era ended in 1998 when the last cattle were removed from Santa Rosa Island[1]; however, San Clemente's ranching era ended much earlier, in 1934, when the navy took control of the island from the Department of Commerce. But the navy's termination of the lease with the San Clemente Wool and Sheep Company did not prevent feral goats from feeding on endemic plant species, trampling fragile habitats, and eroding steep cliff faces, nor did it prevent cats, once kept as ranch pets, from hunting native mice, birds, and baby foxes. Rather, the damage wrought by ranching only supplemented that of the island's potentially newest threat, the U.S. military.

Even before ranching began—perhaps during the last days when island Gabrielino seafarers hauled their sturdy wooden plank *ti'ats*, or "canoes," ashore, seams sealed with tar and slender bows built to slice through waves—San Clemente Island already bore the scars of humanity. These scars were caused by smugglers as well as seal, sea lion, and otter hunters who ravaged the furred animals' island colonies. Until recently, the Chinese abalone fishery had also been lumped in with these pillagers, unjustly blamed as the cause of the dramatic decline of abalone populations. While it is true that the Chinese harvested this easy-to-gather gastropod, whose single, fleshy foot clung to the rocks in the island's shallow tide pools and offshore areas, new research proves that the Chinese fishers were only harvesting adult abalone. This likely helped to maintain populations until over-harvesting by Euro-American abalone fisherman[2]—and, more recently, the spread of abalone withering syndrome caused the well-documented decline in abalone numbers.

This history of heavy human use continues on San Clemente Island today. The navy, marine corps, and other non-DOD (Department of Defense) government units use San Clemente as a multi-threat warfare training site. It is the navy's only live ship-to-shore firing range, and its naval airfield (completed in 1960) includes special training features that allow pilots to practice nighttime landings, simulated blacked-out aircraft carrier conditions, touch-and-go landings, and other maneuvers. In addition to the main runway's use for navy carrier training, several specialized training facilities are located on and around the island, including mine exercise areas, an anti-submarine warfare range, seven submarine areas, a shallow water undersea training range, two laser training ranges, and a simulated embassy. It is widely rumored that U.S. Navy SEALs trained for Osama Bin Laden's capture in a replica of his compound built on San Clemente Island specifically for that purpose.

Despite years of ranching followed by eighty-plus years of heavy military occupation, San Clemente's canyons harbor vestiges of its once rich floral diversity, including 300 native taxa and 135 nonnative plants. Of these plants, 15 can be found only on San Clemente Island,[3] making this military island home to more single-island endemic floras than any of the other Channel Islands. Conditions have become so dire that 6 of these single-island plants are endangered, with 4 of those being the first plant species added under the 1973 Endangered Species Act.[4] However, with the navy's financial support, all feral goats and pigs have been removed from the island and vigorous plant restoration projects have been initiated. The result is that San Clemente's endangered plants are recovering and branching out from their strongholds onto terrain they once abundantly occupied.

Though the island's use as a live firing range makes it notorious on its own, for a time San Clemente was also famous for being home to one of North America's most endangered animals, the San Clemente loggerhead shrike. While the loggerhead shrike's range covers much of the continental United States, the San Clemente Island subspecies lives only on San Clemente's fifty-eight square miles. In 1998, the once-thriving population of loggerhead shrikes dwindled to fourteen birds.[5] Similar in size and general coloration to a northern mockingbird but with blacker wings and a strikingly broad, dark eyepatch that extends above the eye and across its powerful hooked beak like a mask, this predatory songbird possesses a number of unique characteristics that merit its reputation as a "bird of a different feather." "Loggerhead" means wooden block, or blockhead, which is a reference to the large size of its head in comparison to its body. Though noticeable, this isn't the shrike's standout characteristic any more than its melodious warbles and harsh, squeaky notes or its ability to seize and carry prey off in a raptor-like manner (minus the talons). Rather, its most distinguishing trait is its gruesome habit, which led to its common name: "butcher bird." Loggerhead shrikes deliver stunning blows to their prey—sometimes while in flight—and then skewer their intended meal on barbed wire or cactus barbs while still alive.

Recognized as endangered in 1977, the San Clemente Island loggerhead shrike faced numerous threats to its wellbeing. Not only had sheep ranching from 1862 through 1934 destroyed much of the island's unique maritime sage scrub, coastal salt marsh, and endemic island grassland in which the shrike lived, but feral goats further contributed to habitat degradation, feral cats and rats preyed on the medium-sized passerine, and, worst of all, its primary habitat lay smack in the middle of the navy's live bombing range. Thus, when its habitat wasn't being trampled or small mammals weren't eating it, the shrike's nesting habitat was being blown to smithereens and then set on fire by explosives. In the 1990s, saving the San Clemente Island loggerhead shrike meant the U.S. Navy would have to adhere to the Endangered Species Act, something that would likely restrict training activities. Uncertainty surrounding the military's willingness to adhere to the ESA made environmentalists fearful for the shrike's continued existence.

To be fair, federal management of the Channel Islands, including San Clemente Island, has in many cases benefited the islands' natural resources. This is because the military funds natural and archaeological resource assessments, limits access to the islands (thus reducing vandalism), and in other ways protects the land. In mainland California, for instance, some of the largest remaining swaths of undeveloped land—which act as nurseries, fly-over resting spots, and open rangeland for a variety of large and small plants and animals—exist because they are military bases off-limits to the civilian populace. On San Clemente Island, it is estimated that only around 20 percent of the island's landmass has been affected by the military's use, leaving the rest relatively undisturbed.[6]

When it came to the San Clemente loggerhead shrike, the navy came through, funding a monitoring and captive breeding program in cooperation with the U.S. Fish and Wildlife Service, the Zoological Society of San Diego, and the Institute for Wildlife Studies, among others. The first birds were released in 1999. By 2009, a wild breeding population of ninety-two adult shrikes and one hundred juveniles gave voice to a successful start of species recovery.[7]

Upon arriving at the naval training base at Wilson Cove, located on the northeast tip of San Clemente (the opposite side of the island from where the survey was headed), Hancock, Comstock, and Meadows went ashore. The commanding officers of the fleet training base promptly presented the CIBS with a lengthy list of requirements worthy of 1939's pre-war paranoia, such as a request for copies of the survey's goals and objectives, censorship of CIBS photographs, and detailed CIBS personnel information, including citizenship status. Another provision, seemingly innocuous, stood out from the others: CIBS staff were to not only abstain from collecting any specimen that appeared "to be the only specimen in the vicinity," but to inform the navy of the specimen's whereabouts so that protective measures could be taken.[8] This small provision demonstrates that, as early as 1939, the military was aware of the need to protect San Clemente's fragile ecosystem, an awareness that some observers might suggest waxed and waned over the years but eventually preserved several species from annihilation.

In addition to this list of requirements, the navy wanted details pertaining to the *Velero III*, including its power supply, the nature of the small boats she carried, on-board communication equipment, cruising range, identifying numbers, and so forth. Of course, the ship's captain complied, but one wonders if this information may have piqued the government's later interest in the *Velero III* when the United States entered World War II. An undated, unsigned, typewritten memo tucked into NHM's 1941 files on the CIBS's thirteenth expedition records the *Velero's* last civilian sailing: "The outgoing trip on the VELERO III will long be remembered. It was probably the last voyage which this celebrated laboratory schooner will make in the interests of science, as it was taken over by the Navy the following day as part of the preparedness program."[9] On December 15, 1941, rechristened the USS *Chalcedony*, the *Velero III* joined the war effort. Truthfully, it may not have been its fine equipment alone that sealed its fate; in February 1939, the sight of the sleek cruiser at anchor in Wilson Cove proved tempting to the officers in charge of San Clemente Island, who boarded and toured the boat prior to releasing it to the southern tip of the island. Perhaps it was its visage alone that gave reason enough to recruit the cruiser into the Pacific fleet. By 1949, the ship would fly the Kuwaiti flag.

Captain Hancock offloaded the CIBS members at Pyramid Cove, a wide bight of water on San Clemente's southwestern end. Crescent shaped, Pyramid Cove's two miles of sandy shoreline curve gently like a smile blighted only by a small, rocky outcropping near the center of the cove, the only possible landing site in inclement weather. The cove's most notable landmark besides this outcropping is Chinetti Canyon, a deep ravine located a half-mile back from the beach that trickles fresh water into the sea.

Beginning at the beach line and ringing the entire cove up to an altitude of five to six hundred feet, dense mats of cactus cover the dry ground. CIBS staffers negotiated this hazard, taking care to avoid the abundant and very thorny cholla cactus that threatened passersby with its paddle-shaped leaves covered with sharp, stiff spines. Equally as obtrusive, two other types of cactus choked the hillsides leading away from the beach: tuna cactus, also known as prickly pear cactus; and snake cactus, a tree-like species with cylindrical trunks that can grow a meter high. Meadows noted these conditions in the progress report wryly writing, "field work was greatly retarded, and at times made impossible, by the heavy cactus growth."[10]

When the first expedition of the survey set out from Long Beach, California, their goals were simple. They hoped only to scout out the next expedition's campsite at Pyramid Cove and bring home information useful to their colleagues who were busy planning the second expedition's specific field objectives. George Willett, senior curator of ornithology, reported that "the few hours spent on shore at Pyramid Cove . . . were mostly occupied in general observation, looking for water, camp sites, etc."[11] They managed to not only successfully locate "water holes" that they thought "should have useable water until late spring," but "a Pleistocene deposit of invertebrate fossils" and plentiful "signs of foxes and white-footed mice of races indigenous to the island."[12] By all accounts, Pyramid Cove appeared to be a good spot for the next, more robustly staffed expedition that would begin the real work of the Channel Islands Biological Survey.

When Willet, an experienced field collector adept at using all of his senses to spot his quarry, stepped ashore, his keen ears would have picked up the ethereal, flutelike notes, *zreeeeew cheedila chli-chli-chli*, emanating from the scrub brush surrounding the cove—notes that would have revealed to him the presence of an Alaskan hermit thrush. Just as quickly, he would have heard *jaaa, teen raad raad raad raad raad*, the sharp, two-syllable call of a loggerhead shrike scolding the human trespassers. His sharp observational skills would also have allowed him to spot the flurry of the Allen's hummingbird's thin, thrilling, whistle-like wingbeats and the sparkling flash of its iridescent orange-red gorget as it hovered over a rubiacaeae flower. However, though Willett *thought* he saw an Allen's hummingbird, it could just as easily have been a Rufous hummingbird, since the two are indistinguishable except by measuring the length of their tailfeathers. Given the very few hours he spent upon the island, it is nonetheless a tribute to the ornithologist that in addition to the thrush, shrike, and hummingbird, he recorded desert quail, bell sparrows, meadowlarks, mockingbirds, and ravens as well as collecting a thrush, song sparrow, wren, and three house finches for the museum's collection.

What did Willett do with these six specimens? If he had caught them in the hillsides of Palos Verdes—a peninsula that juts out toward Santa Catalina Island just thirty-five well-traveled miles from his Los Angeles laboratory—or while on a month-long trip to one of the Channel Islands instead of on a two-day voyage aboard Captain Hancock's well-provisioned cruiser, his actions to preserve them might have been different. If they were shot within a day's journey of the museum, for instance, he'd simply have brought them to his lab, delivering them either to trained volunteers who knew their way around the skinning process or, if volunteers weren't available, to a freezer that could preserve the carcasses until he or someone else had time to prepare them. If, however, he was on a multi-day fieldtrip, concern that the specimens would deteriorate before he could get them back to LACM would have prompted him to skin them as quickly as possible.

As it was, the *Velero III* was fully equipped to house Willett's six small birds for the short journey back to Los Angeles, and it is likely that the ornithologist merely deposited the specimens in the ship's freezer. Less likely, he used the few hours devoted to the channel crossing to skin them for the collection, thankful for the *Velero III*'s good lighting, ample tables

A midden and surrounding cactus on the south coast of San Clemente Island, looking toward China Point. Photo taken during the CIBS. The entire area around China Point, China Canyon, China Cove, and Pyramid Cove has been used as one of the navy's primary ship-to-shore firing ranges since World War II and today looks very different from what the CIBS researchers saw. Courtesy of Department of Anthropology, NHM.

for working, running water, and rooms free of flies. What Willett actually did with those six birds is unknown, other than the fact that he recorded their takes. Likely, he bore them back to LACM, where they were accessioned as the first specimens of the first expedition of the Channel Islands Biological Survey.

After barely two short days on San Clemente, the researchers were steaming back to Los Angeles aboard the *Velero III*. Meadows might have made a few last notes in journals he later used to prepare the progress reports he submitted to Comstock, or perhaps he discoursed with the crew, angling his way onto the bridge to discuss matters of importance with Captain Hancock himself. It's wholly possible that Willett, a tall man with a dry wit, together with Meadows, reveled loudly in the yacht's music room, sipping champagne and trading guesses about the discoveries they soon would make, or equally as likely that they sat quietly on the deck watching Mount Thirst disappear into the sea as they contemplated the gravity of what they had just begun. Whatever occupied the researchers' time, one thing is certain: John Adams Comstock sailed on that ship, smoking a cigar, planning the next expedition, oblivious to the roadblock that would soon emerge.

Chapter Five

CAMP CHINIGCHINICH

"Senators Hit Japan War Trade Ban: Adoption of Plan Seen
as Possibly Leading to Strife." Washington—Criticism of the
Pittman proposal to ban trade with Japan came today from
several members of the Senate Foreign Relations Committee, some of whom declared its enactment probably would
lead to war.

—*Oakland Tribune* (Oakland, California), April 28, 1939

Back on the mainland, the first expedition complete and the second in
the short-straw planning phase, the CIBS's first major impediment arose:
they had no passage through the San Pedro Channel and the Gulf of
Santa Catalina. Hancock and his cruiser would be in the South Pacific
when the survey team planned to return to San Clemente Island. Comstock couldn't fault the oil baron for his absence—the gentleman captain
had forewarned him of this possibility—but the director of science hadn't
prepared for such a quick realization of this reality. He had no backup
plan and the lack of transportation placed the entire survey in jeopardy.
They had to find someone with a ship who would transport them for free
to San Clemente Island.

Left landlocked and desperate with just over a month until their
intended departure date, Comstock scrambled for a means to cross the
forty-nine miles separating San Clemente from the mainland. His first
choice, the U.S. Coast Guard, declined his request within days of its

making—a new public resolution forbade them from ferrying civilian passengers aboard Coast Guard craft. Comstock, determined to keep the survey going, made his next appeal to the California Fish and Game Commission, who agreed to provide the CIBS with free transport aboard one of its two cutters. Thus, not only had Comstock resolved the expedition's first setback, but he had also initiated a relationship that served the museum well over the course of the next several years.

While Comstock worked to resolve these problems, the board of governors wrestled with their own. Declining attendance, and perhaps other factors as well, caused the board to state "that the Museum has . . . been more or less at a standstill for the past few years."[1] Additionally, the director of art, who had served for the past year, was dissatisfied with the museum's intractability and financial limitations and therefore tendered his resignation, effective June 1, 1939. To replace the outgoing art director, the board of governors quickly named a candidate, Roland J. McKinney, formerly the director of the Baltimore Art Museum. Known equally for growing the Baltimore museum from just a few floors of loaned art exhibits to an institution housing art objects valued at $4.4 million as well as for his work integrating museum art into public, private, and parochial school classroom curricula,[2] his successful hire would be a coup for art-loving Los Angelinos eager to boost the county's national art presence.

With this as an impetuous, before the second CIBS expedition pulled away from the dock in April, the Los Angeles County Board of Supervisors approved McKinney's appointment as director of art with a salary of $10,000 annually, an amount not only double that of the highest paid of his fellow museum directors, but also far exceeding all Los Angeles County civil service positions of an equal level. To fund the $5,000 salary shortfall, the LACM's board of governors turned to private donors, an act that set the stage for art's eventual dissociation from the LACM.

Many letters from Los Angeles art patrons supported the hire, but one exchange between Daniel Catton Rich, director of fine arts at the Art Institute of Chicago, and Preston Harrison, a well-heeled, well-established Los Angeles art collector, warned the board of governors that some people had heard that McKinney was "difficult to get along with."[3] In the same letter, Rich references both "the Baltimore smash-up" in which McKinney was apparently engaged, and some sort of difficulties, justified or not, that arose during his tenure as the head of the American

The *Yellowtail* and the *Bluefin* sit at sea as the explorers offload dunnage. The chore required many round trips from ship to shore before all gear was landed. Courtesy of Department of Anthropology, NHM.

art section of the San Francisco World's Fair. In conclusion, Rich wrote, "while McKinney is full of strong purpose," Preston "would not find him uncooperative . . . in executive relationships."[4]

With the survey's second expedition departure date looming, excitement mounted. Comstock called all members of the upcoming expedition to his office for a Saturday morning meeting. Every man had a job, and some had two. The expedition's mammalogist, Jack von Bloeker Jr., pulled together supply lists, while the director of history and anthropology, Art Woodward, scoured written records about earlier excavations[5] and prepared detailed plans for his own digs. Another member contacted the press, which produced a handsome, front-page article in the *Los Angeles Times* entitled "Savants Will Explore Island." It stated, "Eight members of the Los Angeles Museum will invade San Clemente Island. . . . With permission of the Navy, which since 1936 has forbidden civilian craft to approach within 300 yards of the highly secret base, the eight-man party will comb the island for rare bird, animal and plant life. Always they will be probing the relationship of this volcanic island's strange flora and fauna to the mainland's."[6] It was an auspicious and welcome announcement covering the museum's survey activities that portended future news coverage.

An interesting assortment of men composed the second expedition's survey roster. Some were museum staffers: Woodward, archaeologist and second officer; Lloyd Martin, entomologist; and von Bloeker Jr., mammalogist. The others were Long Beach teacher cronies of Don Meadows: Meryl B. (M. B.) Dunkle, botanist; Theodore (Theo) Reddick, herpetologist and supply officer; and Russell (Russ) Sprong, cook. Over time a subtle undercurrent of professional jealousies would arise between Meadows and either Woodward or von Bloeker, but on this departure day any tension on board sprung purely from anticipation.

On the first day of April 1939, a still morning greeted the survey party assembled on the Fellows & Stewart dock at Terminal Island. The port's waters, dead calm, mirrored the morning sky, and Meadows surely paced the forty-five-foot deck of the California Fish and Game Commission cruiser, the *Yellowtail*, checking and rechecking supplies, inspecting the lashings, and questioning his fellow explorers about whether they had completed all paperwork and could produce proper identification when necessary. Whether he or anyone else on that dock that morning had heard about Hitler's growing aggressions against Poland is uncertain, but the rest of the city wouldn't have missed the *Los Angeles Times*'s front-page headlines: "Britain Gives Nazis Warning, Backed by 2,000,000 at Arms"[7] and "President Discloses Fear Hitler to Spread Domination."[8]

When the *Yellowtail* pulled away from the dock, Meadows, Woodward, Martin, and Dunkle were on board. The others—von Bloeker, Reddick, and Sprong—were aboard the *Yellowtail*'s companion cruiser, the *Bluefin* (nicknamed the *Tuna*, as in bluefin tuna). Without the enormous piles of gear weighing the *Yellowtail* down, the ship might easily have exceeded its twenty-knot speed, but the craft made its way steadily and surely to Wilson Cove, located near San Clemente Island's northerly tip. Art Woodward described the channel crossing thus:

> The sea was calm, deep blue like indigo dye and we had no rough water. . . . Off the east end of Catalina [Island] the sea lions were piled on the rocks like so many logs of wood—the island looked green. . . . The north end of Clemente [Island] is low and

sandy—and the entire east side of the island rises precipitously from the ocean— ... at one place ... evidences of Indian occupation were seen in front of a cave—of which dozens were visible.[9]

It is easy to imagine the archaeologist leaning against the ship's rail, his hair blowing away from his face, his eyes squinting at the islands they passed, scouting sites to explore and, if the swells were rolling, looking forward to regaining solid ground beneath his feet.

As required, the *Yellowtail* and her crew checked in with the navy at Wilson Cove, but were quickly dispatched to Pyramid Cove at the far southern end of the island, where the reconnaissance team had previously located a suitable base campsite. Naval authorities gave permission for the *Tuna* to bypass Wilson Cove and join her sister ship directly.

Now the participants needed to ferry a week's worth of food and supplies to shore aboard small, rowboat-like dories. Each one would have been loaded with care in order to keep the small crafts balanced. Woodward apparently took some pleasure from this manly task, stripping down to his trunks right along with Martin. Later he wrote that "Coming thru the surf was an exciting business" that required them to develop a "technique— ... head in for shore bow on—then reverse the procedure and land stern first timing your efforts to avoid the big rollers and thus ... a spill."[10] In this manner, with Woodward's and Martin's help, Dunkle managed to keep his boat afloat without incident, but the same couldn't be said for the *Tuna*'s greenhorn sailor, whose efforts may have suffered at the hands of the island gods playing an April Fool's Day joke on the researchers. Twice the sailor swamped his craft, the first time empty of supplies, but the second, "of all items to get wet—it was the sugar."[11]

The duffel landed and the marines pitched in with the arduous job of moving gear to the basecamp. While working, Woodward noticed two ravens circling high overhead. Recognizing them to be revered creatures in the native island Gabrielino Chinigchinich religion due to their ability to carry messages to the spirit world, he dubbed their base of operations "Camp Chinigchinich."

Six hours after the unloading began, tents were up, the camp was established, and dinner was served at six o'clock. Rain started shortly thereafter, and with no solid structure in which to retreat, the explorers huddled within their canvas tents and hoped they wouldn't leak. The rain melodiously splattering above their heads lulled the researchers to sleep until two o'clock in the morning, when a strong ocean wind pulled at the rigging of the tent von Bloeker and Martin shared. The pair arose to battle with the lines and tent stakes, darkness and wind-driven rain hampering their efforts and causing their nocturnal antics to awaken the entire camp. A half hour later, they returned to their sleeping bags, miserable wet rats.

The next day, mist clung to the island as the scientists spilled out of their tents and into the field like ants in search of a picnic. Carrying salami and peanut butter sandwiches made on hardtack bread; apples and bars of chocolate for lunch; nets for insects; bags for stashing Indian artifacts, lizards, invertebrates, and snakes (if they were lucky); and traps to be laid in long, carefully set lines—von Bloeker set one hundred of them the first day—they were ready for work.

Several of them toted guns, too, though not for protection, as no madmen or dangerous carnivores roamed San Clemente's rugged cactus-studded hillsides; rather, firearms constituted an essential part of a scientist's collecting gear. Birds were shot for their skins and the island foxes for pelts. Feral cats, considered nonnative pests capable of decimating the local bird, mammal, and herp (herpetological, or reptile) populations, were frequently shot on sight, their carcasses sometimes used to bait traps.

Across the world, animals are treated differently depending upon a host of customs, social mores, cultural practices, species, and religious beliefs. In India, cows are sacred and never eaten, while in other countries beef is a dietary staple. Cats brought good luck and were considered magical by the ancient Egyptians, while farmers almost everywhere use them to control pests, and today they rule the internet. Some people do not eat fish, meat, or fowl, and others further limit their intake of animal products by eliminating milk and eggs from their diets. Some refuse to wear or use leather products, yet in certain societies whale meat is a delicacy and endangered rhino horns are sought for their medicinal properties. Many countries have banned the unethical treatment of animals for testing products, but bull, cock, and dog fighting still have their enthusiasts. These few practices and beliefs demonstrate the wide range of behavior that mankind today deems acceptable with respect to animals.

Jack von Bloeker Jr. with San Clemente Island fox specimens and a feral cat. Courtesy of Department of Anthropology, NHM.

Don Meadows sitting at the head of Camp Chinigchinich's cloth-draped mess table, Pyramid Cove, San Clemente Island, April 1939. Pictured from left to right: Art Woodward, Jack von Bloeker Jr. (mostly obscured), Theo Reddick (partially obscured), Don Meadows, Russell Sprong (standing), and Lloyd Martin. Courtesy of Department of Anthropology, NHM.

M. B. Dunkle's plant blotters drying in the foreground of Camp Chinigchinich. Staff members pictured: Dunkle and von Bloeker (center) with San Clemente's formidable hills in the background. Courtesy of Department of Anthropology, NHM.

This moral perspective has a role in discussions regarding the ethics and importance of taking animals into museum collections—but it is only one facet of the conversation. To some, the practice of "taking," or killing, animals for museum collections is revolting, while other professionals working in both museums and the conservation biology field feel it is imperative. This is because collections contribute essential information to help understand and conserve populations. Current and historic collections play a vital role in ensuring biodiversity and are a fundamental part of the sciences of systematics, taxonomy, comparative biology, and immunology.

The heyday of collecting spanned from the late 1700s to the early 1900s. It was a basic process that catalogued the existence of plants and animals living in certain areas and provided information on the relative abundance and biodiversity of the particular area. While collecting—flowers, leaves, insects, birds, invertebrates, fish, and mammals—continues to this day, the process in the United States is different from that practiced in the time of the CIBS. Much of this change is due to government regulations and requirements that have been driven by social pressures, changing attitudes towards living organisms, and advanced technologies.

Although collecting permits were required in 1939, the process today is more involved and permits are increasingly difficult to obtain. Some of the difficulty stems from the public's concern for individual animal welfare as well as fear that endangered species may be further threatened by collecting efforts. While these are both legitimate apprehensions, many biologists maintain that there is a difference between individual animal welfare and an entire population's welfare. Further, permits are not issued for the collection of any plants or animals that are threatened or in danger of extinction.

There are many reasons to continue the practice of collecting specimens. Historic collections, for instance, provide an important baseline from which to make comparisons to modern animals. By studying changes in appearance, distribution, and genetics, scientists are able to spot warning signals before an entire population is decimated. Foxes collected during the CIBS are currently being used by researchers at the University of Southern California to determine genetic diversity and population health. Old bird collections were instrumental in banning the pesticide DDT by allowing scientists to compare historic and modern eggshell thickness (DDT thins eggshells, which break prematurely and prevent the young from developing). Analysis of eggshell thickness pinpointed the cause of the decline of both the California condor and the brown pelican, allowing wildlife managers to appropriately focus conservation efforts and thus save both species from extinction.

Another benefit of historic collections is that they are useful in constructing baseline measurement systems against which contaminant levels can be compared in order to identify the origins of agricultural pests and track epidemics. In the early 1990s, the southwestern United States experienced an outbreak of the sometimes-deadly-to-humans hantavirus. Genetic studies of museum specimens found that deer mice were historic carriers of the virus, which caused the following questions: Why were deer mice, who for decades hosted this virus, suddenly becoming significant transmitters of this disease to humans? What changed the status quo? Additional fieldwork discovered a spike in deer mouse populations following the wet El Niño event of 1992. From this lead, scientists confirmed that the risk of human contraction of hantavirus increased when heavy rains swelled deer mice populations. Knowing this, health officials can now predict when a hantavirus epidemic may occur and can better manage outbreaks. And this is not an isolated example. The swift die-off of the Costa Rican golden tree frog, the black abalone die-off along Southern California's coastline, and many other ecological disasters are examples of how historic museum collections help people understand what is happening and how to prevent or curtail it. For collections to continue to perform in this way, they must continue to grow.

Edward O. Wilson—professor and honorary curator at Harvard, two time Pulitzer Prize winner for nonfiction, winner of more than 150 awards, and the world's leading proponent to save half the planet's land and sea in order to save most of its biodiversity from extinction—encourages current research efforts designed to "discover, describe and conduct natural history studies for every one of the eight million species estimated to exist but [which are] still unknown to science." Wilson believes that new technologies such as genome sequencing, satellite imagery, and species distribution analysis can exponentially speed up species discovery, but that "it must be supported by more 'boots on the ground,' a renaissance of species discovery and taxonomy led by field biologists."[12]

In 1939, the members of the CIBS were intent on cataloguing species, finding new species, and better understanding relationships between island creatures and mainland animals. They could not have known how scientists more than eighty years in the future might be able to use their work. They only knew it must be done, and they were ready with "boots on the ground."

The second expedition's first day collecting yielded water striders, tiger and water beetles, a San Clemente Island night lizard, and a San Clemente Island fox. Both the fox and the lizard are distinct subspecies found only on the Channel Islands, but the fox is definitely the most well known of Channel Island creatures due to its sheer cuteness and winning personality. Its calendar-worthy appeal lies in its sharply pointed face, dark dollop of a nose on a snout streaked by black bars on both sides, and white cheek patches that run down to the chest. A broad, cinnamon-colored collar extends to its belly and legs, and a black racing stripe running along the top edge of its tail completes its furry ensemble. Yet, as cute as it is, what makes the Channel Island fox truly memorable is its fearless heart.

Because this animal evolved in isolation and without predators, the Channel Islands fox, sometimes called the coast fox or island grey fox, will approach humans in broad daylight, scavenge beneath picnic tables, and sit just outside the fire ring waiting for scraps of food. They are wholly unaccustomed to hiding from larger predators or hunting with the protection that dusk, night, or dawn could afford them. The foxes are so tame, in fact, that more than one scientist kept a Channel Island fox as a pet in their home, including Jack von Bloeker Jr.

The Channel Islands fox is morphologically and genetically distinct on each of the six Channel Islands it inhabits: San Miguel, Santa Rosa, Santa Cruz, San Nicolas, Santa Catalina, and San Clemente. Until recently, the prevailing belief was that foxes never lived on either Santa Barbara or Anacapa Islands, but fox remains have recently been documented on Anacapa Island, though whether they were brought there alive or dead has yet to be determined.[13] Physical differences between the subspecies of Channel Island fox include size, coat coloration, muzzle shape, and tail length.

The Channel Islands fox arrived on the islands as the northern mainland grey fox, a hearty omnivore that ranged in size from thirty to forty-five inches and between eight and as much as twenty pounds. Within just two thousand years,[14] it evolved into one of the world's smallest canids, standing just twelve inches off the ground, weighing between two and six pounds, and measuring nose to tail no longer than twenty-four inches. This top Channel Island land-based predator eats ground-nesting birds and their eggs, lizards, insects, shellfish, or any other seafood they can find, as well as seeds, nuts, fruits, and other types of plants.

There continue to be lively discussions among scholars regarding how and when the grey fox got to the Channel Islands. At one time researchers believed the fox "rafted" on logs from the mainland prior to the islands' human colonization. The close proximity of Santarosae to the mainland and the fact that no large fox fossils, only dwarf forms, have ever been found (meaning it reached the islands so long ago that all evidence of it has disappeared) supports this theory. On the other hand, it is known that native people introduced domestic dogs to the islands and that Channel Islanders had special relationships with foxes, including using their pelts and burying them ceremonially. Thus, it is not hard to believe that native peoples brought grey foxes to the Channel Islands, transporting them in their *tomols* (wooden plank canoes) with the express purpose of colonizing them on the islands. Advanced genetic analysis has even reconstructed the evolutionary relationships between the six distinct subspecies of fox and thereby traced the canid's interisland migratory trajectory. This analysis supports the introduction of foxes onto the northern Channel Islands roughly between 10,000 to 7,500[15] years ago and their later transport to the southern islands by native peoples.

As mentioned, no fossils of large or medium sized foxes have been found. Interestingly, the absence of such fossil records can be used to support both the rafting theory of island colonization and the human introduction theory. This is because the lack of large or intermediate fox bones could be due to the grey fox's swift two-thousand-year evolution from its bigger self to its present petite, island size. This compressed timeframe meant there was not much opportunity for the larger bones to accumulate, which gave nothing for modern-day researchers (so far) to work with. If such specimens are ever discovered, scientists will be better able to determine how the fox first came to the island, when they arrived, and how long it took for them to evolve into the adorably sized, frisky little critters they are today.

One aspect of island living that Channel Island foxes exemplify is the disastrous results that introduced diseases or plants and animals can have on island-evolved animals. In the late 1990s, all Channel Island subspecies of this miniature canid faced sure extinction as a result of human-introduced animals, human-caused environmental changes, and diseases that were often carried by man's best friend. Understanding how conservation managers prevented the Channel Island fox's annihilation is worth knowing about because it is one of the best island restoration success stories in existence.

During the last decade of the twentieth century, the Channel Island fox faced a questionable future as fox populations plummeted on several of the Channel Islands. On Santa Rosa Island, the fox population declined from as many as 1,800 individuals to only 15, on Santa Cruz Island it dropped from 1,500 animals to as few as 50 or 60, and on San Miguel Island it decreased from 450 to 15. The fox's falloff was first detected in the early 1990s, but the cause was not readily apparent. Concerned citizenry and scientists went on red alert to determine the reasons behind the decline.

The first step in saving them consisted of a scientific survey to detect whether disease, changes in food supply, or habitat could be causing the high mortality rates. A breakthrough came in 1999 after researchers discovered a golden eagle nest on Santa Cruz Island that contained feral pig, island fox, and bird remains. Golden eagles were relatively rare visitors to the Channel Islands and had not previously nested on them. The discovery of additional golden eagle nests on Santa Cruz and Santa Rosa Island led scientists to believe that golden eagle predation was pushing island foxes to extinction on their three northern island habitats.

Because golden eagles are not indigenous to the Channel Islands, scientists had to figure out why this raptor populated them in the 1990s and not in the eons before. The reasons, they discovered, are complicated and differ by island. On Santa Cruz, the story of the fox's twentieth-century decline began in the mid-1800s with the introduction of domestic pigs that later became feral; on Santa Rosa, it began with introduced mule deer; and on San Miguel, with introduced domestic sheep. Like the golden eagle, none of these ungulates were native to the Channel Islands.

Up until the mid-1990s, no predators on the Channel Islands were both large enough to hunt foxes or interested in them. While it is true that bald eagles are indigenous to the Channel Islands and are big enough to not only hunt foxes but also young deer and piglets, they are primarily fish eaters and thus did not represent a great threat to island ranch animals or foxes. Additionally, bald eagles likely predated foxes on the Channel Islands and have coexisted with them since they first appeared. Because bald eagles did not aggressively hunt deer, sheep, pigs, or foxes, these animals' numbers multiplied. This changed, however, when the ungulates' populations grew large enough to lure golden eagles to the islands' shores. On Santa Cruz, Santa Rosa, and San Miguel, pigs, mule deer, and sheep represented a new food source for the carnivorous golden eagle raptors. As a result, golden eagles began commuting from the mainland to the islands to take advantage of this plentiful bounty.

The timing of the golden eagle's arrival on the Channel Islands is an important story, too. During the latter half of the twentieth century, both golden and bald eagles were extensively hunted on the mainland for their supposed livestock predation. With the passage of legislation in the early 1960s protecting birds of prey, golden eagle populations flourished in the Los Padres Forest in Ventura County, which is not far from the northern Channel Islands. At the same time, bald eagles became extinct on the Channel Islands due to dichloro-diphenyl-trichloroethane, or DDT. Manufactured by Montrose Chemical Corporation of Torrance, California (near the Palos Verdes Peninsula), DDT was a miracle pesticide, initially able to utilize low doses to kill insects.[16] As part of the manufacturing process, Montrose dumped wastewater from the chemical's production into the sewer system, which then drained into the ocean and settled in the sediment, where worms and microorganisms absorbed it. Thus began DDT's ugly journey up into the pelagic food chain: worms were eaten by small fish, larger fish ate the small ones, even larger fish ate those, and then marine birds and marine mammals such as dolphins and whales ate the fish. With each DDT meal, the toxin accumulated within the consumer until its body filled with poison. Female dolphins' first offspring often die because the mother dumps her own toxic chemical load into her milk, thus cleansing the maternal body and allowing her to effectively nurse subsequent offspring. Bald eagles, who are at the top of their food chain, consumed the poison through the fish they ate, but they do not have the ability to dump their own toxic load.

One tragic side effect of DDT is that it causes eggshell thinning. When the heavy-bodied bald eagle parent incubated its eggs, the shells cracked and the unborn young died, causing the population to dwindle on both the islands and the mainland. As a result, the mainland became overpopulated by golden eagles, causing this large mammal-eating raptor to spread its territorial wings and take flight for the Channel Islands, where the fish-eating bald eagle no longer chased it away.

Fox population declines would not have occurred had the golden eagles limited their hunting to pigs and deer, but this did not happen. Rather, golden eagles began preying on the daytime-active foxes who did not know to protect themselves from their winged predators. Channel Island spotted skunks were on the golden eagles' menu, too, but their nocturnal habits helped protect their populations. After realizing that golden eagles were the primary cause of fox depletion on Santa Cruz and Santa Rosa, scientists decided to remove the birds from the islands. While sound in theory, it had one major flaw: even if they successfully eradicated the birds, what would prevent mainland golden eagles from repopulating these islands since their prey, deer and pigs, remained abundant? This conundrum meant that in order to be successful, golden eagle removal had to be done in tandem with prey removal *and* bald eagle reintroduction.

On Santa Cruz it took eight years, from 1999–2007, to live capture and remove thirty golden eagles. In 2006, Santa Cruz Island became pig-free for the first time since the mid-1800s after six thousand pigs were eradicated. On Santa Rosa Island, the last elk and mule deer were removed in 2011. The doors on these two islands were immediately opened to ecosystem recovery efforts that included captive fox breeding programs and bald eagle reintroduction.

Complicating matters was that separate captive fox breeding programs needed to be initiated for each island experiencing decline since each was home to a distinct subspecies of island fox. Bald eagles were introduced in the northern Channel Islands beginning in 2002, and four years later scientists found the first successful bald eagle nest in fifty years. Today there are at least eight breeding bald eagle pairs on Santa Cruz, Santa Rosa, and Anacapa Islands and over forty bald eagles in total living on the northern Channel Islands. The removal of golden eagles, the eradication of ungulates, and the reintroduction of bald eagles together created a successful ecosystem recovery program that saved the Channel Island fox.

Parallel to the decline of foxes on the northern Channel Islands was a 90 percent decline of fox numbers on Santa Catalina Island. After investigation, scientists determined that golden eagles were not to blame on Catalina; rather, canine distemper virus was responsible for the deaths. While dogs seemed the most likely cause of this disease transfer, the discovery of four "stowaway" raccoons found both on the island as well as swimming to Catalina between 2007 and 2009[17] plunged this into question as the distemper virus strain that endangered the Santa Catalina Island fox was more closely related to that found in raccoons than dogs. In response, foxes were trapped, vaccinated, and then, as on the northern Channel Islands, bred while in captivity.

Today, fox populations on all islands are stable. However recent drought conditions have impacted foxes negatively on San Nicolas Island. Surely the species has lived through droughts and genetic bottlenecks before, but today the Channel Islands fox has the added protection of being monitored by conservation managers alert to imminent disasters.

Sometime during the CIBS's first afternoon on San Clemente Island, Woodward stole off to do some reconnaissance on his own, walking two miles to the marine camp for a cup of coffee and some nosing around. When he returned to camp, he surprised the CIBS staff with a ten-pound bag of sugar the servicemen had given him to replace what they'd lost when the skiff capsized. He didn't stay in camp long, however, as his meanderings next took him westward towards China Point, where he scouted out Indian middens—i.e., ancient trash dumps filled with the castoff items of everyday life, such as charred bones of fish and mammals, discarded shells, broken fishhooks, mortars, pestles, and other tools.

Sorting and sifting through these ancient debris piles was the reason Woodward had come to the Channel Islands. Middens provided him with clues. Their depth and size could indicate the length of time a location had been occupied, while the items found within them told stories about what the people ate (through mammal and fish bones), how they hunted (fishhooks or spear points), what technological advances they had made (canoe planks and tarred basketry), and something of their cultural and religious practices (pottery shards, jewelry, stone effigies, or ceremonial pipes).

Woodward took note of the depth at which the collected items were found in order to create the timeline for when different items were deposited. Changes in the color of the earth helped him determine this, as did changes in a midden's contents, the latter of which also revealed broad technological and environmental changes. For instance, if a midden was distinctly layered by different kinds of shellfish, Woodward might conclude that near-shore ocean temperatures had fluctuated significantly enough during the years the midden had been used that different species of shellfish were available to the people for harvesting. Knowing this, archaeologists today work with climatologists, ocean chemists, and other experts to date various shellfish layers.

Changes in midden content may also be due to technological sophistication. When different types of fishhooks are found near the bones of deep ocean foraging fish, for instance, an archaeologist might conclude that advances in boat technology and fishhook construction allowed people to successfully fish further offshore than they had previously. The presence of exotic items made from materials unavailable on the islands—such as woven cloth or soapstone items on San Clemente Island where no soapstone quarries exist—indicated that natives might have traded with people living elsewhere. In conclusion, the clues found in middens provide both information and a cultural timeline that can be matched with other evidence in order to tell a more complete story of human life throughout history.

Before returning to basecamp that day, Woodward searched for a site where he could leave a message for prosperity. In the rocks near the expedition's tents, he inscribed:

Camp Chinigchinich
Los Angeles Museum Party 7 men
pitched first camp here April 1, 1939.[18]

Not content to leave it at that, he perversely scored another message, this one also in stone. Scratched in Spanish, he wrote, "Pasó por aqui Don Fulano de Tal. 1560,"[19] and near it he cut a crude coat of arms representing Carlos V,[20] Holy Roman emperor who oversaw the Spanish colonization of the Americas. Translated, Woodward's message reads, "Passed by here John Doe in 1560." With these few words, he seems to mock mankind's fleeting impact on the world, in essence saying that even a great ruler, over time, is only a John Doe despite efforts to dominate and take what he finds in the world as his own.

Monday, April 3 dawned sunny and warm. Fish, courtesy of the U.S. Marines who had dropped off a catch the night before, was cooked for breakfast. Each scientist pursued daily activities with zeal. Dunkle botanized while von Bloeker laid traps, catching another fox, nineteen mice, and a big, wild house cat that day. Woodward followed the plans he had drawn up back at his lab, walking around the island with his pencil, maps, and notes, making sketches, recording locations suitable for landing canoes, or noting where the Indians might have had success collecting shellfish. Many days Woodward found time to "chin" with anyone who might offer insights or information, including the marines he chatted up whenever he passed through their camp.

In the evenings, the crew worked late into the night pressing foliage in plant blotters, pickling lizards, and skinning small mammals. If the wind settled down and the air felt warm enough, they set up moth sheets (white sheets hung on clotheslines that were illuminated with lantern light), the perfect low-tech devices to capture winged nighttime Lepidoptera. Other nights, they went to the dark beach in search of grunion, impossibly clever, five-inch-long, silvery fish that during the highest tides lay their eggs on the sand, trusting that the next high tide will unbury their offspring and return them to the sea.

Over the next few days work became routine, but minor setbacks reminded staff that this exploring business was fraught with misadventures. The first mishap left three of the explorers adrift at sea for a couple of hours when the engine on Dunkle's boat stopped working. No real damage done, but in retribution the men beached the wretched little craft for the remainder of the expedition.

Theo Reddick ran into a bit thornier misfortune. While scouring the dry, cactus-choked hills for the endemic *Xantusia riversiana*, the San Clemente Island night lizard that spends most of its ten- to thirty-year life living within ten feet of a single large stone, the herpetologist reached down to grab a rock. When it unexpectedly broke free, he rolled backwards through a patch of heavily armored cholla cactus. With each rotation, thick spines pierced his hands, arms, back, and thighs. When he could stand to examine himself, he found his hands so thoroughly covered in barbs that he couldn't pull the offending thorns out without help. With no other options, he limped a mile back to camp, a human pincushion picking his way around loose rocks and more cactus plants. It took two staff members nearly an hour to pluck the sharp needles from his skin. "Thorns seem to burn terribly,"[21] he drolly noted in his journal.

There were satisfying events, too. Woodward, for example, found "his" cave and discovered places where currents, acting like oceanic shipping lanes, deposited logs ferried over from the mainland that could be used to make canoes, other tools, or fires for warmth, cooking, or cremating their dead. Martin collected near camp in Chinetti Canyon, where water flowed down a deep gorge and foliage rotted on the steep banks, conditions that attracted a variety of insects, especially beetles—though very few butterflies. To rectify this lack, one evening the staff erected two moth sheets in the vicinity of Chinetti Canyon that yielded more than one hundred specimens before that night's 8:15 p.m. moonrise put an end to this activity. Dunkle botanized all around Pyramid Cove and China Point, collecting three new plants he would feature in a paper published in December 1940. One of these plants, a type of lotus (*Lotus argophyllus*), he designated *Hancockii* in honor of Captain "G. Allan Hancock because of his interest in scientific research, and because he has made possible the author's [Dunkle's] botanical and ecological research on the Channel Islands."[22]

On April 5, early morning temperatures dipped down to the high forties, and when the explorers left the relative comfort of their tents to begin their day, wet fog moistened their hair and clothing. Despite a restless night due to stubbornly embedded cactus thorns, Reddick was up and about as usual that morning. Ignoring the lingering pain that made turning over rocks where lizards hid difficult, he wandered the hills that day, his self-sacrifice rewarded when he learned of a marine's account of a snake killed the day before. A search of the particular area ensued, but no carcass was found, leading them to conclude that a raptor had carried away the eighteen-inch, brownish-gray serpent Reddick surmised to be a San Diego gopher snake. What makes this sighting noteworthy is that there are no records of snakes—*ever*—on San Clemente Island,[23] save this one. As no actual specimen was found, it is anyone's guess as to what this snake was and how it got to the island. One possibility is that it arrived as a stowaway in a shipment destined for the marines' camp.

As for the other researchers, perhaps they were tired and sore after five nights spent in sleeping bags, or perhaps the small mishaps of the past few days dampened their enthusiasm, but regardless no one wandered far from camp the morning of April 5. Thus, when the marines rolled in offering rides to Horse Beach Cove, Martin, von Bloeker, and Meadows were still in camp, happy to spare themselves another grueling hike. Von Bloeker took advantage of the two-mile trip to pepper the servicemen with questions about where he might find bats. This conversation led the three of them to follow one marine up a bluff to the cliffside cavern that became known as Big Dog Cave.

Throughout the remainder of the week, all of the scientists helped Woodward excavate "his" cave, yet none abandoned their own fieldwork. Their results accumulated into a fine and varied assemblage of plants and animals. Meryl B. Dunkle collected plants with gusto, each day growing his collection until it comprised 3,500 individual plants representing 125 plant species, including 3 he believed new to science. Lloyd Martin captured 2,945 spiders, crustaceans, butterflies, and moths, while Jack von Bloeker Jr.'s contribution numbered 59 small mammals, some of which he thought were new species. Theo Reddick hunted for reptiles, and though he found neither frogs nor snakes he collected 158 specimens, 2 of which he believed to be new to science. He also captured 60 live lizards, all but 2 of which survived the channel crossing to take up residence in his Long Beach classroom. As for Woodward, in addition to Big Dog Cave, he mapped 32 archaeological surface sites and found fragments of grass, hemp, fishhooks, and much more.

All in all, by the time the explorers broke camp on Saturday, April 8, more than seven thousand specimens were packed and ready for transport to the LACM—a respectable load considering they had only covered 10 percent (just six square miles) of the island. Their experiences drove home the vastness of the terrain they were attempting to explore and the almost insurmountable task their quest represented. Limited resources and mainland day jobs required them to move on, but they knew they would return. They had found success on the "Island of Caves" and could rightfully claim they had made the first complete scientific expedition of San Clemente Island. Who knew what they might find next?

The explorers on San Clemente Island, April 1939. From left to right: Meadows, Reddick, Woodward, von Bloeker, Martin, and Sprong. Courtesy of Department of Anthropology, NHM.

Lloyd Martin adding a wooden crate to the dunnage pile. Courtesy of Department of Anthropology, NHM.

Chapter Six

THE ROCK ISLAND: SANTA BARBARA

"'Important Step' against Poland Hinted by Nazis: Warsaw Warned She Is Going Too Far; Berlin Says Britain, France, Promoting War."

—*The Morning Call* (Allentown, Pennsylvania), May 3, 1939

The Channel Islands Biological Survey chose little Santa Barbara Island for its third expedition (May 27–30, 1939), and again for the seventh (March 16–23, 1940). These visits yielded a total of eleven collecting days, a paucity that made this little speck of land the second least visited island during the survey's thirteen expeditions. Only lonely San Miguel saw fewer CIBS collecting days.

No reason for choosing Santa Barbara Island as the second island of the survey is contained within the archives, but there are a couple of possibilities. First, in 1939 Santa Barbara Island had been in the U.S. government's possession for ninety-one years, far longer than San Clemente, yet it did not have any active duty bases. With Hitler building momentum across the Atlantic and the American public's rising concern over the safety of their mainland Pacific border, it's possible that Comstock and his gang considered Santa Barbara island's "base-less" state temporary. If that were to change, then the concerns the survey had regarding the military's use of San Clemente Island would equally apply to Santa Barbara Island, which may have heightened the importance of conducting a Santa Barbara Island survey prior to the military's arrival.

Secondly, just the year before, President Franklin Roosevelt had designated Santa Barbara and Anacapa Islands as the Channel Islands National Monument and placed them under the jurisdiction of the National Park Service (NPS). This meant that the NPS would be interested in the survey's findings, an interest that Comstock could use to demonstrate the importance of the science department's activities to the board of governors. Furthermore, any increased publicity arising from the NPS connection might serve to capture local newspapers' attentions and consequently generate increased public interest, museum attendance, and donor support.

Then again, maybe it was more practical than that. It is no great secret that grazing animals wreak havoc on flora and fauna. Perhaps the CIBS just wanted to go to Santa Barbara so they could document the destruction and inventory whatever had yet to be lost or, more hopefully, saved. Besides, after tackling San Clemente Island, Santa Barbara Island was bite sized in comparison and might just have felt right.

As the scientists approached Santa Barbara Island on May 27, 1939, they motored toward a small protuberance of land with gently sloped, saddle-shaped peaks bubbling up and out of the Pacific Ocean like a partially inflated ball. At the time of their visit, this pinch of land—named by the first white man to see it on Saint Barbara's Day, December 4, 1602— would have appeared nothing like the uniform, low-to-the-ground coat of sparrow brown vegetation that Sebastián Vizcaíno saw on that December day. Rather, when the LACM scientists arrived Santa Barbara would have been dressed for spring and fairly glowing against the blue of the sea. While the island is devoid of both trees and freshwater, the season's rains would have coaxed flowers to sprout across its sprawling hillsides—a velvet covering of vibrant green grasses, bright yellow daisies, and patches of purple morning glories. Even the prickly pears would have offered large blossoms of brilliant pink, yellows, and oranges.

Notes found in NHM's archives, written in von Bloeker's hand, evocatively name their two Santa Barbara Island campsites, *Campo de los Conejos* ("camp of the rabbits," third expedition) and *El Campo de los Gatos* ("camp of the cats," seventh expedition).

With only one square mile to its name, Santa Barbara is the smallest of the Channel Islands and is situated thirty-eight miles from the mainland and

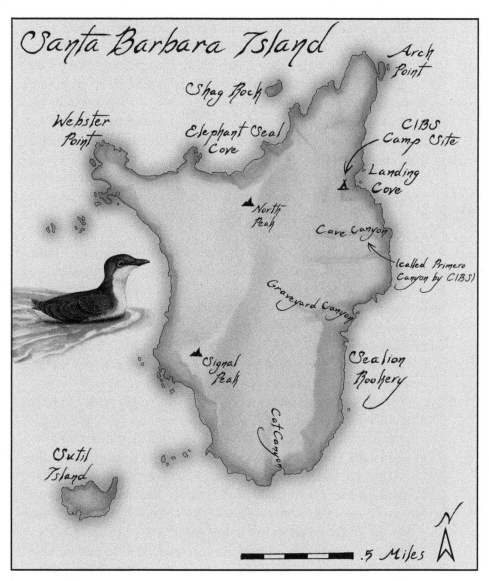

Santa Barbara Island.

twenty-four miles from Santa Catalina Island, the nearest terra firma. Two small outcroppings, Sutil Islet on the southwestern side and Shag Rock on the northeast, are included as part of the island on assessors' maps. Because the island is nearly completely encircled by towering sea cliffs, the CIBS accessed it via Landing Cove on the island's northeastern shore.

Few archival documents detail the two trips the CIBS made to Santa Barbara. Only Don Meadows's overview report, a few pages from Jack von Bloeker's handwritten journal, M. B. Dunkle's record of the plants he collected, and an unpublished description of the island's geological makeup written by James DeLong (a non-museum geologist who accompanied the survey on the 1939[1] trip) provide any insight into the survey's Santa Barbara Island visits. Missing are Art Woodward's and George Willett's vivid descriptions of the island, as neither scientist went to Santa Barbara Island with the CIBS.[2]

Because the island is relatively free from natural terrestrial predators such as skunks, foxes, or snakes, it is an important breeding area for eleven species of ground nesting seabirds, whose only historic native predators were peregrine falcons, barn owls, and occasionally bald eagles. In 1939, von Bloeker's Santa Barbara fieldnotes documented the future troubles the nesting sea birds would encounter due to the presence of introduced predators—cats, mice, and rabbits, the latter of which eat nesting habitats and can compete with birds for burrows.

Had Willett been with the survey in 1939, he would surely have commented on, and perhaps collected, the Scripps's murrelet, known until August 2012 as the Xantus's murrelet.[3] This slight, ten-inch bird—with its wary, dark eye; short, slender beak; striking black back; and snow white chin and breast—spends its entire life at sea except when it lands to breed on one of ten islands off the coast of Southern California and Mexico. These days scientists estimate that springtime breeding season brings up to 2,600 Scripps's murrelet pairs to the Channel Islands of California. Eighty percent of these pairs choose little Santa Barbara Island as their nesting site, literally flocking the smallest of the Channel Islands and making it an extremely important habitat for their future survival. Threats from predation by introduced rats and cats, as well as the murrelet's small breeding range, prompted the International Union for Conservation of Nature (IUCN) to list this pretty little bird as a vulnerable species. In the United States, conservation managers have also considered listing it as a threatened species under the Endangered Species Act.

Humans have utilized Santa Barbara Island for at least 4,500 years, dramatically changing the natural ecosystem throughout history. Although Vizcaíno gave Santa Barbara Island the name we know today, the island Gabrielino and island Chumash peoples were the first to land on its shores thousands of years ago. Meadows noted that the survey party found two midden deposits, one two hundred feet directly above the survey's landing site on the island's eastern shore and a half mile south of Arch Point, and the other "at the Graveyard, elevation 50 feet."[4] He does not elaborate on what or where "the Graveyard" is and reveals few details about the middens other than they were shallow and contained black soil, abalone, and top shells. Archaeologists today believe that there were likely no permanent native villages on Santa Barbara Island, though it served as a stopover spot for voyagers from adjacent islands and the mainland. Questions about the early occupants of Santa Barbara Island are many and remain unanswered, primarily because, until recently, only limited archaeological work had been done on Santa Barbara Island.

As to more modern uses of Santa Barbara, this federal outpost attracted a host of people the likes of which one might expect to find living on a tiny island far out at sea. One of the more fanciful, hoped-for uses of the island came in the early 1900s, when J. G. Howland, the island's lessee, attempted to propagate pearls in abalone. Abalone rarely produce pearls, and when they do it is as a result of intestinal disturbance, so it is not clear how Howland expected to contrive this bit of univalve biological engineering. His plan must have failed, however, since at the conclusion of his five-year lease he did not renew with the Department of Commerce and Labor.

Both prior to and after Howland's time, lobster fisherman, egg collectors, and sea otter, seal, and sea lion hunters all squatted on Santa Barbara's shores, each in their own way abusing the isle's abundant natural resources. Farmers and ranchers took their chances, too. In 1914, the Alvin Hyder family secured a $250 per year lease from the government to utilize the entire island. Hyder arrived in 1915 and eventually brought fifteen family members to the island, most of whom remained until 1922, three years beyond the lease's legal expiration.

While on the island, Hyder constructed two concrete cisterns to hold imported mainland water for the family's and the animals' use, as well as eleven other structures, including a house that he and his brother lashed to the ground with cables to keep it from being blown away and joining Auntie Em's home somewhere over Kansas. When the survey arrived on Santa Barbara Island, all of these structures, save Hyder's house, were gone.

Hyder's ranching activities included raising Belgian hares for meat and fur, importing hundreds of the black and white rabbits and setting them loose to breed on the island. He also brought 300 head of sheep to graze freely across Santa Barbara's gentle slopes and he kept dogs, horses, mules, goats, pigs, chickens, turkeys, and geese. In 1918, he burned much of the island's grasslands in order to plant nonnative barley, potatoes, and hay. Needless to say, these farming activities damaged the native vegetation as much as his animals' hooves and appetites. None of his ventures panned out, however, so per the terms of his original lease, seven years after he arrived he and his family dismantled the buildings and took their dogs, horses, and 300 sheep back to the mainland. The rabbits remained, however, and did what rabbits do—eat and procreate, their numbers significantly assaulting the native flora. Incredulously, Hyder's adventures on Santa Barbara Island didn't end when he left, as years later, with no lease to grant him legal entry, he returned to the island with 250 sheep he intended to fatten up.

As the CIBS prepared to venture out to Santa Barbara Island, they found scarce written records about it. This made their work both more challenging and more exciting. Challenging because scant published information, scientific or otherwise, meant they had little to build upon. Exciting because, as every graduate student knows, the best way to become an expert in one's field is to write a thesis on a subject no one knows anything about. Once it's done, the student becomes an overnight, instant expert on that topic, the ultimate resource for further study.

The opportunity to achieve notoriety and do what no one else had done before would have appealed to both Meadows and von Bloeker. Indeed, within the first paragraph of Meadows's report on the biology of Santa Barbara Island, he succumbs to a bit of chest beating when he writes, "Very little has been published on the biota of [Santa Barbara]. . . .

While not exhaustive, this report will be the first to record the fauna and flora in any detail."[5] As for von Bloeker, he too understood the importance of the work he undertook on the islands, and he had similar goals, though different motivations. Whereas Meadows's aspirations were steeped in ambition, recognition, and the attainment of financial and societal rewards (a new job, scientific publications, etc.), von Bloeker's seemed to hail from a more personal place: fear and love.

In 1909, in Sacramento, California, John "Jack" Christian von Bloeker Jr. was "born under an unlucky star,"[6] the product of a shotgun marriage between John Christian von Bloeker and Winifred West. Von Bloeker likely counted the circumstances surrounding his birth as the first strike against him. Little is known of his Sacramento and San Diego childhood other than one incident that informed his life, especially regarding loss. At the age of eight, young Jack escorted his mother to the bus stop, she perhaps coughing and feverish from the bacteria infecting her lungs, and he wondering why they waited there. No one knows whether they spoke at that time, whether Mrs. von Bloeker hugged her young Jack and whispered a life-changing inspiration into his ear or turned stoically away from him, unable to bear the sight of her son standing alone and small at the side of the street, knowing his eyes would grow wide with fear as they followed her frail form up the steps and into the bus that would take her to the tuberculosis sanatorium.

Between von Bloeker's letters and records as well as stories told by his sixty-five-year-old son, we know that when Mrs. von Bloeker boarded that bus, her departure gouged a permanent hole into her little boy's heart that affected him profoundly throughout his life. Her leaving contributed to a psyche prone to keenly feeling losses, separations, and failures, and it drove him to form long-lasting and deep relationships. It also likely triggered, or at least compounded, his undiagnosed bipolar disorder[7] as well as fostered his incredible focus and drive. Was his fanatical devotion to fieldwork and academic success a manifestation of his attempts to seek his mother's approval and love? Did he want to prove that he had been worthy of her love, that she should not have left him, or were his maniacal work habits an avoidance strategy that kept him too busy to acknowledge the loss he felt over his mother's leave-taking? Either way, when many years later he told his daughter, Elsie Ruth, that he "never understood why his mother had to leave him,"[8] the lasting affect her departure had revealed itself fully.

At the start of the Great Depression, a year after dropping out of high school to seek work, von Bloeker's career at the LACM began when he accepted the job of chief taxidermist. He relished his position as a "museum man," stuffing specimens, skinning birds, sorting through bones, and (mostly) going out into the field to bring things back to the lab to study. Years later, Jack Couffer, von Bloeker's protégé and a high school student working in his museum laboratory during the time of the CIBS, wrote a book about the two Jacks' World War II exploits participating in a project they thought would save the world. About his mentor Couffer wrote, "v. B. was essentially a collector, one of that old-fashioned breed of naturalists to whom a new specimen of any category ... was a treasure ... a modern-day Charles Darwin."[9] True enough, throughout his life von Bloeker assembled like objects no matter their nature. He stashed accumulations of coins, stamps, scarab beetles, bats, and swizzle sticks in nooks and crannies throughout his house and outbuildings. This extensive and varied assemblage of objects made it a challenge to amass the natural history items in one place after his death.[10]

Along with two thousand other employees, Los Angeles County laid von Bloeker off its payroll in 1932. But, having already enrolled in Los Angeles City College, he instead used the forced "break" as an opportunity to continue pursuing a college degree and think about his future. At age twenty-four, he declared his life's goal in his application to the college's scholarship committee, writing, "I began to realize that if I were going to advance further in my scientific studies and attain a permanent position I must get a higher education. It is for this purpose that I plan to study for the Ph.D. degree at the University of California, Berkeley."[11]

True to his word, he pursued this degree relentlessly and with all the vengeance of someone with a compulsive behavioral disorder. Over the course of the next decades, his correspondence files provide detailed status reports on where he stood vis-à-vis his progress toward this goal. Early indicators looked favorable. In four years he went from high school dropout to authoring more than twenty scientific articles, in addition to earning his associate's degree from Los Angeles Junior College in 1935 and later his bachelor's and master's degrees in zoology, entomology, and paleontology from the University of California, Berkeley. By the time he received his master's degree, he had published thirty-three scientific articles.

Success came at a cost, however, and his unlucky star shone brightly. At twenty-six, he was carjacked and robbed, his mouth taped and legs bound with piano wire before he was knocked unconscious with the butt of a pistol.[12] By twenty-nine, he had divorced twice and married thrice. His second wife left him because he "seldom removed his eyes from his books and . . . [had] developed an irritable temper,"[13] allegations she contended amounted to "cruelty." One beloved mentor, upon learning of his pending second divorce, wrote, "I heard today of your wife's action and was considerably moved knowing how much you loved her. I suppose this is one of the many sacrifices you must make to get to that goal which you have set for yourself. . . . And maybe what has happened is for the best of all concerned including the cause of science."[14] It is a wonder that a mentor and friend could find "the cause of science" a silver lining in the dissolution of von Bloeker's marriage, but such was von Bloeker's drive—nourished, encouraged, and understood by his colleagues and mentors. He was endlessly working toward his bifurcated goals: long-lasting love cemented in place by exterior successes.

Tenacity, ambition, an impressive CV, and supportive friends and colleagues made up only half the man. Von Bloeker had vices. He expected perfection, smoked cigarettes compulsively, played cards obsessively, and had a temper—a bad one. Von Bloeker's grown son recounted that his dad was given to fits of rage, once provoking him as a fifteen-year-old to knock his father out cold, the only way the younger von Bloeker could think to make his dad stop hitting his sixteen-year-old sister. While nothing in the archives, von Bloeker's personal journals, museum personnel records, or voluminous collection of old letters portrays this dark side, two decades after von Bloeker Jr.'s death, his son and namesake, Jack C. von Bloeker III, described his father's paranoia, bipolar tendencies, propensity for stretching the truth, and compulsiveness. Surely his recollections were filtered through not only time but also a lens colored by today's perceptions of parental discipline (e.g., spankings). Yet, when coupled with von Bloeker's second wife's statement about his temper as well as an understanding of his unrequited anger and pain over his mother's abandonment, von Bloeker III's statement rings true even if others experienced a vastly different persona.

One individual who seemed to know a different von Bloeker was Jack Couffer, the young man who began volunteering at the LACM in 1939 while a sophomore at Glendale High School. With the approval of his principal, young Jack left class each day at noon to commute twelve miles each way to the museum. He hitchhiked from Glendale to Eagle Rock, California, whereupon he boarded streetcar no. 5 for fifteen cents, which took him straight to Exposition Park and the museum's laboratories. Couffer volunteered in all of the museum's science departments—archaeology, paleontology, entomology, herpetology, invertebrates, and ornithology—but mammalogy was his "favorite niche" and Jack von Bloeker Jr.'s enthusiasm for chiroptera, or bats, soon got to him too.

While working in the combined department of mammalogy and ornithology, Couffer learned the art of making study skins. He recalls making hundreds of them from the animals he collected in traps that he baited with peanut butter and Quaker oats.[15] Seventy-three years later, when he speaks of his LACM days, Couffer slowly raises his hands to head height and his voice quiets to a whisper: "You go to bed and you start hearing."[16] He snaps his fingers open and shut, open and shut, slowly at first, then gradually faster until the pads of his fingers pop like castanets in a fine imitation of a line of traps firing closed in rapid succession. "*Snap! Snap!* We got 'em!" The now octogenarian laughs and his blue eyes sparkle so brilliantly that even the large, metal-framed glasses he wears cannot detract from his mirth. In the next moment, deep crow's feet emerge at the corner of his eyes, their crinkling quickly spreading to his mouth like deep canyon gorges cut by years of enjoyment and frequent, genuine smiles.

So powerful is this memory that Couffer seems to drift from the room to a dark night many years ago where he slept beneath a white canvas tent pitched in the desert, or in the San Gabriel Mountains, or maybe on Santa Rosa Island. After a few moments, he rouses himself, continuing, "In the morning, you go around and collect the specimens. . . . They have to be made into study skins. . . . I became quite good at it. I mean, I could really make good study skins. Mammals are easy [to skin] but birds are a little more difficult. I feel that I earned a certain degree of fame for the quality of my bird skins."[17] Fifty-four skins within the NHM bird collection, each prepared between 1941 and 1948, bear Jack Couffer's name. There are probably many more that should be attributed to him as

well, but because up until the 1980s only the collector's, not the preparator's, name was listed on the specimen tag, there is no way to ascertain
the true contribution Jack Couffer made to the LACM's ornithological
collections.

For his part, von Bloeker took a liking to young Jack Couffer, indel-
ibly inculcating him with his own interest in bats, a bond that paired the
two together during World War II when they joined the army as part of
a crazy crusade to save the world. Couffer and von Bloeker's wartime
escapades became the subject of a book Couffer authored entitled, *Bat
Bomb: World War II's Other Secret Weapon*. Codenamed "Project X-Ray"
and blessed by President Roosevelt, the true-life plan involved bats, bat
caves, a tiger, and an unconventional group of men working to devise
a method for attaching small incendiary bombs to millions of bats that
would be released over Japan's wood and paper cities. The plan depended
on the bats roosting in the eaves and then, when the bombs ignited, the
cities would burn from the top down, a scenario resulting in minimal loss
of life (except for the bats) because the people had time to escape. The
bat bomb's builders believed in their project and expected to deploy it,
but then they burned down a secret U.S. military base during a trial run.
Soon thereafter, top military brass selected "Little Boy" and "Fat Man,"
codenames for the atomic bomb, to replace their pet project.

Couffer was not blind to his mentor's quirks and eccentricities.
Indeed, he recognized the scientist's overzealous collecting habits and
addictive tendencies, writing, a "cigarette forever dangl[ed] ... from
his lips" and his right hand was "stained a sickly yellow-brown.... His
clothes reeked with the pungent odor of tobacco."[18] Yet von Bloeker's
faults did not turn Couffer away. In the end, the bat scientist's great academic passions and wonderful curiosity sparked his student protégé's
future interest in science and bound them together as longtime friends.
Couffer explains, "[m]y tutor in this compulsive study of flying animals
was thirty-three when I was seventeen, and he treated me and my fellow
student assistant, Harry Fletcher (who was as fascinated with fossils as
I was with bats), with all the understanding and perhaps more worldly
insights than if we were his own sons."[19]

In the journal he kept while on Santa Barbara Island, von Bloeker's
prose is not a straightforward recitation of the events as they occurred;

rather, it feels curated and grand, reading as though directed to an audience, or at least a hoped-for one. In the six and a half pages he scribed, von Bloeker devotes more than a page to bemoaning both the dearth of fieldwork on the Channel Islands and the resulting lack of publications. "As many of us know," he begins, "outside the fields of Ornithology and Botany, there has not been a great deal of work done on the Channel Islands in the past as regards scientific investigations. And even in these two fields there appears to remain much to be discovered."[20] Who is he speaking to? Who is "us?"

To prove his point, he cites one obscure article published in an 1897 Canadian journal, recording in his fieldnotes the journal's full name, the author's name, and the document's title. He also lists the page numbers where nine species of beetles hailing from Santa Barbara Island are catalogued. (These details are impressive as he either had these facts memorized or brought the article with him to the island to aid in his work.) Next, with the flair of a magician whipping off the black scarf covering the hat to expose the rabbit within, he makes the exciting promise that, "in contrast with"[21] the Canadian journal article, he would offer a summary of the animals they collected while on Santa Barbara Island. He then expounds upon the three species of land snails found on the island while assuring his readers that his account will be more complete than any written before him. He is especially interested in finding *Binneya notabilis*, a species of land slug recorded only once, sixty years prior, but after searching the island extensively with the aid of his colleagues, none were located. As if in recompense, they found plenty of examples of the other two species.

Now, it is important to note that absence, while it might be an indicator that something is not present, is not proof that it does not exist. Take peregrine falcons, for instance. Von Bloeker spent parts of all three days of the third expedition watching a pair of peregrine falcons protect a nesting site located just offshore on Sutil Islet. This sighting is unusual because, well, they were supposed to be extinct on Santa Barbara Island.[22] No one had seen a peregrine falcon on the island in years, yet there they were.

Both Meadows and von Bloeker were serious about their work. They sought recognition for it—even, apparently, if it could only be found in their own handwritten or typed out words. In contrast to their kind of braggadocio, one gentleman within Meadows's Long Beach gang, a schoolteacher and botanist (formerly the principal of Santa Catalina Island School in Avalon), comported himself quite differently. Tall and bespectacled, Meryl B. Dunkle appears unpretentious as he stands straight-backed and closemouthed in photos, a Mona Lisa-like smile often playing on his lips. He exudes a quiet self-assurance grounded in humility and gratitude, a gentle soul who published a book of poetry in 1964 entitled *Songs of the Trail*. In this slim collection, he wrote a poem entitled "The Byways of Life" that in part reads:

> Let us then not seek the brightness
> That would seem to come from far;
> Nay, let us undertake to search for,
> Find the light that in us lies;
> Seek the light that shines about us,
> Making clear our ways and lives.
> Let us not seek for things beyond us;
> Let us see the world we live in;[23]

Dunkle's modesty, however, did not detract from the seriousness with which he approached his work. During the third expedition alone, he collected 1,200 plant specimens of roughly 48 species,[24] which contributed to the eight articles he published covering the plants of the Channel Islands.

Dunkle documented his work on Santa Barbara Island in an unpublished typewritten draft report located in NHM's archives. This report contains information about the island's botanical state eighty years ago. In it, Dunkle described three distinct botanical zones on Santa Barbara Island. Stretching across the island's terraces and rounded central ridge, he wrote of the "temporary grass lands" that thrived in the deep, rich soil cultivated and burned by Hyder two decades before. This habitat remained home to a "scattering" of "indigenous plants that [were] ... working slowly back into the area,"[25] as well as many introduced species such as false barley, crystalline iceplant, and wild oats. By the time of Dunkle's March 1940 visit (during the seventh expedition), the native *Coreopsis gigantea* was rapidly reclaiming the previously burned and cultivated areas, but most of the other indigenous plants had been pushed out by introduced grasses and icicle plants and could now be found only "in the shallow soil and steep slopes of the seaward cliffs."[26] Writing that the "smaller annual plants [could not] . . . successfully compete with the grasses as yet,"[27] Dunkle revealed his hope that the indigenous plants would meet with a better future.

Dunkle's second plant zone lay between 50 and 250 feet above the waterline within "a belt of broad, flat ridges and shallow canyons lying along the lower slope of the eastern terrace."[28] He described dense vegetative scrub "dominated by the grotesque *Coreopsis gigantea*"[29] growing adjacent to prickly pear cactus, low lying mats of morning glories, boxthorn (the endemic island sagebrush), and wild cucumbers that sprouted inedible, prickly fruits. He described this zone as being "very difficult to penetrate" because of the thickness of the growth, "and the stubby branches of the Coreopsis . . . borne at right angles."[30] Despite these challenges, the botanist's perseverance paid off. Once he made it through these plants, he found short, shallow canyons where plants found nowhere else on the island still grew, including: *Aphanisma blitoides*, a flowering plant that today is listed as rare, threatened, and endangered in California and elsewhere; the distant scorpionweed, another flowering plant; the thimble clover; a fern known as the California polypody; and the coast range melic, a dense tufting clump grass.[31]

The island's cliffs, bluffs, benches, and headlands, all of which drop precipitously off into the sea, comprised the third of Dunkle's botanical areas. Plants in this location had specifically adapted in terms of wind, sun, and salt exposure. Most lived in shallow, rocky soil, and their distribution was limited to very particular areas. Emory's rock daisy, desert wishbone bush, green echeveria succulents, and an aster known by its lyrical common name, silver bird's foot trefoil (*Lotus argophyllus ornithopus*)—some variants of which today include the word "Dunkle" in them, indicating that M. B. Dunkle had a hand in locating a type specimen of this plant—all preferred southern exposures. Dunkle could only locate tarweed on the southern and eastern bluffs below the coreopsis bands, and the rare Trask's milkvetch (known only from Santa Barbara and San Nicolas Islands) and California saltbrush in those areas that received the "full sweep of the wind." Finally, the botantist found *Baeria hirsutula* (a member of the sunflower family) and the leafy desert dandelion on the island's "high rounded shoulders where the soil is a little deeper."[32]

M. B. Dunkle standing amongst his beloved plants on San Clemente Island, April 1939. Courtesy of Department of Anthropology, NHM.

In 1938, President Roosevelt placed Anacapa and Santa Barbara Islands into the Channel Islands National Monument, within the National Park Service's purview. Over the years, a smattering of letters exchanged by von Bloeker and the NPS demonstrates the Department of the Interior's keen interest in Santa Barbara Island, particularly regarding nonnative and introduced species. Von Bloeker's 1939 field journal highlights the abundance of feral house cats, Belgian hares, and oats, information he shares with his government colleagues. Curiously, when the CIBS returned to the island in March 1940, the rabbits had disappeared and the cats were nearly gone as well.[33] How and why they vanished is unclear, though this improved state did not last long enough to benefit all of the islands' native plants and animals.

Between 1942 and 1946 the military brought rabbits back to Santa Barbara Island to serve as a food source for soldiers stationed on this island outpost. By the early 1950s, hundreds of rabbits had nibbled to near decimation the native vegetation, especially the shrubby habitats preferred by the Santa Barbara song sparrow, a sweet-singing, six-inch, short-winged, greyish-brown bird[34] that lived only on little Santa Barbara Island. A rabbit eradication effort began in 1954, but a fire that burned two-thirds of the island in 1959 destroyed much of the song sparrow's remaining crucial scrub and coreopsis nesting areas, a crushing blow to this species. Sometime during the 1960s, this bird, whose pleasant, rhythmic trills and clear notes abundantly greeted early island explores such as Joseph Grinnell in 1897, disappeared. Extensive monitoring surveys failed to locate it, and in 1983 the Santa Barbara song sparrow was officially deemed forever silenced.

The CIBS did not collect any Santa Barbara song sparrows during their third expedition, but von Bloeker's field journal notes their presence.

Ten years after President Franklin Roosevelt designated Santa Barbara and Anacapa Islands as a national monument, the monument's boundaries were expanded to stretch one nautical mile off of the islands' shorelines, thereby protecting the rich kelp beds surrounding them as well as Sutil Island and Shag Rock, which are important seabird rookeries. Today, Santa Barbara Island is part of Channel Islands National Park, as are San Miguel, Santa Cruz, Anacapa, and Santa Rosa. In recent years, considerable efforts to eliminate rats, cats, and invasive plants from Santa

Barbara Island have been expended, with the result that it is seeing signs of ecological recovery.

At the conclusion of the CIBS's first Santa Barbara Island expedition, the scientists seemed not only satisfied by their efforts, but they better understood the enormity of the task before them. Von Bloeker aptly lamented, "Though we have . . . added materially to the knowledge of the fauna and flora of Santa Barbara Island, it may readily be seen that there remains much to be done in regards to investigations on this one island alone, to say nothing of the other islands."[35]

The day the explorers returned to the mainland, the *Los Angeles Times* reported Roland McKinney's arrival at the LACM. During the preceding spring months, the museum's board of governors had worked with the county board of supervisors to create, by county ordinance, a new museum management position that he would fill. Thus, when the governors welcomed McKinney to the museum at their May 31st board meeting, they welcomed not only the museum's new director of art but also its new director-in-charge, whose responsibilities included overseeing and managing the entire museum. McKinney envisioned creating a new institution consisting of curated art exhibits, an education department catering to school children (much like the one he successfully created in Baltimore), and a new exhibitry division that would meld science, history, and art by utilizing personnel currently employed by the science and history departments. His position of authority over all museum departments gave him the latitude to make these kinds of changes to the museum's organizational structure.

Nothing in the museum's files provides insight into what Comstock thought of his new boss or the changes he sought, but Comstock was not the kind of man who aired his grievances in public. Thus, when Meadows put before him an ambitious suggestion for the next expedition, Comstock went to work figuring out the details. Meadows's plan anticipated a month-long survey coinciding with his summer teaching break, a ten-man contingent representing all disciplines, and a week of fieldwork on each of four islands: San Nicolas, San Miguel, Santa Rosa, and Santa Cruz. He requested Comstock coordinate transportation with Captain Hancock and that he secure the necessary permits from island owners and lessees. "Respectfully yours," the professor signed off, "Don

Roland J. McKinney, LACM's new director-in-charge. Courtesy of NHM Archives.

Meadows, Leader of Expeditions, Los Angeles Museum-Channel Islands Biological Survey."[36] It is clear from this proposal's tone, direction, and spirit that Meadows had fully assumed the survey's leadership role, a role he seemed to relish and believe he fully deserved. At this early stage of the expedition, territorial skirmishes had yet to arise and no one thought to warn Meadows that he trod a path strewn with loose scree.

In keeping with the positive and productive nature of Meadows's letter, the director of science congenially attempted to comply with his requests, but obtaining permits turned out to be harder than a straight-forward administrative task. He wrote letters that were returned and postmarked undeliverable, made phone calls that yielded more phone calls but little else, and wasted his time chasing down worthless leads. No one, not even Comstock, fully appreciated the labyrinth of own-ers, lessees, and managers that controlled the various Channel Islands. By early July, the museum had not heard back from the owners of Santa Rosa or Santa Cruz Islands and had no transportation secured. In sum-mary, it wasn't going well and the chances of launching the grand expedi-tion Meadows envisioned were dwindling.

Because Comstock and Meadows had not yet corresponded about the status of the expedition and its many setbacks, Comstock dutifully sat down at his desk on Saturday, July 15, to update his fellow lepidopterist in writing. Meadows did not take the same tack, however, before agree-ing to be interviewed by the *Long Beach Press Telegram* for its Sunday edition the following day. Thus, the paper reported that "Don Meadows is off again chasing butterflies"[37] and leading "a staff of 10 scientists"[38] to San Nicolas, San Miguel, Santa Rosa, and Santa Cruz Islands, when in reality no firm plans were in place to mount such an expedition. The professor had done nothing to corroborate the status of his proposal with Comstock or any museum personnel, yet he spoke to the press as though it was all set. It was bad form, bad management, and bad public-ity. The release of these plans could have compromised the institution and led to any number of bad results. Island owners or caretakers may have seen this news article and felt they were being backed into giving the museum their permission to visit, or Meadows's presumptive belief that the navy would hand over permits for San Nicolas Island could have struck some paper pusher the wrong way. Not only could the museum's request be denied, but the scope of the survey dramatically reduced. With the damage done, the "fox" out of the bag, Comstock could only hope to get his scientists, along with the needed permits, on a boat and out onto those islands—fast.

Miraculously, five days later the *Los Angeles Examiner* captured the crew standing aboard the *Bluefin* in Long Beach harbor just before she shoved off toward distant San Nicolas Island. Comstock had done it—sort of. When Meadows, von Bloeker, Woodward, Martin, and Kanakoff (the museum's invertebrate specialist) left port, none of them held in their collecting-happy hands permits for Santa Rosa or Santa Cruz Islands. But Comstock, like a bat echolocating safe passage through a dark and twisting cave, would not lose his way. He would secure those permits and avoid any embarrassing meetings with his new boss Roland McKinney, who was two months into his new job.

Chapter Seven

THE LOST ISLAND: SAN NICOLAS

"F.D.R. Acts to Aid Refugees: Roosevelt to Aid Jewish Refugees." President Roosevelt today invited the leaders of the International Committee for Refugees seeking to find havens overseas for Germany's 400,000 unwanted Jews, to confer with him in Washington the first week in September.

—*Daily News* (New York), July 20, 1939

It was now a little over six months into the survey and the winds of change so common on the Channel Islands were beginning to blow through the cork-floored hallways of the LACM. In a letter Comstock penned to Nathan Vail, owner of Santa Rosa Island, Comstock revealed a telling detail that delineated the beginning of the tightening of the CIBS-museum reins.

As originally structured and approved by the LACM's board of governors, nonmuseum survey members were allowed to keep a small percentage of the specimens they collected for their private purposes. This provision served as both an incentive and a form of nonmonetary compensation to those participants who did not receive a salary for their contributions but who nonetheless incurred costs for food, gas, and camping supplies. Among the individuals who benefited most from this was Don Meadows, the original drafter of the provision. While other nonmuseum staffers may have viewed it favorably, it does not appear to have been a primary motivating factor in their participation. Don Meadows, on the other hand, had a vested interest in growing his already sizeable Lepidoptera collection, not only because it provided him with cachet as a private collector of import, but also because he intended to use new specimens garnered from the CIBS as the basis for his doctoral thesis. Additionally, physical possession of the specimens gave him control over their future use, including the ability to regulate who had access to them.

Six months into the survey, however, Comstock's letter to Vail clearly indicates that this provision—and one other—had changed. He wrote, "all specimens collected are now pledged to the Museum" and the responsibility for "the financing and equipping of the field parties"[1] now lay with the LACM. These two significant changes indicate the increased level of control the museum was beginning to exert over all aspects of the survey, including its participants and scope.

Another, more subtle change that highlights the shift of power away from Meadows and toward the museum is found in Meadows's progress report of the fourth expedition. In it, Meadows lists the names of all participating personnel, including Comstock, whom he designates "Director," and himself, whom he designates "Entomologist, in Charge." Compare this to the title he selected for himself in his first progress report—"Entomologist and Leader of the Expedition"—and it is evident that something prompted this self-demotion. No documentation explaining these changes is found in the archives, but it is possible that his recent misstep with the *Press Telegram*, combined with someone (perhaps von Bloeker or Woodward) complaining about him, may have played a role in this early curtailment of Meadows's authority. Von Bloeker, just thirty years old and equal in status to Meadows in terms of their Berkeley master's degrees (and certainly "more equal" in terms of their employers), had the pluck to take the likes of the Long Beach lepidopterist on. So did Woodward, a man no one ever faulted for shying away from confrontations, and as a former director of the museum he would have had ample opportunity to air any grievances, real or imagined, to Comstock.

Eight men boarded the *Bluefin* on Friday, July 21, 1939, headed for San Nicolas Island: Meadows, Woodward, von Bloeker, Kanakoff, Dunkle, Martin, Sprong, and Jewel Lewis, a student. John Adams Comstock planned to join the party later for a week's worth of fieldwork on Santa Cruz. As the crow flies, the *Bluefin*'s berth lay about eighty-five miles

Prior to shoving off for San Nicolas Island on July 21, 1939, the explorers pose aboard the *Bluefin* in port at Terminal Island with the Richfield Oil Company marine terminal in the background. From left to right: George Kanakoff, Jewel Lewis, Don Meadows, Captain W. B. Angelke, Captain H. R. Groat, Russell Sprong, Art Woodward, M. B. Dunkle, Lloyd Martin, and Jack C. von Bloeker Jr. Courtesy of Department of Anthropology, NHM.

from San Nicolas Island, but naval requirements mandated that the ship detour to San Clemente Island in order to pick up permits and drop off specimens, which cost them many hours.

Aboard ship, Meadows and Woodward immediately began recording their thoughts. Meadows sent a letter to Comstock and another to his "Dearest Ones" (his wife and son, Donald), and nothing in either of them suggested that he harbored any feelings of disillusionment or the slightest loss of enthusiasm due to the recent administrative changes. Perhaps Comstock had handled any discussions with Meadows in an exceedingly congenial manner, never revealing the reasons—or personnel—behind the changes. Or, perhaps Meadows's collegial attitude and buoyant spirit simply reflected the lepidopterist's enthusiastic pursuit of whatever endeavor he engaged. He certainly was a man of positive

energy, and he seemed not to have allowed any curtailment of his responsibilities to diminish the possibilities the survey continued to provide
him, choosing instead to embrace his opportunities.

The journal Woodward kept during the fourth expedition brims with
relevant and seemingly irrelevant information. At times his notes devolve
into minutiae—how he got to the boat and with whom, who drove, who
was late, what he did when the boat shoved off (read in his bunk), and
what he ate for dinner (roast pork, ham, string beans, potatoes, bread,
butter, coffee). At other times, the details of his finds—"I tested the crest of
a midden overlooking Rocky Beach and found layers of sea urchin shells
and spines. These had not been roasted. The shells had not been burned.
All of these sites are similar in their lack of chipped implements"[2]—illuminate the lives of the people who once lived on the island.

With sixty-one miles separating it from the continental United States,
San Nicolas is the furthest Channel Island from the mainland. Its twenty-
two square miles of semi-arid landscape supports few edible plants, only
three reptiles, and two terrestrial mammals (deer mice and the San Nicolas Island fox), and its geology includes no high-quality stone toolmaking
materials. Today, the U.S. Navy uses the island as part of a missile proving
ground and, except under special circumstances, it is closed to civilian
personnel.

Likely, no more than 200 island Gabrielino, or Nicoleño, ever inhabited San Nicolas Island,[3] but this is still a sizable population for such a
remote and desolate place. Evidence points to human visitation of San
Nicolas beginning 8,500 years ago, as verified by a single radiocarbon-
dated mussel shell, but multiple sites dating to more than 6,000 years
ago suggest that the population grew over time.[4] The disparity between
these two time periods could have arisen because San Nicolas lost one-
third of its land mass between 9,000 and 7,000 years ago due to rising sea
levels,[5] which may have swallowed landscapes containing archaeological
artifacts associated with measurable evidence. Even so, the more than 550
archaeological sites found on San Nicolas to date attest to the thriving
maritime culture that once occupied this island.

Life for the Nicoleño—and all coastal California tribal people—
changed dramatically after Spain began settling California in 1769 during the mission era. Over the next fifty-three years, twenty-one missions
sprung up between San Diego and Monterey on what had been Native

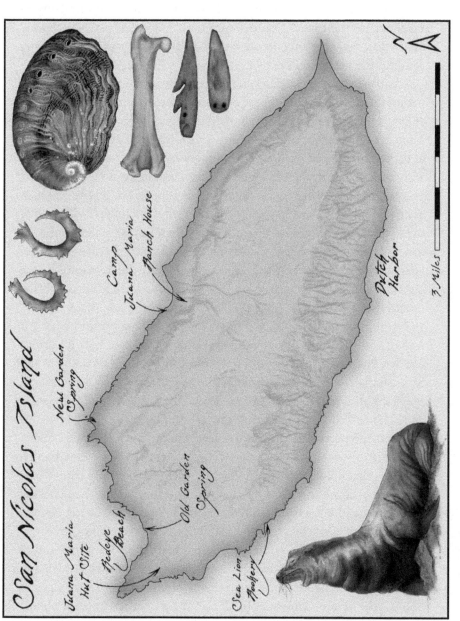

San Nicolas Island.

American land. In order to build the missions and work the fields, the Spaniards recruited tribesmen, who were given food and housing in exchange for their labor. Neither commodity, however, was necessarily better than what the Indians were used to, and in many cases the living conditions were far worse.

As time progressed, more and more Native Americans came to live within the missions. Some came because of the enticement and "magic" of Spanish culture—livestock, candles, trumpets, bells, and iron. Others came to seek refuge from the tyranny of Alaskan natives who had come to the region to hunt sea otters. Still others came either more forcibly or without family or hope—having had their land taken away and having watched their fellow villagers suffer and die due to exotic diseases such as measles, typhoid, and influenza—because they felt they lacked alternatives. Regardless of the reason, most found themselves virtually enslaved in a movement from village to mission, so swift that, only fifty years after Spain began building the missions, no island Gabrielino remained on the once-thriving Santa Catalina Island,[6] whose peoples had greeted Cabrillo so enthusiastically.

Beginning in 1803, Aleut hunters, often working with Russian fur traders, came to Californian waters seeking otters for their luxurious fur. San Nicolas Island supported great colonies of these sea mammals because they favored the lush kelp forests that surrounded the island. Inevitably, this led to interactions between the Nicoleño and the Aleuts, and in 1814 a well-known massacre orchestrated by the fierce Aleut against the Nicoleño people resulted in the deaths of most of the island's men.

By 1830, the remaining Nicoleño were the only native Channel Islanders that the mission padres had yet to "evacuate" from California's southern offshore islands. This changed in 1835 when, at the behest of the mission fathers, a boat[7] from San Pedro harbor sailed to San Nicolas to remove the Nicoleño from the island. Had one woman not remained on the island, that relocation would have marked the absolute end of the island Gabrielino and island Chumash era on the Channel Islands. Instead, for eighteen years one person continuously inhabited the island—she became known as the "Lone Woman of San Nicolas Island."

Several theories circulate regarding how and why the Lone Woman was left behind. One popular theory suggests that she boarded the ship as it hurriedly prepared to make weigh in order to outrun an incoming storm. Upon realizing that her baby remained ashore, she begged the captain to turn the boat around, but when he didn't she jumped into the water and swam back to the island for the infant.[8] The story goes that wild island dogs ate the babe, but there is no mention of either evidence or retribution against the offending dogs. Another theory postulates that she simply did not want to sail to the mainland and therefore hid from the captain and his crew, more willing to risk fending for herself than leave her island home.

Recent unpublished research supports a different theory, one pieced together through careful examination of source documents and accounts of her brief time in Santa Barbara after her "rescue," including her attempts to communicate via spoken words and mime. This theory claims the woman did have a child, a son who may have been between the ages of six and eight years old and who possibly hid from the captain and his crew. In the midst of the commotion his mother lost track of him, but she returned to the island after discovering his absence and they lived together there for some time. At some point, during which time the boy had grown tall, he had a boating accident and died, possibly as a result of a shark attack.[9] After this the mother was truly alone. She had only the wind and her dogs for company.

Regardless of the theory, the Lone Woman proved she was resourceful, eating dried abalone meat and seal blubber, drinking fresh water from San Nicolas's springs, and sheltering in either a cave that offered her protection from the wind and cold or in a hut she assembled from the rib bones of whale carcasses she found on the shore. Her presence on the island was widely known, as demonstrated by an 1847 *Boston Atlas* newspaper story entitled, "A Female Crusoe." Newspapers in New York, Vermont, Hawaii, South Carolina, and elsewhere picked the story up, but no effort to reunite her with her people was made until 1852, when a mission father asked Captain George Nidever, a Santa Barbara-based otter hunter, to fetch her. Nidever made two unsuccessful attempts to do so. In 1853, during his third rescue mission, Nidever's first mate, Carl Dittman, found fresh human footprints in the sand and eventually located the Lone Woman, where she sat cleaning a sealskin, her dogs pacing, sniffing and barking at the intruders they sensed nearby. When the otter hunters approached, the dogs' displeasure grew louder, but with one word the Lone Woman silenced her hounds. After about a month, during which time Nidever and his crew hunted otters, she willingly joined them on their return trip to Santa Barbara, where she took up residence with Nidever and his family.[10]

In 1878, Nidever dictated his life's story to a research assistant of the American historian Hubert Howe Bancroft, an account later edited and published as a memoir entitled, *The Life and Adventures of George Nidever, 1802–1883*.[11] Among other stories, this book chronicled Nidever's discovery of the Lone Woman. According to Nidever, the Lone Woman apparently found her new mainland surroundings to her liking; she reportedly smiled frequently, played endlessly with his children, and spoke often in a language no one understood. This account may not be entirely accurate, however, as new scholarship indicates that there were people who did understand her (which is how the story of her son, his death, and her isolation on the island came to be known).[12] Additionally, Nidever's account of her apparent happiness may have been either wishful thinking on his part or simply justification for his role in removing her from her island home.

Though it has been criticized for containing mythic tropes (such as the "girl Crusoe") and promoting anti-Russian sentiment,[13] Scott O'Dell's Newbery Medal-winning fiction book, *The Island of the Blue Dolphins*, immortalized the Lone Woman's story of survival through its enduring messages of resilience and resourcefulness. First published in 1960, the book quickly became a childhood favorite with children and youth around the world. That 8.5 million copies of the book were in print in the United States in 2015 attests to its popularity.[14]

The true-life story of the Lone Woman of San Nicolas Island ends with her death in Santa Barbara, seven weeks after her arrival. Dysentery, caused by her new diet rich in fruit and vegetables, is blamed for her short life on the mainland. Baptized Juana Maria, she is buried in an unmarked grave at the Santa Barbara mission, where a plaque on the mission wall commemorates her life.

It's not hard to imagine the Lone Woman of San Nicolas Island walking barefoot with her dogs across her island's sand dunes, rolling hills, or terraced plateaus. How often did she make her way up the gentle peak that rises less than one thousand feet above sea level? From there, on a peaceful day, when the winds that frequently blow between twenty to thirty miles per hour quieted and the persistent fog burned off, she could

Portrait of the Lone Woman by Holli Harmon. This is the first painting of the Lone Woman based on historical facts. Courtesy of Holli Harmon.

have surveyed the land below her, all fourteen thousand acres lying within the ten-mile length and four-mile girth of her island home. On a day like that, the single skin she wore to clothe herself may have been enough to keep her warm. She may have even needed to shield her eyes with her hand as she scanned the horizon in search of the ship that left her or surveyed the beaches for dead seals and whales that she could eat. Or, she may simply have enjoyed the vista before descending down again and pausing at a lovely rock oasis created by one of the island's many naturally flowing springs and seeps. There, she may have taken a drink of fresh water or wandered to a nearby shady spot beneath giant coreopsis[15] to rest or sleep.

Heavy ranching activities began in 1857, four years after Juana Maria's "rescue," and by 1865 the sheep—whose numbers would grow to thirty thousand by 1890[16]—had eaten 90 percent of the island's native vegetation.[17] The hillsides eroded and the island's six inches (or more) of average annual rainfall shredded them into deep, ribbon-like ravines.

In 1933, the U.S. military took possession of San Nicolas, pushing the battered little island into a new era: leased sheep ranch *and* gunnery range. Ranching continued until the government revoked Roy Agee's sheep ranching lease in 1943, the year the U.S. Army Air Corps took over active military use of the island as part of the coastal defenses during World War II.

The progress report of the CIBS's fourth expedition outlines the island's deteriorated state: "San Nicolas is exposed to strong northern winds which are rapidly wearing away the soft sandstone composing the island. Great sand dunes cover the northern end, and the upper parts of the island are almost destitute of vegetation. . . . Sheep have been run on the island for many years and as a consequence the island is badly eroded and vegetation is sparse."[18] Lloyd Martin and Meryl B. Dunkle concur with Meadows's assessment. Martin's report corroborates Meadows's analysis and elucidates that sheep contributed to nonnative plant growth by introducing foreign species through seeds that they brought with them in their wool. He further noted the heavy erosion that negatively affected the island's native vegetation. Both of these factors played into the dearth of diversity in San Nicolas's insect populations. A note deep within the archives of NHM nicknames the island the "Dying Island"—such a sad name for a place that had been home to so many for so long. With such a bleak landscape, the CIBS's prospects for collecting seemed dim, but it grew worse as wind and fog hampered their progress.

Upon reaching San Nicolas Island, twelve hours after departing Long Beach, foggy conditions and thick beds of kelp kept the survey party from landing in the dark. To amuse himself aboard ship that evening, Woodward took a Russian language lesson from George Kanakoff. Born Yuryi/ Georgii Pavolvich Kanakov in Crimea, Russia, Kanakoff immigrated to the United States in 1923 at the age of twenty-six with an insatiable appetite for life. When he wasn't appearing in a theater production, collecting specimens, or writing scientific articles, he read nine different languages, spoke six, and taught Russian language and the history of the Russian theater at East Los Angeles College.

The following morning, in the gray light before daybreak, the survey party rose and began rowing successive skiff-loads from ship to shore. Each boat they filled with collecting equipment, camping gear, food

Pictured in this photo taken on July 23, 1939, are, from left to right: Jeanne Lamberth, Jack von Bloeker holding two live foxes, Lloyd Martin, and Dennis Lamberth. Compared to foxes on the other islands, the San Nicolas Island fox subspecies is typically lighter in color, has longer legs, and has the most vertebrae in its tail—averaging twenty-two—compared to the short-tailed San Miguel Island fox that averages fifteen. Courtesy of NHM Archives.

(including 150 pounds of potatoes, 100 pounds of wheat flour, and 1 ounce of cinnamon), clothing, and other necessities. The island caretaker, Reggie Lamberth (along with his wife and two young children), greeted them where they pitched their tents on the north side of the island.

Lambreth congenially offered both his assistance as a guide and the use of the horses whenever needed. Woodward, of course, chatted him up, learning that Reggie worked for Roy Agee, the island's current lessee who ran about 1,600 sheep on the island. Woodward also discovered that the navy could revoke Agee's lease at any time, the possibility of which likely caused the caretaker some sleepless nights as German aggression increased in Europe.

By eight thirty that morning, Camp Juana Maria—or *Campo de la Juana Maria*, as von Bloeker colorfully referred to their San Nicolas Island base—had been erected atop the island's soft sandstone ground.

Camp Juana Maria with the American flag flying on the left and a small boat at the ready on the right, San Nicolas Island, July 1939. Courtesy of NHM Archives.

Woodward's first find that morning was a message cut in stone near camp, dated January 1938. In all likelihood, he likely wished he had not found it—better yet, he probably wished that the person who'd left it had never stepped foot on this island, much less any of the other Channel Islands—but it came as no great surprise that he did. The name etched in stone, A. R. Sanger, was known to Woodward from his first archaeology job at the LACM in early 1925. He ran into the name again during his days at the National Museum of the American Indian in New York City,[19] and then yet again in 1928 when the LACM rehired him. Both organizations had items in their collections that had come from San Nicolas Island, and Woodward may have handled the artifacts, studying them carefully to try and understand their provenance.

Woodward (and others) knew Arthur Randal Sanger as a "pot-hunter," or graverobber, who made his living looting and selling treasures he found in Native American sites, many of them burial spots. Sanger owned a boat named *Dreamer*, had a following of wealthy social-ites and Hollywood-types, and an overblown opinion of himself. Wood-ward didn't trust Sanger or any of his ilk, contemptuously claiming that if pothunters didn't have "the provenance of the artifact, they ... would make it up."[20] Years later, accused of fabricating artifacts—some from the Channel Islands—that he passed off as authentic, Sanger became widely thought of as charlatan. Woodward was right.

Together with Lamberth, Meadows and Woodward began surveying sites. About a quarter of a mile east of camp, near the southern point of the ranch house landing cove known as Coney Island Point, they found several of Sanger's pot-hunted sites, one particularly badly vandalized. Woodward's fieldnotes for this expedition mention several such digs, but no photographic records of them are found in NHM's archives. However, the CIBS archaeologist did photograph a wide area destroyed by Sanger on San Miguel Island. The typewritten caption on the back of that photo reads, "Pot hunter's pit. Screens and bones left by Arthur Sanger and party on site on $$.st [east] end of Cuyler Harbor San Miguel I[slan]d. This p[oin]t we named Lester Point. The pit was 15' in dia[meter]. The human remains were scattered. We gathered them together. Later, after we left the island I understand Strandnt and another chap dug under the pile looking for burials and scattered them again."[21] Woodward recorded vandalized sites, photographed them, and then reported these finds to John Adams Comstock, who in turn reported them to the U.S. Navy. Comstock, a long time Indian rights advocate, fired off several letters to naval officials and the U.S. National Museum (i.e., the Smithsonian) imploring their help in curtailing Sanger's illegal activities. Finally, the museum's efforts on Native Americans' behalf paid dividends when, in the spring of 1941, the navy requested the LACM's assistance in reporting "unauthorized diggers" to them.

Long enamored with her story, Woodward first wrote about the Lone Woman in 1930 and then again in 1931. His fascination with her eventually led him to his main objective on San Nicolas Island: finding the Lone Woman's whalebone hut. He began by walking to a rock seep used by Lamberth and his family—as well as Juana Maria—for fresh water. Called Garden Springs, it received its name from the driftwood fence someone erected around a small crop of lettuce, beets, and squash.

In the vicinity of the garden, Woodward casually surveyed the many midden sites he found, occasionally stooping to pick up bone awls, fishhooks, a red arrowhead that looked interesting or asphaltum-covered pebbles. The pebbles, though smaller than those found on the mainland, were the byproduct of watertight vessel manufacturing that began with the creation of baskets. Into the baskets the Indians tossed heated pebbles and chunks of naturally occurring tar. Then they rolled the tar and pebbles together until the tar melted sufficiently to seal the basket's interior and therefore make it waterproof. Also that day, Woodward located human remains, several very old whalebone huts, and an abundance of red abalone shells. These he noted because he knew that red abalone could no longer be found in the island's shallow tidepools, but he didn't know why, though researchers today understand that red abalone prefer cool water. At the time of the CIBS, waters were warmer than in earlier times, which caused the red abalone to retreat to deeper, cooler therms. In their place, black abalone arrived that could thrive in the warmer, shallower waters near the shore.[22]

As Woodward collected, he never lost sight of the fact that the things he found might not be in their proper places—i.e., the items deposited last in the middens were not necessarily on top, and those deposited first not always on the bottom. He explains,

> During the course of the years the wind has shifted the sands allowing the heavier objects to remain on top.... In time these objects slide or rather sink to a common level—the present surface. As the process continues the sandbar proper will gradually disintegrate. The dark sand and charcoal will blow away leaving the specimens. These will then be mingled with the others now on top. In time, as it has already occurred in many places—the stone and some heavy bone and heavier shell objects will remain, resting on the old hard beach level.[23]

This passage describes something that archaeologists often encounter: sites that cannot be taken at face value. The location and depth of found items, especially those exposed to wind and water, may not be as originally deposited and could have come from a different place altogether. Thus, making inferences about these sites based purely on what was found and where is fraught with problems.

While on San Nicolas Island, Woodward filled his journal with names, addresses, and stories. Anyone might find themselves a star for a sentence, a paragraph, or a page or two. Nothing seemed too mundane to record: addresses, inscriptions on grave markers, or the names and hijinks of fishermen, ranchhands, and the naval man stationed on the island to tend the radio. These musings represent Woodward's personal brand of historical archaeology mixed with a flare for the dramatic and a flourish of fancy and fun, and while they might not contribute to archaeological scholarship, they make Woodward's journals wonderfully personal and help readers understand his curious nature and genuine interest in people.

On July 25, 1939, the CIBS's archaeologist turned his attention away from recent residents and to the one who left San Nicolas Island eighty-six years before, the Lone Woman of San Nicolas Island. Woodward wanted nothing more than to locate her whalebone hut, and on that day he set upon his quest in earnest.

Chapter Eight

THE SEARCH FOR THE LONE WOMAN'S WHALEBONE HUT

"Japs Defy U.S. on Pact: Demand O.K. on Grab in China."
The United States threat to cut itself off as a source of Japanese war-making supplies drew from the Government today a defiant announcement that if America wants a new treaty of friendship and commerce with Japan she will have to negotiate it "in conformity with the new situation in East Asia."

—*Daily News* (New York), July 28, 1939

That morning, under partly cloudy skies, Woodward mounted an island steed named Blaze. He carried with him a copy of the *Life and Adventures of George Nidever*, the sea captain's account of the events leading up to his first mate Carl Dittman's "discovery" of the Lone Woman, and set out with Meadows and Reggie Lamberth in search of Juana Maria's whalebone hut. They made their way toward the northwest end of San Nicolas Island, closely retracing the route Nidever took eighty-six years before. When Meadows peeled off to pursue his own activities, Woodward and Lamberth continued their search without him. The pair made their first stop at a spot where Nidever had drunk freshwater issuing forth from rocks at low tide. The island shepherds knew of this spring—its water tasted better than at Garden Springs—and five or six large abalone shells were strewn about from which they drank during low tide. Reggie, wearing a big floppy cowboy hat, knelt next to the rocks at the spring to pose for a photograph taken by Woodward. Click.

Reggie Lamberth posing for Art Woodward at Abalone Spring. Freshwater spots such as this attracted foxes and mice when canyon springs stopped running in the late summer. Courtesy of NHM Archives.

In his journal Woodward notes "J. Roca 1902" and "F. Murray," both names he found cut into the rocks nearby. Roca's identity is unknown, but one Edward F. Murray had some interest in the Channel Islands. He transcribed mission records for the prominent California ethnologist Hubert Howe Bancroft, and later took by dictation the life story of George Nidever and others.[1] However, whether this is the same F. Murray as the one who cut his name into the island's rocks is not certain.[2]

Woodward and Lamberth moved on. They rode past Garden Springs to Old Gardens on the northwest portion of the island, from whence another clear freshwater source bubbled forth from rock shelving located at the very edge of the tideline. Here they ate lunch and Lamberth watered the horses. While they rested, Woodward looked about, mentally noting the presence of crevices within the rock oasis where Juana Maria kept her caches of seal meat and blubber cool and out of reach of her dogs. Click. After this photograph was developed, Woodward captioned it, "Old Garden Spring or Juana Maria's Spring ... [the spot where] Juana Maria had her first food cache."[3]

Old Garden Spring is located in Redeye Beach, a deeply bowed bay that Woodward referred to as Honeymoon Beach. He described this expanse of coastline as a place where Japanese glass fishing floats washed aground, where driftwood collected in the winter, and where a rocky offshore reef supported thousands of abalone. It is "one long sand dune covered with middens ... acres on extent,"[4] he enthused. The shell middens to which he referred extended away from the water and up toward a hilltop, their abundance nothing short of overwhelming. Before turning away from the beach to gaze toward the ridgeline, where he believed he would soon find Juana Maria's home, he took a moment to pen his thoughts: "No wonder this well watered island with its teeming sea life was a favorite haunt in spite of the drawbacks of fog and wind."[5]

As Woodward looked at the wealth about him, he may have conjured up images of Nicoleño people hauling abalone up from the beach, grinding roots, and preparing fires over which they would roast the tough flesh of the univalve gastropod. The Lone Woman herself may have feasted here with her people. Would returning to this site have caused her to grieve the loss of community, friends, and family? Was this a sacred or ceremonial site, a place where whistles sounded and people sang together? Or, was this just a pretty beach, a nice place to gather where good smells and the waft of grey smoke in the wind comforted? Woodward's journals do not pose these questions, but he likely wondered about the area's use.

Before departing their lunch spot, Woodward took his camera out again to photograph the ridge from the east. Click. This is at least the fourth picture he took, and a note in his journal accompanies each one. His careful documentation, written and photographic, makes it clear that Woodward considered this more than a simple outing. He was chronicling, in detail, his quest to find Juana Maria's whalebone hut and essentially creating a photojournalistic documentary, a new type of storytelling technique U.S. periodicals were only beginning to use.

The black and white image that resulted from the last shot immortalized the multitude of middens on San Nicolas Island. Each midden location is marked by dark shells festooning the rounded sand hills like lost leopard spots. The knolls are etched against the firmament as clearly as if an artist sketched in the curved dune line distinguishing land from dove grey sky. Looking more closely at the photo, the snowy fingers of a fog bank crawling up and over the ridge are just barely visible. Had Woodward waited a few more minutes to take the picture, the photo would have no horizon line at all.

The men remounted and moved on. Soon they picked their way amongst whale rib bones scattered across the ground. The bones were sun-bleached and broken, their surface pocked by the now visible pores that once housed blood vessels and nerves. Click. This is not the spot Nidever indicated in his memoir as being Juana Maria's whalebone hut. They are not the bones Woodward was searching for. They continued on.

After riding further up the ridge, Woodward may have pointed with his hand or his chin and said to Lamberth, "If Nidever was right, then we should find the remains of Juana Maria's house on that high point."[6] Surely eager to find what remained there, they must have urged their horses onward. Upon reaching the top, they saw Honeymoon Bay (Redeye Beach) to the east, Rocky Beach to the west, and to the southwest, obscured by the point, a seal rookery, the animals' guttural barking audible in between gusts of wind. All around lay more shell mounds. Their profusion impressed Woodward, who described "the entire area" as "covered with acres of shell debris,"[7] and confessed to having "never seen anything to equal the extent of these areas." There were so many, in fact, that he concluded that although "pot hunters may have worked some of these sites ... one could work [here] for many years and still have more work to do."[8]

Woodward's journal is anything but straightforward at this point. It is circuitous, skipping in time, a mass that separates and comes together the way an amoeba moves within a microscope's viewfinder. His words jump from this water seep to another one, to the ridgeline and then to Honeymoon Bay. The journal must be read over and over again before the order of events is clear. Each noted detail seemingly gives life to another, but the chronology is off. Sometimes he repeats himself. Sometimes he backtracks. Any sight or sound might evoke a thought that he wished to give voice to. Sometimes it feels rushed, as though he didn't have the time to record everything he feels compelled to note.

Reading the journal raises questions about the times at which he penned his thoughts. Did he commit his impressions to paper at the very moment he experienced something? For example, whilst on horseback, or upon first seeing something of importance. Did he wait to scribe his beliefs until the moment he took a break to drink, eat, or photograph? Or did he give himself time to reflect and absorb, choosing to wait until evening, when he could sit at a table sipping the hot cocoa or tea that was served nightly at nine o'clock? It is possible that he waited even longer— a day or two—before jotting down his assessments, though that seems unlikely given the immediacy of his words and the vivid details he provides.

Everything in his journal about the day he searched for the Lone Woman's hut gives the impression that he is stunned by the abundant evidence of life that lies before him on the ground, as well as the archaeological magnitude of what he is documenting. There is a brooding, low-key hum of excitement that exudes from this section of his fieldnotes. As he moves closer to his quarry, his writing takes on the feel of a novel building to its turning point, and his words assume a dramatic edge: "The barking of the seals comes to us and the north winds blows steadily[,] a barren wind swept port. The fog hangs out at sea shrouding us but the horizon's clear."[9] His choice of the word "clear" is an indication that he knows he is onto something. Each piece has fallen into place. Each step is accurate. The fruits of his thoughts and efforts are almost within reach. The way is "clear" for him to make another discovery.

Woodward and Lamberth continued up the hill along the broken ridgeline until they "came to the high point from which the visibility ...

Reggie Lamberth in the saddle, holding the reins of Woodward's mount, Blaze. Scattered in front of him are nineteen whalebones, the remains of what Woodward believed was Juana Maria's hut. Courtesy of Department of Anthropology, NHM.

[was] good. On the apex of the hill were the many ribs, scapulae etc. of a whale—definitely a hut site."[10] Click. "This site tallies perfectly with Nidever's acc[ount]"[11]; since it "was the only evidence of any shelter on the site which corresponded to Nidever's description, it seemed logical that ... [it] was the wreckage of the whale-bone and brush shelter once occupied by the lost woman of San Nicolas."[12] Click. Click. Click. Woodward dismounted, handing Blaze's reins to Lamberth before stooping toward the ground, where he found a weathered bone barb from a fish harpoon. Again, he notes the abundance of red abalone shells lying around the midden site.

Before leaving Juana Maria's hut site, Woodward sketched the bones lying on the sand and took one last photograph. This one is a lovely shot featuring Reggie astride his mount, holding the reins of the riderless Blaze. In the background, land, sea, and sky nearly merge as one, with only faint lines delineating their boundaries. In the foreground, the shell middens are abundant, and on top of these lay nineteen long, white whale ribs, scapulae, and vertebrae—Juana Maria's hut. Click.

Woodward's discovery of Juana Maria's whalebone hut represented another charismatic find for the CIBS, and staffers took note. Von Bloeker mentioned it in a letter to Comstock, and Meadows included it in the body of the fourth expedition's progress report. At least one newspaper picked up on it, too. The article's headline read, "Shack Site Found," followed by, "Director Arthur Woodward ... located the forgotten site of the shack in which Juana Maria, the Lost Woman of San Nicolas, lived alone on the island for 18 years."[13]

The Lone Woman's story clearly resonated with the researchers and the public as well. But perhaps the person most smitten was Woodward himself. In December 1940, during the tenth expedition, he staged a reenactment of George Nidever's account, including photographing a dark-haired female archaeologist sitting inside the resurrected whalebone hut and posing as Juana Maria. Over the years, Woodward wrote two articles about this find, participated in an oral interview, and on at least one occasion corresponded with Phil Orr of the Santa Barbara Museum of Natural History on the subject.

Modern scholars have several bones to pick with Woodward's discovery of Juana Maria's whalebone hut. Most consider it a romantic notion, contending that there is no way to distinguish Juana Maria's hut from all the other hut sites in the vicinity.[14] In addition, because the Lone Woman lived so long on the island and moved freely about it, researchers believe that she likely would have used several of the huts as windbreaks depending upon her needs. Thus, claiming that one particular hut "belonged" to her makes no sense. Further discrediting Woodward's theory, most Nicoleño houses were semi-subterranean, a style that provided protection from the island's strong winds. A whalebone hut would not have afforded enough protection to warrant its use as a permanent home. However, far from being the last word on Juana Maria, Woodward's romantic find instead heralded the emergence of an entirely new generation of researchers eager to know her. They have made impressive progress.

One hundred and fifty-five years after Juana Maria left San Nicolas Island, three scientists discovered a time capsule dating to her time there. Inside was a collection of artifacts so personal that if there was something to match it to they might have found either her fingerprints or those of someone in her community.

This time capsule, found carefully stashed in a steep hillside beneath a whalebone rib marker, is comprised of two handmade boxes configured from recycled redwood boat planks that hold tantalizing clues to the Nicoleño's world in the 1800s. Consisting of over two hundred artifacts associated with the Nicoleño, Native Alaskan, and Euro-American peoples, scientists believe that the contents—shell pendants, abalone dishes, lovely carved fishhooks, effigies, a brass button, and flaked glass hand axes, among other items—represent both finished products as well as the raw materials for producing other items for future use.

The evidence suggests that the cache was created either in the early 1800s, while a small population of Nicoleño still lived on the island, or in the years coinciding with Juana Maria's lone existence there. Though researchers cannot definitively associate this find with the Lone Woman, it is possible that she may have been the one to make, fill, and bury the boxes.[15] It certainly is romantic to imagine her saving a favorite possession (a brass button, perhaps?) just because she admired its artistry, storing away a knife she knew she would need later to survive, or crafting an intricate and beautiful fishhook during the long days she spent alone.

One archaeologist who had a hand in discovering and evaluating the cache has a theory about this box. This individual notes its careful construction and the wonderful items within, many of which took considerable time to manufacture before being sensibly placed into a box and then stashed beneath a large white whalebone that made finding it again easier. The Lone Woman was in no hurry to leave the island with Nidever and his men, perhaps because she wished to visit her boxes a few more times before leaving the island for good. At least one archaeologist speculates that the Lone Woman may have constructed these boxes, possibly together with her son, as a toolbox of sorts. After all, they contain both finished items and works in process. Maybe before she left the island with Nidever she wished to add a few more things to the boxes, or select an item or two to take with her. If she believed she was leaving the island forever, her thoughtful review of the contents is logical, even if it cannot be proven.[16]

Another remarkable find was made in 2012. Having spent nearly twenty-five years searching for the Lone Woman's cave, a navy archaeologist got a new lead after reading the journal of a nineteenth-century government surveyor. The surveyor wrote that his own field station lay "100 yards eastward of the large cave formerly inhabited by a wild Indian woman who lived there alone for 18 years."[17] Using this clue, the navy archaeologist located a sand-filled cave beneath a rock overhang in the vicinity described in the surveyor's journal. While there was no physical evidence linking the cave to the native islanders' use of it in the past, the abundance of archaeological items found throughout the island supported an excavation. During this process, some forty thousand buckets of sand, a few historic artifacts, and a seemingly modern engraving on the cave wall were found, which deepened the mystery of what might be inside and who might have used the cave. With excitement rising, the researchers believed they were within inches of exposing strata containing artifacts that would provide a greater understanding of the lifeways of the island's inhabitants at the time of Spanish contact. They also hoped to tie the cave's occupation if not to Juana Maria, as this was nearly impossible, then at least to her time on the island. However, their work was suddenly halted when the U.S. Navy ordered a stop to all excavation at the cave site.

This directive resulted from naval officials' response to the receipt of a mainland Indian tribe's critique that the work being done was not in compliance with federal historic preservation laws. This same Indian tribe also concurrently made a claim of cultural affiliation with San Nicolas Island under the NAGPRA (Native American Graves Protection and Repatriation Act). Of concern were at least 571 human remains and over 1,000 associated funerary objects removed from San Nicolas Island over the past century, which are now housed in museums throughout the state of California. Due to these circumstances, the navy elected to cease excavation of the cave in order to minimize controversy while it consulted with the tribes involved.

The current state of the NAGPRA process indicates that, at some point in the future, the human remains and associated funerary objects will be returned to San Nicolas Island and "consolidated there with those held in the Navy's on-island repository."[18] It is expected that "after this consolidation, representatives of the four Indian tribes consulted with under NAGPRA will prepare the remains and objects for reburial and then conduct a joint ceremony"[19] in a manner keeping with their cultural practices. To date, the NAGPRA process is nearing completion for the cultural items; however, future plans for the cave remain undecided.

Some scientists involved in the search for Juana Maria's cave, as well as some interested professionals, are frustrated at the inability of research activities to continue at this cave. Other interested parties—including researchers, Native Americans, and other citizens—are supportive of tribal interests and the NAGPRA process, both of which aim to repatriate certain types of cultural items to the appropriate Indian tribes. Either way, the tension the navy's decision sparked between Native American groups and archaeologists is indicative of the ongoing struggle to balance science with human rights.

As for San Nicolas Island? Named in 1602 after Saint Nicholas of Myra (the prototype Santa Claus), it continues to give gifts that make us pause and wonder how we got to where we are today. And Juana Maria? Her allure remains as potent as any shaman's magic.

Chapter Nine

THE LONELY ISLAND: SAN MIGUEL

"Jap-German Treaty: Tokyo Announces Trade Pact Soon after Cut by U.S. Action Seen as Threat to Draw Closer to Italy, Germany." "Oriental Gesture: Japan Aims Her Announcement at Great Britain and France."

—*Hope Star* (Hope, Arkansas), July 29, 1939

Meadows conveys his satisfaction with the fourth expedition in a letter he wrote to his wife and son from Camp Juana Maria on San Nicolas Island: "Dearest Sweetheart and Sonny Boy.... The grub is good, the camp comfortable and the weather mild. A wind blows continually from the north west but clear skies keep the temperature up to comfort."[1] But despite his apparent contentedness, a melancholy then fell upon the expedition leader and he revealed a soft and tender side of himself, a bit of his personality infrequently seen in his official CIBS correspondences. It is a part of him, however, that is very much in keeping with the opinions of those who would one day know him as "the dean of Orange County historians." He wrote,

> Even though I've been very busy and happy I still have been a slight bit homesick at times. You, Donald and I have been out together so much that an out of door undertaking doesn't seem quite right with just me.... Lots and lots of love and kisses to both of my pals. Even though I'm realizing a dream of boyhood

days I still feel lonesome and incomplete without you both. Bye bye sweetheart. I love you. Kiss Sonny for me, and keep a lot for yourself. Signed, Daddy.[2]

The degree to which Meadows pines for his wife and son is endearing, but also surprising given that he had left home only the week before. Perhaps San Nicolas Island's remoteness and stark landscape seeped under the professor's skin, twisting his emotions and making a week feel like much longer.

Back on the mainland, Comstock scrambled to stitch together the loose ends of the fourth expedition. An important piece of this included the missing island permits. The Santa Cruz Island permit had finally been secured and Comstock had it delivered aboard the *Bluefin* when she ran to San Nicolas to transport the researchers to San Miguel. As for Santa Rosa Island, though Comstock obtained the Vail family's promise that written permission would be forthcoming, the CIBS did not yet have it in hand.

On the eve of the survey's departure from San Nicolas Island, the staff tuned in to NBC's *Kraft Music Hall* radio show. They listened to the rich bass and baritone voices of Bob Burns and Bing Crosby as they struck their tents and packed up cots, bedding, and supplies. After finishing their chores, they laid their bags on the ground to spend a last night on the Rock Island without cover save the shelter provided by their sleeping bags and a thick blanket of fog. Rising at four in the morning, they loaded up and began the run to San Miguel Island.

Begg Rock, named after the sailing ship *John Begg* that hit it in 1824, clears sea level from a depth of fifty fathoms (three hundred feet) eight miles northwest of San Nicolas Island. This rocky pinnacle juts just fifteen feet above the waterline, but below the surface it extends north and south for more than one hundred yards in both directions. Today, it's a magnet for scuba divers due to the challenging open ocean topography and the abundance of beautiful filter-feeding organisms that cling to the steep, rocky outcropping and swing wildly in the haphazard currents. Dive boats don't make this trip regularly, but when they do they frequently cancel the dive right on the spot, the conditions too perilous.

Begg Rock is also reputedly the inspiration for Tall Rock, the outcropping in Scott O'Dell's novel *Island of the Blue Dolphins*. In the book, the heroine, Karana, and her dog, Rantu, explore a burial site in a sea

Readying to shove off San Nicolas Island on July 28, 1939, with the *Bluefin* in the distance. Courtesy of NHM Archives.

cave within Tall Rock. They become trapped overnight inside the cavern when the tide rises, preventing their escape, and the experience unsettles Karana because she realizes that the dead inside the cave are her ancestors. Furthermore, the seated skeleton Karana sees on a ledge within the cave is holding a pelican bone flute to its mouth. Coincidentally, a similar flute was found in 2009 by a prominent Channel Islands archaeologist working on nearby San Nicolas Island.

The fourth expedition headed along a northerly, mostly open ocean route to reach San Miguel Island. Even on the mildest of days, the waters here are unpredictable. From the *Bluefin*'s roiling deck, von Bloeker wryly noted, "the trip has been a little rough so far and some of the boys are wishing for about a square foot of solid dry land to stand on for about an hour or so."[3] Von Bloeker was too polite to call the green-gills out by name (though Meadows had done so previously in other letters), but Art Woodward would certainly have been one of those boys needing to keep his eyes fixed to the forward horizon. If that didn't work, his would have been the torso bent over the stern railing, a strategic spot that allowed the wind to blow any organic matter he might give up away from the ship.

The *Bluefin* paused at Begg Rock just long enough for the scientists to record its life: no plants, two California sea lions, two western gulls, and five Farallon cormorants. Already homesick, the sight of this barren outcropping deepened Meadows's longing. In the letter he penned to his "Dearest girl" while aboard the *Bluefin*, he said he'd "never seen anything more lonesome."[4]

Continuing, the California Fish and Game Commission cruiser motored northwest until it reached the San Miguel Passage, the inhospitable waters separating San Miguel from Santa Rosa Island. Here the vessel turned east to shoot the narrow, passably deep gap before following the island's northeasterly shoreline. At Prince Island, a forty-acre outcropping just offshore of San Miguel, the *Bluefin* turned left into gently curving Cuyler Harbor, the large bay on the island's northeastern side. Tucked behind Harris Point and Bat Rock to the north, Cuyler Harbor is the island's only protected anchorage.

San Miguel Island is forbidding—cold, foggy, and windswept. It is the most northern and western of the Channel Islands, the third smallest in the eight-island archipelago, and definitely the most battered. Scientific literature often describes its terrestrial landscape as depauperate or impoverished. The island's fourteen square miles take the brunt of the harsh Northern California winds that drive down the coastline and whip past Point Conception to frequently howl across the bowed highlands, viciously blowing away the island's topsoil and driving sand dunes before them. Only twenty-six miles separate the island from the mainland, but these seas are among the West Coast's most turbulent and difficult to navigate due to strong, conflicting currents, heavy winds, and frequently foggy conditions.

Approached from sea on a calm day, San Miguel appears a gently rounded isle, essentially two eight-hundred-foot-high hills surrounded by tablelands. However, upon drawing closer to Cuyler Harbor, a steep, craggy coastline emerges. Headlands whose profiles resemble worn granite gargoyles appear to stretch over the sea, beckoning fresh ships to join the known twenty-nine already ringing its shoreline like a macabre necklace of broken timbers, loosened anchor chains, and lost lives. Even some headland names memorialize the dead men who perished there. It can be a stark island, one subject to wind and waves that continue to shape its future as they have its past. Even so, on sunny days blue ocean

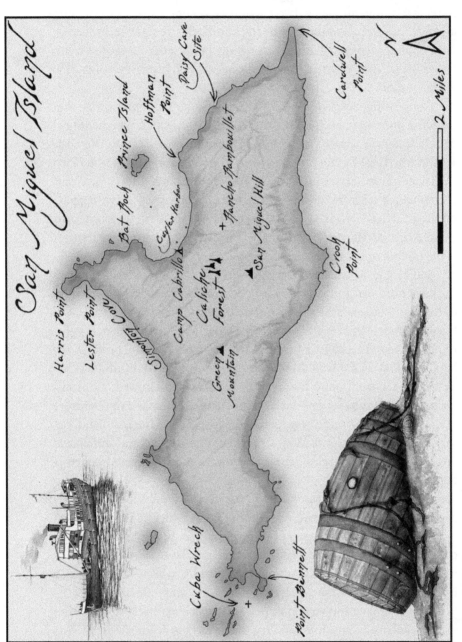

San Miguel Island.

vistas and a serenity born of solitude mix with wild smells to create a powerful potion of pure island magic strong enough to draw people to its shores for thousands of years.

Meadows described the island's basic topography and condition in the fourth expedition progress report:

> Roughly diamond in shape.... Precipitous cliffs rise from narrow sandy beaches to an average height of 250 feet, except toward the eastern end, where, at Cardwell Point, a long sand spit runs into the sea.... All of the west end is sand covered. There are many springs on the island.... Once fairly large groves of trees and shrubs were on the island, but only a few indications of their former extent now exist. Considerable vegetation is found on protected cliffs and slopes that are inaccessible to sheep.[5]

One indication of the large groves of trees to which Meadows alludes is the island's caliche forest, a terrain dominated by thick, ghostly white skeletal stalks, the root remnants of fir trees and both Torrey and bishop pine trees. These trees thrived in cool environments and provide an indication of the island's former, more lushly landscaped self. As the world warmed after the last ice age, the island's cold-loving trees died, and subsequently the island's constant winds buried the lifeless trunks beneath up to thirty feet of sand. Over the years, sparse rainwater reacted with the dissolving bits of shell strewn across the land to create a calcareous soil. The mixture leeched down to the remaining tree roots and there, beneath the surface, magic happened. The shell and rainwater combined to form calcium carbonate, a cement-like natural concrete substance called caliche that is brittle and hard. Eventually the root inside died, leaving a sheath filled with concrete, an underground caliche cast. Blowing almost ceaselessly, San Miguel's fierce winds eventually exposed the buried rhizomes, revealing an eerie white graveyard of upwardly twisting root stumps, commemorating a forest that died out thousands of years ago. In a shamanistic way, the caliche forest foreshadowed the future demise of an entire culture.

Based on research conducted during the last quarter century, we know that the people who lived on San Miguel witnessed the development of the caliche forests over many generations, beginning when they lived on the mother island, Santarosae, before she became four separate landmasses. Early Channel Islanders also witnessed the extinction of the flightless duck, the giant mouse, and possibly the pygmy mammoth.

Much of this knowledge as well as the timeline of human occupation on San Miguel Island came from excavations of a single cave that for many years was one of the most important archaeological sites on the Pacific Coast of North America: Daisy Cave. Located on the northeastern shore of San Miguel, researchers from the CIBS trod all over this area, perhaps walking right past Daisy Cave, never dreaming that late in the 1960s a LACM archaeologist, who began working at the museum long after the CIBS concluded,[6] would be the first to "well-document"[7] this site and later—along with a colleague from the University of Santa Barbara— conclude that the cave had been used for three thousand years. Following his and others' explorations of Daisy Cave, an archaeologist from Oregon and his colleagues further investigated this site in the latter part of twentieth century. They discovered and documented evidence that maritime peoples with advanced seafaring technologies built boats capable of navigating Santa Barbara Channel's treacherous waters and lived in, or at least utilized, Daisy Cave for roughly twelve thousand years. The early occupants thrived, and their society grew in size while advancing culturally and technologically. Evidence of this growth includes: active trade with mainlanders; development of shell bead money; crafting of fine ornaments, beads, and circular shell fishhooks; production of asphaltum coated baskets; and utilization of the many maritime resources at their disposal.

Significantly, various people frequently occupied this cave over the millennium, choosing Daisy Cave because it provided shelter and was sited near abundant marine resources such as shellfish, kelp beds, and (most importantly) fresh water. Enhancing its attractiveness were the nearby quality chert sources that supplied the raw materials for making tools. In short, these attributes made it the "best house in the neighborhood." Of great interest to archaeologists and anyone desiring to understand the peopling of America is the fact that the date of Daisy Cave's earliest documented occupation (11,700 years ago[8]) and that of nearby Cardwell Point (between 12,250 and 11,200 years ago[9]) are among the earliest known Paleocoastal occupations in California.[10]

The dates of these finds place human occupation of the Channel Islands as contemporaneous with mainland Clovis sites while also providing further evidence that humans with advanced maritime econo-mies capable of making strenuous seafaring voyages occupied at least some of the northern Channel Islands. This, then, begs the question: Did Channel Islanders populate California instead of the oft-assumed other way around? Did they perhaps move eastward and inland, bringing their technologies with them? Most likely, yes, they did—but, naturally, it is more complicated than that.

Long after Juan Rodríguez Cabrillo's arrival in 1542, Russian and Aleut hunters learned of the Channel Islands' large sea otter populations. Sea otter fur, being the thickest fur of any animal in the world, became known as "soft gold"—just one inch of this marine mammal's pelt can include as many as one million silky hairs. Eager to supply Europe's aristocracy with lush otter pelts that artisans would make into coats, hats, and boots, the Russians and Aleuts swarmed southward, unleashing a killing spree that drove the Southern California otters to near extinction by the early 1800s. Aleuts didn't limit their destruction to otters, however, as they used sophisticated weaponry in their clashes with the island Chumash and island Gabrielino. Both tribes suffered at the otter hunters' hands, and by approximately 1820 the few island Chumash who remained on San Miguel were removed to the missions.

As Southern California's otter population diminished and the Chu-mash islanders were expatriated from San Miguel, this northern Channel Island became a resting place for other hunters, who soon pointed their heavy oak clubs and other weapons at the heads of the next sea mammals slated for decimation: northern fur seals, northern elephant seals, harbor seals, California sea lions, Steller sea lions, and Guadalupe fur seals. All of these pinnipeds were once abundant on San Miguel, hauling out on the beaches to breed, hunting fish in the island's rich kelp beds, and rest-ing on the sand. But by the late 1800s, the seal trade brought them all to near extinction. Today, as a result of Mexican and U.S. conservation laws, some of these pinniped species have rebounded, but the Steller sea lion and Guadalupe fur seal have yet to recover.

In 1850, San Miguel Island's first sheep rancher "sold"[11] his interest to George Nidever, an accomplished sea captain with a boat capable of navi-gating the treacherous waters separating Miguel from the mainland and the man who removed the Lone Woman from San Nicolas Island. For over ten years, ranching proved profitable for Nidever, who occasionally worked and lived on San Miguel while growing his operations to include two hundred cattle, one hundred hogs, thirty-two horses, and six thousand sheep. However, on an island whose vegetation could only support half as many livestock, the "shear" number of mutton-on-the-hoof made the ranch wholly unsustainable. A yearlong drought in 1864 pushed Nidever's herd to denude the island, eating every bush, tree, and edible root they could reach. But even this could not sustain the animals, whose grisly starvation deaths not only presaged the end of the Nidever era, but also pushed the island into danger. Without the benefit of grasslands and shrubbery, northwest winds (which average between twenty-five and fifty mph or more) swept the topsoil into the sea, leaving exposed bedrock and sand dunes.

Despite its poor ecological condition, two brothers from San Francisco bought San Miguel Island from Nidever in 1869. Eighteen years later, they sold a 50 percent share to William G. Waters. With hopes that the sea air would cure Mrs. Minnie Waters of tuberculosis, the Waters family moved to the island on January 1, 1888. When Minnie did not recover, William hired a ranch manager to take over operations and returned to the mainland, where Mrs. Waters died. For the few months that she lived on San Miguel, however, Minnie kept a detailed diary of island life in the late 1800s, which was later published by the Santa Cruz Island Foundation.[12]

After Minnie's death, Waters returned to the island, eventually purchasing it outright. In 1906, Waters—now in his sixties—began building a large ranch house in a meadow six hundred feet above Cuyler Harbor that under future ownership would became known as Rancho Rambouillet. He demonstrated his industriousness and ingenuity during the construction of his island fortress by utilizing wood scavenged from shipwrecks and the spilled cargo of lumber schooners that had unsuccessfully navigated the treacherous currents swirling around San Miguel. Over the years, lumber from any number of wrecks was recycled for fencing, outbuildings, a wharf, a warehouse, and (of course) the constant repair of all the structures. The house, inspired by Waters's efforts and imagination, included modern conveniences and unique features such as a 120-foot double wall to withstand the northwest winds, sliding doors between rooms to save on space and eliminate hallways, and five bedrooms equipped with running water and washbasins.

Ironically, both Waters and a future island dweller, Herb Lester, would declare themselves "King of San Miguel." Waters, however, wasn't joking in this claim (unlike Lester), going so far as requesting San Miguel Island's sovereignty from presidents Grover Cleveland and William Howard Taft. His requests met with no success.

After nearly thirty years on the island and just four months before his death, the first "King of San Miguel" sold his lease to a twenty-five-year-old rancher, Robert L. Brooks, and his partner. In time, Brooks bought out his partner and became the island's sole lessee, but titling issues spanning back to the Treaty of Guadalupe Hidalgo that ended the Mexican-American War in 1848 clouded his ownership rights.

When the young rancher reached an annual lease agreement with the U.S. Lighthouse Service, a new, modern era of ranching on San Miguel commenced that would include the charismatic second "King of San Miguel." This king, Herbert Steever Lester, also known as the island's "Deputy Sheriff"—and who, along with his family, *Life Magazine* dubbed the "Swiss Family Lester"—would come to dominate this period in San Miguel Island's history. Much later, the captivating stories of both kings of San Miguel would populate the pages of T. C. Boyle's historical fiction novel, *San Miguel*.

Chapter Ten

THE KING OF SAN MIGUEL BEFRIENDS THE CIBS

"Curbing Power for War Asked." Senator Nye, Republican, North Dakota, told the senate today that this country could stay out of war "if we curb executive power to secretly move toward war."

—*Arizona Republic* (Phoenix, Arizona) July 30, 1939

A quirky, quiet sense of humor led Herbert Steever Lester to claim the titles "King of San Miguel" and "Deputy Sheriff." Yet, all jesting aside, Lester did possess quality stationary with letterhead that read "Herbert S. Lester/Deputy Sheriff/Rancho Rambouillet/San Miguel Island, California." Whether his wife gifted the stationary to him as a joke or not is uncertain, but he used it nonetheless. On this fine paper and in lovely inked cursive lettering, Lester replied to Comstock, who had written to Lester about the CIBS's desire to survey San Miguel Island. Assuring Comstock that he and his wife would welcome the museum party, Lester offered them lodging in "the Ranch house, and if we cannot find room enough for all ... the Sheep Shearer's Barn."[1] His congenial letter was an auspicious beginning to a productive week of fieldwork on San Miguel Island.

Lester met the island's lessee, Robert Brooks, at Walter Reed Army Hospital in Washington, DC, when the pair were recuperating from injuries sustained in World War I. After recovering from his wounds, Brooks hightailed it west, back to his island and mainland California ranching operations, while Lester returned to a job requiring extensive travel. During the years that followed, Lester "continued to suffer symptoms from the poorly healed shrapnel wound in his side, and was profoundly psychologically scarred by his wartime experiences. . . . [He] felt a desperate need to escape from congested city life and he shared this growing desire with Bob [Brooks], from whom he particularly enjoyed hearing about the adventures of island ranching."[2] In 1929, Brooks offered Lester a temporary position as the island's resident manager, and by the spring of 1930 Lester had married Elizabeth "Elise" Sherman and moved his bride to their new San Miguel Island home. Soon, airplane pilots, newspapermen, and pothunters (such as Art Sanger) flocked to San Miguel, all drawn to the remote location by the twosome's special blend of magnetism.

Upon the CIBS's arrival on the Lonely Island, Lester and Arno Ducazan, Lester's full-time ranch helper, met the *Bluefin* on the beach. With the aid of a horse-drawn sled of Lester's own design, the two dragged the CIBS's dunnage across the sand and up to a small beach shack Ducazan had built seven days prior. Von Bloeker dubbed their San Miguel Island camp *El Campo del Cabrillo* ("Camp Cabrillo"), a fitting name given Woodward's forthcoming hunt for the Spanish explorer's gravesite. Despite the propitious camp name and von Bloeker's belief in his colleague's ability to locate the grave, Woodward himself lacked conviction about his chances of finding it. While the archaeologist's skepticism was aptly placed, it was not, as Woodward believed, because rising seawater had subsumed Cabrillo's resting site over the course of the past four hundred years, but because Cabrillo most likely died and was buried on Santa Catalina Island.

Still, Woodward didn't let the prospect of failing in this endeavor keep him from walking the island searching for midden sites and dutifully mapping them in his journals. Rather, he set his well-trained blue gaze on the sand, mentally picking through the bits of rubble and riches he found strewn about while bending his aching back to examine them closely before slipping what he considered to be the best treasures into a bag. He may have furrowed his brows a time or two when he picked up chalcedony fragments and wondered why these rocks were so abundant on San Miguel, yet completely absent on San Nicolas. Without a ready

Camp Cabrillo, Cuyler Harbor, San Miguel Island, July 28–August 4, 1939. From left to right: the tent belonging to George Kanakoff and Jewel Lewis; the cook shack and quarters of Russ Sprong; Don Meadows and Art Woodward's tent (half hidden); Meryl Dunkle's tent (white); and Jack von Bloeker and Lloyd Martin's tent. Courtesy of NHM Archives.

answer, he nevertheless recorded the existence of this quartz—just as he noted its absence on San Nicolas—right alongside the shellfish remains he encountered in the middens: mussels, abundant quantities of red abalones, and some black abalones.

Red abalones thrive in cool oceans. Scientists can track historical ocean temperature fluctuations in order to deduce the period in which a midden formed. For example, if native people collected red abalone near shore, then water temperatures had to have been very cool, even in shallower depths. On San Miguel, red abalone evidence indicates that one site was utilized during the Middle Holocene, or about 7,000 to 3,500 years ago. This information can help scientists begin to build a chronology of human activity in and around the site.

Walking farther east and south (toward Cardwell Point) to a site he calls "#7," Woodward writes,

> [the site] occupies the crest of the ridge at the extreme tip of the [island] nearest Sta. Rosa. Here . . . was a work shop. The material used were chalcedony and cherts.

Thousands of flakes, broken pieces, and the inevitable hammer stones littered the ground for some distance along the top of the hill. In the sandy area at the end of the ridge where it slopes downward to the long sand spit is an occupational area covered with mussel and some abalone. . . .

The occupational area near the workshop site on top is scattered among low hummocks. . . . I judge the material used is found on this ridge which appears to be old conglomerate weathered out on top. The sand spit and the large breakers rolling in from two sides reminds me of the extreme east point of San Nicolas. Sta. Rosa is plainly visible beyond. It appears that at one time these 2 islands must have been joined together.[3]

In these passages, Woodward correctly speculates that Santa Rosa and San Miguel were once one island, something that science had yet to prove, and he also describes the location of a chert source in the ridge at Cardwell Point. The seemingly innocuousness of the latter belies its significance. Chert is a type of stone important to Chumashans because it can be made into any number of tools, including flakes (a simple tool useful for scraping and cleaning animal hides), arrows, and knife blades. Additionally, high-quality chert played an important role in producing microblade drills, which were used to make shell beads, the Chumash currency. As a result, chert was valuable and tradable not only between Channel Island dwellers, but with mainland tribes as well.

In 1993, a group of scholars hailing from the University of Oregon, University of California–Santa Barbara, and California State University–Long Beach "rediscovered" the Cardwell Bluff chert site on San Miguel Island that Woodward documented in his journal. They named the stone "Cico chert," which is an abbreviation of Çiquimuymu,[4] an island Chumash word for a village once located on San Miguel. Unlike Woodward, these scientists were quick to recognize its significance. Namely, analysis of Cico chert informed scientists that it had been used on the Lonely Island beginning more than ten thousand years ago and that most previous analyses of trade routes based on chert could no longer stand unchallenged.[5] That is, earlier assumptions about trade and use patterns needed to be reevaluated because researchers now knew that Santa Cruz chert is *not* the only chert source on the northern Channel Islands. The lesson to be learned here is that not only do scientists need to conduct more research on the distribution of mineral resources used by island Chumash, but also that care must be taken to adhere to the scientific principles of testing hypotheses and questioning assumptions when interpreting artifacts.[6]

Ironically, Art Woodward specialized in trade good dispersal patterns—how things were made, an object's importance to a tribe, what it implied regarding social structure, and whether or not it was an actively traded item[7]—yet he did not directly evaluate or publish anything about San Miguel chert. Still, his fieldnotes include thirteen references to chert items found on San Clemente, San Nicolas, San Miguel, and Santa Cruz, an indication that his gut told him this material was important even if he never published articles that future scientists could mine. Today, Woodward would be impressed to learn just how important the San Miguel Cardwell Point chert site is. Given his personality, he might have thunderously cursed himself for not putting his name in print next to its discovery and then he may have spun a nice long yarn about what he found that day.

In a letter to his wife, Meadows retold a story he had heard from Herb Lester. It may have resonated with the lepidopterist not only because of its cautionary tale, but also because of the academic status of its protagonist, Ralph Arthur Hoffmann. Hoffman—a Harvard graduate, ornithologist, and esteemed botanist who collected prodigiously on the Channel Islands—was the director of the Santa Barbara Museum of Natural History for the nine years preceding his death. In his museum staff photograph, he appears approachable and thoughtful, though more genial investment banker than botanist, but regardless he possessed the job, professional acclaim, and academic achievements to which Meadows aspired. When Hoffman arrived on San Miguel Island on July 21, 1932, it was at least his eighth collecting trip to that island and approximately his twenty-fourth trip to the islands altogether.[8] That particular July day ended foggy and windy with Hoffman having gone missing. Near midnight, Herb Lester located the botanist's plant press at the base of a cliff east of Cuyler Harbor. A few feet away lay Hoffman's body, facedown, one eye ripped from its socket, his back and neck broken, his skull fractured in several places. Dead for hours, his pulse silenced.

Meadows disparagingly described "the accident" as being Hoffman's "own fault" as he "was noted for his carelessness and recklessness."[9] While this description strikes as more begrudging than necessarily accurate, something else in the letter he sent to his wife was even more disturbing. In that letter, Meadows wrote, "San Miguel is interesting. It shows signs of several ship wrecks, violent storms and tragedy."[10] On all counts, his assessment was dead-on—within three years of the CIBS's visit, tragedy would befall the island again.

Woodward spent Sunday morning (July 30) helping von Bloeker empty his traps, after which he penned three letters. One to Ralph Beals (a University of California anthropology professor), another to an unknown gentleman by the name of Lee Shipping, and a third to a mysterious "M." The transcriber of Woodward's journals suggests this was Marion Hollenbach, an archaeological graduate student at USC who also worked at the LACM curating the pre-Columbian art and Pacific Islands exhibits. There is nothing untoward about writing a colleague, but it is unclear why he chose to keep her name undisclosed in his journal and on the exterior of the envelope.

In the afternoon, Woodward and the gang prepared for Sunday dinner with Herb Lester by shaving and donning clean clothes. Their feast of fresh lamb, green peas, potatoes, coffee, bread, and fruit also included a tour of their host's home, which von Bloeker described as "a veritable museum ... in which Lester has gathered collections of fossils (including tusks of a Miocene? Elephant), Indian artifacts, Fire-arms," and an "ample library on history, archaeology, and whaling." But more than just a home, Rancho Rambouillet was almost like a self-contained city, replete with a blacksmith shop ("Ye Olde Forge"), a harness shop ("Ye Saddlery"), a small schoolhouse (dubbed the "smallest in the world" and where the two Lester girls attended classes taught by Mrs. Lester), a radio weather station Lester operated for the navy, and a bar ("Ye Saloon"), in which von Bloeker said Lester "display[ed] ... one of the finest collections of empty bottles and kegs in the world."[11]

Not every bottle in Lester's "Killer Whale Bar" sat empty, however. Seven years after the 1923 wreck of the 308-foot steamliner *Cuba*—which carried 115 passengers, 65 crew, and $2.5 million in gold and silver bullion when it ran aground 500 yards from Point Bennett, San Miguel's westernmost point—and seven years after the ship's contents were auctioned off and its bullion and passengers saved, Lester salvaged a fifty-gallon keg of whiskey buried in the sand. He siphoned the spirits out a few gallons at a time, keeping his cache hidden until he had emptied the keg and Prohibition ended. Then, the barrel, minus the hoops and hooch, took up a place of honor in a corner of Rancho Rambouillet's living room.[12]

The gang enjoyed a fine time that afternoon in Lester's company. Meadows declared it "one of the most pleasant experiences on San Miguel Island."[13] To reciprocate, expedition members invited the "King of San Miguel" and his helper, Ducazan, to Camp Cabrillo for dinner the following night. After they arrived, staff and guests huddled around an island map and created names for some unspecified island sites: Lester Point, Nidever Canyon, and Anchor Beach. As supper stretched into a nightcap of hot cocoa, Woodward worked on his beads, separating the decorated red and green ones from larger *Olivella biplicata* shells while Lester regaled the group with island tales of his children and their little schoolhouse, including an account of his request to the Southern Pacific Railway for a schoolhouse bell that ended with the delivery of a single 350-pound brass carillon now rung twice daily to commence the beginning and end of each school day. The family pets made for good stories, too, including: their beloved collie, Pomo, who lived to be twenty-two and was the island's regular third student in the little schoolhouse;[14] tips on rearing young bald eagles gleaned from Lester's experience raising three of his own—Cabrillo, Lindy (after Charles Lindbergh), and Uncle Sam; and surely, Reynard, their pet fox, named after the French word for "fox." The researchers probably shared some stories, too, but the wind had blown fiercely all day, frothing the ocean and slipping sand into the folds of their skin, clothes, and eyes. Everyone must have been exhausted when the guests departed at nine o'clock that night.

Despite it being July, San Miguel lived up to its reputation. Meadows wrote, "There is more misinformation about the Channel islands than any other place I have ever heard of. San Miguel Island is foggy, cold and wind swept, but not lacking in interesting Biota."[15] Though miserable weather conditions persisted throughout the week, it didn't keep Lester from supplying the scientists with fresh lamb or suggestions for productive study areas. By the end of the week, the CIBS had added eight thousand new specimens to its collection and the gang saw the sun, warm and welcoming, for the first time since their arrival. Taking advantage of the opportunity, they broke away from striking camp to play "Sally

Rand" on the beach. What that meant exactly isn't clear, but it may have had something to do with the burlesque dancer named Sally Rand, who made famous a style of dance in which it appeared as though she were wearing nothing but her birthday suit (a style of island beach undress favored by some CIBS participants in a number of archival photographs). Or, it could be that they were playing football and utilized a play known as the "Sally," in which one misdirects the defense just like the fan dancer, who led her audience to believe she wore far less than she actually did. Either way, on that fine, sunny day they enjoyed the best San Miguel Island could offer.

In a letter to "Doc," Meadows summed up their time on the island, writing, "San Miguel is smaller, colder and more windy than San Nicolas. Herb Lester, the resident manager, is a good fellow who visits camp often and has kept us supplied with fresh meat."[16] On the eve of their departure, Lester once again appeared to offer his help. The following morning he returned, assisting the researchers with moving gear from shack to shoreline. When it was all piled up on the beach, he may have been the one to snap photographs of the gang standing behind the barrels, wooden boxes, canvas-wrapped bedding, collecting kits, and tent stakes. They looked like happy vagabonds, each smiling broadly—all, that is, except for Meadows, his countenance befitting the more serious, lofty endeavor in which he participated.

On August 4, 1939, the CIBS left San Miguel Island with their specimens and rolls of undeveloped photographs, including at least one Woodward took of A. R. Sanger's depredations on the graves of the people who lived long ago. As the *Velero III* slipped from the calm waters of Cuyler Harbor and out to the tempestuous sea, it is easy to imagine Herb Lester standing on the beach and waving farewell, a genuinely warm, mustachioed smile lighting up his eyes. In the end, beyond the specimens and the adventure, the researchers' most enduring impression of San Miguel Island may well have been its king. Meadows proclaimed, "throughout the week his friendship and enthusiastic co-operation was greatly enjoyed by the expedition members."

The truth and depth of this admiration of Lester is corroborated within the archives of NHM, where the photographs of Lester and the CIBS staff outnumber those of any other island caretakers. Lester is there in the yard with the CIBS staff inspecting notes and papers, Pomo, the black Scotties, and horses nearby, with Herb speaking and Meadows smiling. In another, a few of them pose, tired and ragged, with Lester in Rancho Rambouillet's yard. Additionally, the archives are filled with photos of Herb with family friend George Hammond, the pilot who weekly flew mail and groceries to the island; of Elsie ringing the school bell; of Lester in his forge making horseshoes; and of Lester's lovely blond daughters.

The archives also hold many newspaper articles and clippings about the "Swiss Family Lester," with headlines reading, "Lone Family on Tiny Isle Enjoys Full Life Despite Isolation," "Nine Years in Solitary," "Lonely Island Family of San Miguel Soon to Make Visit to 'Outer World,'" and "Children on Lonely San Miguel Island Scan Sky in Vain for Santa's Plane." The latter ran on page six of the *Los Angeles Times* on December 26, 1941, after the bombing of Pearl Harbor grounded West Coast flights and, consequently, Santa's only mode of Christmas transportation to San Miguel Island. Beyond the headlines, the newspaper articles contain other clues to the Lesters' lives. They reveal the burial sites of Lester's beloved pets (each marked with a cross), an account of how the "shell shocked WWI veteran"[17] saved R. L. Brooks's life, the reason why Lester wore red Russian epaulets sewn on the shoulders of his sweater (it has something funny to do with Haile Selassie), and the story of how Lester successfully campaigned to have a granite, cross-shaped monument erected above Cuyler Harbor in honor of Juan Rodríguez's death and burial on San Miguel Island, a burial that future historians knew did not occur on San Miguel Island.

These items, accounts, and stories are all there in the archives of the NHM, and all bear witness to the humanity of Herb Lester. The most indelible items within this particular file are the yellowed sheets of newspaper at the back, which tell of the events of June 18, 1942. Devastated by the loss of two fingers in a ranching accident, suffering from depression exacerbated by his old war wounds and the sulfa drugs prescribed to help him heal, and hating himself for being unable to work that year's sheep shearing, Herbert Steever Lester took stock of his life. Fearing that he faced a future where he would become a burden and an encumbrance to his family, Lester took matters into his own capable hands. He placed a handwritten note inside the family's locked safe. He took his favorite gun to a hilltop where he had once made it known he wished to be buried. He waited for the arrival of a ship in Cuyler Harbor carrying friends dear to him and his family, and then he shot himself.

Chapter Eleven

TO ROSA, THE MYSTERIOUS

"Advisory War Board Chosen." With President Roosevelt's sanction, the Army and Navy set up an Advisory War Resources Board of six prominent industrialists and economists today, to speed up national mobilization in case of war.

—*The Wilkes-Barre Record* (Wilkes-Barre, Pennsylvania), August 10, 1939

When the *Velero III* weighed anchor, it left Cuyler Harbor and the last King of San Miguel (Herbert Lester) in heavy fog and good health. Upon landing in Bechers Bay on Santa Rosa Island, the ranch superintendent, George Haise, offered the researchers use of a three-room shack (with one room being the toilet cubby). Outfitted with electric lights, a worktable, and running water, the fellas found themselves in the relative lap of luxury, quickly converting their digs to laboratory-cum-sleeping quarters and dubbing their new home "Camp Nidever."

Santa Rosa Island has a long history of human occupation. For the modern archaeologist familiar with Santarosae this makes sense, of course, but during the time of the CIBS, detailed knowledge about the chronology of island Chumash and their ancestors prior to European contact was minimal. One scholar who studied and published findings about Santa Rosa Island inhabitants was Alfred Kroeber. Although Woodward was no longer at Berkeley when his former professor published the locations of a number of Santa Rosa villages in 1925, he likely read his well-known mentor's publications and knew about the sizeable village called Niaqla, as well as the existence of six to eight other villages located nearby on Santa Rosa's northwest coast. Curiously, Woodward did not inspect Niaqla himself, nor did he send an expedition to it. Instead he left the future pioneering work at this site to his Santa Barbara colleague, Phil Orr, whose fifteen seasons of fieldwork began in 1947. During these years, Orr excavated ten home sites in Niaqla that were occupied for two thousand years before the historic period of ranching began. Although Orr speculated that as many as seventy homes were located in this one village site, the number is more likely twenty-five—still a sizeable village.

Had Woodward followed Kroeber's lead and visited Niaqla, he may have found evidence of the eighteen-foot-wide, thatched-roof homes that the Chumash islanders built and supported using wooden poles or whalebone ribs. Many homes featured hearths at their centers, a convenience that provided their occupants not only with a cozy place to sleep, but also a place to make shell bead money, stone tools, ornaments, and meals.

Today, reexamination of this site has led to some interesting discoveries. Scientists know that at Niaqla and elsewhere, the presence of certain high-value artifacts—glass beads, swordfish remains, and even chunks of redwood trees that did not grow on Santa Rosa Island and could only reach the islands via ocean currents—were associated with an elite class of people. The presence of these items near certain homes but not others allows researchers to infer the class status of the people who lived in the various houses. In Niaqla, high-status items were fairly evenly distributed among the houses, leading scholars to postulate that in this village wealth may have been shared.[1] Thus, in Niaqla there existed not only a class structure, but potentially a cultural propensity to distribute wealth among the people.

When the Europeans encountered people living on Santa Rosa, island Chumash culture was thriving. However, their culture came under pressure when introduced diseases, malnutrition caused by a diet high in carbohydrates and lacking in iron, and violence amongst themselves caused the population to decline. In the early 1800s, the remaining few Santa Rosa Chumash were removed to the missions and the island's ranching era began.

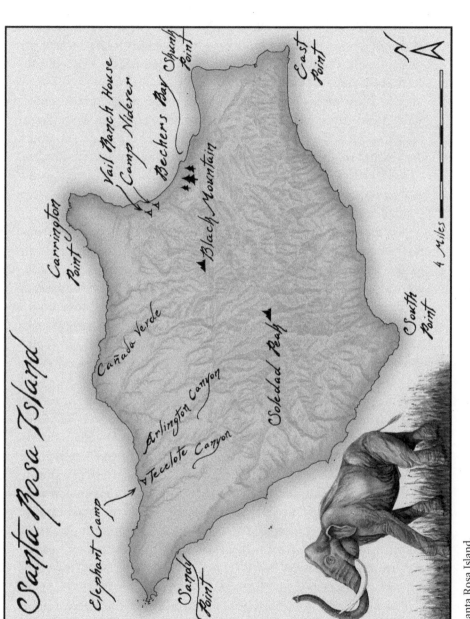

Santa Rosa Island.

An early archaeological explorer of Santa Rosa Island described the island's shape as a rough parallelogram. Meadows called it a rhomboid, but an artist or fisherman might describe its shoreline more picturesquely as that of an ocean sunfish (also known as the Mola mola), where the contours of the animal's nose, fins, and tail demark the major north, south, east, and west landmarks.

The Mola mola's nose is the island's westernmost protuberance, Sandy Point. The creature's anal fin, on the southern tip, is South Point, the dorsal fin is Carrington Point, and from there the island's contours dip southward, forming Bechers Bay, the landing site and base for the CIBS's fourth and thirteenth expeditions. Skunk Point, the island's northeastern protuberance, and East Point, the corresponding southeastern point, denote what would be the Mola mola's stubby caudal tailfin.

As the explorers cruised the passage between San Miguel and Santa Rosa, some of them may have leaned over the *Velero*'s handsome rails to note the similarities between these bookend easternmost and westernmost points of both islands. Here, the low-lying sandy beaches of Cardwell Point on San Miguel and Sandy Point on Santa Rosa stretch across the three-mile channel like two lovers straining, but unable to make contact. Given that Woodward had stood at Cardwell Point on San Miguel and considered that the islands might once have been connected, might his perspective from sea have strengthened that opinion or changed it in some other way? The islands are quite different, after all. At eighty-four square miles, Santa Rosa is six times San Miguel's size. Vail Peak, at roughly 1,600 feet, is nearly twice as high as Green Mountain on San Miguel, and Santa Rosa's vegetation is not as threadbare as San Miguel's. What Woodward thought when he made this voyage can never be known.

The passage eastward from Cuyler Harbor took captain and crew past Carrington Point, from whence they entered into the broad expanse of Bechers Bay. Here, deep indigo ocean waters turn translucent as six hundred-foot depths give way to a shallow white sand bottom. Nearing the pier, the bay's narrow beach is lined by low, vertical sandstone cliffs whose faces are etched with horizontal ripples cut by wind. This expansive cove, observed from atop one of the island's wave-cut terraces, makes Bechers Bay look like a rimmed punch bowl, a crescent beach that meets flat tablelands and ascends to rounded peaks and rolling hilltops sliced by steep canyons flowing with fresh water. Beneath the August sun, Santa

Rosa Island's fifty-three thousand acres would appear cloaked in a soft brown velvet of dormant grasses. All in all, Santa Rosa Island presented a very different visage compared to its more barren, wind-blown neighbor, San Miguel.

But Santa Rosa Island's topography, just like its weather, is as impetuous as the wild colts the *vaqueros* once broke on its pasturelands. Eighty years ago, a springtime ride around the luscious landscape would have revealed broad plateaus covered by grasslands and every color of flower, gorges cut steep by streams, oak groves shaded and quiet, tidepools stuffed with abalone and lobster, and narrow beaches abutting steep cliffs or stretching lazily toward the hills. The island's northeast corner contains hillsides with two groves of what is likely the world's rarest pine tree, the Santa Rosa Island Torrey pine, a subspecies of the Torrey pines found only on the San Diego coastline. They are majestic trees, each trunk supporting a sweeping, umbrella-like canopy of needles that Woodward found clinging "to the rocky hill sides."[2] He wrote that the seeds were "very large.... The shells ... heavier than pinons," and "the meat ... sweet and good," concluding, "no doubt in times past the Indians found these acceptable foodstuffs."[3]

Like neighboring San Miguel, Santa Rosa's winds blow incessantly and, together with rainfall and fog, have eroded much of the island. While caustic to the landscape, these inhospitable factors are a boon to paleontologists and archaeologists, who sometimes benefit from Mother Nature's constant cleansing. Natural erosion brings long-buried treasures to the surface. Of course, this has its drawbacks, too: bones, beads, fossils, arrowheads, and other finds become sun-bleached and weathered; high winds often carelessly redistribute lightweight items so that the clues imbedded in their original location are lost; and heavy rainfall can wash away items and redeposit them in other places, where they might become erroneously associated with the wrong artifacts, buried under sand and mud and silt until the next millennium's treasure hunters happen upon them, or, worse, dragged by storm waves into one thousand-foot-deep submarine trenches just offshore where they are lost forever.

Woodward devotes several pages of his journal as well as a detailed sketch to illustrate the effect of wind erosion on Santa Rosa. He observes, "Along the edge of the bluffs the sites disappear by erosion of the entire cliff.... Chunks fall off into the sea—the entire content of the mound

A photograph of majestic Santa Rosa Island Torrey pine trees, taken August 1939. Courtesy of NHM Archives.

vanishes hence ... there are few very old sites left.... Possibly ... some of the older may be preserved further inland."[4] Though Woodward was wrong about old sites having mostly vanished—there are at least twenty-eight on Santa Rosa dating to eight thousand or more years ago, and many are along the modern-day coastline[5]—the last sentence in that passage speaks to the need to search inland for sites that would further illuminate island Chumash life. Three days later, after completing surveys along the beach, Woodward reiterated his own advice, writing, "Now for the inland sites ... if any"[6]—unfortunately, he never sought them out or studied them in detail. Such work waited for his other contemporaneous and future colleagues.

Phil Orr of the Santa Barbara Museum of Natural History investigated inland sites in the 1960s, National Park Service archaeologists did the same within the last decade, and in 2013 a team of researchers investigated elevated inland marine terraces on Santa Rosa's southwestern end to determine if people congregated there in order to exploit resources such as chert sites, fresh water, or edible plants. What those researchers concluded in 2013 is that in addition to these draws, people thousands of years ago—just like today—wanted a room with a view, the more expansive the better.

So compelling were these views, apparently, that the researchers surprisingly found nine new inland sites likely dated to more than eleven thousand years ago. Studying them provided evidence that Terminal Pleistocene people found resources, such as chert, at interior sites that were not available on the coast, and that they carried food—fish, shellfish, aquatic birds, and marine mammals—several miles inland to very particular locations where they ate their meals.[7] Imagine people hiking miles up to the marine terraces, each person hauling baskets or nets laden with fish and shellfish, then sitting down to gut the fish with a chert tool, removing its head and discarding the entrails in a pile nearby. Someone else may have shucked mussels and pounded abalone, tossing the empty shells onto that pile. When a knife blade broke or a tool cracked, the useless item was tossed into the same heap. Over the years, the organic matter that the people threw away disintegrated, but animal bones (including fish vertebrae used to identify the species eaten) and such items as castoff stone points broken inside an albatross did not. These items, when found, tell stories.

Even though Phil Orr and a few other esteemed archaeologists investigated some inland sites, most archaeological research during the twentieth century emphasized coastal areas. Thus, it is left up to conjecture as to whether or not a published note from Woodward suggesting the need to rigorously pursue investigation of inland sites would have encouraged either his current or future colleagues to do just that. If he had, no one knows what artifacts may have survived the trampling of thousands of hooves, or what clues may have been revealed. At the very least, the process might have started sooner and be further along than it is now. However, Woodward did not write about his suspicions concerning inland sites, and nearly sixty years passed before such work commenced in earnest.

Cattle and sheep ranching began on Santa Rosa Island in 1844, one year after the Mexican government granted the island to two brothers. When their sibling relationship ended acrimoniously in the 1860s, they sold their ownership shares to Alexander Peter More. Initially, demand for wool to make uniforms for Civil War soldiers helped More's ranch thrive, and he responded by increasing his stock to an unsustainable one hundred thousand sheep. When the wool market collapsed, More's business did, too, and by 1901 Vail and Vickers, an established mainland ranching operation, began buying up shares. Twenty-one years later, they owned the island outright.

During the Vail and Vickers era sheep were replaced by cattle, and in the 1920s imported Roosevelt elk, Siberian snow deer, and mule deer supported a big game hunting business as well. When the CIBS arrived in August 1939, the island sustained five thousand head of cattle, five hundred deer, three or four hundred elk, and sixty-five head of riding stock. A year-round ranch crew of eight maintained the operation, augmented by additional hands during branding season or when the cows were driven to market. This latter chore was fraught with challenges, one of which was persuading the cattle to step onto the pier where the boat waited at its end. Cattle have an innate fear of walking in areas that have gaps or seams in them because the bovine eye detects places through which a hoof or leg could fall and break. The wharf's wood planking mimicked seams that are not dissimilar to the painted roadway strips that keep cattle from crossing an unfenced road. Partially as a result of this fear, getting the naturally slow-moving cows onto the boat required predawn cattle gatherings that culminated in all-out charges through the corrals and chutes onto the wharf and into the boat.

Despite the island's ranch usage, Meadows felt that "grazing is kept under control, there are no sheep on the island, and . . . the island nearly approaches the original ecological conditions."[8] How Meadows could realistically draw this conclusion is uncertain, since the first botanists to arrive on Santa Rosa came in the 1850s after sheep ranching had already begun. Thus, no pre-ranching record of the island's floristic condition was available for him to compare to its 1939 state, yet this is the assessment he made.

The Vail and Vickers ranching era on Santa Rosa Island is legendary. It is filled with vaqueros, months-long family vacations, early morning cattle drives, horses, cows, and boats, of which there were three. The schooner *Santa Rosa Island* was the first, its fate after being replaced by the *Vaquero* unknown. Fully loaded with cattle, this second boat could make the crossing to Wilmington, California, in twelve hours, though in foul weather it might take twenty-three. In 1942, the *Vaquero* joined the ranks of the *Velero III*, both taken over by the U.S. government under the War Powers Act. After this, the island ranch managed without a vessel until 1958 when the *Vaquero II*, the last wooden cattle boat on the "west coast of the Americas,"[9] was commissioned.

Though noteworthy, this wouldn't be the only time the Vail and Vickers ranch featured in a singular "last" event. The "last-last" began in 1980 when the island ranch was included within Channel Islands National Park. Six years later, Vail and Vickers signed a deed of sale granting the island to the U.S. National Park Service for just under $30 million while retaining a twenty-five-year right of personal use of the ranch house and approximately eight acres surrounding it. Subsequent negotiations resulted in the NPS issuing a series of five-year special use permits allowing Vail and Vickers to continue cattle ranching and big game hunting.

A lawsuit brought by the National Park Conservation Association (NPCA) against the NPS in 1996 alleged that the island was not being managed per the requirements of the Clean Water Act, National Environmental Policy Act, Endangered Species Act, and other federal environmental laws. Vail and Vickers countersuit of the NPS led the three involved parties to reach a voluntary, court-sanctioned settlement. This agreement stipulated that cattle ranching would cease by the end of 1998, that Vail and Vickers would manage the deer and elk herds down to zero animals, and that they would terminate their hunting operation by the end of 2011. When these conditions were met, the last privately owned island cattle ranch in the Lower 48 successfully transitioned to the people of the United States of America, thereby heralding Santa Rosa Island into a new era of stewardship designed to preserve and protect its natural and cultural resources.

Von Bloeker worked hard on Santa Rosa Island. He set trap lines and shot mammals, skinning them for their pelts and preserving the skeletons as best he could. He also judiciously collected birds, sifted through midden sites, and helped collect amphibians and reptiles. He did a nice job bagging representative samples of both of Santa Rosa's native amphibians, the California tree frog and the Channel Islands slender salamander, but

Unknown artist's caricature of Jack von Bloeker Jr. baiting a mousetrap while a curious Channel Island fox looks on. Courtesy of Department of Anthropology, NHM.

he didn't do as well with endemic reptiles, catching only the island fence lizard plus some nonnative lizards. In retrospect, most disappointing is that he did not secure a Santa Cruz Island gopher snake. This serpent, once thought to exist only on its namesake island, is known today to live on Santa Rosa as well. Jack would certainly have enjoyed catching one of these slithery critters.

As if to make up for this unknown lack, he collected six very interesting specimens, which he astutely predicted would prove to be the remains of the extinct island giant deer mouse, a rodent 35 percent larger than the other species of deer mice found on Santa Rosa. In 1939, only a single jawbone (also found on Santa Rosa Island) bore witness that a "giant" mouse once lived on the Vail and Vickers ranch. Even today, specimens of the giant mouse are rare, making the six von Bloeker collected an especially good find. However, for this Chiroptera enthusiast, von Bloeker must have most enjoyed collecting a solitary California brown bat, the first ever bat recorded on Santa Rosa Island.

If bats didn't keep von Bloeker busy, Channel Island foxes certainly did, and they proved irresistible to the researchers. "He is a friendly little cuss and does not snap,"[10] Woodward wrote about Zorrito, the young male fox Kanakoff brought into camp. This breed's pleasant personality came in handy when one female fox who had been transported to the mainland achieved some notoriety after escaping from her cage located atop the LACM's Beaux Arts building. Von Bloeker's pursuit of this little rascal, named Rosie in honor of her island home, proved irresistible to the *Los Angeles Times*, which ran a cartoon and a front section article spoofing the scientist. The paper wrote, "on the roof of the Exposition Park institution Jack Von Bloeker ... sat and panted.... Almost ready to confess that the roundup job was beyond him ... [he] was wondering whether a pack of hounds, a few red coated fox hunters and a barrage of 'Tallyho!' ... might not turn the trick."[11] It took von Bloeker four days to capture the sly Rosie, but upon her return to her rooftop digs he reported that she abandoned her wild dog ways and ate directly from his hand.

Three weeks into the expedition, a letter Meadows's posted to his "Dearest little Sweetheart" illustrates that his melancholy persisted. He wrote, "Another nine days and I'll have you in my arms again, and I'll hold you so tight you'll never get away. I dreamed about you last night. You were on a river bank with no clothes on; I was on the other other, waiting for a roaring flood to subside. We couldn't talk to each other because of the noise, but you kept beckoning to me."[12]

While the lepidopterist pined for his love through romantic and picturesque dreams, Santa Rosa's pine forests and varied environments inspired Woodward's artistry. He filled pages of his Santa Rosa Island journal with illustrations: a hand-drawn map, a site stratigraphy, a land-scape drawing, and even a schematic depicting the entire layout of the Vail ranch. Another of his charming sketches resembled a hobbit home, though it was actually a drawing of Captain George Nidever's cave. Modest on the outside, inside it was large enough to fit one hundred men. Purportedly, the Aleuts attempted to take over Nidever's cave, but Nidever and his men successfully defended their provisions by killing a few of the marauding northerners in January 1836. This battle was pivotal in reducing the Aleut Indians' reign of terror on the Channel Islanders, and Woodward hoped to find this storied storage cellar. To improve his chances of doing so, he thoroughly read Nidever's account of the skirmish. His prep work proved unnecessary, though, because Mr. Smith "Smitty," the ranch superintendent and a friend of Nidever's son, led Woodward straight to the cave. When Woodward saw it, the cave was no longer the site of a battle; rather, it ignobly served as a duck house on the Vail and Vickers ranch, and before that the sheepherder's bunkhouse. Nonetheless, the site inspired Woodward to create a sketch of the Nidever/Aleut battle plan, complete with markings indicating the spots where island Chumash guards stood, where the Aleuts landed near the pier, and so forth.

While scouring the island, Woodward recorded the locations of various sites and findings. One that received only a brief mention in his journal was a broken obsidian blade fragment he found near Lobo Canyon. He obviously recognized the volcanic glass material, and he probably knew it was prized the world over for making stone tools and that this material had been found in previous mainland sites. He likely further deduced that this scrap of stone found its way to Santa Rosa Island via trade routes, which is probably why the shiny object piqued his eye in the first place. This piece, and one collected in the spring of 1940 on San Nicolas Island—crudely made with a good chipped point that had been sandblasted to a dull finish—are the only obsidian tools Woodward found during the CIBS. Despite not journaling much about these shiny objects, this rare material managed to whet something in his subconscious, even if it wasn't the important story that obsidian on the Channel Islands has to tell.

Because Woodward did not write about obsidian on the Channel Islands, the telling of this story waited until the early 2000s, when researchers confirmed the mineral's rarity there. In 2011, another study focused on one bit of obsidian found in situ (i.e., resting in the spot in which it had been deposited) on Santa Rosa Island. Geochemical analysis revealed not only that this bit of stone debris originated from a region in the eastern Sierra Mountains of California, but more importantly it also confirmed that the Channel Islands people actively conducted trade beginning at least twelve thousand years ago.

Woodward's work on Santa Rosa between the eastern end of the island and Cow Canyon on the island's northern shore resulted in his mapping of thirty sites, including a beadmaking site near Skunk Point. Viewing that much of the island led him to conclude that Santa Rosa was the least pothunted island of those visited during the fourth expedition.

As the researchers' week on Santa Rosa Island drew to an end, Woodward devoted several journal pages to the Vail and Vickers families, including the stories ranch hands and family members shared with him, as well as descriptions of the island's picturesque canyons and vistas. Though this information might not contribute directly to the archaeological record, Woodward's ear and gift for gab did serve a purpose. For instance, someone told him that he could find "elephant bones" near the beach at the mouth of Tecolote Canyon. Dutifully recording and apparently passing the comment along to the paleontologists at the museum eighteen months later when the CIBS returned to Santa Rosa, two separate paleontological teams headed directly to Tecolote Canyon with the express goal of bringing fossil mammoth remains home.

Another tip, the last he recorded in his Santa Rosa Island journal, came from Mr. Smith, the ranch superintendent. It read, "He says Arlington cañon site has not been touched."[13] That he wrote down Smith's words indicates Woodward recognized the island's archaeological significance and suggests he wished to note the location for possible future excavation.

Arlington Canyon is on the northwest end of Santa Rosa Island, two canyons northeast of Tecolote Canyon. Woodward had been told that both canyons might yield interesting finds, yet the CIBS followed up only on Tecolote canyon. Why wasn't an exploration of Arlington Canyon undertaken during either of the two trips the CIBS made to Santa Rosa island in 1941? Did Woodward forget the nine words he jotted down in his journal? Surely he would not have had he suspected that someday Arlington Canyon would figure as the central character in a find so spectacular it would change the course of archaeological thinking forever.

Chapter Twelve

THE FORESTED ISLAND: SANTA CRUZ

"Germany Reports Pact with Hungary for Aid in War." Adolf Hitler received Count Stefan Csaky, Hungarian foreign minister, at his Obersalzberg mountain retreat today and semi-offical sources hinted that an agreement was being reached for Hungary's cooperation in case of war.

—*Reading Times* (Reading, Pennsylvania), August 18, 1939

While Captain Hancock navigated from Santa Rosa toward Santa Cruz Island, staffers standing aboard the deck would have noticed the "irregular" shoreline "and many sheltered coves . . . indented in the steeply rising sides of the island."[1] They also would have spotted the island's "highest point, Picacho Diablo, near the center of the island," along with "many other peaks" rising "over 1700 feet."[2] And while they could not see "the interior of the island" where the island's owner lived in the "approximately seven miles long" valley that "runs east and west," perhaps they would have welcomed the lush sight of Prisoners Harbor, the "side canyon"[3] that drained the great valley where they would anchor after taking a last luncheon aboard the *Velero III*.

Edwin L. Stanton (the island owner), sixteen-year-old Carey Stanton (his youngest son), and Stanton's wife, Mrs. Evelyn Carey Stanton, met Dr. Comstock and the explorers at the Prisoners Harbor dock. Edwin warmly welcomed the group in the same manner he had received the

The *Velero III* approaching Prisoners Harbor, Santa Cruz Island, August 11, 1939. This sheltered harbor received her name after prisoners from Mexico were offloaded here in 1830. Left with a small supply of food and livestock, the prisoners were expected to fend for themselves. Legend has it that they built rafts and returned to the mainland. Courtesy of NHM Archives.

many other scientists with whom he shared his land. Over the course of the following week, Evelyn and Carey increased the esprit de corps by escorting the researchers on various explorations and excavations.

The researchers, well-fed and happy to have their "Doc" with them for their last week in the field, set up camp in the pine grove lining Prisoners Harbor. Their site, Camp Murcielago, or "Camp Bat," offered a cool and breezy locale with a view of the ocean, beach, and shoreline. Meadows described the island as being "much like Catalina—high peaks, deep canyons and lots of vegetation . . . by far the most beautiful of all the islands."[4] He later supplemented this description, writing that Santa Cruz is "the roughest and most densely wooded of the Channel Islands" where "forests of Santa Cruz and Monterey pines and scrub oak" blanket "large portions of the Island and" its "steep slopes . . . are covered with chaparral."[5] Meadows's conclusion was that Santa Cruz "more closely resembles mainland conditions than any other of the Channel group." Woodward enthused more simply about Camp Murcielago, declaring it the "best camp yet."[6]

Camp Murcielago, or "Camp Bat," Prisoners Harbor, Santa Cruz Island, August 11–19, 1939. The camp is nestled in a stand of nonnative Italian stone pines on the beach. Courtesy of NHM Archives.

Santa Cruz is a superlative island. Once, its ninety-six square miles made it the biggest exclusively privately owned island off the continental United States. Today, the largest of the Channel Islands chain is jointly owned by a public/private partnership consisting of the U.S. National Park Service and the Nature Conservancy. The island is twenty-four miles in length and as much as six miles wide.

If Santa Rosa Island is shaped like an ocean sunfish, then Santa Cruz is a seahorse stretched for a westward sprint. On the island's northwesterly end, Fraser Point and West Point form the tip of the seahorse's tubular snout. Moving eastward along the top of its head, the island boasts one of the world's largest and deepest sea caves, Painted Cave, so named for its colorful display of lichens, algae, and natural rocks.

Southeast and inland from here is Picacho Diablo (Devil's Peak), which, at 2,450 feet high, is the tallest point on any of the Channel Islands. Returning to the northern coast and following the shoreline east for a few miles, a series of freshwater springs emerge that empty into coves, harbors, and bights, a coastline imaginatively evocative of a Hippocampus's[7] fan-like, frilly dorsal fin. The origin of this "appendage" is Arch Rock, its apex

Santa Cruz Island

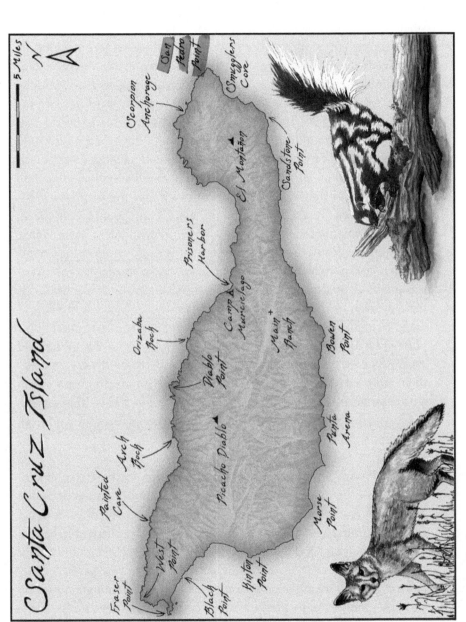

Santa Cruz Island.

is Diablo Point, and its terminus is Orizaba Rock. From there the coastline moves southeast past Prisoners Harbor until it narrows at the island's smallest girth, just two miles wide, before bending northward to curve into a tightly curled, prehensile seahorse tail whose easternmost locale is San Pedro Point, just eleven miles from the mainland. Moving south from San Pedro Point, the tail slopes down past Smugglers Cove, Middle Anchorage, and Sandstone Point before running westward to reach its narrowest girth again. Then the island elongates slightly southward and builds in thickness until it reaches Bowen Point, the brood pouch of a male spiny fish. From there, the belly (or keel) dips and bulges past Corral Point, Punta Arena, Morse Point, Near Point, and Kinton Point. Passing Christy Point, the shoreline slopes northward and the island narrows at the seahorse's imaginary pectoral fin. Black Point could be the cheek spine, from whence the circumnavigation completes itself at Fraser Point.

Topographically, the Forested Island is the most varied of the Channel Islands. Its well-watered, long central valley—created by an east-west running fault that spans much of the island's length—makes Santa Cruz the only Channel Island with a true interior whose climate is not dominated by marine conditions. Temperate, Mediterranean weather supports grasslands, chaparral, oak woodlands, and pines. Boggy, almost swamp-like areas appear seasonally at the mouths of freshwater streams, their moist environment appealing to a variety of insects that in turn attract birds and some of the island's eight species of bats. This variety of ecosystems contributes to a diversity of flora and fauna found only on Santa Cruz.

In 1939, Woodward and his contemporaries did not have the benefit of decades of meticulous scientific research behind them to conclude, as modern day archaeologists have, that people occupied Santa Cruz Island beginning about ten thousand years ago (and perhaps even before that).[8] Paleocoastal and then island Chumash people lived on the island continuously, but after European contact their numbers began to decline due to the spread of introduced diseases and even, it is thought, violence amongst themselves. By 1822, the mission fathers brought the last of the Santa Cruz Island Chumash to the missions.[9]

However, ten thousand years ago the Santa Cruz Island people's culture rested on the cusp of change that would bring them great technological advancements, cultural richness, and more formalized spirituality. The environmental changes that the end of the Ice Age heralded—melting glaciers, flooding of low-lying lands, decreasing intertidal shellfish habitats, declining species of cold-water animals, the arrival of different warm-water species, generally warmer terrestrial temperatures, less rain, fewer freshwater sources, and new flora zones—required people to react nimbly to their changing environment.

People living on the larger northern Channel Islands utilized many different landscapes, including temporary inland homes and permanent residential sites throughout the island. About 5,500 years ago, Santa Cruz Island people continued to have fairly mobile settlement strategies, migrating relatively short distances between the coast and inland and then back again. Had Woodward known about this, he might have irreverently called them "snowbirds" who exchanged their beach houses for temporary inland "vacation digs" that they occupied for a few days (or more) at a time. Notwithstanding this short-term occupancy, these vacation pads weren't picked at random. Rather, modern researchers believe that these sites were used for stopovers or meal breaks during longer journeys from one part of the island to another, generally because they provided something the people desired: plant foods, such as pine nuts, acorns, or blue dick corms (bulbs) that could be harvested and eaten; reliable freshwater; and chert stone for toolmaking. As a result of these mini-migrations, middens at some of these vacation pads grew larger. Apparently, the desires of these early island inhabitants were not unlike our own. What Palm Springs vacationer doesn't know how beneficial a change of scenery, some tasty food, and warm sunshine can be?

The nutritional diversity of the people living on Santa Cruz Island expanded as a result of the development of more sophisticated tools—metates for processing increasing varieties of plant food, harpoon spears, circular fishhooks (500 years ago), and later the plank canoe.[10] Around 3,500 years ago, and maybe as many as 8,500 years ago, people learned to make stone tools that they used to grind plants into edible flours and mashes. For example, the basket mortar Woodward found buried alongside human remains at the Prisoners Harbor site is similar to other tools scientists have found throughout the island. (Basket mortars are mortars with bottomless baskets attached to their tops or sides so that seeds, nuts, or other plant food could be better contained as they were pounded with a pestle.) Additionally, Santa Cruz Islanders supplemented their basic diet of mussels, abalone, and other shellfish with dolphin, sea lion, other marine mammals, and pelagic fish species such as tuna and swordfish. By about 2,500 to 2,000 years ago, fish and sea mammals provided even more protein to the Chumash islanders' diets than did shellfish. However, despite technological advancements, the easy to gather mussel remained an important food item, a reality attested to by the abundance of mussel shells found in middens dating to every era.

Over time, evidence of cultural, spiritual, and ritualistic behaviors became more complex on Santa Cruz Island. High status individuals, for instance, possessed beads, cut abalone pendants, and *tomols* (plank-sewn canoes), but commoners did not. Additionally, items of ritualistic significance—including stone pipes, bone whistles, quartz crystals, chunks of red ochre hematite, and eagle claws—have all been found in burials on Santa Cruz Island.[11] There are also numerous rock features on the island that are believed to be possible shrines.[12]

On El Montañon, the highest peak on Santa Cruz Island's eastern end, some of these rock features may have been used to stabilize feather poles. On the mainland, feather poles were made by affixing raptor feathers to wooden poles that the Chumash pounded into the ground and then surrounded with piles of rocks in order to anchor them in upright positions. Symbolizing a connection between the earth and sun, feather poles were used during winter solstice ceremonies to help predict the coming year's climate and bring the sun back onto its northerly course, among other uses. Most of Santa Cruz Island's rock features are found on high ridgetop saddles on either El Montañon or North Ridge. These settings usually come with good sightlines (viewsheds) and provide sufficient flat land around them on which people can gather. Modern scientists surmise that these types of locations are similar to mainland mountaintop sites and are spiritually significant because of their close proximity to the "upper world," thus representing gateways to power.

Santa Cruz Island's North Ridge runs east to west and bounds the northern side of the central valley. On it are several high peaks, including Red Peak and Mount Diablo. Some believe that both the entire North Ridge as well as El Montañon on the island's eastern side represent sacred geography due to their expansive viewsheds. Supernatural properties may have been attributed to these ridgelines because they provide a far-reaching view of the Chumash mainland territory. Specifically, aggregated sightlines from the triumvirate peaks—Red Peak, Mount Diablo, and El Montañon—allow a person to see the entire extent of the Chumash Middle World, or the earthly world of the living. This world is defined by Point Conception, California at the northern boundary, Mount Pinos (Ventura County's highest peak, located within today's Los Padres National Forest) at the southern boundary, and Santa Rosa and San Miguel Islands at the western boundary. Today, this triangle contains parts of Santa Barbara and Ventura Counties as well as the two most northern Channel Islands.

As a result of the panoramic views these Santa Cruz Island peaks provide, the ridgelines could have been "part of a larger supernatural landscape that may have connected members of different island villages not only to El Montañon and the North Ridge, but also to the topography of the mainland and its sacred locales."[13] This viewshed, together with rock features found on Santa Cruz, speaks to the possibility that the land supplying these vast views held special spiritual significance for the island Chumash and may have been "analogous to those ... used throughout the Chumash mainland in historic times."[14]

By five hundred years ago, Chumash islanders became more sedentary. Though they still traveled inland to utilize sites that were meaningful previously, their coastal villages grew larger, functioning as more permanent settlements. Reliable oceangoing canoes and advanced fishhooks that allowed them to hunt oceanic fish supported their robust maritime lifestyle. Still, they didn't abandon their inland sites completely, occasionally walking to them to fetch water in tarred baskets, collect chert to make bead money, and practice rituals. They may have even gathered at inland sites in large numbers for communal feasts.[15]

What might Woodward have done with this information? Would he have filled his journals with speculation? During hikes across El Montañon's ridgelines, or while traversing the land connecting the historic island Chumash village Xaxas (near Prisoners Harbor) and Red Peak on the North Ridge, would he have trained his gaze to the ground in search of postholes, piles of rocks, and incised stones? Would the possibility of finding evidence in support of ritualistic practices have goaded him out of whatever lethargy he felt on Santa Cruz Island? It seems likely, since he loved figuring out how people lived, what they thought about, and what they believed in, but nothing in his journals indicates that he searched for or even thought about these types of clues. With uncharacteristic lack-luster, he declared in his journal, "I do not anticipate doing much work on this island."[16] Unsurprisingly, he concluded that Santa Cruz produced "the least results of any [of the islands]."[17] It is hard to be sympathetic to Woodward and his apathy, however, as scientists today estimate that Santa Cruz harbors over one thousand midden sites.

When Europeans first encountered Santa Cruz Island, more than 1,800 people lived on the isle's lush, diverse landscape, mostly in coastal villages. By the mission period (late 1700s to early 1800s), ten villages on Santa Cruz were known and named. Two such villages that were particularly well identified were on the eastern part of Santa Cruz, one each bounding the northern and southern coasts on either side of San Pedro Point. Nanawani was a medium-sized village located in the Smuggler's Cove area of the island's southeastern shore, and Swaxil—believed to be the largest village on any of the northern Channel Islands, and probably all of the Channel Islands—was located at Scorpion Anchorage on the northeastern shore. Xaxas was also well known both as the economic center of Santa Cruz Island and the gateway to its interior.[18]

In determining where these villages were located, today's archaeologists do what Woodward frequently did: consult ethnohistoric accounts made by Spanish explorers, mission records, oral histories, and records of interviews with Chumash people who either once lived on Santa Cruz or whose relatives lived there. Additionally, items such as glass beads, microblade drills used to make shell bead money, and metal artifacts that were traded amongst the various Indian tribes are reliable sources for placing the village sites into a meaningful chronological timeframe.

The Channel Islands continue to provide researchers with the best preserved and most abundant records of human lifestyles and lives in the Southern California bight and beyond. Connecting written and oral accounts of life in island villages with the actual villages and artifacts located within them, such as what has been done at Swaxil and Nanawani, uniquely aids scholars and ancestors to better understand the culture of the people who lived there, just as examining sites located throughout the island helps to reveal motivations, cultural changes, and the effects of new technologies on island life. Modern scientists know much more about Chumash islanders than Woodward did, but much of the work they do is similar to his, though more thorough and refined.

Legend has it that Santa Cruz Island received its name in 1769, when Spanish explorers came ashore at Xaxas, near today's Prisoners Harbor. After exchanging gifts with the Chumash islanders, they re-embarked, inadvertently leaving behind an iron staff decorated with a cross at its top. Though iron was highly coveted by the natives, the next day the Indians paddled out in their tomols to return it. Sufficiently impressed by this demonstration of friendliness and honesty, the Spaniards named the island *La Isla de la Santa Cruz*, "Island of the Holy Cross," the name the island still carries today.

In this same year, the mission era began with the construction of *El Presidio Real de San Diego*. As interactions between the natives and the Europeans increased, so did the spread of diseases for which the Indians had little or no immunity. In 1803, consideration was given to building a mission on Santa Cruz Island, but by 1807 measles and other diseases had reduced the population to the point that construction of an island mission no longer made sense. The last island Chumash left Santa Cruz Island in 1822.[19]

When Mexico gained independence from Spain one year earlier, the country claimed the former Spanish territories of Mexico, Baja and Alta California, including the Channel Islands, for itself. During the following decades, in a bid to populate these territories, the Mexican government gave out more than 750 land grants. In 1839, the grant for all of Santa Cruz Island was given to Andres Castillero, a native Spaniard and captain in the Mexican Army. During the eighteen years Castillero held the island, his sheep ranch became part of the United States as a result of the 1848 Treaty of Guadalupe Hidalgo, which included all of Santa Cruz Island. After failing as a rancher, Castillero sold his island to a local Santa Barbara businessman, who made a go of it until the drought of 1862–1865 decimated his livestock and caused him to sell in 1869.

Ten businessmen, including Justinian Caire, a merchant and banker who dreamed of one day owning the island outright, purchased the land and established the Santa Cruz Island Company. When a series of financial missteps and improprieties, a suicide, and a bank liquidation reduced both the resolves and fortunes of his fellow shareholders, Justinian Caire began buying up ownership interests until he realized his dream in 1886.[20] He then "threw himself into land husbandry . . . with its roots in the early pastoral vision of colonial America . . . based on . . . subduing nature and creating a controlled, fruitful environment in the face of an untamed howling wilderness."[21] He expanded the sheep and cattle operations, further developed and improved existing ranch buildings, and built newer outlying ranch facilities. Additionally, he planted two hundred acres of grapes—mainly in the island's central valley but also some at the east end of the island by Scorpion Ranch—and built two large, brick winery buildings to house the crushing and fermenting cellars.

Amidst the vineyard growing in the island's broad and picturesque central valley, and not far from the main house, Caire also built a charming small chapel. During crushing season, the pleasant clanging of the church's bell sounded across the valley and the delicate, slightly rose-like smell of the late-season apple blossoms that Caire planted in the main ranch's fruit orchard wafted through the valley on island breezes, mixing freely with the sharp odor of wine must.[22] By the time Justinian Caire died and was buried in the chapel's cemetery in 1897, the Santa Cruz Island Company had become a thriving, successful enterprise, one immensely satisfying to him and his family.

Unfortunately, a few years after the patriarch's death, Mrs. Caire and the grown children began feuding over the division of ranch profits, management rights, and ownership interests. The bitterness between them grew during the twenty years the heirs waged a costly litigation battle, causing them to put 90 percent of the island up for sale. Santa Cruz's acreage languished for several years on the real estate market until someone with the wherewithal to complete the priciest real estate deal ever transacted in Santa Barbara County saw the island's potential. In 1937, forty-two-year-old Edwin Stanton—a former University of California track star and Olympic contender who became a successful manufacturer and Long Beach, California oilman—closed the deal to purchase that 90 percent for $750,000. The eastern 10 percent remained in the hands of Ambrose Gherini, a Caire heir.

Under Stanton's hands, winemaking ceased and sheep ranching flourished. From the beginning, the family recognized that their elder son, Edwin Locksley Jr., would follow in his father's footsteps and take over the island ranching operation, while young Carey Quillian would be free to choose his own profession. As a result, Carey studied medicine at Stanford University and became a doctor. After Edwin Locksley Jr.'s unexpected death during World War II, the youngest Stanton pursued his medical calling while his father continued managing the ranch. During those years, the senior Stanton converted the labor-intensive sheep business into a cattle operation, until in 1957, at the age of sixty-two, his health began to fail and he called upon his only living son to come to the island full-time to assume its management.

Nurtured by his father's predilections, Carey Stanton presided over the island with a keen interest in its history and an appreciation for the various scientific studies he allowed on the island. During his nearly thirty years managing Santa Cruz, Carey welcomed scientists to its shores and collaborated with the University of California, Santa Barbara, in 1966 by establishing a university research station near the main ranch house. To quench his intellectual curiosity, Carey was active in any number of philanthropic organizations, including serving on the boards of the Santa Barbara Historical Society, Santa Barbara Museum of Natural History, California Historical Society, and others. Intensely private, a bachelor, and a bit quirky, he collected a cast of beloved island characters around him that included Henry Duffield, a ranchman who knew a fair bit about cattle, and Joe Fidler Walsh, a guitarist who didn't.

Duffield met Stanton in 1959, not long after Carey assumed full-time management of the island and shortly after polio paralyzed the thirty-eight-year-old cattleman from the waist down. At Stanton's invitation, Henry came to the island for a short visit in 1960 and remained until his death. Despite his paralysis, Henry was a capable rancher, "known by many as the cowboy in the red jeep with hand controls, never without his rifle in a scabbard, a flask of Ancient Age Bourbon in his glove box, and several dogs at his side."[23] During the twenty-six years the wrangler helped manage the cattle ranch, he and his boss became close friends. In 1986, a stroke further paralyzed sixty-five-year-old Duffield, immobilizing his upper left body. Pride and practicality probably played equal parts in what happened next: Henry, rancher at heart, shot himself while sitting in his chair in the ranch office. Carey, deeply moved by Duffield's suicide, buried him in the cemetery of *La Capilla del Rosario*, the little chapel in the big valley of Santa Cruz Island where Stanton himself was interred a year later.

What began as an unlikely friendship between Carey Stanton and Joe Walsh of the Eagles in the mid-1970s grew into the rock-n-roller's passion to preserve the Channel Islands. In the 1980s, Walsh began serving on the board of the Santa Cruz Island Foundation (which Carey established to protect Santa Cruz Island in perpetuity) and later became chairman of the foundation, a position he still holds today. Since 1988, every May 3rd Walsh faithfully attends, sings, and plays guitar for the annual Feast of the Holy Cross that is held in the little island chapel where his friend is buried. In 2016, at the conclusion of this private mass, he dedicated a solo rendition of "Desperado," a well-known Eagles hit, to three of his friends: "Carey, Henry and my brother, Glenn."[24] It seems fitting that a man associated with a band named after the U.S. national bird, which once used all eight Channel Islands as its own "Hotel California" for nesting and hunting, has become a leading advocate for preserving all of the Channel Islands for future generations.

There are many more Carey Stanton stories than this, but when the story of his life—though not his legacy—ended on December 8, 1987, the half-century Stanton era (1937–1987) came to a close. Prior to his death, Carey agreed to pass his land to the Nature Conservancy and his personal estate to the Santa Cruz Island Foundation (SCIF), which he founded in 1985. The SCIF continues to work in the public's interest for the preservation of not only Santa Cruz Island but all of the Channel Islands. The 10 percent eastern portion of the island that remained in the hands of Justinian Caire's heirs eventually sold to the U.S. National Park Service. These transitions account for the island's joint management and inclusion in Channel Islands National Park.

When the CIBS party landed on Santa Cruz Island on August 11, 1939, they surely looked bedraggled and tired, and if they didn't admit to being sore, after more than twenty days in the field—hiking, digging, lifting, and sleeping on the ground—they must have been. Returning to the mainland and their families may have consumed their thoughts had their congenial leader, Dr. John Adams Comstock, not bunked with them on Santa Cruz Island. Throughout the week the survey staff accompanied Comstock both in the field and while he fished from the dock or cobbled beach. Sometimes the researchers fished even if Comstock did not, dutifully turning their landed catches over to the cook, the sweet meat surely a welcome diversion from lamb. All in all, the tempo of their time on Santa Cruz changed. It may have been the island's lush environment or the raucous antics of the Santa Cruz Island jay, a "conspicuous endemic, quite common around camp,"[25] that affected their attitudes, or perhaps it was Comstock's paternal presence. Either way, the group seemed to coalesce while on the Forested Island, benefitted by Comstock's congenial manners and sharp scientific mind that surely drew the savants together, thick as bats in a belfry, during each evening's fireside discussions.

Collecting activities began on the group's first day when Woodward, snooping and sleuthing, crawled into the attic of an old two-story former hotel[26] in Prisoners Harbor and found a colony of three hundred insect-eating lump-nosed bats, the first ever of this species recorded on Santa Cruz Island. Following his lead, Comstock reached into a crevice of an old bungalow building, also in Prisoners Harbor, and captured a pair of California myotis bats, the first species of big-eared myotis bat ever taken on any of the Channel Islands. Not to be outdone, von Bloeker collected large-eared pallid bats from within Justinian Caire's defunct brick winery building in the island's central valley. This bat is the largest of the Channel Island bats, with a wingspan of up to sixteen inches, and sensitive ears that measure nearly half its body length and are capable of hearing the falling footsteps of its grasshopper or spider prey even while in flight. So numerous were these bats that each fall the Stantons collected two tons of guano to use as fertilizer for the flower and vegetable gardens surrounding the ranch house.

Despite Woodward's belief that there was little to occupy him on Santa Cruz, the archaeologist couldn't stop himself from digging, not even in the muck and mud at the mouth of the creek leading into Prisoners Harbor, which is where he spent most of his time. At fifteen feet deep, this site was the largest dig of the expedition, yielding six burials and numerous artifacts. He complemented his Prisoners Harbor journal entries with rough schematics of these burials, site maps, and sketches of artifacts.

While on Santa Cruz, Woodward took a liking to Carey Stanton, describing him as "smart as a steel trap."[27] The attraction appeared mutual, too, as the future owner of Santa Cruz Island genially escorted Woodward on horseback trips to view gravesites at distant middens, suggested boat outings where they could travel farther afield, and excavated in the

A rare candid shot of the gang relaxed at mess, Prisoners Harbor, Santa Cruz Island, August 1939. Pictured from left to right: Jewel Lewis, George Kanakoff, Lloyd Martin, Meryl Dunkle, Russell Sprong, Don Meadows, Art Woodward, and (seated on the ground with pipe in mouth) John Adams Comstock. Courtesy of NHM Archives.

mud right alongside his new archaeologist friend. Ultimately, Carey Stanton spent a week in the field with the charismatic Woodward serving as teacher and tutor.

Carey's father, Edwin, seemed to enjoy the scientists as well. He welcomed them to the main ranch house, where he showed them photographs and allowed his wife and son to help the researchers with their work. One night, upon learning that the Russian-born scientist George Kanakoff had come up missing, the elder Stanton gathered his Santa Barbara evening guests and Woodward into the station wagon and set out to find him. Shortly, they saw him limping along the trail. After giving Kanakoff a drink, Edwin drove the researchers back to Prisoners Harbor, staying long enough to join the gang for hot chocolate and conversation.

Except for the setback suffered when first mold and then an infestation of the minute black midge fly completely ruined several tin boxes of specimens, insect collecting was wildly successful on Santa Cruz. Out of over seventeen thousand insects collected during the fourth expedition, nearly 30 percent came from Santa Cruz Island—once again, the varied ecosystems allowed the land to support more species of insects than the other islands. In terms of sheer numbers, beetles were the most collected insect on the biggest Channel Island, followed by Lepidoptera and true bugs, Hemiptera such as aphids, cicadas, and leafhoppers.

These bugs feasted on the plants Dunkle prodigiously collected on Santa Cruz as he walked from Prisoners Harbor west to Pelican Bay, inland to the main ranch, and eastward from there. Because of its size and variety of ecosystems, it is not surprising that 40 percent of all the plant specimens amassed during the fourth expedition came from Santa Cruz. On the surface this would seem to indicate the island's relative health, but Dunkle felt otherwise, explaining that "heavy grazing and fire ... [had] been quite destructive," but that "water erosion in the cultivated area ha[d] ... been well controlled by a series of check dams constructed about twenty-five years ago." In conclusion, he wrote that "immediate restriction of grazing ... [could] still be very beneficial in erosion prevention on the higher slopes, and in the saving of most of the indigenous flora."[28] While Dunkle assessed Santa Cruz's botanical condition as salvageable, he asserted the best flora stewardship belonged to Santa Rosa Island, where carefully controlled grazing preserved lush ferns and highlands dotted by California live oaks, cherry trees, bishop pines, and the rare umbrella-shaped Torrey pines.

Throughout the week, Woodward intermittently dug in the Prisoners Harbor midden. Messy work, to be sure, but the strands of patterned black and white beads, serpentine beads, abalone shell pendants, and bracelets found buried in the mud alongside human remains held Woodward's interest as much as the steatite vessel clasped within one set of skeletal fingers did. Each time he dug into the mud and dirt he uncovered something new: a red stone bead, a bone fish barb with tar at its base, a chert drill, chunks of red paint, or abalone shell dishes, their holes plugged with tar. In addition to these human-made offerings, Woodward found natural objects deliberately placed with the dead: fish bones, whale ribs, whale scapula, porpoise skull fragments, and sea otter femur bones (which accompanied almost every burial). His journal offers no suggestions regarding the otter bones, but their inclusion might concern their relative rarity, especially if the cemetery dated to historical times—by the mid-1800s sea otters had been hunted to near extinction.

"The only criticism of Kanakoff: he works too hard,"* Don Meadows wrote. Anonymous artist's caricature. Courtesy of Department of Anthropology, NHM.

*Donald C. Meadows to John Adams Comstock, written from San Miguel Island, California, August 2, 1939.

John Adams Comstock, right, and von Bloeker, left, pose with a line of salted fox skins "hung out to dry in the shade of a grove of introduced gum trees (*Eucalyptus* sp.) at Prisoners Harbor.... This represents part of the series of foxes captured on San Nicolas, San Miguel, and Santa Rosa islands in July and August, 1939."* Photo taken August 15, 1939. Courtesy of Department of Anthropology, NHM.

*Jack C. von Bloeker Jr., unpublished and undated report located at Santa Barbara Museum of Natural History.

The CIBS staff gathers for a group shot on Santa Cruz Island commemorating the fourth expedition, August 1939. Standing from left to right: Don Meadows, Lloyd Martin, Meryl Dunkle, Arthur Woodward, Russell Sprong, Jack C. von Bloeker Jr., and John Adams Comstock. Seated from left to right: George Kanakoff and Jewel Lewis. Courtesy of NHM Archives.

During the course of the week, von Bloeker assisted Woodward in the middens, finding a bay porpoise skull and remains from California sea lions, steller sea lions, and a harbor seal. Based on this, the scientists could deduce that Chumash islanders supplemented their diet with high-protein marine mammal flesh and that they possessed the technologies required to hunt them. He also managed to collect three species of snakes on Santa Cruz. Most interesting is that within this take were three slender, mildly venomous, but non-lethal spotted night snakes, a species that has never again been seen on any of the Channel Islands. The easy capture of this species on Santa Cruz yet subsequent absence from all future collection efforts is quite the mystery. Did von Bloeker serendipitously collect the only three night snakes *ever* on Santa Cruz Island? Did the fact that only three were ever found indicate that island living was unsuitable for the nocturnal foragers, or did the island's birds, skunks, and foxes prey on them? Had the snakes only recently been introduced to the island, perhaps buried in a shipment of livestock feed, hiding in plants intended for the Stantons' garden, or concealed in someone's luggage? It's hard to say, but modern scientists continue to wonder about the single remaining, albeit poorly preserved, little serpent.

But von Bloeker, whose greatest interest was bats, must have most enjoyed adding 225 bats to the museum's collection. Of these, all hailed from Santa Cruz save the one specimen of brown bat from Santa Rosa Island. Von Bloeker's cache represented five different species—golden long-eared, California brown, lump-nosed, Pacific pallid, and Mexican free-tailed—and four "first records" from Santa Cruz. Camp Murcielago certainly lived up to its name.

George Kanakoff, the survey's shellfish, snail, jellyfish, and worm expert (otherwise known as the invertebrate scientist, or chonchologist), collected more than seven thousand specimens during the month-long expedition. Most of his take were snails, clams, octopus, scallops, and squids (collectively called Mollusca), as well as spiders, millipedes, crabs, shrimps, krill, and lobster (designated as arthropods).

On August 19, 1939, when the researchers rolled up their bedding and cots, folded their chairs and tables, pulled their tent stakes, and packed up lanterns, empty water barrels, and plant presses, bound for home and at last aboard the *Velero III*, the CIBS had accumulated over thirty-one thousand specimens and mapped out over one hundred archaeological sites. A good month's work, and something for which they could be proud. Despite this pride, each one wanted more than a scant week on each island to conduct complete surveys of species within their discipline. They noted this desire in their journals, they complained about it in their letters, and they documented it in the progress report. They wanted one month, at least, for every island.

Chapter Thirteen

THE EXPEDITION CONTINUES

"Churchill Denounces Hitler in Blasting All Talk of Peace."
First Lord of the Admiralty Winston Churchill tonight blasted
talk of peace and mediation in the European war with a blunt
announcement that the Allies will fight until "that cornered
maniac," Adolf Hitler, and his Nazi regime are crushed and
destroyed.

—*Los Angeles Times*, November 13, 1939

Throughout much of the spring of 1939, the museum suffered declining attendance. This started to change when Roland McKinney, newly appointed in May 1939 as art director and director-in-charge, set a course to counteract the slide. Cultivating a relationship with Harry Chandler, publisher of the *Los Angeles Times*, was one key component of his plan, and it resulted in the museum's receipt of much-needed regular newspaper coverage. Not only did Chandler publish regular articles spotlighting the work of a museum staff member, but in collaboration with the museum he selected an "object of the week" to consistently feature in the paper's high-circulation Sunday edition. Together with a public seeking refuge from the daily dark news of war in Europe, this publicity resulted in over sixty-six thousand people visiting the museum in the month of August alone, a healthy 5 percent increase in attendance compared to the prior August.

By late September, the researchers were deep into planning a well-orchestrated, month-long trip to San Clemente Island for that coming November/December. According to the itinerary, Woodward would encamp near Horse Beach Cove in order to resume work on Big Dog Cave, Willett would set up near Pyramid Cove to complete studies on the island's late autumn bird life, and Dunkle and Meadows would resume botanical and entomological work. Even though the two Long Beach men were restrained by their high school teaching schedules and could therefore only devote their brief Thanksgiving school vacations, November 23–26, to the work of the survey, this arrangement allowed the museum to conduct an expedition covering four distinct fields of study—archaeology, ornithology, botany, and entomology—thus placing a nicely staffed, well-rounded team on the island. A rather significant change occurred in the expedition's structure, however, when Comstock did not give Meadows oversight of the entire expedition. Rather, he parsed leadership responsibilities to each man for his own specific fieldwork. Thus, Willett took responsibility for ornithology, Woodward for archaeology, Dunkle for botany, and Meadows for entomology. In this manner, Comstock effectively wrested more of the survey's management out of Meadow's hands and back into the museum's.

A fortnight prior to the fifth expedition's departure, Comstock directed a letter to the commandant of the Eleventh Naval District in San Diego, ostensibly to confirm survey arrangements, but more pointedly to decry the exploitation of Indian graves and artifacts by "untrained persons" and "pothunters." He cited current national and statewide laws prohibiting such activities and beseeched the navy to more closely regulate digs by restricting permits for archaeological activities conducted on military land. Only "accredited representatives of museums, scientific societies and qualified governmental officials"[1] should be awarded such permits, he implored. This letter became the first of several Comstock wrote during the survey years requesting assistance with preserving native sites. Winning meaningful support for his endeavor would not be easy.

"Tonight Kanakoff and I are remaining aboard the *Velero III* as guests of Capt. G. Allan Hancock,"[2] von Bloeker rather proudly proclaimed in his fieldnotes for November 7, 1939. The fifth expedition would depart Long

Beach Harbor bound for San Clemente Island the following day, but until then the two researchers were free to do as they pleased. To amuse themselves, "after supper" he and Kanakoff "visited the Japanese settlement on Terminal Island on a sightseeing tour."[3]

The excursion was easy for the two scientists to accomplish since the *Velero III* lay berthed at Terminal Island, a gritty, industrial port that at the time housed Southern California Edison's steam station, Ford Motor Company's Long Beach assembly line, Richfield Oil Company's (now known as ARCO) marine terminal, a naval air station, and a federal prison. Though such notorious inmates as Al Capone, Charles Manson, and Timothy Leary were incarcerated in this federal penitentiary, Terminal Island is perhaps most famous for being home to 3,500 first- and second-generation Japanese Americans living in tidy houses located in a four-and-a-half-mile wide mudflat known as Fish Harbor. It was here that numerous Japanese, mainly abalone fisherman and their families, took refuge prior to World War I, when discrimination forced them from their Los Angeles area homes.

Curiosity about this community led von Bloeker and Kanakoff to make a brief visit to Fish Harbor,[4] a neighborhood that consisted of neat bungalow homes with Japanese street signs that read Mackerel, Tuna, and Sardine. Residents spoke a combination of Japanese and English, kids played baseball and mastered judo, and families celebrated Christmas and Boy's Day (a Japanese holiday) on May 5, stringing carp-shaped kites on bamboo poles and flying them outside homes. Oblivious to the fate of the people whom he visited that evening, the last entry in von Bloekers's journal that day read, "Returned to ship by 7:30 PM. Played chess for three hours. Shaved and retired by 11:30 PM."[5] Today, none of what the CIBS participants saw in 1939 remains. Fish Harbor is a distant memory, a casualty of WWII, its neat, muted-red shingled homes razed by the U.S. Navy and the residents remembered as the first to be evacuated and committed, en masse, to U.S. internment camps after Pearl Harbor was bombed.

The *Velero III* arrived in Horse Beach Cove, San Clemente Island, late in the afternoon of November 8 to find it clogged with military cruisers, battleships, and destroyers. After dropping anchor, Captain Hancock instructed the CIBS staff to load a single rowboat for a trip ashore and

then return for dinner and a last night of comfortable bunking. Following directions, staffers landed and offloaded bedrolls, tents, one sack of
potatoes, and a bag of onions. As they worked, night fell and the surf grew
heavy. When they attempted to return to ship, "the search light from the
Velero III played in" their "eyes and" they "couldn't see to launch the skiff.
Rather than take a chance," they "decided to remain ashore."[6] Making
the best of it, "Willet set up his tent, Kanakoff built a fire, the Wood-
wards [Art and his brother, Barker] got a pail of brackish water and"
von Bloeker "found dry clothes for Harry, the sailor who was marooned
with" them.[7] They "had no water to drink, but the potatoes and onions
kept" them "from going hungry ... and for dessert" they "had candy
which Willett had accidentally bought along in his coat pocket."[8] For
von Bloeker, the sight of a single bat flying over the evening's campfire
provided more than enough compensation for the night's lost bunking in
the *Velero III*'s comfortable sleeping quarters. The same couldn't be said
for the others, however, who must have spent a restless night listening
to the muttering of guns far out at sea and the hooting of the many burrowing owls living near camp.

Morning dawned without noise relief. Circling high above *El Campo
de las Cholla*, "Camp Cholla," white-feathered California gulls took up
the previous evening's racket. Dipping their substantial fifty-four-inch
wings toward the water, their hoarse, scratchy shrieks might momentarily
have blocked out the drone of the *Arizona* launching a pair of surfboats
from which sailors and officers noisily practiced landing exercises on
the beach, but the birds could never completely block the clamor. Shots
fired from cruisers lying close by at anchor reminded CIBS staffers that
the war rumbling in Europe had reverberated across the pond, the entire
continental United States, and westward to this remote Pacific island.

Over the next month, the navy's maneuvers were as tireless as those
of the researchers, who, if they became bored of their work, need only
glance toward the cove for distraction. There, airplanes took off from
aircraft destroyers and navy ships towed targets to the horizon line.
The *Relief*, a regular presence anchored in the middle of Pyramid Cove,
reflected sunlight off its sleek white hull, giving it more the appearance
of a passenger liner than a military hospital ship. At night, frequent and
loud, nighttime military exercises intruded on the scientists' sleep. Day-
time disturbances included the misadventures of a half-dozen marines

who couldn't manage their way back to the *Oklahoma* after landing practice, a failure that required the CIBS's assistance and the loss of a good chunk of a field day. On this desolate island, military exercises vied with bald eagles, Farallon cormorants (now known as double-crested cormorants), spotted sandpipers, killdeer, snowy plovers, lizards, mice, and archaeological artifacts for the researchers' attentions.

Even though the military's battle presence was unrelenting, beginning on that first night in Camp Cholla, the war the scientists waged had nothing to do with Hitler, gunboats, or "aero planes." Rather, its sole focus and murderous intent lay with the salt marsh mosquitoes that invaded the staffers' tents, buzzing, dive bombing, and biting exposed noses, necks, and ears.

While CIBS staff scoured San Clemente Island, Comstock learned of a setback that would increase his administrative burdens and make execution of the CIBS more difficult. The $88,000 *Bluefin*, one of the California Fish and Game Commission's survey boats that regularly provided transportation to CIBS staff, foundered in Mexican waters when it hit a submerged reef during foggy conditions. After the nine-member crew was rescued by a U.S. Coast Guard cutter, a commercial tug began towing the *Bluefin* to San Diego Harbor for repair. The future looked promising for the eighty-six-foot vessel until it took on water one mile outside the harbor. Unwilling to risk going down with its charge, the tug cut the *Bluefin*'s lines and the damaged ship sank to the bottom of the ocean.

With the *Bluefin* out of commission, the CIBS lost one-third of its former transportation services. Now the challenge would be trying to schedule expeditions around both Captain Hancock's and the *Yellowtail*'s intensive research programs—no easy task, and Comstock knew it.

In addition to the lengthy duration (thirty days) of the fifth expedition's single island survey, the trip was noteworthy for another reason. Between November 7 and December 7, 1939, Mrs. Ora Willett accompanied the field party to San Clemente Island. Serving as expedition cook and field assistant to her husband—both areas in which her skills were abundantly refined—she became the CIBS's first female staff member. George Willett's views about women could be genteelly classified as "conservative," but when it came to his wife he happily modified his stance, changing the old adage "a woman's place is in the home" to "a woman's place is with her husband."[9] Without a doubt, George Willett preferred to have Ora's company whenever he went into the field. She was "an excellent sailor, and experienced camper . . . capable of carrying her share of the work on ship or in camp," and she was completely comfortable "stalking grouse by day, setting mammal traps by night, searching for snails under rocks in the desert, or working over manuscripts at home."[10]

Over the next two years, their devotion to one another accounted for Ora accumulating eighty-one collecting days in the service of the CIBS—more days in the field, even, than Donald C. Meadows. During the thirty-day trip on San Clemente, the couple tirelessly traipsed across the island's hillsides in search of avifauna to add to the museum's collection and together collected over 150 birds. At the time of a take, George or Ora would have pulled out a preparator's notebook to record the date, place collected, and catch method (most likely gunshot, with either a pistol or a rifle, depending upon the bird's size, since netting didn't become widely used until the 1950s). The information thus recorded would then accompany the specimen in whatever final form it took: skeletal, fluid, or skin. But before stashing the specimen in a collecting bag, one of the Willetts would most likely have stuffed cotton into the mortal wound to keep blood from staining the feathers and reduce the risk of damage to, or loss of, the specimen.

This simple act also minimized the chance of needing to spend precious minutes cleaning the feathers at a later moment. Under the best laboratory conditions, it takes a skilled preparator twenty minutes to skin a small bird, not counting additional cleaning or drying time for soiled plumage. Given that the Willetts bagged over 150 specimens, twenty minutes per specimen translates into fifty hours of preparatory work— more, actually, since the conditions under which George Willett and his CIBS colleagues operated were nothing like the well-lit, comparatively spacious, insect-free, windless, sand-free, rain-free labs at the museum. Field preparators such as von Bloeker and Willett did not have freezers in which to store specimens for skinning at a later time, nor bright lights, various sorting trays, fresh hot and cold running water, or a ready supply of clean, sharp tools. But by keeping their birds clean and free from blood, the CIBS's avian fieldworkers avoided the need to both wash the specimens and dry them. Eliminating these steps is vital because during the time-consuming drying process the bird's skin moisture may attract pests that could attack and ruin it, ultimately causing the loss of a hard-earned take. But even if the field preparator worked smart and was skilled, unfavorable field conditions such as heavy fog, rain, or humidity might conspire against his (or her) best efforts.

It's easy to imagine the gang straggling into camp in the afternoons, dusty, thirsty, and weighted with the day's finds. Mrs. Willett, camp cook, would probably have started washing up and preparing the evening meal that afternoon while the men hunched over their specimens, trying to get as much sorting and prep work completed before November's early sunsets stole the natural light from the sky, thus requiring them to carry on by lamplight. Von Bloeker and Willett needed to prepare their specimens as soon as possible because, lacking refrigerators and freezers, the best way to preserve an animal is to properly prepare the skins. This task, when done correctly, ensures their survival for a hundred years or more. Through scientific processes, a dead animal can outlive its mortal self.

The importance and scope of the preparation tasks in front of him would certainly have spurred George to get to work as early as feasible each afternoon. To begin, he may have tented his work area with insect netting to keep the flies away. Next, he likely ducked under the covering, laid a bird on his worktable, and reached for his ornithologist's kit. In the museum's modern-day skinning lab, a kit like the one Willett may have carried sits next to an assortment of newer ones. This particular old oak box is nicely aged to a golden color, fitted with worn brass corner brackets and a handsome brass lock that remains fully operable and capable of keeping its contents safe from spilling forth in a tumble down a steep slope or during a rough sea passage. Atop the approximately eight-inch-high by nine-inch-wide box a worn wooden handle waits to be lifted and taken back out into the field.

Upon opening the box, the little oak chest reveals its contents neatly arranged much like a sewing kit. The first layer consists of small items: specimen labels, a pen, sewing needles, scissors, a ruler, measuring tape, and tweezers. Removing the tray exposes the bulkier necessities: cotton, spools of thread, a scalpel or knife with a metal blade that could easily be sharpened in the field, forceps, and these days a small, lightweight scale for weighing specimens. Willett's kit likely didn't contain a scale suitable for weighing birds since science only devised such a field-friendly device in the 1950s, which resulted in many modern-day ornithologists lamenting the lack of avian weight data for their older collections. This particular wooden kit holds a little bit of magic, too—or at least a surprise, which if not borrowed from a shaman was surely some biologist's idea of a bad joke. Resting beside the carefully provisioned items is a shriveled, desiccated dead frog, whose home the box has probably been for decades.

When making a study skin, George would have carefully picked up a bird and held it breast up with its beak pointed toward his stomach. Then he might have brought it near his mouth and blown at the breast feathers whilst parting them with his thumbs. The skin thusly exposed, he likely wetted the plumes, pushing them aside to help ensure the feathers remained free of blood or bodily fluids in case he cut too deeply. Next, using the knife or scalpel, he would have incised the skin, *just* breaking through the membrane before drawing the sharp instrument through the exposed area toward the cloaca, the bird's waste orifice. Working carefully, Willett would have removed the innards, adroitly working his fingers between skin and muscle to separate them. When done properly, this process is surprisingly "clean" as the membrane surrounding the organs keeps the blood contained. The only concerns are puncturing the membrane or having the intestines or stomach contents squirt out of the mouth or cloaca, both occurrences that could soil the feathers. To guard against this, these orifices, along with the throat, would have been plugged with cotton, too.

At this point, Willett would coat the body cavity with corn meal to absorb blood and grease, another step aimed at keeping the exterior feathers clean. Then he would proceed to the knee, pushing from the outside and then cutting between the femur and tibiotarsus (shin). Following this step, he would cut the knee joints and discard the thigh along with the innards. The leg below the knee, which includes the bird's foot, ankle, and fused shin, would be retained. Skinning would have continued as Willett carefully separated the end of the vertebral column without dismembering the tail from the rest of the specimen. Reaching inside, he could then peel the skin from the bird as though preparing an orange.

Next came disarticulating the wings from the body. Willett would have cut close to the shoulder, through the humeri, well above the elbow. Had it been summertime or early fall, Willett may have noticed short, dark tubes under the wing's skin. These would have been the bird's new feathers, each fed by its own blood supply. Eventually, the molting feather "sprouts" through the skin, where it continues to grow bigger and longer. Once it is fully grown, the life-giving capillaries atrophy and leave a completely formed feather, dead but lightweight and perfect for flight. The presence of molt and the relative age and type of feather being molted tells scientists much about the species, its migration patterns, and sometimes even its age. However, given that it was November, Willett's specimens had most likely completed their molt.

Another condition that gives researchers information about a bird is the amount of fat found on it. A very fatty bird might mean that it was a migrant, requiring the considerable fuel derived from its fat stores for long flights. Conversely, a leaner bird might indicate that it resided on San Clemente Island.

It would now have been time for Willett to turn his attention to the skull, the skinning of which requires considerable skill and knowledge. He had to extract the ears, eyes, and tongue, severe the skull from the neck vertebrae, remove the soft palate from the mouth, and clean and dry the brain case. After completing these tasks, now might have been the perfect time for Willett to admire his handiwork, lifting the specimen, blowing on its feathers, fluffing them up, and then ballooning the bird's cavity with another puff of air. All together the bird would look very realistic. Willett could now stuff the bird with cotton, sew the belly together with thread, and carefully store the completed skin for transport to the mainland. Only after he repeated this entire process five or six times a day could von Bloeker successfully draw him into an evening game of bridge that would last until someone protested the late hour.

Among the birds Willett collected were San Clemente wrens, a subspecies of the more widespread Bewick's wren. Four and one-half inches long, this soft, gray-brown bird sported a long white eyebrow, a pointy and curved bill, and a tail tipped in white that it held upright behind it like a popsicle stick. Abundantly resident in cactus stands and dense brush, the Willetts surely heard the sweet songbird voices of the males and females as they sang to each other with effervescent *churrs* and *pishes*. Willett noted that this insect-eating bird was easy to catch, even calling it "tame," while he found other San Clemente Island avian species wild, wary, and difficult to capture, behaviors he attributed at least in part to the military's bombing activities. Residing only on San Clemente Island

and nowhere else, this little bird went extinct as early as the 1940s due to habitat destruction caused by introduced sheep and goats, which was likely exacerbated by bombing.

Von Bloeker diligently laid trap lines, placing them in the mesa above Camp Cholla's tents, in brush and cactus patches near the beach, and in the salt grass and pickleweed marsh bordering the slough on the east side of Horse Beach Cove. Over the course of the month, he experimented with a variety of fruitful locations, moving his traps regularly in order to catch lizards, foxes, birds, and mice—meadow, harvest, and white-footed—all with great success. Sometimes he found only "parts," the mangled remains of critters who escaped the traps by leaving behind toes, feet, legs, or tails, or those who, after succumbing to the trap, were preyed upon by feral cats, peregrine falcons, or common kestrels (known then as sparrow hawks), the most diminutive of raptors. But even the "bits" gained a place in von Bloeker's field journals, for after inspecting and identifying them he dutifully recorded the species and its condition before discarding the remnants or making use of them as bait.

Von Bloeker didn't limit his collecting activities to traps, however. He spent time collecting beetles from carcasses that he purposefully left out just for that purpose, and he wasn't above straining sand or crouching beneath bushes to find insects for his entomological friends. He also regularly assisted in Woodward's cave, digging, sifting, and troweling through debris to add to the museum's collection. He frequently took his gun into the field as well, honing his marksmanship skills by shooting birds, mammals, and feral cats.

One afternoon von Bloeker fired at and missed a feral feline in the wash near camp, and that night a curious kitty visited the mammalogist sleeping in his tent. Feeling the weight and warmth of the creature settling in near his feet, von Bloeker directed his "torch" toward the uninvited visitor, who wisely bolted, never realizing just how close it had come to donning a museum specimen tag for a collar charm.

Big Dog Cave was a mess when Woodward and his brother Barker first inspected it that November. The pegs Art had left in place during the prior expedition were gone, the trench they dug in the early springtime had caved in, and, worst of all, evidence of fresh digging by pothunters or military men had destroyed the chronology of at least part of the trove. Even so, the pair extracted cloth fragments, burned basketry, several toys, a broken whistle (possibly associated with shamanistic rituals), feathers, beads, shells, and wads of fur that contained a chicken.

"The more I dig in this heap the more I am impressed with the idea of seasonal occupation. The layers of windblown sand impregnated with salt spray sandwiched between the matted layers of trash ... argue for a series of reoccupations,"[11] Woodward reasoned. Additionally, he recognized that "the scarcity of certain types of implements[,] even broken ones[,] seemingly indicates a lack of such items during residence in the cave."[12] Ultimately, Woodward began to believe that the cave's "intermittent occupation" may also have meant that it "was used as a temporary refuge from time to time by the inhabitants of the open camps on the bluffs," and that the "several sandy layers in the deposit ... [were] between 100 and 120 years in the forming." Thus, "Using this as a basis the deposit in the cave might easily be estimated at 600–700 years or more."[13] Scholars today might agree with this assessment.

Woodward also mused over the reason he found many charred materials, but few ashes, at the site. This puzzle eventually led him to wonder if human and animal remains were burned elsewhere and carried to Big Dog Cave for burial. While Woodward's journal leaves this question open, other speculations are more fully addressed, such as the unearthing of an iron blade and glass scraper. These items, which could only have been manufactured by Europeans, corroborated Art's belief that the Indians traded with white men and that the cave's occupation dated to historical times, perhaps within one hundred years of the CIBS's visit.

Another aspect of San Clemente Island Indian life that Woodward contemplated was diet, the staples of which were tuna cactus fruit and opuntia cactus. However, based on finding sheepshead (a fish), bat ray, sea mammals, and bird remains in the cave, he also knew that an array of protein sources were important to the diets of these island inhabitants. Additionally, he noted that sea mammal and bird remains were more frequently found in the first layer of debris, a detail that might chronicle not only what people ate during various periods of the cave's occupation, but also indirectly substantiate the technological advancements that allowed a change in diet to occur. That is, as hunting technologies improved beyond shore-based, opportunistic marine mammal takes, the

Indians' diets expanded to more frequently include food items such as seal, sea lion, and various pelagic birds that they could now hunt because they had developed more advanced circular fishhooks and plank canoes suitable for open-ocean fishing. Alternatively, one modern-day San Clemente Island archaeologist believes the occurrence of sea mammal and bird remains provides circumstantial evidence that these animals used this site for refuge during periods of abandonment by humans. This could mean they were not necessarily hunted, butchered, or eaten more frequently in later periods than in earlier periods, and that the presence of their remains does not necessarily signal changes in these animals' population numbers over time.[14]

On Thursday, November 23, 1939, the second wave of CIBS staff arrived on San Clemente Island. Meadows, Dunkle, Sprong, Reddick, Martin, and E. C. Williams (a "one-trip pony") comprised the sixth expedition. While they hustled to set up *El Campo de los Mosquitoes* above Mosquito Harbor, Camp Cholla residents took the day off—it was Thanksgiving, after all.

Accordingly, they "loafed all day," and George Kanakoff yarned and rode "his Jewish hobby horse [*sic*] as usual." Later, to clean up, George took "a dip in the surf" and "Jack Von B.... a bath."[15] The day had all the makings of a great holiday. When the navy mail truck arrived at Camp Cholla late that afternoon, the gang piled in for a ride to Camp Mosquito, where they feasted on a Thanksgiving meal complete with all the trimmings: "turkey, mashed potatoes, cranberry sauce, dressing, gravy, plum pudding and coffee."[16] The cost of such an extravagant meal fell beyond the responsibilities of the museum and its board of governors; therefore, without hesitation the men and woman of the CIBS each ponied up four bits—four quarters, or one dollar—for their holiday meal.

During his last days on the island, Art Woodward found within Big Dog Cave a "large piece of a pine carved canoe prow or stern ... pierced with 6 holes [with] part of cordage still in place [and] Tar covered on edge." Declaring, "Hooray!"[17] he dubbed it the best artifact of the trip, as good an indicator as any that the island Gabrielino were capable seafaring people with a rich maritime heritage. The cave yielded additional telling items, including: bone whistles, which are associated with ritualistic practices;

El Campo de los Mosquitoes, the Long Beach gang's "Mosquito Harbor Camp," San Clemente Island, November 23–26, 1939 (sixth expedition). Courtesy of NHM Archives.

abalone pendants, which could signify the development of class structures; bone fishhooks indicative of developing technologies; a portion of a low-heeled, leather Spanish shoe, proving the natives traded with Europeans and further supports occupation in historic times; and one more piece of wooden canoe.

After more thorough examination of the burials in Big Dog Cave, scholars noted that male and female burials were treated differently regardless of whether the burial was animal or human. Prior to interment, both the adult human burial as well as the dog and rooster, all male, had been wrapped in sea otter fur, whereas the female human burials and the hen were wrapped in mission cloth. Due in part to preservation issues at other burials, it is not certain whether this treatment was consistent during historic times or whether it was an anomaly at Big Dog Cave. Regardless, Big Dog Cave is a multicomponent site of historic and possibly older age that contributes to researchers' better understanding of maritime technologies and ritualistic practices, including the significance of the relationship between humans and animals. Its treasures make today's archaeologists wish the unexploded ordnances standing

George Willett inspecting a fossil whale head at Horse Beach Cove, December 1939.
Courtesy of NHM Archives.

sentry outside Big Dog Cave could be safely detonated or removed so they could get back inside.[18]

As the calendar year drew to a close, Director McKinney delivered his status reports and hyped his educational reforms during board meetings. He praised Mr. Chandler's publication of the museum's "object of the week" in the Sunday *Los Angeles Times* and cryptically reported to the board of governors that he had been "slowly reorganizing the Museum and inaugurating" functions that would "be of value in strengthening the organization."[19] Results were already evident, he crowed, and would become more so as time passed. During the December board meeting, McKinney presented an eleven-point list of activities he had initiated since his arrival. The first three of these succinctly illuminated his vision for recreating the museum into one focused heavily on significant art exhibitions, publicity, and programming targeting school children. His fourth point consisted of a veiled hint of the plans he was making to raze the history and science departments. It read, "reorganization of the executive office."[20]

Chapter Fourteen

FIELDWORK, FIRST HALF OF 1940

Tokyo—The Japanese army and navy asked the diet today to approve a new seven year arms program costing about $671,000,000. This sum would be in addition to the nearly two billions of dollars already approved for this purpose. It would also be in addition to the China "War and Domestic Military Budget" totaling $1,500,000,000.

—Honolulu Star-Bulletin, February 1, 1940

In January 1940, Jack von Bloeker took over management of the mammal collection. Though no change in pay or title ensued, he seemed pleased with the change, swiftly reporting his new responsibilities to his former employer, Professor Hall at the Museum of Vertebrate Zoology at the University of California, Berkeley. The thirty-one-year-old LACM scientist perhaps envisioned his new role as a precursor of better things to come, a positive new direction, and the replacement of his unlucky star with a newer, brighter one. As a result, he may have approached the logistical planning for the 1940 fieldwork—figuring out expedition dates, determining camp locations, unraveling permit issues, obtaining transportation, and securing staff—with renewed enthusiasm.

While von Bloeker toiled over these responsibilities, McKinney labored over his own—namely, a report he would present at the February board meeting that requested a 25 percent increase in the annual budget.

More ominously, it also contained a plan that was poised like a hurricane ready to make landfall in the Departments of Science and History, a plan that would wreak havoc at the museum.

When McKinney unveiled his plan at that February meeting, he informed the board of governors of the "imperative need" to conduct "a careful [policy] study ... with a view to correcting the ... hap-hazard development of the collections."[1] This step was necessary, he asserted, because "the History and Anthropology Division was covering too much territory and should confine its activities to Southern California history and ethnological sources concerning this region."[2] He specifically recommended that work be limited to "the Pacific Basin cultures, Mexico and Central America."[3] This scope, McKinney assured the board, was sufficiently broad.

As for the science department, McKinney felt that it, too, "covered too much ground," with the result that it lost its opportunity to be unique. "All sections of the Science Division would bear checking over,"[4] he submitted. What McKinney strategically left out was that, when enacted, his proposal would flatten the Departments of Science and History the way gale-force winds level island villages.

This wasn't the first time the director had brought up the notion of curtailing science and history. Months before, at an administrative council meeting, he presented his idea to the other directors. But both Comstock and Woodward sat on that council and, as might be expected, no action ensued.

After McKinney's presentation, the board discussed the proposal, and though they were generally in agreement with his ideas, they instructed him to confer with the administrative council and present that group's recommendations for later board consideration. Perhaps at this suggestion, McKinney briefly cast his gaze downward and stifled a grimace before raising his head to gamely acknowledge the governors with a halfhearted smile before he agreed to carry out their wishes.

When the seventh expedition pulled away from Long Beach Harbor on March 16, 1940, headed for Santa Barbara Island, on board the *Yellowtail* were von Bloeker, Kanakoff, Martin, Meadows, Sprong, and Dunkle. Von Bloeker hopped off the cruiser at Johnson's Harbor, Santa Catalina

Island, to conduct a one-day insect-collecting foray, forgoing the CIBS's second and final visit to the Rock Island.

His decision to eschew Santa Barbara Island, for whatever reason, may have been a wise one, because for the length of the survey's eight-day stay the researchers were hampered by fog, rain, and clouds. Even so, when the gang returned to the museum, their insect catches exceeded those obtained on the same island during the third expedition the previous year. They also reported seeing a single sea otter asleep on the rocks on northwest side of the island,[5] and they added more than a dozen elephant seal sightings to the twenty-two spotted the previous May. These mammal tallies were exciting because both species were thought hunted to virtual extinction by the late 1800s. Seeing them gave the scientists hope that one day their numbers might grow. (Today, northern elephant seal populations have rebounded and are thought to be at their pre-exploitation levels, while the southern sea otter is still listed as "threatened" under the Endangered Species Act and "endangered" on the IUCN Red List.)

Two and a half weeks after returning from Santa Barbara, the scientists reboarded the *Velero III* bound for San Nicolas Island. Von Bloeker, Kanakoff, Woodward, and Comstock (who could only spend the first two days of the trip with his staff) comprised the core of the eighth expedition's participants. Conspicuously absent were Meadows and Dunkle, whose names had appeared on the museum's roster for the nineteen-day trip departing April 10, 1940. No reason for their absence is available, but their vacancy left unmanned the fields of entomology and botany, a gap Comstock partially filled by entreating LACM entomologist, Chris Henne, to join the expedition. (Thenceforward, Henne regularly accompanied the survey members.) The remaining scientific positions were rounded out by two non-museum individuals who functioned as archaeological field assistant and botanist/entomologist.[6] Ona von Bloeker, Jack von Bloeker Jr.'s wife, was the second female to join the expedition and served as the camp cook, eventually logging more days on the islands than any survey participants other than her husband, George Kanakoff, and Art Woodward.

While a few "stray" individuals accompanied the survey's 1939 expeditions, the museum archives reveal that beginning in 1940 increasing numbers of these "one-trip ponies"—student biologists, assistant scientists, and women—appeared on expedition rosters. Eventually, the museum recruited a total of eighteen people—sixteen men and two women (Barbara Loomis and Carol Stager)—who participated in only one expedition. This is more than the number of reoccurring participants, twelve of whom were men and three were women (Ona von Bloeker, Ora Willett, and Marion Hollenbach), and demonstrates the great lengths the museum took in order to achieve multidisciplinary scientific representation.

One of the reasons the museum increasingly needed to invite "outside" participants to join the expeditions was Meadows and his associates' reduced participation in the CIBS, a situation likely attributed to the limitations of their school teaching schedules compounded by personnel tensions that surfaced within the first six months of the CIBS's launch. Comstock responded to the initial frictions by more narrowly defining Meadows's leadership responsibilities, but by 1940 the Long Beach professor's leadership role vanished altogether. This power shift is briefly but concisely documented in a March 1940 letter Comstock sent to von Bloeker concerning staffing. In it, Comstock assured his staff mammalogist that no "inhar[m]ony will develop, as Don knows that the Museum is in charge now, and you are in authority when Willett is not along."[7]

On the eighth expedition's outbound trip, characteristically nasty springtime oceanic conditions nauseated Woodward and delayed the researchers' arrival at San Nicolas for a full day. But even after waiting out the worst of the weather, large waves swamped von Bloeker and Woodward's skiff during landing, making off with the archaeologist's tennis shoes like a cat with a slab of bacon. Along with high surf, spring weather brought rains that transformed parched San Nicolas Island into rolling green hills but provided little relief from air temperatures that registered eighty degrees at 7 a.m. on their first field day.

It was only late April, but on those sunny days the clear horizon prompted Woodward to note that both Santa Barbara and San Miguel Islands were visible during the day, and that at night lighthouse beacons on Anacapa and Santa Barbara Islands shone clearly in the distance. Researchers believe that such long-range visibility may have been important to Chumash islanders living on Santa Cruz because it played a role in their spirituality and connection with their mainland kin. While research does not yet support such a supposition for San Nicolas Island, it seems reasonable that it could apply, and in any event such good sightlines would certainly have assisted with navigation between distant islands.

Some days, weather conditions at San Nicolas Island's *El Campo de los Borregos*, "Camp of the Sheep," made fieldwork miserable if not completely untenable. Heavy fog occasionally shrouded the island, and on other days a thirty mph northwestern wind caused small craft advisories and drove sand into the researchers' faces. On many nights, stiff winds or the full moon thwarted them from setting out moth sheets.

Nonetheless, Woodward dug test trenches and collected awls, arrowheads, and a chipped obsidian point. One day he located two holes eighteen inches apart that were filled with debris, speculating that these may once have supported poles thrust inside them. While the holes' purpose is unknown, they may have contained feather poles such as those that modern-day researchers believe were used on Santa Cruz Island for various rituals. Alternatively, they could have supported house roofs or were perhaps dug for other reasons.

A week into the expedition, Woodward discovered a pet cemetery where four dogs were shallowly buried. Nearby, a small cache of olivella shells and a human also lay buried. After photographing this site and sketching the locations of the skeletons and shells in relationship to one another, Woodward collected the canine bones for the museum.[8] He noted that no offerings accompanied the dog burials, though he allowed that "the olivella shells may be considered as such."[9]

Woodward, like his contemporaries and those who came before him (Shumacher, 1877; Bowers, 1890; Wagner, 1929; Nidever, 1937),[10] knew that Native Americans brought dogs to the Channel Islands and that these animals were sometimes sacrificed and buried ritualistically. The lone canine in Big Dog Cave, wrapped in cloth and interred with birds swathed in otter fur, potentially fits within this ritualistic burial pattern. In contrast, no obvious grave offerings of abalone beads or pendants accompanied these four dogs, though they had been carefully positioned when laid to rest.

The lack of such offerings stands in stark contrast not only to Woodward's "big dog" but also to other dogs buried on San Nicolas Island. One double dog burial found some sixty years after Woodward unearthed the four-dog cemetery consisted of two young female dogs sacrificed and interred with one dog embracing the other. Analysis of their stomach contents revealed that their last meal consisted of the same foods that their human companions ate. Additionally, right next to their resting site were unusual groupings of stacked stones made of both non-island and native-island materials together with calcite crystals—stones known to have been used by California shaman—and an unfinished soapstone piece that one modern-day researcher speculates might symbolize the dogs whose lives had been cut short and were thus likewise unfinished.

One year after these two dogs were found, a triple canine burial composed of older dogs was located just thirty feet away. These mature dogs lay curled on their stomachs, their bodies arranged in a circle, heads over paws, with tails deliberately folded to the side. Buried with them were exotic and native artifacts. Most interestingly, the bones of these old boys showed evidence of having worn harnesses that would have allowed them to pull sleds across the island. Additionally, one animal showed extreme trauma to its scapula (shoulder) that could only have healed with human care.

Woodward may have suspected that the dogs he found buried were not wild animals but domesticated canine pals that today are thought to have served as religiously important sacrificial beings, hunting companions, sentinel animals, pets, offal scavengers, and potentially status symbols. Only occasionally were dogs eaten.[11] Dog domestication is corroborated in George Nidever's memoir, wherein he described finding the Lone Woman of San Nicolas Island surrounded by her dogs who barked loudly as his men approached. They quieted, however, as soon as she uttered a command—her dogs were most certainly not wild.[12]

All of this demonstrates that dogs and Channel Islands people maintained a special relationship that began at least six thousand years ago when Native Americans first shepherded them across the channel. But traveling with their canine friends was not just a one-time event; rather, the fact that there are no clearly distinct Channel Islands dog breeds (as there are distinct species of foxes), indicates that throughout the ages both islanders and mainlanders may have traded dogs with each other. If so, these canines were not just beloved pets but living commodities emblematic of the robust and active trade routes in existence at the time. Today, the archaeological history of the islands includes ninety-six dog burials, with twenty-nine—the most of any island—occurring on San

Nicolas. Only Anacapa and Santa Barbara, the smallest of the islands, lack evidence of dogs.

During their nineteen days on the windswept island of San Nicolas, the CIBS enjoyed certain luxuries. The ranch managers made sure the crew never lacked fresh milk or cream, while the navy gave the CIBS gasoline when needed, use of a shelter with electrical lighting, and daily weather reports. On Thursday, April 18, 1940, Art Woodward celebrated his forty-second birthday, complete with a cake baked in his honor by Ona von Bloeker and a rendition of "Happy Birthday" belted out by his colleagues like a "crew of Crosbys."[13]

The day after his birthday, Woodward began excavations on a mounded midden site located in Dutch Harbor on the southeast side of the island that he called "site #1." Today it is known as SNI-51, or colloquially the Dutch Harbor site. As with Big Dog Cave, Woodward thoroughly excavated this midden area, his efforts rewarded by a rich assortment of fish and mammal bones, abalone shells, mussel shells, and uncooked sea urchin spines. As interesting and important as these dietary remains are, the numerous intact pieces of grass textiles, mats, and skirts that were recovered—soft goods that typically do not preserve well and that continue to provide researchers with significant information on what types of textiles the islanders made, what materials they used, and how they utilized them—are the real treasures of this site. Dutch Harbor's baskets were made from twined seagrass, a naturally occurring material found abundantly in the waters surrounding San Nicolas Island, while the ones Woodward found in Big Dog Cave on San Clemente Island were made from juncus, or the common marsh rush plant used frequently on the mainland for basket weaving.

Woodward immediately recognized that the abundance, quality, and variety of items he found at Dutch Harbor set the artifacts apart from earlier collections. Thus, his compulsive journaling—five pages and three sketches of site #1 alone—can surely be forgiven, but his emboldened questioning of noted cultural anthropologist Alfred Kroeber's theories requires a closer look.

In 1925, Kroeber authored *Handbook of the Indians of California*, a hefty tome of nearly one thousand pages that not only secured Kroeber's place as the most preeminent California Indian expert of the time, but also squarely cemented this status well into the modern era. The handbook is still cited by archaeologists today, and Woodward most certainly had a well-worn copy or two, but despite Kroeber's credentials the CIBS archaeologist writes confidently that "Kroeber has been refuted on the following points,"[14] which he then enumerated.

While the questioning of scientific theories is always good science, it is Woodward's tone that calls unwanted attention to his suggestions, especially since a closer reading of the handbook reveals that Woodward's assertions, if not plainly wrong, are at least unjustified. For instance, immediately after his comment about refuting Kroeber, Woodward states, "Basketry is definitely island material,"[15] implying that Kroeber believed the opposite, that basketry was made of mainland materials. Kroeber does not say this, however; rather, he writes that island baskets are "of the type ordinary in Southern California,"[16] by which he meant that "they were often asphalted" and that "water baskets were in plain twining."[17]

Secondly, Woodward writes in his journal that, except for cremation (which would align the Nicoleño with the island Gabrielino/Tongva or Shoshonean peoples), everything else points to the Nicoleño's affiliation with Chumash islanders. Granted, these are just musings in his journal, not a published article, but later he expounds on his point of view in a letter to his colleague, Phil Orr of the Santa Barbara Museum of Natural History, writing,

> I am hoping to be able to either confirm or disprove the cultural affiliations of the Islanders with the Chumashan group as a whole.... So far, with one or two sporadic exceptions it seems to me that all of the Islanders were more closely allied in culture to the Chumash than to the Shoshonean areas.... The distinction between the Gabrielino [the terms Nicoleño, Gabrielino, and Shoshonean all refer to the people that today are called Gabrielino/Tongva or island Gabrielino] and the Chumash seems to be almost imperceptible. This deduction is made on the basis of a combination of material cultural elements present on all the islands and the adjacent mainland from Orange County north to the San Luis Obispo region. The few characteristic Shoshonean traits ... such as cremation burial while occurring on San Clemente and San Nicolas do not seem to be general for all of the

Islands. On the other hand the canoe—fish hooks—steatite ornaments—extensive use of sea mammal bone—grass basketry (sea grass)—use of small tarred pebbles for water proofing—bead making techniques—abalone shell ornaments, etc, are common to all of the Islands and the Channel mainland, but not present further south in Shoshonean territory. The Gabrielino are Shoshonean of course, but . . . more Chumashan than anything else.[18]

Although the letter to Orr does not mention Kroeber, Woodward's journal entry clearly implies that he believed Kroeber was wrong about the San Nicolas islanders cultural affiliation being Gabrielino/Tongva, an assertion Woodward's more esteemed colleague comfortably made based on an analysis of language alone. Today, researchers agree with Kroeber, not Woodward, that the people who inhabited San Nicolas Island were more closely related to the southern Channel Island Gabrielino than the island Chumash.

Before leaving the island on April 28, Woodward spotted another midden in Dutch Harbor that he thought would provide more textiles. Eager to obtain more of these rare materials, he began plotting a third trip to the island, one that would put him on San Nicolas in late fall of 1940. But first, the CIBS planned to venture to Anacapa Island, an expedition in which some of his twenty-first-century colleagues wished Woodward had participated.

Chapter Fifteen

SUMMER 1940

"London Battered Six Hours: German Planes Circle Capital in Long Attack." For more than six hours the German air force hurled slaughter and destruction in and around London last night and early today in the longest air raid of the war.

—*The Los Angeles Times*, August 27, 1940

In 1933 Joseph Grinnell, the University of California biologist under whom von Bloeker studied,[1] published "Review of the Recent Mammal Fauna of California." In this article, the Berkeley scientist and founding director of the Museum of Vertebrate Zoology at Berkeley speculated that the white-footed mouse living on Anacapa Island "probably" belonged to the same subspecies as the one inhabiting Santa Cruz Island, *Peromyscus maniculatus santacruzae*. But Grinnell never examined, nor even saw, a white-footed mouse from Anacapa. His thesis rested entirely, as he freely admitted, "on the basis of probability as no specimens were available."[2]

Five years after Grinnell's publication, President Franklin D. Roosevelt placed Anacapa and Santa Barbara Islands into the Channel Islands National Monument, but even with this distinguished designation, Anacapa's three rocky islets were still "very poorly known,"[3] and no mice had ever been collected from them. Furthermore, "little, if anything . . . [was] known of the insect and land snail fauna . . . [and] ornithological work . . . [remained] in an incomplete state."[4] In short, natural history knowledge about these islands had not increased since Grinnell published his paper seven years prior.

As the CIBS prepared to visit Anacapa for the first time, von Bloeker recalled his professor's paper and recognized an opportunity in it. The island's incomplete scientific record played nicely into the LACM mammalogist's desire to collect, analyze, discover, and publish. On the whole, he had everything to gain and nothing to lose when it came to Anacapa's mice. Moreover, he fully recognized that whether he confirmed or disproved Grinnell's theory regarding the progeny of Anacapa's *Peromyscus*, his name would claim a spot in the biological sciences where none existed before. In short, anything he learned would be meaningful.

In the spring of 1940, with the chance to affirm or repudiate Grinnell's supposition dangling before him like catnip, von Bloeker's letter writing, telephoning, and list-making activities became infused with a sense of urgency necessary to surmount a number of obstacles. Finding suitable transportation topped the list of chronic complications. Neither the California Fish and Game Commission, likely still hampered by the sinking of the *Bluefin* in San Diego Harbor the prior November, nor Hancock were available to transport the research team. As a result, von Bloeker recommended that the museum seek passage aboard the Los Angeles County Forestry Department vessel, the *Gray Gull.*

While the CIBS awaited word on this request, von Bloeker sought to solve another major hurdle for completing a successful Anacapa expedition: finding a small skiff to transport the researchers to all three islets. Anacapa is notoriously difficult to land upon due to the nearly uniformly unbroken, sheer cliff faces that make up its isles. Only a small boat would provide access to its precious few landing sites. Understanding this reality, von Bloeker drew up two plans, each with a mainland departure date of May 18 and a duration of two weeks. The first assumed they would find a small craft to transport them from a single basecamp to the other islets. While clearly optimal, if a boat was not available they would camp for one week on each of two islets. The drawbacks to this plan included the amount of administrative time needed to secure a ship large enough to complete their transfer, the time and energy needed to move from one basecamp to another, and the research constraint it put on the scientists whose scientific conclusions could apply to only two of Anacapa's islets.

But unless they could get to Anacapa in the first place, a small boat was small potatoes. When the museum received word that the *Grey Gull* could not accommodate the CIBS's request, the museum temporarily put off the Anacapa expedition. By late May, the trip's status was changed to "indefinitely postponed until sometime the next fall."[5] While representing a significant setback for the CIBS, it turned out to be a trifle compared to the next issue they would face, this one with the potential to stop the expeditions altogether.

The year 1940 proved to be one of considerable upheaval, reorganization, and cost containment at the museum. At the June administrative council meeting, Director Roland J. McKinney advised Comstock to seek legal counsel regarding utilizing the "services of non-paid volunteer workers"[6] for CIBS expeditions. The suggestion must have surprised Comstock because no one had questioned this practice before and the board of governors originally approved the survey knowing that Meadows and other non-museum staff would play a significant role in the expeditions. Why did McKinney bring this up? Had someone on the board of governors asked him about it? Did this line of questioning indicate the deepening power struggle between Comstock and McKinney? McKinney had already made it known he wanted to curtail the science and history departments' activities, so it's possible he was also trying to derail the CIBS.

Nothing in the archives provides any clues about McKinney's reasoning, but Comstock's response is informative because it demonstrates both his conviction in his beliefs as well as a fundamental difference between the two men, namely that Comstock stayed the course. He thoughtfully came to conclusions and did not change his mind merely because it suited the situation. In this case, Comstock believed complete scientific representation formed the cornerstone of the survey and that achieving it behooved the CIBS's successful execution. It is a belief he remained true to throughout the length of the survey. He made this point clear in a reply to his boss, responding that since "the regular staff of the Museum is not sufficient to cover many phases of the work ... and that outside help ... directly [benefits] ... the County, [it] should be obtained, when ... needed."[7] He also used this opportunity to remind McKinney that the science and history departments were understaffed, a situation that would worsen under McKinney's tenure long before it got better.

Nothing further about this topic is recorded in the meeting minutes, and there is no evidence that suggests Comstock checked on the legality of the issue. However, less than one year later, McKinney reversed himself on this issue and pushed Comstock to hire outsiders to keep the survey going. The reasons for McKinney's reversal are also unknown, but it further demonstrates McKinney's unpredictability, a character trait wholly at odds with Comstock.

Under the banner of creating greater efficiency, as summer wore on, McKinney pursued the initiatives he laid out at the close of the prior year, aggressively advancing his agenda month by month. One item that may have been part of this—though it is unclear who instigated this action—was an accounting of the CIBS's total expenditures during the survey's first eighteen months of operation. The results revealed that the county's outlay for staff salaries and groceries had amounted to $2,778.49, of which only $335.91 had been spent on foodstuffs and not a dime on lodging or transportation. Thus, if McKinney had initiated this report hoping to find lavish expenditures, it was all for naught—per the board's original approval, staff salaries were the survey's primary expense.

Regardless, McKinney's promised reorganization began to take shape in July when he formed the new Division of Education. To solidify his plan, the following month he requested that the board seek approval from the county "to amend the ordinance creating the Department of History, Science and Art so as to include therein a Division of Education,"[8] and in September he requested and received approval for the creation of a new, high-level position, curator of exhibits, who would be responsible for the formulation and production of all exhibits within the museum. Before that meeting adjourned, he fired a last potshot at the history and science departments by reporting that the history and science committees "seldom met," but that he "personally felt it important"[9] that they do.

An interesting scrap of information within the archives adds to this story. It is a typewritten list of individuals and their job titles during the time William A. Bryan was director. Handwritten comments accompany the list, including the date (September 1940), the approximate salary of the people holding each job, and the names of any replacements and

Anacapa Island.

their salaries. Additionally, another handwritten note in the document's top right corner reads, "13 [or] 14 gone since former list."[10] Who drew up this list? Who asked for it to be made, and who examined it? Perhaps it provided a roadmap for staff reductions in the departments of science and history.

Anacapa Island, the only Channel Island to retain its Native American name, *Eneepah* or *Anyapax* (in Chumash "deception" or "mirage"),[11] is actually not one island, but three steep-sided volcanic islets, all once part of Santarosae Island. Occasionally, during extremely low tides, ephemeral sand and rock causeways temporarily connect Anacapa's islands, but usually they are completely inaccessible from one another except by boat.

Altogether, the Anacapa islets are about six miles long and comprise nearly seven hundred acres, sixty more than the smallest Channel Island and its sister in the former Channel Islands National Monument, Santa Barbara Island. While each of the three islets share sheer cliff faces and a lack of fresh water, they differ in terms of height and shape. West Anacapa's angular bulk and 936-foot Summit Peak loom above Middle and East Anacapa, which are flat-topped and rise 325 feet and 250 feet, respectively, above sea level. Whereas West Anacapa remains frequently visible from the mainland shore, the two smaller islands regularly melt into the fog and mists that often surround the island, contributing to the shifting, mirage-like visage and name.

Twenty-seven recorded shipwrecks ring Anacapa's little fortress islets. One of these, the *Winfield B. Scott*, which ran aground in 1853, is remembered not only for the captain's master seamanship that saved all 250 passengers and crew, but also for the boatload of rats it deposited on the island's shores. It is also the wreck credited for highlighting to the Bureau of Lighthouses (now part of the U.S. Coast Guard) the need to construct a light on Anacapa Island. Thus, the following year, the U.S. Coast Survey visited Anacapa Island in order to select a site upon which to construct a lighthouse, but concluded, "It is inconceivable for a lighthouse to be constructed on this mass of volcanic rock—perpendicular on every face, with an ascent inaccessible by any natural means."[12] However, after losing more ships over the years, the U.S. Lighthouse Bureau eventually succeeded in building a lighthouse on East Anacapa Island. On March 25,

1932, when the Anacapa Island Light shined for the first time, it became the last lighthouse constructed in California.

In 1959, the Department of Anthropology at the University of California, Los Angeles, described East and Middle Anacapa as: "2 plateaus ... rimmed by vertical cliffs which sometimes drop off directly into the sea.... East Anacapa is the most inaccessible of the 3 island segments.... Middle Anacapa is a flat plateau ... over 3 miles long ... very narrow [and] averaging 100 yards wide.... At ... places ... little more than a ... spine."[13] The report also states that West Anacapa has "no good landing" sites except for West Fish Camp (not to be confused with East Fish Camp on Middle Anacapa) at the extreme east tip of the isle and LeDreau Cove, also known as Frenchy's Cove. After offering these landing suggestions, the report declares, "even in a calm sea it is difficult to land [on West Anacapa] because of swells and rock."[14] Moreover, even when a boat or skiff successfully lands on Anacapa Island, the miles of virtually unscalable cliffs form a perimeter only the most agile and determined visitor can surmount.

Mr. Richard "Dick" M. Bond of the Department of Agriculture's Soil Conservation Service (precursor of today's Natural Resources Conservation Service) exchanged lengthy letters with von Bloeker covering many aspects of exploring the Anacapa islets. As a government biologist and an ornithologist, Bond offered von Bloeker a number of suggestions to help him maximize the time he spent on the island. He told the LACM mammalogist that the CIBS should contact Raymond "Frenchy" LeDreau about their survey plans, and that they should be prepared to present him with the Park Service's written permit as the hermit kept a look out for unwelcome island visitors. The Frenchman lived in a shack on a little spit of beach located on the northeast end of West Anacapa, one of the island's only landing sites (today marked as Frenchy's Cove). He moved there in 1928 after his wife died, sustaining himself through fishing, catching lobster, and trading abalone to the many island visitors who stopped by for conversation, libations, and frequently songfests and lofty literary discussions around his campfire.

After Anacapa became a national monument in 1938, Frenchy's tenure on the islets would have ended except that his extensive natural history knowledge and convivial personality persuaded park personnel otherwise. By 1941, the park superintendent had developed a habit of copying LeDreau on relevant correspondence, a good indication of just how respected his services were. For nearly three decades Frenchy acted unofficially as the island's caretaker, keeping illegal egg collectors and "people with guns and dogs off the island."[15] When the eighty-year-old Frenchman took a bad fall that prevented him from negotiating Anacapa's demanding environment, he exchanged island life for city life, living in Santa Barbara until his death in 1962.

Bond also told von Bloeker that if he wanted to "make a collection"[16] of mice, the top of West Anacapa's difficult-to-access north side would be a good place to do it. Getting there wouldn't be easy, he acknowledged, especially since he would have to haul sufficient gear for "spending a night or two on top of this island."[17] He suggested that von Bloeker utilize a boat to land on some rocks situated on "the north side of the extreme west end"[18] of the island and warned him that landing could only be accomplished when waters were calm. For a summer fieldtrip, he advised alighting between "dawn until about 10:00 or 11:00 a.m." and that he bring "a camp outfit and ample water," which he would need to "pack . . . up over the rocks and guano and cactus to the plateau."[19] Bond concluded, "It is a tough place to get to any way you make it."[20]

As May wore into June, the correspondence between the two biologists moved beyond landing sites to the evils wreaked by Anacapa's feral rat, cat, and rabbit infestations. Around the globe during the last four hundred years, rats infested 82 percent of the world's islands and are responsible for 40–60 percent of recorded bird and reptile extinctions.[21] In his role as chief of the Regional Biology Division of the Soil Conservation Service, Bond felt a responsibility for the health of Anacapa Island's ecosystem, including feral animal removal if warranted. Bond told von Bloeker that he thought a "violent cat control campaign"[22] might save Santa Barbara Island's seabirds, but he thought that "no amount of control [rat or cat extermination] would help"[23] Anacapa's alcid and petrel bird populations. His reference to these birds was probably directed at Cassin's auklets, ashy storm-petrels, and Scripps's murrelets, whose eggs young black rats preyed upon. In reality, a few of these seabirds likely managed to survive on Anacapa's rock crevices and ledges inaccessible to rats, but after residing for more than eighty-five years on the island, *Rattus rattus* had ravaged populations of burrow-nesting seabirds, native mice, reptiles, amphibians, and even intertidal shellfish such as mussels.

Bond's support of eradication on Santa Barbara Island was unquestionable, and both he and von Bloeker agreed it was essential. However, their opinions differed in scope, both geographic and taxonomic. Von Bloeker campaigned for including Anacapa in all eradication efforts. He also strongly voiced his disagreement with Bond's statement that an unavoidable side effect of cat extermination would be the unchecked growth of the rabbit population, which Bond believed would be "relatively harmless to native bird life."[24] The LACM mammalogist felt otherwise, citing rabbits' devastating effects on Laysan Island in the early 1900s, where in less than thirty years introduced bunnies ate nearly all of the island's vegetation, thereby reducing the overall bird population to one-tenth its former size and causing twenty-six native plant species and the Laysan millerbird to go extinct. In summary, von Bloeker "strongly recommend[ed] that a stern campaign of control, with extermination the end in view ... be instituted ... on the islands of the Anacapa group."[25] Von Bloeker wanted to see the island cat, rat, and rabbit free.

The LACM mammalogist also recommended using poison for this extermination. He conceded that it would initially hurt the very birds they hoped to save, but he rationalized that since seabirds were already "doomed to elimination by the cats and rats," no true further damage could result by using poison. Once the exotic mammals were eliminated, von Bloeker felt that the birds might "re-establish themselves" and thereby "regain the status they enjoyed before the non-native mammals were introduced."[26]

The ideas Bond and von Bloeker wrestled with in 1940 continue to plague conservation managers around the world. As for Anacapa, it took thirty years to declare the islets cat-free and double that to be black rat-free. Coincidently, just as von Bloeker suggested, modern conservation managers used rodenticide (rat poison) to eradicate *Rattus rattus* from Anacapa Island.

As von Bloeker predicted, once cats, rats, and rabbits were eliminated from Anacapa, seabirds returned. In 2014, twelve years after the last rats were expunged from Anacapa, Scripps's murrelets were removed from candidacy for protection under the Environmental Species Act. The relatively high numbers of occupied nests, clutch sizes, and hatchings gave evidence of this seabird's improved breeding conditions.[27] While conceding that the status of Scripps's murrelets "may warrant downlisting to a

lower threat category," the ICUN Red List of Threatened Species continues to list the bird as "vulnerable" because of the species' small nesting
range and susceptibility to oil spills and predators.

Of importance, too, West Anacapa supports the largest breeding
rookery in the western United States of the once highly endangered
California brown pelican. Though delisted in 2009 from the Endangered
Species Act, the disappearance of Pacific sardines—the bird's primary
food—is once again threatening the status of these birds, and their Anacapa Island rookery remains closed to public access.

Whereas von Bloeker discerned great opportunities in the three islets
located a short boat ride from the mainland, Art Woodward did not.
He never went to Anacapa. Few archaeologists had.

Even today, notwithstanding Anacapa's being the closest Channel
Island to the mainland and by far the most frequently visited in Channel
Islands National Park, archaeological lethargy has only recently begun to
wither. Between the CIBS's time and now, only a smattering of archaeologists have worked on Anacapa, with most of that research occurring
in the late 1950s through the late 1970s. During that period, six burials and twenty-seven archaeological sites spread across the three islets
were discovered. Despite this success, after 1978 over twenty-five years
passed without the publication of any formal archaeological research
about Anacapa Island. Recently, research on small islands has been on the
upswing throughout the world. For Anacapa, the hiatus finally broke in
2006 when a researcher from Southern Methodist University in Dallas,
Texas (working together with an archaeologist from the National Park
Service), radiocarbon dated material from Anacapa Island that positively
placed people on 'Anyapax at least five thousand years ago.[28]

Native people used Anacapa's two main landing sites most frequently:
Frenchy's Cove on West Anacapa and Shepherd's Landing on Middle Anacapa.[29] Their time on the island has been documented through a few olivella beads, bone gorges and barbs, chert pieces derived from both known
sites on Santa Cruz Island as well as unknown locations, projectile points,
and shell fishhooks.[30] The natives ate mostly California mussels supplemented by red and black abalone, various types of fish, birds, and several
species of seals, sea lions, and dolphin, and research indicates they lived
on or used the island as recently as the early 1800s (the historic period).[31]

Many questions surrounding Anacapa's role in the greater Chumash subsistence and trade systems remain,[32] but some have been resolved. For instance, researchers have determined that Chumash people used Anacapa as a stopping point and rest area when journeying from the mainland to the islands—or from island to island. They also think that the island may have provided an alternative living space when factors such as overcrowding or fighting pushed them from their homes. Other new studies ascertain that people made bone and chipped tools on Anacapa, harvested shellfish and cetaceans, and transported deer parts and island foxes or their remains to the island.[33] As continued scientific discoveries mount, a better understanding of Anacapa's human history will hopefully unfold.

As von Bloeker pieced together the details of the ninth expedition, again to Anacapa Island, the Nazis invaded France, Belgium, Luxembourg, and the Netherlands. In May 1940 the commander in chief moved the U.S. naval fleet from San Diego, California, to Pearl Harbor, Hawaii. In June he established the National Defense Research Committee, a think tank committed to studying and improving devices of war, including radar and the atomic bomb. Newspaper and radio broadcasts brought daily reports of Hitler's advances to the U.S. citizenry, and in 1940, responding to the war publicity, Hollywood released eleven war-themed films, including Hitchcock's *The Foreign Correspondent* and Charlie Chaplin's *The Great Dictator*. Across the continent in Washington, about as far away as one could get from the Hollywood sign, President Franklin D. Roosevelt came to terms with the United States' inevitable involvement in the war.

By mid-June, Belgium, Norway, and Holland surrendered to German forces and Italy declared war on Britain and France. Before the month was out, France signed an armistice with the Nazis, and Hitler, after meeting with Mussolini in Munich, toured Paris and then ordered his U-boats to attack merchant ships in the Atlantic. The attacks that began on July 1 eventually sank three million tons of merchant goods. Stateside, Congress approved $16 billion for defense spending and enacted the first peacetime draft in America's history. In the skies above England, Hitler initiated the Battle of Britain, the world's first primarily aerial battle, a firefight that lasted from June to late October.

The Führer pressed on.

As European countries fell to the pressure of the German *Wehrmacht* (Hitler's army, navy, and air force), LACM's art department publicly mused over the fate of the forty-two European Old Masters paintings on loan for display in the museum. The concern focused on the age-old practice of confiscating art as spoils of war. If that played out, what might happen to the Masters' works? Would the pieces by Rembrandt, El Greco, Constable, Hogarth, Turner, Vermeer, David, and others—worth millions and loaned from the Rijksmuseum in Amsterdam, the Louvre in Paris, the National Gallery in London, and museums in Antwerp—soon belong to "Mr. Hitler" because "the countries from which they were borrowed ... [had] fallen before the blitzkrieg"?[34] It wasn't a trifling question, and it's one the world grappled with for decades into the future.

In the museum's mid-July newsletter another reminder of war surfaced. This time the history department drew a comparison between Hitler and Napoleon, writing that LACM's three-thousand-item Napoleon exhibit "outlines the life of a former great European conqueror, ambitious for world dominion," and that it "invites striking comparisons to the situation on the Continent today—particularly to the person of Adolph Hitler."[35] This similarity, the full-page article not so subtly proposes, gave new significance to the museum's long-standing exhibit and thus warranted another look, even if one had toured it before.

Whether through communications with its members or the need to reach out into the community to staff the CIBS expeditions, the threat of war resoundingly crackled throughout the laboratories and marbled hallways of the Los Angeles County Museum of History, Science, and Art. What further effects would this looming war have on the museum?

Sometime before the ninth expedition's departure on August 15, 1940, Comstock made arrangements with Meadows and Dunkle to join museum staff on Anacapa. Serving as entomologist and botanist/meteorologist, respectively, their presence rounded out the scientific team consisting of von Bloeker (vertebrate zoologist and leader), Henne (entomologist), Kanakoff (invertebrate zoologist), Jack H. Van Nordheim ("student assistant biologist"), and Mrs. Ona von Bloeker (cook). The expedition manifest is noteworthy for two reasons. First, it indicates that Comstock overcame Director McKinney's concern about non-museum participants in the CIBS. Second, because von Bloeker held the title of expedition "leader," it serves as further corroboration of the continued diminishment of Meadows's role in the survey.

Finally, after more than three months of planning, the CIBS secured transport to Anacapa—their old friend, the California Fish and Game Commission, came through. The *Yellowtail* would deliver CIBS staff to Frenchy's Cove on the west island of Anacapa.

With the biggest piece of the transportation puzzle in place, the last dangling, niggling, irksome detail—procuring a small boat for shuttling between Anacapa's islets—likely prompted von Bloeker to light up count-less packs of smokes. He needed a boat, and he needed one badly. Where it finally came from is anyone's guess, but the researchers loaded the "small launch powered with an outboard motor"[36] onto the *Yellowtail* and headed out. Once on the island, staff scrambled, climbed, waded, and boated to all parts of it. The insect contingent, Meadows and Henne (assisted by Kanakoff), proved particularly industrious, plucking fleas, millipedes, and various types of larvae from beneath eucalyptus bark, stripping them from milkvetch pods, and even examining other tiny specimens in search of parasites. Preserved in alcohol, dried in the sun, or captured alive and reared to adulthood in the museum, these animals provide much fodder to work with. As a result of these efforts, several new species were found and several papers published.

Dwight Pierce, a museum staff entomologist whose interest and laboratory-based involvement with the CIBS never vacillated, was one such author. Within a year's time, Pierce published two papers in the bulletin of the Southern California Academy of Sciences that focused on insects found on Anacapa Island during the ninth expedition. One insect he named *Diozocera comstocki* "in honor of . . . [his] friend and associ-ate Dr. John Adams Comstock, Director of Science of the Los Angeles Museum, under whose direction the Channel Islands Survey is being conducted."[37]

In another paper, Pierce's writing oozes with emotion uncharacter-istic of dry scientific publications and incongruent with the subject of his admiration—squirmy, wriggly, creepy critters most people eschew, or at least step on at sight: millipedes. More specifically, he wrote about "beautiful little creatures"[38] from Anacapa Island, *Polyxenus anacapensis*, a rare new myriapod (millipedes, centipedes, or the like). The opening paragraph of Pierce's scientific publication reads, "The Anacapa Island

Expedition of August 1940 turned up a little colony of creatures, looking like Dermestid larvae [flesh eating bugs], which set the writer's heart into high speed, for only twice before in over 40 years of collecting had he ever seen any other specimens of the rare Diplopod genus Polyxenus Latreille."[39]

While Pierce's excitement might seem laughable, if not just plain odd, anyone who has conversed with or listened to a group of scientists discourse about their specialties—worms, whales, anthropology, etc.—knows that the dry prose of scientific papers is nothing but a great facade. Behind all those big words are fierce dedication, keen curiosity, an intense interest in the subject matter, and lives dedicated to the pursuit of answers to questions that may not yet have been posed. Scientists can be a wacky, wicked bunch, full of passion and bravado, egotistical or quiet, thoughtful, and often damnably right about almost everything. But most who have had the privilege of spending an evening in such company couldn't recommend the activity highly enough, no matter the quirky, offbeat nature of the conversations.

As expedition leader, upon arrival to the island von Bloeker could have left the grunt work of unloading the *Yellowtail*'s dory and setting up camp to the others, but he was a field man and he relished this part of his job. He almost certainly pitched in with zest, unloading and carrying crates, bags, and boxes to Frenchy's shacks until the work was done. Von Bloeker delighted in every aspect that being out-of-doors and camping entailed. Additionally, his compulsive nature meant he likely had a planned layout for the supplies and tools that made them easily accessible yet kept them clean and orderly in the midst of potential chaos. It would have been a plan he wished strictly adhered to and quickly consummated so that their real work could commence.

It didn't take long before the traps von Bloeker set began doing their work. Snap, snap, snap. Fish Camp, the name von Bloeker gave to the researchers' home base (probably known today as Frenchy's Cove), eventually yielded eleven deer mice, including one particularly large male mouse captured on the second day that was destined for great things (more on that later). Eleven mice might sound like a lot from just one location, but it wasn't nearly enough to satisfy von Bloeker. He was hungry to prove—or disapprove—something. The first step in this process required collecting mice from as many different places on Anacapa as possible so that he could determine whether mice on Anacapa Island exhibited geographic variations. To do that he needed to examine dozens of mice *in exacting detail.* He would examine their physical traits and, if different, he might be able to conclude that Anacapa had not one, but two or even three subspecies of mice living on its three shores. What if some of the mice were Santa Cruz mice, as Grinnell speculated, and some of them weren't? What would that mean? How would that change their evolutionary story as well as that of the island?

Von Bloeker didn't know the answer to these questions, but he did know that in order to find out he would need to get to the top of West Anacapa, probably to Vela or Summit Peak, as his colleague, Bond, had instructed him. To accomplish this feat, he scrambled and slipped 930 feet up the west island's talus and pelican-guano encrusted slopes encumbered with mouse traps, water, and camping gear. *Ahh. What a joy. What a job,* he may have thought even as his footing gave way and he slid downwards many feet. Getting dirty, breathing the fresh ocean air, collecting animals—von Bloeker loved this. Upon gaining the ridgeline he sought, he surely would have searched for the signs of mice Bond told him existed there. Bending low to the ground, he may have located the little trails the tiny rodents' feet wore into the dirt and through the vegetation. He would have perhaps examined the land for the minuscule piles of scat they left behind. Finding either, he might have placed his traps near these signs of life.

In all, von Bloeker laid traps in six locations on the west island: Fish Camp, Anacapa Peak (known today as Vela or Summit Peak), a spot he called Middle Peak (likely Camel Peak today), Middle Saddle, Cherry Canyon, and Oak Canyon. From these sites he collected a total of nineteen "moderately large ... long-tailed, darkly colored ... *Peromyscus maniculatus.*"[40] Elsewhere on Anacapa he used the small boat he and Comstock had worked hard to secure to reach Middle and East Anacapa, where the traps he laid yielded larger numbers of deer mice. The plateau surrounding the east island's lighthouse provided him with thirty-three little grey omnivores, and the traps he set near Old Ranch Landing on Middle Anacapa, the site of a former sheep ranching operation, yielded another thirty-seven dark grey-backed, black-eared, and white-footed *Peromyscus.* By the end of his two weeks on the islets, von Bloeker had captured eighty-nine deer mice that he accessioned into the museum's collection. This was enough to study and compare to the specimens collected on the other islands, and enough to prove or disprove Grinnell's theory regarding their affinities.

Over the course of the next year, while inhaling packs and packs of cigarettes, von Bloeker examined deer mice through a haze of smoke. He weighed and measured them from tip to tail and the length of their tails, too. He measured their hind feet, ears, cheekbones, skulls, and so much more. He looked at the differences between males, females, and juveniles. He used Ridgeway's *Color Standards and Color Nomenclature* published in 1912 to evaluate and describe the hair colors on the little mammals' backs, stomachs, cheeks, ears, feet, and even the fur at the base of their tails. And then, when warranted, he distinguished color variations, delineating strands, for example, as "dorsal hairs with terminal portions black, narrow subterminal bands light drab, broad basal portions deep mouse gray."[41] After learning all he could about the mice he had caught on Anacapa Island, he compared his findings to at least four different subspecies of *Peromyscus maniculatus* who lived elsewhere, including, of course, on Santa Cruz Island.

Having completed his examinations, a little over a year later he achieved the goal he set out to accomplish during the ninth expedition: he published his findings, concluding that Anacapa, like all the Channel Islands, had its very own subspecies of white-footed mouse. He named it *Peromyscus maniculatus anacapae* after its island home. As for Grinnell's speculation, the well-known biologist correctly conjectured that the mice on Anacapa would be the same species as those found on Santa Cruz, *Peromyscus maniculatus*, but he incorrectly attributed them to the subspecies *santacruzae* when actually they were their own subspecies. Von Bloeker must have been thrilled to improve upon the work of his famous professor.

As for the large male mouse von Bloeker caught at Fish Camp on August 17, 1940, that animal's skull and skin, now known as no. 7335, became the holotype specimen, or the representative of the subspecies for which all the deer mice on Anacapa are named. Some of his eighty-eight other brethren, each a paratype of their subspecies—i.e., similarly representative, but also providing an example of differences within the subspecies due to sex or age variation, for instance—were deposited by

After completing the ninth expedition in August 1940, Donald Meadows never participated in another CIBS trip. Anonymous artist's caricature. Courtesy of Department of
Anthropology, NHM.

von Bloeker at the Museum of Vertebrate Zoology at Berkeley (which
Grinnell founded), the Allan Hancock Foundation (across the street from
LACM at the University of Southern California), and the Smithsonian.
Von Bloeker placed these specimens in these particular institutions so
that future scientists might study them.

Don Meadows, however, would never study any of these mice, and
not because his training and interest didn't lie with mammals. Rather, the
ninth expedition would be the "father" of the Channel Islands Biological
Survey's final trip. By the end of the decade, he shed the title of scientist,
hanging up his pith helmet, butterfly net, and lab coat forever.

Chapter Sixteen

A FLURRY OF LETTERS AND THE END OF THE 1940 FIELD YEAR

"Germany, Italy and Japan Sign Pact Designed as Warning to U.S. In Europe, Far East Affair. Hitler Is Present at Ceremony." Germany, Italy and Japan signed a 10-year military and economic pact today which axis spokesman said was aimed at forestalling possible entry of the United States into the European war.

— *The Kingston Daily Freeman* (Kingston, New York), September 27, 1940

The museum's weekly newsletter reported that the conclusion of the Anacapa expedition marked "another mile-stone" for the CIBS: the end of the preliminary eight-island survey. This allowed Comstock to cleverly rebrand future trips that would likely be understaffed as "follow-up" excursions needed for "more intensive study" of specific flora and fauna.[1] In this way, the survey could move forward without having a full scientific contingent onboard.

For Don Meadows, the Anacapa expedition marked different milestones, ones he discussed with John Adams Comstock. Their discourse ventured into some tender areas that left the professor doubting he had successfully persuaded Comstock to support his propositions. His concern had merit, too, as Comstock ended their discussion with the admonition that he would take his fellow lepidopterist's points "under advisement,"[2] a conclusion that must have been deeply unsatisfying to the Long Beach schoolteacher.

Not content with this outcome, Meadows directed a two-and-a-half-page, single-spaced letter to Comstock in which he laid out his opinions about the survey's shortcomings and presented his recommendations for rectifying them. It began inappropriately with an insulting salvo—a reminder that the survey was Meadows's idea, one that Meadows successfully presented to the board of governors for approval. After making this demeaning point, the professor restated the survey's objectives, as if Comstock may have forgotten. Meadow's next point may have caused Comstock to lay down the letter and push back his chair. Never had the survey's staffing been characterized in quite the way Meadows portrayed it when he pointedly states that the originally proposed survey envisioned it being "carried on by persons not associated with the museum, together with certain members of the museum staff."[3] In placing the museum's contribution to the survey as a modifying clause to the work conducted by non-museum staff, Meadows relegates the museum to a position of lesser importance and implies that the LACM was helping Meadows and his Long Beach gang, not the other way around. Comstock, undoubtedly, did not see it this way.

In the third paragraph, Meadows's tone grows pricklier when he hints that the museum has not lived up to its end of the agreement regarding distribution of specimens intended to serve as dispensation for non-paid survey participants' work efforts. He insinuates that non-museum staff were to be allowed to hold onto specimens, only giving the museum its share "at the conclusion of the survey."[4] He also declares that, to date, the distributions to non-museum staff have "been extremely low,"[5] a scathing insult to Comstock's evenhandedness. Surely, if the doctor had held a pipe in his hand he would have brought it to his lips and inhaled deeply, holding the warm smoke in his mouth a good long time while considering Meadows's unfounded reprobation. To begin with, the original proposal *never* contemplated the museum receiving its share of specimens at the conclusion of the survey. Secondly, he and Meadows discussed the possibility of Meadows keeping specimens at his home, but because Meadows did not own a fireproof safe in which to keep them secure, they mutually agreed that the museum provided the best storage facility.

The fourth paragraph reiterates that the survey was to have been conducted "outside regular museum activities," even though the objectives were "quite in line with the desire of the museum to gain public co-operation and support."[6] With these words, Meadows once again relegates the museum to a minor role in the survey, while also positioning its interests as being solely for publicity and financial gain rather than scientific advancement, as Comstock likely believed. While it is true that scientific endeavors are often arranged and carefully developed with an eye toward achieving donor funding, Comstock asked neither donors nor the county for a penny of support. In fact, his own men bore the cost of their work on the islands, and occasionally Comstock personally reimbursed staff or other participants for expenses he knew the county would not cover. And yes, Comstock certainly wanted his scientists to publish both peer-reviewed journal articles and pieces intended for public consumption, in addition to developing exhibitry for museum display, but these goals matched the museum's fundamental mission; they were not ploys or actions that could in any way be considered untoward.

Relentlessly, Meadows's fifth paragraph insinuates that the museum failed to properly catalogue, sort, or classify the fifty thousand or so specimens collected during the ten expeditions completed thus far. Of course, there had only been nine expeditions, and of these Meadows's had participated in seven. After making this blunder, Meadows unwisely chooses to give the director of science some advice on how to conduct his business. He instructs Comstock that "more field work is necessary," but that it should not be undertaken "until the material already gathered is so organized that it may be seen in perspective and future collecting will not be a duplication of work already done."[7]

In his final shot, Meadows states that the survey has lost its focus and that the expeditions were being conducted "more in the nature of field days rather than a part of a preconceived plan." He condemns the survey participants, who view their work as "part of their everyday job with no other purpose than to do what they are paid to do."[8] Meadows's complaint displays a snobbery that is quite surprising. All of the participants, including Meadows, were focused on collecting specimens out in the field—in fact, Meadows and Chris Henne, the two Anacapa expedition entomologists, had just gathered up a bunch of millipedes that set Dwight Pierce's "heart into high speed." Why would Comstock find anything disagreeable about that?

By this point, Meadows's tone is that of a manifesto—rambling, repetitive, contradictory. With every click of a typewriter key, he pins his metaphoric wings ever more securely, and in most unfavorable positions, onto the CIBS's foam core storyboard. He eventually advises Comstock that in order for "the Survey [to] be carried to a successful conclusion . . . that the motives, purpose, objectives, organization and administration be understood. Definite policies must be established, ideas and interest must be coordinated, and unselfish attitudes shown. Obviously unity is necessary, and unity necessitates an administrative head."[9]

Were Comstock the type of man prone to anger, upon reading this he might have pounded his fist and sworn loudly at his colleague, or perhaps picked up the phone to give Meadows a piece of his mind. But Comstock was not that type of man. Rather, as he sat at his desk shortly after Labor Day reading this letter, he likely leaned back into his chair, lit his pipe, and thought for a moment. After sending a plumb of smoke into the air, he may have asked himself, "What the dickens has gotten into Meadows? And how in the devil did this high school biology teacher get the idea that he could tell the Los Angeles County Museum of History, Science, and Art how to conduct a scientific expedition?"

John Adams Comstock was nothing if not a focused, consistent professional, the kind of person who thoughtfully puzzled over issues in pursuit of optimal resolutions and then stuck with his guns unless thoroughly convinced that a change was necessary. He was a fiercely loyal man, too, and would not have stood for his employees to be disrespected or brushed aside as Meadows suggested in his letter. No, Comstock would need to explain a thing or two to the Long Beach professor. He would do it skillfully, of course, so as not to burn bridges, but he would not waste time nor allow bad feelings to further fester and risk spoiling the good results the survey enjoyed already. Comstock surely knew what that solution would look like, but it wouldn't be the one Meadows had in mind.

However, before getting to that, he owed it to Meadows to finish reading the six recommendations his colleague had neatly indented and numbered "a" through "f" on the next page and a half. Among the recommendations the professor makes is a call for all survey participants to reacquaint themselves with the objectives of the CIBS, including how the survey was "associated with the museum," again implying that the survey was outside the museum's regular activities. Of course, Comstock could not more heartily disagree with this conclusion, nor did he believe for a moment that the researchers weren't amply aware of the survey's goals.

Next Meadows recommends that he, Don Meadows, "be recognized as director of the Survey, with full authority to select, approve and direct personnel ... with power to delegate ... authority during my absence, to control the time and activities of all expeditions, and to maintain supervision of all Survey collections."[10] Comstock may have found this request equally jarring and insulting, but it was not the most absurd request the professor made. That honor belonged to Meadows's recommendation that archaeology be jettisoned from the survey altogether, though he provides no reason for making the suggestion. Nothing in the survey's notes, memorandums, or letters gives a clue either, yet Comstock might have surmised that a personality clash between Meadows and the museum's archaeologist prompted the idea. Both men had large egos, and both men considered themselves "in charge" of the expeditions.

Indeed, in various letters and memorandum, Comstock designates Woodward as being in charge and then addresses at least one letter to "Mr. Don Meadows, In charge—Channel Island Biological Survey."[11] As for Meadows, he frequently claimed the title, choosing to close his letters using the designation "Leader of Expeditions" typed right below his name. The press didn't get it right either, variously dubbing Meadows or Woodward as the leader of the expeditions. Considering all this confusion about which man held the title and responsibility, it is understandable that Meadows would want to clarify his role. From his point of view, the most expeditious way to accomplish that would be to drop archaeology from the survey—that would cull the competition, at least. However, archaeology was an important part of the survey, and its inclusion ensured scientific representation across all disciplines. Additionally, the board of governors supported it and the public was keenly interested in it. Archaeology would not be dropped. Period.

Had Meadows been savvy about communicating his desires to Comstock he would have worded his entire letter differently, and he surely would not have concluded it with the following affected, unctuous, and repetitive statements:

Since the Survey was organized as an extra-museum activity, and since I was the person who was instrumental in bringing it into existence I feel a great responsibility in seeing the undertaking succeed. To gain that success I need and want the support

and co-operation of everyone connected with the museum. Your
own co-operation and friendship has been splendid. Without it
I would be tempted to "chuck" the whole undertaking.

... In the meantime, consider my suggestions as a means
toward harmony, good fellowship, efficiency and success."[12]

Meadows probably knew nothing of the pressure the museum's senior
management and board were putting on the science department, and
Comstock in particular; he likely knew nothing of the clandestine
changes to the museum's management structure, staff reallocations,
or salary reviews. However, even if he did know about these nasty internal conflagrations, Meadows's apparent lack of office acumen would
likely have precluded him from taking any of these factors into consideration before making these egregious recommendations to his supposed
colleague and friend.

In addition to the professional slight, Comstock must have felt the
sting on a personal level, too, as Meadows's requests indicated a lack of
appreciation for the work Comstock had put into what he considered a
joint endeavor between the two of them. After all, Comstock had demonstrated his commitment to the Long Beach teacher by steadfastly including Meadows and his Long Beach colleagues in the survey, working to
accommodate their schedules, and backing their inclusion even when
Comstock's boss thought otherwise. Did the professor not understand
that his petitions undermined all of the goodwill and camaraderie the
pair had created in moving the survey this far?

Comstock was no stranger to scientists' egos, and it couldn't have
been the first time he'd run into one whose self-image loomed inappropriately large. Besides, he wasn't one to strip a man's contributions away
from him, regardless of his subsequent actions, and Meadows had been
the one to approach him with the idea of an eight-island survey in the
first place. The survey remained a very good idea and a noble endeavor
of which the museum could be proud. Comstock owed the man the courtesy of a reply.

As summer waned toward autumn, Meadows wasn't the only survey
member writing inappropriate letters. Woodward wrote an angry letter
to someone named Dorr who worked for the Los Angeles County Civil

Service Commission. He begins the typed, rambling missive with a blasphemous tirade: "Jesus H. Christ! Who is that red tape loving guy sitting in a swivel chair as asst. director of Region IV. . . . This isn't an official letter so I can squawk as loud and hard as I damned please but just the same I wish you'd pin a tail on that donkey and ask him why the hell he has to be sooo-oo technical when technicalities aren't called for."[13] Woodward's ire stemmed from an official request for his birth records, records he did not have—"no birth certificate, no physicians certificate, no official records of any kind."[14] In lieu of this, Woodward supplied the county with a self-made affidavit prepared following official instructions given to him. The county returned these documents because they wanted more information and notarization, but Woodward refused. "[I am] holding the documents here," he informed Dorr. "They are perfectly legal. . . . If and when Region IV decides they can follow the instructions laid down by Civil Service, I'll mail them back otherwise they can take this damned job and shove it . . . there's no money in it anyhow." A threat, but an idle one, he admits: "I'll probably go on working for you guys even if it isn't legal."[15]

The tone of Woodward's letter isn't surprising, but the lack of consideration he gives to the impetus of the request, however, is. Could the internal reviews, scrutiny of titles, salaries, scope of work, and levels of authority have had anything to do with it? Or, could Woodward's arrogance and cocky mannerisms have attracted unwanted attention from McKinney and others, attention for which he would pay a price in the future? Given the dissatisfaction with which the director-in-charge held the Departments of Anthropology, History, and Science, it is within the realm of reason to suspect that inquiries into Woodward's employment record and official transcripts had something to do with McKinney's larger plan.

Comstock gave Meadows's letter a week of "long and careful study"[16] before composing his own single-spaced reply that mimicked the form and style of the professor's. In this two-and-a-half-page rebuttal, Comstock carefully addresses his colleague's grievances and recommendations, attempting, but not always succeeding, to conceal his irritation. And, why should he, anyway? After all, the Long Beach schoolteacher denigrated Comstock's staff, relegated the museum's role to one of lesser importance, and proceeded to tell him (several times, in fact) how to conduct museum business. In response, Comstock's tone is clipped,

business-like, direct, and written in legal parlance, sprinkled throughout with phrases such as "unalterable policy" as well as quoted references
like "in paragraph 3 of your letter you state that...," or "if you will refer
to your letter of December 20, 1938, you will note on item 6, page 2, the
paragraph covering...,"[17] and so forth.

Comstock efficiently dismisses all of Meadows's requests for a variety of good reasons. First and foremost, he explains that LACM policy
precluded any organization from using the museum's name unless an
approved museum staff member supervised the activity. This meant
"that the only person who can function as 'Director' of the Survey is the
Director of Science of the Museum"[18]—that would be Comstock. Next,
he handily dispatched Meadows's wish to have specimens distributed by
reminding him that the two of them had previously discussed the matter and Meadows had conceded "the inadvisability of keeping any large
amount [of specimens] ... in ... [Meadows's] studio ... [because it was]
a fire hazard."[19]

In conclusion, Comstock allows that the interference of personnel
issues—or "certain inharmonies," as he terms them—caused "tempera-
mental differences" to plague the expeditions. These, he suggested, "are
very unimportant in comparison with the ... possibilities ahead for real
achievement," and therefore the parties involved should "frankly face" the
issues and keep their differences "out of the picture."[20] This comment corroborates that Meadows had clashed with someone. In sum, the professor
would not become the director of the survey, he would not receive any
specimens right away, and no changes in staff composition would ensue.
On top of that, anyone who wanted to be involved with the survey had
best get along.

The day after Meadows penned his grievances and recommendations
for Comstock's perusal, he wrote another letter that indicates he expected
to hear a very different response from the one he would receive from the
director of science in a week's time. In this letter, he addresses the commanding officer of the U.S. Coast Guard in San Francisco, asserting that
he could represent the museum's point of view and speak "personally,
and on behalf of the Survey party."[21] At its conclusion, he boldly assigned
himself the title, "Don Meadows, In charge of Expeditions, Los Angeles
Museum–Channel Islands Biological Survey."[22] It is clear that Meadows
assumed Comstock would assign him a formalized leadership role.

In retrospect, this letter reveals not only a lack of common sense on Meadows's part as it pertains to office politics, but also his overinflated belief regarding his status within the survey team. Meadows could easily have waited for Comstock to reply before he wrote to the Coast Guard, but he did not. Tellingly, this is the last letter penned by Meadows that bore his signature in tandem with any leadership title relating to the Channel Islands Biological Survey.

Saturday, November 23rd was clear and cool when members of the tenth expedition left Terminal Island aboard the *Velero III*. One of the primary purposes of this expedition was to complete Woodward's earlier work at the Dutch Harbor site by collecting as many grass textiles as possible. Given this focus, three assistants accompanied Woodward: John Shrader (son of Roscoe Shrader, director of the Otis Art Institute at the LACM), Howard Keller, and Marion Hollenbach, the mysterious "M" Woodward wrote to while on San Miguel Island who was the third woman to participate in the expeditions and probably the first trained female archaeologist to work on the Channel Islands.

The ship's clock read 3 p.m. when Hancock landed the researchers on the southeast curve of San Nicolas Island. Staff unloaded in jig time and without incident, establishing Camp Zorro as their island home for roughly the next two weeks. Their arrival on the island fell on the Saturday immediately following the country's "new" Thanksgiving Day, designated the prior year by President Franklin Roosevelt as the third Thursday in November instead of the last Thursday. Political pundits quickly took to calling the new holiday "Franksgiving," but their fun at Roosevelt's expense did nothing to budge his belief that an earlier Thanksgiving would boost retail Christmas sales and help the country move past the Great Depression. Despite the president's views, U.S. citizens were mixed about this new date. In 1940, only thirty-two states and the District of Columbia observed the "official" Thanksgiving Day of November 21, while twenty-two states chose to celebrate the "traditional" holiday date. Three states couldn't seem to figure it out at all—Colorado, Mississippi, and Texas gave residents holidays on both Thursdays.

Not surprisingly, Woodward fell on the pundits' side of this national debate, a position he makes clear in his journal by noting below the date (November 28th, the last Thursday of the month) the words,

Franksgiving Day feast on San Nicolas Island, November 1940; California mussel stew shared with friends. Pictured from left to right: Ona von Bloeker, Art Woodward, Chris Henne, and George Kanakoff. Courtesy of NHM Archives.

"Thanksgiving day B.R.—Before Roosevelt." Then, as if to further bolster the ongoing Franksgiving protest, staff members organized a Thanksgiving Day feast celebrated not with turkey, but California mussels collected and cooked into a stew.[23] They enjoyed the pale, slightly orange meat whilst sitting on a windswept field overlooking the Pacific Ocean, but when Woodward reflected on the meal he advised that they "should have collected smaller" mussels, like "the Indians [who] gathered very few large mussel shells."[24] Perhaps their feast of predominately larger mussels tasted a bit too chewy, or maybe the mussels were overcooked and tough.

Woodward orchestrated a different nontraditional activity, too: a photo shoot staged on the hill where he believed Juana Maria's whale-bone hut sat. There, using the whalebones found at the site, he and his assistants reconstructed the Lone Woman's "home," in which the short-of-stature, dark-haired Hollenback sat, her image a Hollywood-like stand-in for the abandoned woman. Woodward then photographed a "reenact[ment of] . . . the [1853] capture of Juana Maria"[25] in 35 mm stills. Before leaving the island, he augmented those photos by taking "a shot of M's footprints to go with the Juana Maria story."[26]

The researchers photographed this elephant seal pup on San Nicolas Island in December 1940, documenting the existence of this endangered species. Courtesy of NHM Archives.

By the end of the expedition, Woodward and his crew had success-fully collected numerous grass artifacts, including rope (which he specu-lated was part of sailing ships' rigging gear), seaweed grass skirts, grass matting, fishhooks, and whalebone implements, all items the LACM still holds within its collection today. As reported in the *Los Angeles Times*, Woodward described the archaeological items from the tenth expedition as "the most important collection of pre-historic artifacts of primitive character since the survey began 20 months ago."[27] The *Long Beach Press Telegram*, *Oakland Tribune*, and *New York Sun* all carried similar articles about the expedition.

The *Los Angeles Herald-Express* ran a story, too, one it augmented with a photograph of two scientists standing by a large grass mat. In the image, a nattily attired Hollenbach and Woodward—she in a dark, conserva-tive dress, he in a tailored suit, light shirt, and tie—stand a respectable distance apart on adjacent sides of the mounted artifact. Marion holds a small paintbrush within her bejeweled right hand, poised and pointed at a section of the mat. Her carriage is tense, her expression serious, and her gaze sharply focused on someone outside of the photograph to whom she appears to be listening raptly. Woodward's entire focus is on his archaeological assistant. It's clear that not only is he also listening to the question, but that he knows the answer and is trying to *channel* it to her through barely parted lips—a nervous professor worrying his protégé might not get it quite right. Overall, the photograph displays awkward-ness and apprehension, which doesn't make sense given the positive press surrounding the archaeological field crew's work on San Nicolas Island.

An examination of a few of Woodward's contradictory journal entries provides some clues about the tension in the photograph, but they cannot be deemed conclusive. In one, Woodward appears generally pleased with the excavation of the Dutch Harbor site and enumerates the various objects found there. "So far everything has worked out fairly well,"[28] he wrote on December 10th. Two days later, however, his opinion has changed: "Glad this trip is about over. Sundry complications have set in that are disappointing, [but] nothing can be done about it."[29] What sundry complications occurred over the course of those two days? Had he received news from the museum, such as rumors of pending reorga-nizations? Could it have had anything to do with his archaeological field assistants—Marion Hollenbach, perhaps? She was his muse for the photo

This "mystery" photo is located in NHM's files with nothing but Channel Islands Biological Survey noted on the envelope sleeve. Careful examination reveals that this photo was taken during the tenth expedition in November/December 1940 and that it is likely one of the only photos of Marion Hollenbach at NHM. From left to right: Ona von Bloeker (facing away from the camera); Jack von Bloeker Jr.; Art Woodard; Marion Hollenbach (believed); unknown, but either John Shrader or Howard Keller, both student archaeologists; George Kanakoff (standing); unknown, but either John Shrader or Howard Keller; and Chris Henne (back to camera). Note the crate supporting the picnic table that reads "Los Angeles Museums Channel Islands Biological Survey ARCHAEOLOGY." Courtesy of NHM Archives.

shoot, and they had worked, hiked, and swam together over the course of the last two weeks. He had even "planted"[30] a handmade artifact on her to ensure that she "found" an item of interest on an otherwise disappointing day. Or was it something else?

Further illustrating his change of heart is the last entry in his San Nicolas Island journal: "Another trip done—one I shall long remember. More than ever I realize. San Nicolas Id. is a desolate, dreary place slightly cursed. I shall always dread going back to it."[31] What happened during those last days on San Nicolas Island is a mystery that will likely remain so.

The survey members' return to Los Angeles on December 12 marked the conclusion of the 1940 field year, but not of CIBS staff members' hunger to continue exploring and collecting on North America's Galapagos Islands. While Willett set about planning a week-long, late-January trip to Santa Catalina, von Bloeker submitted a proposal for the most ambitious expedition yet, one in which he would be the leader. As von Bloeker envisioned it, the twelfth expedition would last eight weeks and cover all eight Channel Islands. Due to the length and scope of this expedition, the bat scientist took care to fully outline the itinerary, staffing, the complicated permitting process, and the goals of each participating discipline—ornithology, mammalogy, herpetology, entomology, invertebrate zoology, and botany.

Somewhat conspicuously absent from this detailed list was archaeology, but why? Woodward had made it known that he wished to revisit several of the islands, and this would be as good an opportunity as any. Could this simply have been an oversight on von Bloeker's part? Was Woodward being punished for some behavior on San Nicolas? Or was he—as well as a replacement—simply unavailable during the proposed early spring 1941 time period? The answer is still unclear, but six weeks after von Bloeker sent his original itinerary to Comstock, archaeology appeared on the travel plan—Woodward's name, however, did not. In his stead, a student assistant's name, John Shrader, was listed.

At the same time as archaeology's place in the twelfth expedition was being sorted out, a more pressing issue arose. Director McKinney planned to make a stunning—and for the history and science departments, a crippling—recommendation to the board of governors when they convened on January 16th for their first meeting of the new year. The reverberations from his proposition would not only be keenly felt throughout Los Angeles and national scientific communities, but it could change the course of the Channel Islands Biological Survey.

Chapter Seventeen

THE MAGIC ISLE: SANTA CATALINA

"Defense Budget Approved: House Members Endorse Grants for Arms Branch." "Army, Navy, Coast Guard, FBI Appropriation of $267,198,908 Is Allowed as Urged by President."

— *The Newark Advocate* (Newark, Ohio), January 10, 1940

A quorum was present when the board of governors met on January 16th with just one museum representative in attendance: Roland McKinney. The meeting proceeded routinely until discussion turned to the "work being done by the Science Division of the Museum,"[1] at which point McKinney expressed his belief that the Hancock Foundation, located on USC's campus across the street, was "better equipped to carry on research in the [science] fields [than] ... the Museum." As a result, McKinney stated, the science department "should be curtailed." This action, he enthused, would allow for the "building up [of] the recently added Education Department" and put the science staff's time to better use, "furthering the [education] program [rather] than ... expanding ... work in research."[2]

The room must have stilled when McKinney made these proclamations, but when he ceased speaking it burst to life like a lightning storm, abuzz with questions, answers, and exchanges back and forth. One board member pointed out that USC is private and therefore accessible to only a small number of people. In contrast, LACM was open to the "general public who look to its scientists for help with their problems."

Furthermore, he said that the works of public and private institutions are different, and "research by the Science Division of this museum must [not] necessarily be given up because another very different institution had entered the field." This board member concluded by stating that while the education department could utilize science department staff to conduct scientific interpretive work, such activities did not constitute a need to "discontinu[e] the research of the department." During the subsequent discussion, the importance of continuing the Channel Islands Biological Survey was voiced and no oppositions were noted.[3]

McKinney countered these objections weakly. He did not address the differences between public and private institutions, nor did he comment on the advisability of continuing the CIBS. He did, however, call attention to the history department and suggested staffing changes, comments that led to a "prolonged" conversation between McKinney and the board. The meeting concluded with the chairman of the science committee motioning for McKinney to submit a report for further discussion at the next monthly meeting. This was seconded and unanimously adopted. The meeting was adjourned.

When George Willett and his wife Ora—who comprised the entire staff of the eleventh expedition—departed for Santa Catalina Island on January 20th, they probably knew nothing of McKinney's board presentation a few days before. Rather, Willett focused on his priorities: getting to the island, making contacts that the CIBS could leverage during the twelfth expedition, determining where the best collecting locations would be, and bringing back to the museum as many specimens as he could.

With just he and his wife traveling, mobilizing Hancock or the California Fish and Game Commission for passage across the Catalina Channel seemed excessive—thus, the Willetts investigated publicly scheduled transportation services. His options were two. His first was the SS Catalina, better known as the Great White Steamer, a gracious 301-foot steamship capable of ferrying two thousand people in style while making the trip from the mainland to Avalon in two hours and fifteen minutes. William Wrigley built and launched the ship in 1924, and for the next fifty-one years—except during WWII—she provided daily service between Wilmington and Avalon. While aboard the vessel, the Willetts could look forward to dancing to big band orchestra music, lounging on the ship's leather settees, and drinking from the onboard bar. Upon arrival in Avalon, speedboats towing water skiers sliced through the steamer's wake, circling the boat to the delight of all the passengers. When they disembarked, mariachi bands would play in greeting as they walked down the pleasure pier and into town.

Their second option was a luxury, amphibious, ten-seater Douglas Dolphin aircraft operated by Wilmington-Catalina Airline, a Santa Catalina Island Company subsidiary. Designed by Donald Douglas, the twin-engine seaplanes predated the DC-1 as a passenger airplane. Wrigley purchased the first two planes in 1931, immediately putting them into service. Ten years later, having flown thirty-eight thousand times between its two homeports without a single incident,[4] the Wilmington-Catalina Airline held an impeccable record: the world's shortest and safest airline.

Since the county would not pay for the cost of the Willetts' channel crossing, it only made sense for George and Ora to board the *Great White Steamer* at a cost of $2.25 roundtrip per person, a great savings compared to the Wilmington-Catalina Airline's $10 roundtrip charge per person. Both the eleventh expedition and possibly von Bloeker's return trip home from his one-day collecting stint on Santa Catalina Island (March 16, 1940) were the only CIBS expeditions to make use of public transportation.

George and Ora spent the rainy week of January 20–27 on Santa Catalina in a small apartment they used as their island headquarters. During the week, Lester Smith, assistant county fire warden, provided the couple with intra-island transportation to Cape Canyon, Middle Ranch Canyon, the hills east of Avalon, and Avalon Canyon. He not only gave Willett nine foxes and an out-of-season rattlesnake for the museum's collection, but he also assisted the Willetts in collecting fifty-nine birds in good winter plumage. One, an Alberta fox sparrow, was a new record for the Channel Islands. In addition to these animals, the Willets culled hundreds of parasites from the skins they made, agreeably turning the cache over to the entomology department upon their return to the mainland.

In contrast to the Willets' relatively simple Catalina island expedition, the twelfth expedition's robust itinerary included trips to Catalina, San Clemente, Anacapa, Santa Cruz, and Santa Rosa Islands. Its focus was to collect early spring specimens of insects, reptiles, plants, invertebrates, and both birds and mammals in winter plumage and pelage.

Because employees would be traveling outside of Los Angeles County to Ventura County (Anacapa Island) and Santa Barbara County (Santa Rosa and Santa Cruz Islands), Comstock needed approval from the board of governors and the Los Angeles County Board of Supervisors, approval he had received in the past, but which now represented just a portion of the administrative complications associated with this particular expedition.

In preparation for the twelfth expedition, Comstock dropped at least a dozen letters into that January's post. When the chief of staff of the Eleventh Naval District replied, it was to inform the museum that the district intended to forward their permit request to Washington, DC, for approval. Realizing the delay this could cause, Comstock provided Captain Ravenscroft with copies of all previous naval approvals, including some that Ravenscroft had signed himself. Shortly thereafter, the museum received naval permits to work on San Clemente, San Nicolas, and San Miguel Islands.

The Santa Catalina Island Company's response to Comstock's request featured a different twist by prohibiting hunting on the island due to concerns about the safety of company-owned livestock. Because of the nature of the CIBS's fieldwork, the museum couldn't live with such a restriction and thus began a series of letters and telephonic exchanges between the Los Angeles County game warden, the Santa Catalina Island Company, and the museum. Eventually, the museum prevailed, and the survey's plans began moving forward again.

Santa Catalina Island, or just Catalina to most Southern Californians, is the most well known and most visited of all the Channel Islands. It is easily visible from much of the Los Angeles and Long Beach coastlines on clear, crisp days. At these times, from almost anywhere along Santa Monica Bay's shoreline, Catalina looms behind the Palos Verdes Peninsula, appearing not as an island at all but a fingerling extension of the mainland. These are the days when only sailboat masts and squadrons of pelicans obscure the island's rain-cut ravines, their telltale whitewashed rock visible from twenty-one miles away. On other days, fog shrouds the island completely, masking Catalina entirely from view.

Between these two extremes a magical middle ground exists when thick fog hovers halfway down Catalina's two mountaintops like a white veil obscuring the peaks of Mount Orizaba and Blackjack Mountain, each

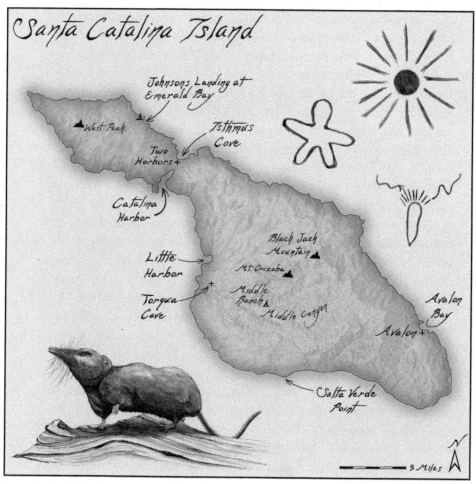

Santa Catalina Island.

two thousand feet high. With only the lower half of the island visible, off-shore winds perceptibly flutter the feathery veil, moving it up and down, back and forth, as though the island were alive and breathing. Ancient mariners might have imagined Catalina's craggy, east-facing profile as a sleeping dragon with white smoke leaching from her nostrils, seawater swells bathing her abdomen with salty foam, briny spumes colliding with the rocks she lies upon and then racing upwards along her blue and green schist flanks.

Catalina is a rugged outcropping of land whose mass is nearly bifur-cated at its western end, where two mountains drop steeply to sea level like décolletage to cleavage to create a half-mile-long Isthmus. The small town of Two Harbors sits smack in the middle of this narrow strip of land, a flat alluvial plain of sand and grasses connecting Catalina's west and east ends. Isthmus Cove, "the only natural, deep, all-weather harbor between San Diego and San Francisco,"[5] forms Two Harbors's eastern edge. Ringed by a white sand and rock beach, Isthmus Cove is a sapphire jewel. On its opposite shore, the shallow, muddy flats of Catalina Harbor (Cat Harbor) slop greedily, edging ever closer to the island's eastern shoreline. In this age of rising sea levels, Cat Harbor and Isthmus Cove must eventually meet, and when they do, Catalina Island will be two.

A varied terrain, a few year-round freshwater ponds, and a mild, Mediterranean climate contributed to Catalina's initial habitation by the *Pimu* (or *Pipimar*) people, today known as the island Gabrielino. These people, who lived on Catalina since at least eight thousand years ago, called their island *Pimuu'ngna*, *Pipimar*, or simply *Pimu*. Although Catalina is the closest southern Channel Island to the mainland and the easiest to get to, little is known about these ancient people, especially compared to what is known about the early inhabitants of Santa Rosa, Santa Cruz, and San Miguel Islands.

This lack of knowledge is not due to a shortage of archaeological sites (more than two thousand[6] have been found so far) or from a dearth of professional interest (archaeologists began work on the island as early as 1873), but because most early published research lacked context.[7] Ironi-cally, this is the same criticism levied against Art Woodward's research, but in his case it was the lack of specificity in his fieldnotes and the pub-lication of few peer-reviewed, scientific papers that contributed to this lackluster appraisal. In contrast, Catalina's early researchers did publish their findings; however, like Woodward, they tended to use general terms instead of specific, site-traceable ones. For instance, if a dig was identified as being conducted at Isthmus Cove, it is not particularly useful to scholars because the description is vague, encompassing a fairly large physical space that could contain many middens and habitation areas. An additional problem with earlier digs is that many were conducted by pothunters who rarely documented their finds (it behooved them not to) and who sometimes deliberately misrepresented them, mixing "real" artifacts with purchased or manufactured items and thereby muddling the item's provenance and scientific usefulness. Most egregious to Native Americans and others concerned with civil rights is the irreverence with which these profit seekers exhumed burials.

Much of what is known about Catalina's early people can be credited to university- and compliance-driven field expeditions that ran from the late 1950s into the present. Though some scholars find fault with this work, citing that much of it was conducted in haste and/or used student archaeologists whose results may have included inaccurate and incomplete data, beginning in 2007 the Pimu Catalina Island Archaeology Project (PCIAP) began building on this foundation.[8] PCIAP is an organization led by a Gabrielino/Tongva community member, NAGPRA (Native American Graves Protection and Repatriation Act) experts, and scholars from the University of California–Los Angeles and the Southwest Museum of the American Indian. Dedicated to better understanding the cultural and physical life of the Pimu, PCIAP utilizes modern technologies such as GPS and GIS to remap and redocument previously recorded sites, and—like Woodward before them—compile and reanalyze previously acquired data.[9]

Woodward did not travel to Santa Catalina Island as part of the CIBS. Instead, he relied on John Shrader to conduct the survey's fieldwork. Shrader's initial notetaking focused on Catalina soapstone (or steatite), a well-studied commodity. He excitedly informed Woodward that he found this stone at "not just one or two quarries on the island, but practically [in] an infinite number."[10] Indeed, the Magic Isle includes nearly two hundred[11] sites, a quantity of soapstone outcroppings no other Channel Island can duplicate.

This soft stone's scarcity, combined with its heat resistance and malleability, made it a valuable resource. The island Gabrielino carved it into beads, bowls, *comales* (cooking pans or griddles), ollas,[12] effigies, and other ornamental and utilitarian items that were widely traded in exchange for other needed goods. Catalina soapstone pieces have been found on the mainland in several places within the San Fernando Valley of Los Angeles, north of Santa Barbara in the Cuyama Valley, in the Tejon Pass (located roughly ninety-five miles inland from Long Beach), and nearly two hundred miles north along the coast to Arroyo Grande, near the central California town of Pismo Beach. Additionally, soapstone artifacts have been found on all Channel Islands except Anacapa, which some scholars attribute to the comparative paucity of archaeological work having been completed on Anacapa's islets.[13] Researchers have attributed this commodity's widespread distribution to the region's thriving trade networks.[14]

Soapstone wasn't the only thing the Catalina Gabrielino exchanged. They "traded dried fish, marine mammal pelts and meat for … furs, skins, seeds and obsidian,"[15] and they distributed these goods by utilizing a system of pathways they constructed and maintained across their island, or by paddling their *ti'ats* (wooden plank canoes) from one Catalina sparkling bay to the next.[16] A 1969 UCLA study of the village of Nájquqar at Isthmus Cove determined that this site served as a distribution center for island-mainland trade goods. Burials in this village contained a steatite pipe and abalone shells, both typical of island burials, but others contained European glass beads, iron knives, and food items that came from the mainland. One burial included poignant evidence of mainland interactions: two bullet holes in a skull.[17]

Catalina has seven species (or subspecies) of plants found nowhere else on the planet and about thirty[18] that are located only on the Channel Islands. Additionally, there are hundreds of introduced plants that arrived by over-water dispersal, either aboard ships, on shoes, in feed, or by people who brought them to Catalina, including the island Gabrielino. As their use of soapstone indicates, the island Gabrielino knew how to manipulate their resources in order to suit their needs. When they traded island wares for mainland plants and trees, they—like other Channel Island and mainland people—were actively engaged in land management. For instance, in one form or another, Catalina islanders probably imported mainland Indian tobacco that they used ceremonially and as medicine, as well as plants they favored for making baskets.[19]

In addition to Catalina's native plants, the island has five endemic mammals (two types of mouse, a squirrel, a shrew, and a fox), two native salamanders, a native frog, and three single-island endemic bird subspecies. Of course, the ecology of the island is much more diverse than this, as many plants and animals found Catalina so welcoming that they have outcompeted native species. Such was the case with introduced sheep, goats, pigs, rats, and any number of plants.

In 1542 when Cabrillo "discovered" Santa Catalina Island, about five hundred people[20] are thought to have lived there. Though he did not make note of it in his ship's log, had Cabrillo done so he would have perhaps described the autonomous village sites located all across the island in coastal, ridgeline, riparian, and valley terrains. He might have written that related individuals made up each village, with the largest located at Little Harbor on the western shore, Two Harbors at the isthmus, and Avalon on the northeast side of the island. Nearly four hundred years after the island Gabrielino paddled their *ti'ats* out to greet Cabrillo, the CIBS researchers would camp at one of the village sites Cabrillo failed to note: Johnson's Landing at Emerald Bay, located just a few headlands north of the isthmus.

When Sebastián Vizcaíno arrived at Pimu on the feast day of the martyred Saint Catherine of Alexandria, the Spanish explorer did two things that earned him a place in Channel Islands history. First, he named the island Santa Catalina in the martyred saint's honor. Second, he recorded his visit, thus becoming the first white man to document his stopover on Catalina since Cabrillo had arrived sixty years prior. Some scholars believe that merchant sailors who loaded their Manila galleons with goods they traded between Mexico and the Philippines likely set foot on the island in the interim, but no written record of this exists. Regardless, European visitors introduced diseases to the native people that they had never experienced before.

During the island Gabrielino's last years on Catalina Island, they found themselves with fewer trading partners, as native tribes had become smaller on both the Channel Islands and the mainland—thus, the need for island goods diminished. By 1820, and perhaps as early as 1810, no island Gabrielino remained on Santa Catalina.[21] It's possible that they died at the hands of armed Aleut otter hunters, but their decline was also certainly attributed to horrible deaths caused by cholera, rabies, smallpox, and venereal diseases for which they had no immunity. In the end, the few remaining Catalina Gabrielino—discouraged, lacking trading partners, sick, and grieving the loss of so many loved ones—left the island with the mission fathers.

At this point, Catalina, being a mostly unpeopled island, became an ideal spot for smugglers. Traders avoided paying customs duty on their cargo by offloading parts of it onto the island and then smuggling the balance to the mainland later. Chinese immigrants also found refuge and subsistence here, and during Prohibition bootleggers stashed alcohol in various caves and other difficult-to-find locations.

In 1846, two years prior to the Treaty of Guadalupe Hidalgo, in which Mexico ceded the Southwest (including California) to the United States, the Golden State's last Mexican governor, Pio Pico, transferred Catalina to a Santa Barbara resident. Purportedly, the price set for the exchange was one fast horse on which he could escape the approaching U.S. Army.[22] This transfer began a series of island sales whose owners transformed Catalina from a wild island into a resort destination.

In 1891, the Banning brothers, sons of stagecoach baron and founder of the Port of Los Angeles Phineas Banning, purchased Catalina after the prior owner defaulted on his debt. Over the next twenty plus years, they succeeded in making Avalon a tourist destination, but a fire in 1915 that destroyed half of the city (including six hotels), together with the decline in tourism after World War I, saw the Banning's fortunes diminish. By 1919, the island changed hands again.

During the next fifty years, the new owner, William Wrigley Jr., transformed Santa Catalina into the tourism attraction it is today. He improved the island's infrastructure, increased transportation options, built a mansion on Mount Ada overlooking Avalon Harbor (which today serves as an exclusive bed and breakfast), transferred his Chicago Cubs' spring training to Catalina, and in May 1929, the year the Great Depression struck, completed the island's iconic round, red-roof-tiled casino.

During Hollywood's heyday, Catalina earned a reputation for being the place to be and be seen. The Magic Isle became a favorite haunt of movie stars and other famous personalities. Charlie Chaplin, Clarke Gable, Groucho Marx, Marilyn Monroe, John Wayne, and many others came to dance to big bands playing at the casino and fish big game species such as swordfish and tuna. Zane Grey built a pueblo-style home in the hills above Avalon where he wrote, dreamed, and relaxed, and General George Patton summered in Avalon as a child.

Furthermore, it wasn't just the stars that came to Catalina—the production staff came as well. Over two hundred documentaries, television programs, and commercials, as well as three hundred films, have been shot on Catalina Island. Included in this list is the 1925 movie *The Vanishing American*, based on Zane Grey's book of the same title. As part of this western's backdrop, fourteen American bison were imported to Catalina. While the bovines' chances of stardom fizzled when their scenes were left on the cutting room's floor, two hundred of their progeny remain free to roam Catalina Island and have become a tourist attraction in and of themselves. For many years, the restaurant at Catalina's airstrip was one of the few places that served buffalo burgers, a menu staple to this day.

During World War II, Catalina was closed to tourism because the military used Avalon, Two Harbors, and Toyon Bay for training. They also set up a radar communications tower in the interior of the island and practiced underwater demolitions in Emerald Bay. However, tourism returned to Catalina after the war, its Hollywood allure still intact.

In an incident harkening back to Catalina's smuggling days, in 1972 a group of Latino activists raised the Mexican flag on the island. They supported their revolt by invoking the Treaty of Guadalupe Hidalgo, which did not mention the island's transfer to the United States. Thus, they claimed Santa Catalina for Mexico, effectively "smuggling" the island's forty-two thousand acres back into its mother country. For its part, Mexico did not respond nor attempt to repatriate any of California's offshore islands, and the "rebellion" ended without incident.

In the same year, William Wrigley Jr.'s son, Philip Wrigley, established the Catalina Island Conservancy, whose mission is stewardship of the island through conservation, education, and recreation. When he deeded nearly 90 percent of Catalina to the conservancy three years later, the island's current (unofficial) role as an ambassador for all the Channel Islands began. Today, one million people annually visit this lovely island. They arrive by ferry, private boat, airplane, or helicopter, most of them destined for either Avalon (with just under four thousand residents) or Two Harbors (a town of three hundred year-round residents). Few visitors take full advantage of Catalina's seventy-six square miles of rugged, mountainous terrain, sprawling hillsides linked by two hundred miles of trails, or aqua and emerald bays. This is not to say that Santa Catalina Island is pristine. It most certainly has changed throughout time, variously being used as ranchland, big game fishing and hunting playground, mooring spot for large and small vessels, and movie set. Introduced goats, buffalo, cattle, pigs, house cats, rats, horses, and mule deer have also altered the natural environment, ravaging native plant and animal populations and, in some areas, causing erosion. While it is true that these uses have affected the other Channel Islands, none of them are tourist destinations in the same way as Catalina. This makes Catalina unique and requires the conservancy to be vigilant in managing human-caused crises such as the one faced in recent decades by the decline of bald eagles and the Santa Catalina Island fox.

Chapter Eighteen

EARLY 1941

"Yugoslavia and Greece Invaded as Hitler Launches Balkan War: 'Your Hour Has Come!' Fuehrer Tells Soldiers. Italy Backs Ally in Push: Rome Closes Frontier and Mines Fiume International Bridge." The German radio announced today that German armies marched into Yugoslavia and Greece at dawn.

—*Los Angeles Times*, April 6, 1941

As Comstock worked out the details of the twelfth expedition, he remained faithful to the need to fully staff each ambitious trip. To achieve that end, he invited both Meadows and Dunkle to participate if their teaching schedules permitted and sent them the island itineraries and dates, never once bringing up anything about Meadows and Comstock's September exchange. Noteworthy, however, is Comstock's casual mention in his correspondence with Meadows that archaeology would not be part of the expedition. If this is a clue pertaining to any past personality rifts, then its insertion may have been Comstock's subtle way of letting the Long Beach lepidopterist know that Woodward would not be participating and Meadows need not be concerned with any "inharmonies."

On the flip side, the director of science felt no need to mention Woodward's absence to Dunkle, an indicator that any strife existed solely between Meadows and Woodward, but he invites Dunkle for an informal conference the next time he visited the museum. What did

Comstock want to talk to Dunkle about privately? Could it be that he wished to provide the Long Beach botanist with both sides of any story that needed sharing? Or was it for another reason? As it turned out, Comstock requested a meeting in order to urge the botanist "to publish a brief" technical description, something Comstock termed a "Latin diagnosis of the new island plants ... [that Dunkle had] described in the last issue [of the *Bulletin of the Southern California Academy of Sciences*]." Comstock wanted his friend and colleague to rightly benefit from the work he had accomplished as part of the CIBS. If Dunkle did not publish soon, Comstock feared "that ... someone [else] may ... give ... [the plants] a Latin diagnosis ... which will result in crediting them with the species."[1] Comstock "was anxious" for Dunkle to write up the diagnosis quickly so he could publish it in the next bulletin. Meryl dutifully complied, and his description of four new subspecies of plants appeared in the September–December 1940 bulletin, just forty-seven days after Comstock made his request.

N. R. Vail (Nathan Russell II, a Santa Rosa Island owner) wrote Comstock in response to the museum's request for a permit to work on Santa Rosa. In it, Vail not only granted the museum permission to work on his island, but also offered the researchers use of saddle horses, room (a cottage outfitted with ample blankets and mattresses), and board. Vail's generosity caused Comstock pause. He would gratefully accept N.R.'s offer of housing and horses, but not the rancher's offer of a cook. To explain, Comstock wrote back to Mr. Vail:

It would really be too much of an imposition for you to furnish our very individualistic group of scientists with their board in view of the fact that they have very strange and irregular goings and comings. In other words, we have found that once one of these naturalists gets on the trail of any particular animal or insect in which he is interested, he forgets all about time. Thus we have learned to accommodate our cooking facilities and schedules to meet these peculiarities. We could not expect any organization to meet these strange requirements. Therefore, with your kind permission, we will furnish the food and cook with our own outfit.[2]

Comstock's response makes clear how well he understood his scientists and their idiosyncrasies. It also brings to mind Dwight Pierce's publication on millipedes, in which he unabashedly admitted that the sight of the larvae of the rare diplopod *Polyxenus latreille* put his heart into "high speed." In his own gracious way, the director of science corroborated the stereotype: scientists are an eccentric bunch.

Upon learning of Arthur Sanger's plans to conduct excavations on San Nicolas Island, Comstock broke from his administrative work to mail off a three-page, single-spaced letter to the Secretary of the Navy in Washington, DC. He wanted the Secretary to radio Arthur Sanger and demand that he halt his activities until such time as his credentials for conducting archaeological excavations under the American Antiquities Act could be ascertained. Two weeks later, Washington responded with the disconsolate news that Sanger had been properly investigated and authenticated "as a representative of the Museum of the American Indian"[3] (located in New York City) and granted permission by the Eleventh Naval District in San Diego to work on the Channel Islands. Further questions were referred to Captain Ravenscroft in that office.

It wasn't long before Ravenscroft, chief of staff of the Eleventh Naval District, sent Comstock a letter informing him that the Smithsonian had received a copy of Comstock's letter and confirmed that permits were granted to no more than one institution at a time. Furthermore, since the LACM held the only valid permit for San Nicolas Island, the CIBS was "entitled to proceed with its program without interference from Mr. Sanger."[4] It must have come as disappointing news that the navy was unable to "obtain any evidence that Mr. Sanger was working on either San Nicolas or San Miguel Island,"[5] despite the fact that Herb Lester had told the CIBS that Sanger had dug on San Miguel. Additionally, the researchers had seen the pothunter's name carved in stone on San Nicolas, and this led them to believe that Sanger was responsible for at least some of the looted sites found on that island. It may have been some consolation that Ravenscroft requested the museum notify the navy if they found future evidence that Sanger was "engaged in any excavations on . . . any . . . island under the jurisdiction of the Navy Department,"[6] but it was not the response Comstock hoped for.

As scheduled, the twelfth expedition got underway on Valentine's Day 1941, though after this little else went according to plan. Deviations began immediately when the researchers—Jack and Ona von Bloeker, George and Ora Willet, Chris Henne, George Kanakoff, Reid Moran, and John Shrader—landed on San Clemente Island in a pelting rainstorm that unexpectedly kept them in naval quarters for the night. Although a pause in the storm allowed staffers to move gear and set up camp next to a stream at Middle Ranch, the good weather did not last and the crew found themselves working in wet garments throughout the week. The rain did not stop twenty-five-year-old botanist Reid Moran from collecting plants along the gravely banks of the seasonal stream near camp, however, and his efforts made their way into print several years later when Meryl Dunkle determined that a specimen Moran found was a new species. To honor him as the collector, Dunkle's 1943 published account named the purple flowering lupine *Lupinus moranii*.

At the end of the first week, under a heavy downpour, Hancock transferred the researchers from San Clemente to Santa Catalina Island, where Lloyd Martin relieved Chris Henne as expedition entomologist. But even though Henne was going home, he wasn't finished collecting. While the researchers set up the Catalina Island camp, Henne pocketed a few live woolly bear larvae (fuzzy black caterpillars of the type children love to pick up and pet), which he reared "to maturity in the Los Angeles Museum laboratory."[7]

Henne expected the woolly bear larvae to emerge from their cocoons as painted tiger moths that would spread their elaborately camouflaged grey, black, and white forewings in glory and flutter their pink-splashed rear wings like confetti in a breeze. He might also have expected Comstock to inspect the pretty moths, some of which may have measured nearly two inches long. Comstock, being an astute lepidopterist, would not only have observed the moths fold their grey primary wings over their abdomens, thus enveloping the pink hind wings until the blush of color was no longer visible, but would have compared them to other tiger moths in the collection, recording the similarities and differences between them. He surely would have considered subtle variations noteworthy, such as the forewings where "almost no trace of . . . black edging of the grey bands" could be seen, or the hind wings where "the broad gray bands edged with darker gray" were "wider than the pink bands"[8] of the same moth found on the mainland. He also certainly would have noticed differences in the striping of the insect's gray thorax (where the wings and legs attach) and in the gray and black patterns of the sense organ at the base of the wings. Comstock's thoughts may have jumped to the series of painted tiger moths Don Meadows collected on Catalina Island during the years he taught school there that he subsequently donated to the museum.

After carefully examining these moths and noting all their differences and similarities, Comstock concluded that the fuzzy black grubs Henne snatched from Catalina Island represented a new subspecies of painted tiger moth. But it was not for Henne that he named the creatures; rather, recognizing that "the first examples of this race ... were collected by Prof. Don Meadows," Comstock found it "altogether fitting ... to designate [them] ... *Arachnis picta* MEADOWSI."[9]

Although Catalina's rains spoiled the researchers' collecting endeavors, CIBS staffers made the best of it—e.g., handlebar-mustachioed Kanakoff "characteristically collect[ed] nearly every animate object that came under his observation,"[10] Willett recorded a new bird species for the island, and John Shrader not only recorded the seemingly "infinite" abundance of soapstone quarries on the island, but also described rock art.

The term "rock art" is used to describe painted images (or pictographs), etched carvings (also called petroglyphs), and cupules, or shallow holes made in rock that are typically cup shaped and nonutilitarian. (Cupules should not be confused with "bowl scars," which are byproducts of manufacturing processes,[11] not artistic endeavors.) Rock art is widely thought of as one of humankind's oldest forms of expression, though what exactly is being communicated is often up for debate. On the Channel Islands, however, rock art is relatively rare. None are located on Anacapa, San Miguel, or Santa Barbara Islands, and less than twenty sites have been found across the other five islands. Within the Channel Islands archipelago, Catalina is uniquely home to the most known rock art sites on any of the islands. In 2009, the Pimu Catalina Island Archaeology Project located a "new" rock art site on Catalina's southwestern coast, near Salta Verde Point. Here, within a thickly vegetated drainage area, the face of an eight-foot-high "boulder is etched with zigzag lines and cross-hatching" in a style reminiscent of rock art found on the mainland's southwestern coast. A cupule element is present in the image of a snake pecked into the top of the boulder, which "in other Southern California tribal areas" is associated with a "girl's puberty ceremony."[12]

In a lengthy letter student archaeologist John Shrader wrote to "Mr. Woodward," he detailed the rock art he saw when he traveled with Lester Smith (the county fire warden who assisted Willet and his wife in January.) In the letter, Shrader described "a boulder on which had been left some unfinished bowls and some pictographs ... made on a steeply overhanging rock" that he judged to have been "long occupied" based on the quantity of "shell debris on the floor." Another site consisted of "only six or eight" images drawn with red pigment "spread over a big dull yellow face of stone." The paintings were "dulling of color," he explained, and "somewhat vague ... [and] simple in design, one being a whirl, several with radiating lines from an undefined central body, and others of simple straight or curved lines" that did not appear to his untrained eye to lie in any particularly important positions. To his credit, Shrader warned Woodward that a "study of them ... should be done fairly soon" because a "danger" of "losing them through ... weathering" existed.[13] Unfortunately, Shrader chose not to make sketches of the rock art he saw, excusing this lapse by explaining that "only a Kodachrome or actual visitation of the site can give one an idea of them." Many an extant scholar would undoubtedly disagree, wishing for even a poorly sketched drawing or dark, grainy photograph.

As with much of Shrader's reporting, the student archaeologist does not provide sufficient details. For example, he did not provide locations for any of the pictographs, only the vague description that he and Smith traveled through the "the Eastern and bigger end of the island"[14] to reach them. Even so, based on his descriptions, it is possible to speculate that the site Smith showed Shrader may be one of three on Catalina's western shore in the vicinity of Little Harbor. One of these, Torqua Cave, is located south and east of Little Harbor and is considered "the most complex rock art site on all the islands."[15] It is unlikely that Shrader saw Torqua Cave, however, because "Shrader's cave" contained only six or eight paintings, compared to "at least 25 red ochre pictographs"[16] featured in Torqua Cave. The other two sites are at Little Harbor, including one that was not "discovered" until 1985. This site consists of three panels of drawings that remain brightly red in color, proving it is also probably not the dull-colored artwork of "Shrader's cave."[17] It is a shame that the sites Shrader visited are still unknown.

As poor as Shrader's specificity was, it is even more disappointing that Woodward did not revisit Santa Catalina Island with Shrader, or at least seek Lester Smith's counsel in tracking down these drawings and documenting them for future research. Sadder, too, knowing that Shrader specifically recommended further investigation of a number of sites, including the Salta Verde area of Catalina that had "been completely untouched and are of appreciable size and depth." To aid Woodward in the future, Shrader even marked a map with two springs in the "Salta Verde Country" where good sites might be found. Maybe one of them contained the cupule boulder found less than a decade ago, or perhaps something else was there. That Woodward did not follow up is another example of a missed opportunity for the CIBS.

After spending a week on Catalina Island, the itinerary called for the researchers to proceed to Santa Barbara Island, only they didn't want to go. Rain had frustrated their Catalina collecting efforts and they sensed their time would be better spent on the larger island instead of the smallest of the Channel Islands. Comstock and von Bloeker corresponded about this potential change of plans, and Comstock was amenable but insisted that Santa Barbara and San Nicolas Islands be dropped from the itinerary so that the overall length of the expedition would remain the same—anything else would require board approval. In some ways, this was a curious requirement on Comstock's part, as in the past he had gladly accommodated itinerary changes, worked hard to put new plans in place, and made the necessary arrangements with permit and transportation providers. But times were different now. Since January, Comstock had been required to work with McKinney on the director-in-charge's plan to downsize the science department. As a result, it was natural that Comstock wanted to avoid drawing any negative attention to his department. Asking the board to amend the survey's already-approved itinerary may have constituted negative attention in Comstock's mind.

However, Comstock could not explain his reasoning to von Bloeker because staff members were not yet aware of McKinney's plan. Had he been so forthright, this sensitive information may have leaked out to others, crushing moral and leading to inefficient operations and an unfortunate self-fulfilling prophecy. As a result, Comstock explained his decision to cut the two islands from the CIBS itinerary by obtusely telling von Bloeker that it "is not good policy to make very many of these requests in a season," and that "it is particularly bad psychology to have it appear that we are continually changing our minds—even through the weather is at fault, rather than our survey party."[18] In this manner, Comstock cannily avoided divulging sensitive information to von Bloeker and prevented the opportunity for even the slightest negative information about his department to reach the board.

The two directors had not seen eye-to-eye for some time, and Comstock could not have been pleased with his boss's plans to dismantle his department, but the director of science could not have denied McKinney's successes. In his first full year on the job, McKinney's results were laudable: an 11 percent increase in annual museum attendance, totaling a whopping 670,000 people. This impressive achievement was a testament to McKinney's abilities and served to garner the favor of the art-loving members of the board of governors. With his management capabilities secure in the eyes of the board, McKinney next intended to siphon funding away from science and toward art and education.

As letters between Comstock and von Bloeker sorting out the itinerary changes sallied back and forth across the Catalina Channel, staffers relocated to Catalina's Middle Ranch, located in the widest part of the island in Middle Canyon. When they arrived in the broad canyon, they found riparian woodland where red willows vied with huge black cottonwoods for space along the streambed, blue elderberry shrubs thickly dotted green hillsides, and large and diverse populations of bird life thrived. Ona von Bloeker may have picked wild blackberries and watercress from the creek bank to serve with meals, and the researchers likely bunked in the abandoned sheep ranch buildings that now belonged to the Santa Catalina Island Company.

Due to a combination of treacherous seas and communications gaffes, the CIBS's plans changed frequently. Before they knew it, three weeks had passed and the decision to drop San Nicolas Island from the itinerary was made. Santa Barbara had already been scratched.

In what little written documentation exists about the twelfth expedition's third operation on Anacapa Island, no mention of rain impeding their work is made. This does not mean, however, that conditions were entirely satisfactory. George Willett accurately pointed out that "the only available campsite" was located in a "niche isolated by impassible cliffs from the larger part of the island." This small area, he complained, "contained almost no birds of interest." To overcome this handicap, the researchers used a rowboat to get around, but even this proved insufficient when "the wind was so strong that" they "were unable to use the boat to advantage," and therefore "opportunities for collecting"[19] were limited.

On some days, ocean conditions were treacherous, and winds high. If this wasn't enough to deter the ornithologist from taking the rowboat out to sea, surely any knowledge of the "incident" that threatened the lives of three CIBS's researchers during the ninth expedition the previous summer would have. Only a brief letter typed by Meadows describes what happened that day. Around four thirty in the afternoon on August 23, 1940, he and the others working at Fish Camp spotted three of the researchers motoring toward them from the sea. Expecting their arrival within the half hour, they lost themselves in their normal afternoon activities. The summer skies would have been darkening by eight o'clock when they noticed that their colleagues had never arrived. Immediately their thoughts jumped to the dangerous reef located at the west end of Anacapa, where hazardous currents made travel difficult even on the fairest of days. The researchers knew their colleagues would need to pass through this perilous stretch of water in order to land, and it caused everyone to become alarmed. Their concern would only have been heightened by the blast of strong northeast winds and the high seas that pounded the shore.

The anxious CIBS staff consulted with Frenchy LeDreau, concluding they needed to contact the lighthouse keeper. This task entailed using one of Frenchy's boats to motor or row some three miles to the lighthouse situated on the plateau on the far eastern side of East Anacapa. Once they reached the islet, they had to perform a tricky dock connection before beginning their ascent on concrete steps leading to the top of the 100–225-foot cliffs. (Today, visitors still have to scale 157 stairs to reach the island's one-hundred-acre flat plateau.) By now any remnants of sunlight were gone, and though the lighthouse was close, depending on the night's blackness and whether or not they thought to bring torches with them, they needed to take care not to stray from the path or they would risk falling to their deaths like one lighthouse keeper had the decade prior.

When they reached the beacon, they found the lighthouse keeper, Mr. Allen, asleep, but they woke him up. Allen wasted no time before "radiophoning" the mainland lighthouse at Point Vicente (on the Palos Verdes Peninsula) to apprise them of the situation and order the U.S. Coast Guard vessel *Anacapa* to affect a rescue. Together with his second officer, Allen set out to find the lost researchers.

No one knew precisely where to look for the scientists, and no one knew that their colleagues' motor had become disabled when their boat swamped. Without power, the men were left adrift in the Anacapa passage, a treacherous channel where water and winds collide to create high seas, irregular swells, and unpredictable currents. Imagine the shouts and calls the boys must have yelled out to their colleagues on shore when they first realized their craft was unresponsive. How awful it must have felt to be ignored, but there was nothing else they could do—their voices would not carry through the wind and wash.

It took the marooned researchers several hours before they managed to pull themselves up onto some rocks abutting the island's unforgiving shoreline at its west end. Better there, of course, than to spend the night at sea in a swamped, open boat. Still, they must have wondered where their fellow researchers were. Why had their absence gone unnoticed? What was taking them so long? Was the tide rising or falling? If it was rising, should they stay on the rocks and risk the tide swallowing the outcropping, or get back in the boat and hold on as it was swept back out to sea?

With the night fully fallen, they must have been wet and bathed in cold darkness as they sat and waited. They may have even been scared, though surely none of them would have admitted as much. It is unknown which of the CIBS staff were stuck on those rocks that night, except for one clue suggesting George Kanakoff may have been among them: the lighthouse keeper sent his greetings to the staff and to Kanakoff, specifically, when he replied to Comstock's letter of appreciation for his rescue of the staff. The rescue would have been the only opportunity for Kanakoff and Allen to have met.

If, indeed, "Uncle George" was marooned on those rocks, he would likely have attempted to allay the others' fears, spoken or not. He may have used his theatrical talents, perhaps singing to them in Russian,

Turkish, Tartar, Montenegro, or Sart, singing until they begged him to stop. His antics would have made the others doubly happy when, at midnight, the *Anacapa* appeared to rescue them.

In the third week of March, Meadows sent Comstock a letter requesting permission for Dunkle, Reddick, Sprong, and himself to join the survey beginning April 5, sweetening the petition by offering to pay for any increased food costs. This request makes it clear that Meadows's aspirations had not waned—he still wanted to participate in the CIBS. For his part, Comstock was amenable to Meadow's request, though he wisely asked for von Bloeker's opinion[20] before replying to Meadows and letting him know that the museum would absorb any additional costs due to their participation. All in all, Comstock's willingness to accommodate the Long Beach gang was an indication that though Don Meadows's participation in the survey may have lost ground over the past few months, their participation was still welcomed.

The board of governors met on March 20, 1941, and this time McKinney was ready to discuss his report "fixing" the "policy and the scope of the activities of the Science Division."[21] The report, prepared by the members of the science committee (including Comstock), specified that "the territory to be embraced in the activities of the Science Division shall include, 'first ... Los Angeles County and it adjacent zonal areas, and, second ... the Pacific littoral."[22] It further called out the "pivotal" role Rancho La Brea, today known as the La Brea Tar Pits, would play "in developing the earth sciences."[23] Science department employees, the report stated, would be required to create and participate in educational activities with "wide public appeal,"[24] and any work performed outside of the scope spelled out by the proposal would have to be done on an individual's own time. If put into place, McKinney's proposal would curtail Woodward's trips to Arizona and New Mexico as well as von Bloeker's forays north to the mouth of the Salinas River in Monterey County or into the Sierra Nevada Mountains to follow in his mentor, Joseph Grinnell's, footsteps. But for the moment, the inclusion of the terms "adjacent zonal areas" and "Pacific littoral" indicated that the Channel Islands Biological Survey escaped intact.

When the report had been read in full, McKinney interjected his satisfaction with the policy's local focus and logical use of "the La Brea material as the point of departure"[25] for the future activities of the Department of Science. At that point, he may have dipped his considerable double chin and bowed his balding pate in a sort of nod to indicate he was done and that he would wait for either the governors' input or, more pointedly, approval. Although the board agreed that the proposal would make the museum "the unique institution it should and may become,"[26] without a quorum, no vote was taken.

The twelfth expedition continued when the fourth operation moved from Anacapa to Pelican Bay, Santa Cruz Island. It was the survey's second visit to this island.

Woodward continued to mail Shrader weekly written instructions. This week's letters tasked the young man with talking to Herb Lester about archaeological looters once the survey was on San Miguel. Woodward wrote in great depth about the navy's request to have pothunters reported to them, and he provided Shrader with significant information about two men who might claim to be representatives of the National Museum of the American Indian in New York City. He instructed Shrader to tell Lester both "to hold up on any digging" if the two men appeared and to "obtain an official okay from the 11th Naval District"[27] before allowing them to do any work on San Miguel. It was quite a responsibility to hand over to a student. Perhaps the task should have been directed to von Bloeker, the expedition's leader, but Woodward apparently thought nothing of it, genially scribing in closing, "Best of luck fella in your work. You should be quite experienced by the time you return."[28]

After spending eight nights on Santa Cruz, Santa Rosa was next. Preceding the researchers by about a month were a team of nine civilian engineers and surveyors who were sent by U.S. government officials with the aim of examining Santa Rosa Island's "long westerly coastline" that made it suitable "as an anti-aircraft station [because] ... Radio facilities could give warning of enemy approach."[29] The contractors' immediate goals were to start the planning process for building a lookout station and a road that would circumnavigate the entire island, infrastructure deemed capable of "supply[ing] advance information of any naval or aerial attack on the Coast." The military's interest in this near-shore island demonstrates the level of concern the government felt for the populace's safety. Although they were gone before the researchers landed on the

Mysterious Island, their visit would surely have been the subject of speculation when employees of Vail and Vickers came to visit the researchers'
nightly campfires.

The scientists spent eleven nights on Santa Rosa before returning to
the mainland on April 9, and in hindsight their itinerary looked nothing like it had at the onset. Meadows and Dunkle had never joined the
expedition, and the CIBS had not visited San Miguel, Santa Barbara,
or San Nicolas. So much had changed since the February onset of the
survey, and Comstock's only explanation was that "the very stormy condition prevailing for the past eight weeks" made it "impossible to effect
landings"[30] on the three skipped islands—an explanation that was as
unsatisfactory as it was unlikely. The only consolation for the foreshort-
ened expedition was "a new deposit of Pleistocene fossils,"[31] which soon
enough would lure the group back to the Mysterious Island.

Chapter Nineteen

BACK AT THE MUSEUM

"U.S. Forms Civilian Raid Warning Service." The war department announced today immediate formation of a nation wide aircraft warning service to include 500,000 volunteer civilians. Observers termed the move "another step in real preparedness for a possible emergency."

—*Honolulu Star-Bulletin*, April 17, 1941

The board of governors held their regular meeting in mid-April with Colonel Wayne Russell Allen, Los Angeles County's first chief administrative officer, sitting in special attendance. Allen began his career with the county as a purchasing agent in 1936, and after just one year on the job his savvy negotiating skills contributed to county savings that totaled hundreds of thousands of dollars. In the photograph accompanying his Los Angeles County online bio, Allen's closed-mouth smile spans the growing fullness of his face, almost (but not quite) easing the directness of his gaze. He wears a uniform bearing the epaulet of a brigadier general, the rank he attained during World War II when he was in charge of purchasing supplies for the military and Red Cross in the European Theater—budget overruns be damned.

The day's meeting agenda featured a vote on the plan developed under McKinney's direction and presented in the March meeting that proposed limiting the science department's scope. With no further discussion and a quorum present, the board approved it, swiftly moving on to McKinney's budget request, a sum that exceeded the prior year's by 20 percent. Allen had already studied McKinney's numbers and informed the director-in-charge that no increase in budget from the prior year would be granted. To address the budget shortage, the two met several times before Allen requested to appear before the board of governors and propose their joint plan. This all suited McKinney very well, as the director-in-charge could use a man of penny-pinching genius to accomplish his own agenda while maintaining a veneer of even-handed objectiveness for himself.

After being given the floor, Allen presented the plan he and McKinney had crafted. It packed a punch, promising to trim the budget to within allowable limits and also better "the institution as a whole."[1] He began by recommending that the institution drop the words "History, Science, and Art" from its name, leaving only "Los Angeles County Museum" as a "less cumbersome" title. Devious in its simplicity, this recommendation fit perfectly within the centerpiece of the complete reorganization he and McKinney had dreamed up: a streamlined institution requiring only one director responsible for five divisions—business management, maintenance, education, exhibits, and art instruction. The details required the Department of Art Instruction to absorb the Otis Art Institute and to completely eliminate the Departments of History and Science while simultaneously demoting their directors to "Curators and their assistants [to] Curatorial Assistants."[2] Additionally, Allen said "the character of the work carried on by"[3] the employees within the current departments would change because workers in the new Divisions of Education and Exhibits would focus their efforts on interpreting for the public "the wealth of material acquired in the past years."[4]

Budget relief gained through "abolishing . . . five positions in the Science Division, one in the History Division and one in the Art Division"[5] also played a central role in accomplishing their plan. As Allen explained earlier in the meeting, once those positions were eliminated, "the money released . . . would be available for use in the new field of Exhibition,"[6] which "would absorb a certain number of employees."[7]

On the whole, the plan Allen laid out fit perfectly with McKinney's agenda—it reorganized the museum, demoted his strongest opponents, and limited those opponents' scope of work. This coup not only achieved McKinney's goals but also distanced him from the messy details. However, the board did not approve Allen's plan during the meeting, instead requesting a special committee to study it and report back as soon as possible.

On the same day the board of governors met, von Bloeker wrote Raymond Hall, his former boss at the Museum of Vertebrate Zoology (MVZ) at Berkeley, who at that time held the prestigious title "curator of mammals." Like von Bloeker himself, Hall studied as a graduate student under naturalist Joseph Grinnell and was considered one of Grinnell's brightest students. Over the years, von Bloeker maintained a professional relationship with Hall, exchanging information and sharing specimens, but the tone he employed when he wrote Hall about the twelfth expedition seemed out of place. In the letter, von Bloeker boasts that the "expedition to the islands [was] . . . quite successful considering the 'tough' weather" and that "despite almost daily rain or wind" he "collected nearly a thousand vertebrates in . . . eight weeks." He also brags that "there should be some interesting papers forthcoming from the result of this survey."[8] Von Bloeker's bold assertion could have been an attempt to elevate himself—and his institution—to Hall's and the MVZ's level. Or, it is possible that rumors of reorganization and staff cuts had filtered down into the ranks and he was currying Hall's favor in case he needed a job or recommendation in the future. McKinney had been talking of reorganization since early 1941, and matters such as these have a habit of trickling out from behind closed doors.

If this were the case, von Bloeker did not dwell on it. Instead he buried himself in his beloved laboratory, unpacking specimens, sorting, comparing, and seeking out the fantastic. And he certainly found it, though not in the manner he would have expected. His next big discovery arrived special delivery courtesy the U.S. Postal Service: one dead shrew, collected by Miss Ruth B. Eaton, a schoolteacher in Avalon on Santa Catalina Island. Wrapped up, packaged, shipped, and hardly dead, it was the first shrew seen, collected, or definitively discovered on any Channel Island. The shrew's arrival would have come as a huge surprise to von Bloeker. He may well have put out his cigarette before picking up the darkly colored, long-tailed beauty and muttering, "Damn, Willett. You were right."

During the course of many discussions and planning meetings pertaining to the museum's Channel Islands expeditions, George Willett "predicted that shrews would be found on one or more of the larger islands, such as Santa Catalina and Santa Cruz." Even so, von Bloeker "confess[ed] that, although" he "was familiar enough with the topography of the islands to know that certainly there appeared no valid reason why shrews could not exist there," he was "still skeptical that one would ever be found on any of the Channel Islands."[9] Von Bloeker was wrong.

In his 1941 paper describing the new species of shrew, von Bloeker provides delightful background to this discovery. He recounts Miss Eaton's letter, in which she wrote that "she had a small animal which had been captured alive in Avalon Canyon and that she thought it might be a shrew."[10] The poor thing "refused to eat in captivity and appeared to be becoming weak," she explained, promising that "if it died she would send it to the museum for identification. Apparently the animal died soon thereafter, because her letter arrived at 10 A.M. and the shrew at noon of the same day."[11]

So, what did von Bloeker do with his present? What any self-respecting biologist would do: he gutted and skinned the thing, preparing it "as a study skin—with skull."[12] He then examined the four-inch long critter, analyzing it and comparing it to others before diagnosing it as a new species, a determination that gave him naming rights. In the same 1941 paper, he wrote that it was "a pleasure" for him to name the shrew "in honor of the man who predicted its existence," his "good friend and counselor, George Willett."[13] By the time von Bloeker published "Land Mammals of the Southern California Islands" in 1967, he had reexamined Miss Eaton's shrew and determined that *Sorex willetti* was not a separate species at all, but a subspecies of the mainland shrew.

Shrews on the Channel Islands remain rare. More than a decade passed after von Bloeker's first publication before another shrew was sighted on Catalina Island, and by 2002 only nine had been seen or collected. Since then, due largely to the institution of the U.S. Geological Survey's animal monitoring project, shrew sightings have risen to about forty, yet despite Willett's predictions all have been on Catalina Island.

While von Bloeker analyzed the shrew, the special committee tasked with evaluating Allen's budget proposal had a meeting. When the board of governors convened in late April, that committee was prepared to deliver its recommendations for the shrewish evisceration of the Departments of History and Science. The committee endorsed eliminating fifteen positions, only twelve of which would be absorbed by the Divisions of Education and Exhibits. Money for these retained employees would be appropriated in the budget until the end of the fiscal year (June 30, 1941), and if McKinney determined their "ability to deliver lectures, and prepare and give out materials in accordance with the Director's instructions"[14] were "competent," they could "be retained as museum instructors."[15] Allen and a member of the Los Angeles County Board of Supervisors entered the meeting while the governors discussed the implications of the committee's report, and he must have been pleased when the votes were cast unanimously in favor of the cuts. Implementation would begin July 1, the start of LACM's fiscal year.

Talk around the stainless laboratory worktables and office coffee pots must have been bleak during those days. The museum's handwritten employment records outline the demotions: Comstock and Woodward were downgraded from directors to curators and von Bloeker went from curator to assistant museum taxidermist. Comstock termed it "the precarious budget situation,"[16] but von Bloeker flatly stated that there was "little left [at the museum] toward making any real accomplishment in science."[17]

Faced with a demotion, an unrewarding future, and most likely an unwillingness to risk being unemployed (as he had been during the depths of the Great Depression), von Bloeker sought work elsewhere. He applied for a position as assistant curator at the Smithsonian and wasted no time reaching out to his colleagues—Comstock, Hall, and Alden Miller, director of the MVZ—for letters of recommendation. In support of his colleague, in the letter Comstock posted to the Smithsonian he used superlatives such as "very competent . . . in the laboratory and field," "an indefatigable worker," and "a distinct loss to my staff."[18] Hall, curator of mammals at the MVZ, was slightly less enthusiastic, but he assured von Bloeker that he considered his qualifications for the job to be "very high." He also told his former employee that he could "count on" his "appraisal being one that would do" him "no discredit."[19]

Hall's boss, Alden Miller, was not of the same persuasion, however, a fact he disclosed to von Bloeker in writing. Because Miller had already written a letter of recommendation for another applicant, he felt that a subsequent letter from him on von Bloeker's behest would be "viewed as of secondary rank."[20] Nevertheless, if von Bloeker thought "it would be diplomatic and in" his best "interests,"[21] he would write to the Smithsonian and "speak favorably of" von Bloeker's "qualifications."[22]

Von Bloeker must have felt like a mouse crushed in a trap when he received Miller's letter. The MVZ director's sponsorship could make the difference between winning or losing the job. It was imperative that he receive Miller's support. When von Bloeker learned that the Smithsonian would soon have three positions open, not just one, von Bloeker put aside his ego and asked Miller to write that letter of recommendation, regardless of whether the director found him to "place second, third, or even lower in the list of available men." The request sounded desperate, but he would only need to "place among the first three" to "secure a position where" he could "be a credit to the professors and institution responsible for" his "scientific training."[23] He dearly wanted that job.

Miller complied, placing von Bloeker second to the other applicant, Dr. David H. Johnson from the MVZ. Miller did praise von Bloeker's "energy and enthusiasm" but tempered his admiration, noting "his academic background is not as extensive as Johnson's," though "it is good." He closed his letter to the Smithsonian by writing that the LACM applicant was a "decidedly alert and competent mammalogist."[24]

The job went to Miller's man.

Chapter Twenty

HUE AND CRY

"U.S. Ties Up Japan's Funds, Oil and Ships: All Exports Placed under Licensing; $131,000,000 in Holdings to Be Seized Today." President Roosevelt struck back today against Japan for her push in French Indo-China by an executive order clamping a sweeping control on all economic intercourse between the United States and Japan, and freezing Japanese cash, oil ships, silk and other assets.

—*San Francisco Examiner*, July 26, 1941

By late April, the news was out. The *Santa Monica Evening Outlook* was among the first to cover the museum's reorganization, which it characterized as an "attempt to make the museum strictly an educational institution" that "would eliminate or drastically reduce the research staff" and leave the research collection unavailable to other scientists.[1] The Los Angeles County Board of Supervisors was besieged by hundreds of letters protesting the dismantling of the Departments of History and Science at the LACM. Letters arrived from a variety of people including: a reverend; an archivist and historian; the head cataloger of the USC library; owners of construction, hotel, and music companies; bankers; insurance underwriters; professors of anthropology, biology, and geology from UCLA, USC, LA City College, and others; U.S. Park Service employees; surgeons; newspaper editors; electrical lighting contractors; garden clubs; audubon societies throughout the west; museum curators; the Conchological

Club; the California Fruit Growers Exchange; the Wilmington Taxpayers Association; citizens, science teachers, and teacher associations; historical societies; the Native Daughters of the Golden West; the Sierra Club; chambers of commerce; manufacturing associations; mineral clubs; cub scout troops; the Department of California United Spanish War Veterans; members of the Unitarian Fellowship for Social Justice; the president of the Society of Motion Picture Engineers of Eastman Kodak Company; and so many more. They wrote and wrote and wrote.

Return addresses for these letters read: Bakersfield, California; the Old Mission, Santa Barbara; the San Diego Natural History Museum in Balboa Park; Stanford University Zoological Collections; the Steinhart Aquarium, California Academy of Sciences, in Golden Gate Park, San Francisco; Eastern Washington College of Education; the Brooklyn Museum, Brooklyn Institute of Arts and Sciences; the Canadian Department of Agriculture in Ottawa; and, of course, various places throughout the greater Los Angeles area. The letters arrived for months.

A. W. Bell, chairman of the life sciences department at Los Angeles City College and von Bloeker's old friend and mentor, submitted one of the first letters of protest. Signed by ten other staff members, Bell politely objected to the curatorial staff's transformation into docents while lauding the existing science department's importance to the students of Los Angeles City College. He stated, "No other city institution contributes as many useful demonstrations to supplement the teaching in our science classes,"[2] thereby not only complimenting the science department but also subtly criticizing the duplicity of McKinney's new education department with the work the science department had already been carrying out. He closed his letter by reminding the board of supervisors "that in a time of war if there is any aspect of our culture that must not be impaired it is science."[3]

Not all letters were as decorous as Bell's, however. Many railed against McKinney's exorbitant $10,000 salary, "limited" thinking, and single-minded obsession with creating an art museum. In a "Town Talk" column featured in the *Los Angeles Illustrated Daily News*, the newspaper's managing editor, a well-known columnist, leveled that the museum's reorganization "jeopardizes the research of 25 years . . . [and is] guided by the $10,000 a year museum director, a man untrained in science and history, but supported by the board of supervisors."[4] Mistrust over McKinney's motives and disgruntlement about his salary—double that of comparable civil servants with equal qualifications—enraged the populace. Other letters faulted the board of supervisors for dismantling a world-class science museum in favor of art alone, expressing "grave alarm" over a "rash act." They were "perturbed" and "shocked," filled with "consternation" over the "inexplicable," "unwise," and "sad state of affairs" the board of supervisors had plunged the county into. Curtailment of science at the LACM was a "major catastrophe," a "great public loss," and a "grave blow" that was "extremely detrimental to the public good." The whole thing was "tragic."[5]

The volume of letters, the diversity of citizenry, and the public's indignation continued to rise like steam rushing from the stacks on the *Queen Mary's* deck. The torrent of objections led the board of governors to reassess the reorganization, and at the end of May they met to consider the protests. A member of the board of supervisors and the county council attended that meeting, as did several organizations protesting the board's actions. But seeing the gathered crowd, the board of governors dismissed the visitors and adjourned into executive session where, in private, the letters of protest were read aloud. The public's antipathy toward the reorganization became quite clear and made the board so uncomfortable with the previously approved cuts that they resolved to reconsider the matter entirely.

A motion to establish a new committee composed of a much larger group of distinguished board members passed, with nine in favor and five (including the board's president, Rufus B. von KleinSmid) opposed. The executive committee meeting ended and the general meeting resumed, reopening to visitors who occupied the governors' time until well past their usual adjournment hour.

The trouble with the board of governor's decision to reevaluate was that they were too late—the board of supervisors had already acted based on the board's earlier approval of Allen's proposal. As of July 1, the cuts were law and the title changes (approved through the civil service process) were effective. Thus, they really could not change a thing, which put the board of governors in a pickle. Nevertheless, over the next few months, the special committee met on several occasions, but the issue was complicated and no final report was made.

As the esteemed board of governors fumbled with this budget fiasco, a nearly deadly incident occurred on the third floor of the museum.

The issue was so serious that in his explanatory letter to the chairman of the board of governors McKinney included the text of Matt Weinstock's "Town Talk" column from the *Los Angeles Illustrated Daily News*.[6] Weinstock first derided McKinney as a "$10,000 a year museum director, a man untrained in science and history," and claimed that his reorganization was "a step toward tearing away the scientific foundations of the museum."[7] After finishing his rant, Weinstock then explained that the former curators of conchology and sciences—who had lost their positions in the reorganization—were offered, and accepted, jobs "as museum helpers—$100 a month jobs—equivalent to janitors,"[8] and that they were expected to control pests and preserve the collection by conducting normal fumigation of the botany collection. Clearly supportive of the "janitors" and the humiliating position they had been forced into, he wrote, "being inexperienced in such matters, the fumigators failed to take proper precautions and cyanide gas swept through a wing of the building." He then closed the article with the biting remark that "it can kill, you know, in a museum the same as in San Quentin's gas chamber."[9]

McKinney must have cringed when he read this damning newspaper column, another blow to his reputation already battered by the press and populace for his reorganization plans. But because of the incident's severity, he had no choice but to apprise the chairman of it. He must have given the delivery of this news some thought, for he wrote his memo rather foxily, cannily avoiding any culpability while also offering a solution. He began by assuring the chairman that he had initiated an investigation into the incident, which had ascertained that the procedures followed had been in place since 1934, long before his arrival at the museum. Secondly, to avoid recurrence, McKinney recommended that a "County Purchasing Agent" be contracted to engage future fumigation services from a "licensed commercial fumigator." "As a further aftermath of the episode,"[10] McKinney informed the chairman, he had been summoned to appear before the city attorney in connection with a criminal charge filed by the former director of history and anthropology—none other than Arthur Woodward. Woodward had complained to the "City Attorney of the Los Angeles Criminal Division" that "in substance and effect" McKinney was "connected with an alleged violation of . . . Los Angeles Municipal Code[:] . . . Fumigating without giving notice to Health Officers."[11]

The Los Angeles County Museum Beaux Arts Building. Courtesy of NHM Archives.

McKinney was surely furious at Woodward's audacity and blatant attempt to embroil him in a criminal matter. It was an attack that could tear him down professionally and personally, but would he seek retribution?

Continuing his decry of the science department's dismantlement, A. W. Bell wrote an article that appeared in *Science*, a highly regarded scholarly journal. In it he asserted, "the staffs in history and science ... [have been] drastically cut by a system of transfers. Demotions of the professional and technical personnel ... [have been] made in all divisions.... There have been no hearings, no impartial investigations." He declared that the museum had become an institution of "exhibitions, art instructions and 'education'" that primarily provided instruction for schools, a function, he attested, that the departments of history and science had performed satisfactorily in the past.[12]

If there had been any question about the museum's reorganization attracting national attention before, this article in *Science* ensured that museums, academics, and governmental agencies everywhere knew about it. It must have displeased McKinney enormously when he received that article from the news clipping service he employed to track his publicity. Not a single copy of this article, or any having to do with the reorganization he orchestrated at the LACM, are included in his files that were donated to the Smithsonian Archives of American Art.

Chapter Twenty-One

AN UNMEETING OF MINDS

"U.S. Destroyer Sunk: Warship Torpedoed on Convoy Duty
West of Iceland." The United States Navy today had lost its first
warship in action since the war started—the destroyer Reuben
James, which was carrying about 120 officers and men. She
was sunk by a torpedo, presumably German.

—*Brooklyn Eagle* (New York), October 31, 1941

During the last weeks of September, Director McKinney called together
Comstock, von Bloeker, Willett, Stock, Howard, and Pierce—representatives of the science department at large, mammals, birds, Rancho La
Brea, fossil birds, and insects, respectively—to discuss continuation of the
"work in the Channel Islands."[1] No one from the Departments of History
or Anthropology attended. This absence is not mentioned anywhere in
the meeting minutes, suggesting that Woodward's department had been
purposefully left out, potentially at McKinney's behest.

   As the group gathered that afternoon to take their seats or pace about
with lit cigarettes, their exhalations burdening the room with smoke,
most must have shared a silent kinship of defeat. Their departments had
been pared down and their people demoted. The pervading feeling must
have been that senior management didn't give a damn about their contributions to science. Some may have glanced clandestinely at one another
and then with veiled contempt at the director-in-charge, while others
may merely have reached across the table to pour themselves a cup of

coffee in preparation for getting on with it. Upon opening the meeting, McKinney made no mention of the many changes he'd wrought at the museum; rather, he simply expressed his desire to discuss plans for continued work on the Channel Islands because "no expedition had been sent out since April, 1941."[2] He then asked Comstock to offer his thoughts.

Bearing the new, lower title of curator of science, Comstock addressed his male and female colleagues—all of whom had suffered similar degradation—with meticulously conceived remarks. He opened by saying that the museum must proceed with caution when mounting any new expeditions "in view of the present situation"[3] (i.e., the reorganization). He explained that when the CIBS first launched, the museum had been fully staffed (other than geology), and that this allowed them to develop a detailed expedition plan and secure governmental and other required permits. This was no longer the case, however, and if the museum were to "announce ... plans to continue a biological survey" such as the one they had originally initiated, they would "lay themselves open to criticism."[4] He explained that this was because a botany department and an entomological field force are essential disciplines when properly conducting full-scale expeditions. As a result, he urged that future work should proceed through small, focused field studies intended to mop up prior expeditions' unfinished business. If Comstock's recommendation feels a far cry from the glorious undertaking begun less than three years before, it is. But make no mistake, Comstock spoke purposefully.

When McKinney asked for clarification about the role of botany and entomology, Comstock obtusely replied, "an expedition cannot be conducted ... covering the field of biology, without a botanist capable of quick determination of the plants."[5] The curator of science could easily have explained to McKinney that plants and insects are fundamental to understanding any ecosystem, and that their sheer number and diversity means they play an important role in nourishing the larger environment and therefore in creating ecosystems. But he did not, and McKinney asked for no further explanations.

Comstock then turned his comments toward staffing issues for the next expedition, announcing that "if archaeology is excluded" where it "is extremely important ... [such as on] Santa Rosa Island," the museum "would be exceedingly weak" in its "organization and open to criticism."[6] Comstock was not speaking hypothetically about an improbable future situation, but about one that had already occurred. To wit, McKinney had called that day's meeting and excluded any representative from the Departments of History and Anthropology, including Woodward. He had also excluded history and anthropology from the CIBS entirely.

Although Comstock said little more about this during the September science meeting, a month later he railed against the director's decision to not only close down the museum's botanical department, but to "exclude anthropological work"[7] from the remainder of the CIBS. It was a decision Comstock denounced as being, "beyond . . . [his] comprehension."[8] Why did McKinney bar archaeology from the CIBS, a board of governors favorite and a draw for the press and the public? Could his actions have represented a retaliation for Woodward's part in enmeshing him in a criminal lawsuit over the cyanide fumigation situation? Although McKinney's motivations will never be known, the overt omission certainly had a reason, however mysterious.

When McKinney attempted to sidestep Comstock's insinuations about archaeology, Comstock ignored him, telling him instead "that scientists throughout the country had been watching this survey with great interest and . . . the National Park Service had been dependent on [the museum's] . . . work . . . in the furtherance of their own." In essence, the world was watching. Comstock concluded by stating, "It would therefore be most inadvisable to issue a lot of publicity . . . on lines in which we were weak" because it would leave the museum "open to much criticism."[9] A month later he underscored this sentiment, warning McKinney that "the scientists in these organizations [the National Park Service and others] cannot be hoodwinked by promises and pretensions,"[10] and that the LACM's "reputation will stand or fall on the basis of the caliber of our personnel, the dignity of organization and the accomplishments of . . . [our] work."[11] Without a doubt, Comstock held that botany, entomology, and archaeology—frankly, all of the sciences—were vital to any fieldwork undertaken by LACM.

Comstock gave little ground to McKinney that afternoon. When his boss pushed for launching another expedition, he objected, citing lack of sufficient staff. In response, McKinney suggested using student helpers, but Comstock tersely replied, "the usual run of student help was worse than useless."[12] The director next proposed locating an "amateur entomologist to collect insects,"[13] but Comstock asserted that "too, is useless,"[14] as it is just as important to "know what not to collect as . . . to know . . . [what] should be collected. The Museum's field men know the items that are desirable and those which are already in the collections in sufficient quantity."[15] In every way he could think to say it, Comstock repeated his message: the museum possessed the expertise necessary for launching a successful series of expeditions. They did not need students or lay practitioners; they needed their people released back into the hands of science. Anything less, and McKinney doomed the LACM into being a mere distributor of knowledge instead of a manufacturer of it.

Later in the afternoon, the discussion turned toward the evaluation and availability of previous expedition members. Reid Moran? An "A-1 field man"[16] who was well trained but no longer available because of a two-year scholarship at Cornell. John Shrader? Lloyd Martin? Chris Henne? All discussed. When it came to Don Meadows, someone in the room noted that because "Prof. Meadows made no field notes . . . his material was of lesser importance,"[17] a comment that further validated Meadows's diminished role in the survey.

From there, the meeting jumped from topic to topic like a snow-fed stream careening down a mountainside. The group discussed the survey's timeframe, debated which departments should next go into the field, considered the types and quality of publications the staff should pursue, and endlessly revisited staffing needs. As the meeting wore on, von Bloeker boldly "asked if it would be possible to borrow some of the workers from the educational division . . . during the spring vacation."[18] He did not call the "workers" out by name, but he could only have meant George Kanakoff, Chris Henne, and Lloyd Martin. They were good men who could help make the difference between a well-staffed expedition and a poorly staffed one.

It would have been easy enough for a more collegial director to offer to loan back former science department employees for the CIBS's use—what harm could it cause, anyway? The absence of a few docents for a few days, or few weeks at most, during a period of time (school spring break) when the museum wouldn't have as many school groups cycling through couldn't be too damaging. These were the men Comstock also wanted to see working in the verdant grasslands of the islands during the upcoming winter months. These were the men who knew the museum's collections, who knew which items were needed and which were not.

This was exactly the place Comstock was maneuvering toward with his refusal of student and volunteer help. These men were almost within Comstock's grasp, but McKinney, like a two-year-old unwilling to share, left von Bloeker's question unanswered and the staffing lacking. None of those three men ever participated in another CIBS expedition again.

And that is how it went. Talk, talk, talk. The meeting minutes filled seven single-spaced pages. The eight-member group must have been exhausted when they finally came to an agreement, but they cobbled together a plan: Santa Rosa Island in the late fall. At that time of year, Willett and von Bloeker could collect specimens in "prime condition." Comstock, beaten down by this point, promised McKinney he would look into using volunteers or unpaid student museum assistants to round out personnel needs. With these details settled and Comstock satisfied that he'd made his points, he told the group he felt "a good beginning had been made."[19] Gradually, he promised, they could "work toward a real survey"[20] again.

When Comstock wrote N. R. Vail to make arrangements for visiting Santa Rosa Island, the curator of science chose his words carefully in order to make clear that this visit was "supplementary to the work done by the Los Angeles–Channel Islands biological survey"[21] and that Vail and Vickers could expect a small party of six to work in the areas of paleontology, mammalogy, and ornithology during the month of November. What might Vail have thought when he received Comstock's letter, his new, less-prestigious title neatly typed beneath his signature? Being an astute businessman, he surely would have read all about the museum's reorganization in the Los Angeles presses, and though it probably wouldn't have affected his inclination to provide or withhold permission, the politics and power struggles taking place at the museum may have interested the stockman. It was perhaps something the two of them would discuss around a campfire when Comstock joined the gang on Santa Rosa Island. Or maybe, like a saddle sore, it would be too tender a topic to lance.

Provisioning supplies for the thirteenth expedition fell to von Bloeker, only this time he needed to juggle the responsibility with that of securing a new job. After losing out on the Smithsonian positions as well as the internal LACM curator of exhibits and curator of education jobs, von Bloeker applied for a rather familiar position close to home.

On October 5, 1941, he tendered his resignation—he was moving to the Hancock Foundation across the street at the University of Southern California. McKinney wasted no time offering Kenneth E. Stager a position as "curatorial assistant to George Willett,"[22] a title seemingly above the one von Bloeker had just vacated. Stager started the job on November 1 and was associated with the museum until his death in 2009.

Throughout October, Comstock and McKinney continued to clash. Their differences came to a head late that month when Comstock detailed the grievances he had laid out during the September science meeting. He repeated the mantra that small excursions with "limited objectives" were necessary because McKinney's "plan did not include those members of the staff qualified by experience and training to conduct a comprehensive survey." Next he criticized McKinney for closing down the botany department because "the relationship of plants to insects and of insects to their insular environment" was the second most important field of study for the upcoming Santa Rosa trip. He shored up this position by passionately explaining that the museum "cannot claim to be making an ecological study of the area when we have no active botanical department and when our qualified field scientists in entomology are held in the Department of Education." He concluded his reproach with the strong declaration that "a Biological Survey without ecological studies is a farce."[23]

Comstock also told McKinney in no uncertain terms that his decision to exclude archaeology from the Santa Rosa trip was incomprehensible because Santa Rosa Island's "greatest potentialities for original work" lay "in the field of anthropology," a department whose staff "is nationally recognized and" where "no better qualified persons could be secured from any source."[24] Furthermore, the U.S. National Park Service and the Smithsonian would criticize the museum for excluding entomology, botany, and archaeology from its expeditions. He stated that McKinney's deliberate exclusion of anthropology could be especially problematic because some of the museum's permits specifically required anthropology's inclusion. What Comstock found most deplorable, however, was McKinney's urging of two senior staff members to participate in paleontological and entomological fieldwork even though they were primarily laboratory scientists unaccustomed and unsuited to the physical demands of field expeditions. Specifically, Comstock noted that one of these individual's expertise lay outside the fieldwork McKinney had directed the individual to participate in, and the other's "physical condition" made "it a real hazard for him to undertake expeditionary work." It was the museum's responsibility to safeguard personnel, Comstock declared, and he was therefore "personally not willing to assume" the risk of sending that person out into the field.[25]

Before closing his letter, Comstock circled back to the topic of appropriately staffing expeditions, finding the matter reprehensible because the museum had "qualified workers ... who are excluded from participation." He names Chris Henne, Lloyd Martin, and a female botanist, asserting, "their special talents are lost to the Museum."[26] Comstock took his responsibilities seriously. He staunchly believed that the museum's work standard should remain high and that each individual must fulfill their greatest potential. In this letter, Comstock illustrates his commitment to his beliefs and his vocation as well as the injustice he felt over the organizational changes McKinney had imposed.

In closing, Comstock strongly recommended using trained museum personnel when appropriate and threatened that if McKinney found this unacceptable, he would not "assume the responsibility of these expeditions ... nominally under" his "jurisdiction."[27] Comstock had taken the reorganization personally.

Chapter Twenty-Two

SANTA ROSA (AGAIN)

"President Studies Japan's Reply." President Roosevelt promptly gave his personal attention today to a document presenting Japan's reply to his request for an explanation of Japanese troop movements into French Indo-China, a crucial factor in current far eastern tension.

— *The Daily Home News* (New Brunswick, New Jersey), December 5, 1941

Comstock's forcefully worded letter failed to release either Henne or Martin from their educational responsibilities, but miraculously archaeology rejoined the docket, a victory that allowed Comstock to turn his attention to the cumbersome task of organizing the next expedition. It would be a complex series of mini-surveys joined together by an umbrella of four distinct goals: conducting archaeological work at Skunk Point, finding and removing a "dwarf Pleistocene elephant" in Tecolote Canyon, taking additional specimens of the spotted skunk, and collecting a large number of late fall and early winter insects.[1] While this appears to be a relatively aggressive and comprehensive list of goals, neither botany nor geology was represented. Thus, while Comstock did not conceive of it as a "full" expedition, he nonetheless satisfied his promise to McKinney by filling staffing voids with a variety of qualified personnel, though what fit the definition of "qualified" may have been stretched a bit.

Staffers clearly falling under the term "qualified" included: Ken Stager, mammalogist and ornithologist; Stager's wife, camp cook; King A. Richey, a paleontologist with an master's degree from Berkeley who was currently working on his doctorate at the California Institute of Technology; Barbara Loomis from USC's anthropology department; and Marion Hollenbach, a museum curator and an archaeology student at USC. Not everyone participating in the Santa Rosa expedition was as qualified as these individuals, however. One of these was John Chester Stock, the nineteen-year-old son of Dr. Chester Stock, a California Institute of Technology paleontology professor who was heavily involved with the museum's work at the tar pits of Rancho La Brea. Another was nineteen-year-old Harry Fletcher, who had spent the last several years working as a student assistant in the museum, experience Comstock deemed good enough to serve as expedition paleontologist and assistant archaeologist. And a third was Richard Case, a museum employee variously described as "assistant paleontologist," "attendant," "guardian," or "janitor," depending on who was speaking.

Among the last of Comstock's recruits to round out the expedition muster was Jack Couffer. Couffer was known to most members of the LACM scientific staff because of his work in the departments of archaeology, entomology, paleontology, herpetology, ornithology, and mammalogy, as well as for his proficiency at skinning birds and mammals. His inclusion on the mandate stood out from the others because his mother was required to sign a written waiver giving her sixteen-year old son permission to participate. Jack Couffer attended Glendale High School as a junior in November 1941. The youngest member of the CIBS, Jack was itching to get out onto those islands—missing a few weeks of classes was just a bonus.

With four discreet objectives and a staff that included many new members, the logistics were bound to become complicated. To accommodate individual schedules, Comstock arranged six round-trip channel crossings aboard various vessels. The first group of scientists—Comstock, Ken Stager (serving as both mammalogist and ornithologist), Carole Stager (camp cook), King A. Richey (paleontologist), and John C. Stock and Harry Fletcher (assistant paleontologists)—would arrive at Bechers Bay, Santa Rosa Island, on November 8. Of this initial contingent, Comstock, Richey, and Stock planned to return to the mainland on November 15. The archaeological crew—Woodward, Marion Hollenbach, and Barbara Loomis—were scheduled to report to the island on the twenty-first, while Case and Couffer (who would resume paleontological activities) as well as George and Ora Willett would arrive on the twenty-eighth. Woodward would depart the following day, leaving Hollenbach and the woman he would marry six years hence (Barbara Loomis) to assume all archaeological responsibilities. Stager and his wife intended to leave the island on December 1 and the remaining troops would go home on the thirteenth. All in all, this was an intricate plan destined to change in ways no one could imagine.

The first research contingent motored to Santa Rosa Island aboard the *Velero III* on November 8, the last civilians to travel aboard the ship before the navy commandeered it the following day as part of the war effort. After landing at dusk through high winds and surf, the Vails greeted the researchers and offered the use of a tractor, a trailer, and the services of ranch superintendent George Haise while they were on the island.

The next day, the light, airy whistling and rustling sounds of mourning doves taking flight awakened staffers, who emerged from their quarters and were greeted by an emerald island made green by that season's rains. The Stagers got right to work setting traps in places they hoped would snare island skunks, but Fletcher set traps in the camp kitchen, where he caught so many mice that he later joked the mice jumped straight into the traps as soon as the bait cans were opened. "Poor little buggers," Loomis wrote of the doomed creatures.[2]

Birds were abundant on the island, too, and their caws, chirps, and alarms must have been nearly constant. Along Bechers Bay, loons—both common and red-throated—patrolled the near shore while elegantly diving for fish. Blue herons skulked along the shoreline, their long, deliberate steps very much in contrast with the quick running and pausing movements of the black-bellied plovers, whose haunting, melancholy *PLEEooee* calls could have inspired the songs of the first Santa Rosa human inhabitants. At night, the survey members heard occasional burrowing owl rasps carrying through the canyons, startling when a barn owl let loose its terrifying alarm scream. Days brought bald eagle shadows gliding across the landscape, hawks (coopers and red-tailed) hunting for meat, and the trim silhouettes of peregrine and kestrel falcons racing across the sky at high speeds.

Locating and bringing home fossil pygmy mammoths from Tecolote Canyon on the island's far west side was one of the chief aims of this expedition. Responsibility for provisioning food, water, transportation, and the special tools the paleontologists would need for digging and jacketing fossils in plaster—a preparation necessary to ensure their safe passage back to the museum—fell to Comstock, and he worked diligently on these details. Initially, they were to travel via boat from Bechers Bay to Tecolote Canyon, but that fell through. Three days passed before Richey, Fletcher, and Stock mounted up in a light rain to ride single file behind the island vaqueros, their packtrain trailing behind them en route to Tecolote Canyon.

The paleontologists' delay in leaving basecamp meant they only had three days to work their site before their departure date beckoned. Though they did not discover any actual fossils to bring back to the museum, they did not return emptyhanded, as they possessed promising reports of a number of "dwarf elephants" worthy of further work. An unsigned, undated memo within the LACM archives for the thirteenth expedition reveals that finding these fossils would be "one of the most interesting projects of the expedition."[3] Because Comstock, Richey, and Stock all had to leave the island on November 15, these fossils had to wait for the arrival of the next contingent of paleontologists and the survey's youngest member, Jack Couffer.

A week after Comstock left Santa Rosa, Woodward, Hollenbach, and Loomis prepared to travel to the island. The local press got wind of it and latched onto the story, reporting that "according to authoritative sources," Hollenbach and Loomis would "be the first two feminine archaeologists ever to explore"[4] Santa Rosa Island. The paper's source is unknown, but an informal survey[5] of a small number of archaeologists working on the Channel Islands today not only agrees with their statement, but also suggests these two women were likely the first trained female archaeologists to work on any of the Channel Islands.

Barbara Loomis's fieldnotes deliver colorful accounts of her CIBS experiences. She begins her journal with a description of the threesome's arrival at Port Hueneme in Oxnard, California. The city of Oxnard is about forty miles south of Santa Barbara, and its harbor, Port Hueneme, is a working deep-water port that today serves as the U.S. Navy's only western mainland harbor operating between San Diego Bay and Puget Sound in Washington State. In 1941, a kelp dehydrating plant that manufactured food for cows, a fish cannery, a packing plant, and a training school for the U.S. Merchant Marines[6] called the port home.

The archaeologists arrived at the busy port late in the afternoon of November 21 expecting to travel to Santa Rosa Island that evening. Like a Groucho Marx skit, they searched the harbor for the *Yellowtail's* whereabouts, repeatedly running into a "decrepit" old man whose appearance came to signal they had gone awry. Afternoon turned to dusk as they scouted out the many marinas, commercial fishing docks, and launch ramps, hoping all the while to find the *Yellowtail* with cabin lights blazing and engines lazily idling in readiness for their departure. It was after nightfall when they located the cruiser moored in the yacht basin (of all places), berthed and locked for the evening. Realizing that no one would be coming to ferry them to Santa Rosa Island, they trundled off to a hotel, booking two rooms, each decorously occupied.

The next day the little group learned the cause of their delay: the *Yellowtail* had orders to stay in port. Strong easterly winds made the channel crossing perilous, and the California Fish and Game Commission wasn't taking any more chances, not after losing the *Marlin* the week before on Catalina Island. The bad weather kept the archaeologists ashore until six in the morning on Sunday, November 23, when they finally boarded the *Yellowtail* expecting to make the Santa Barbara Channel crossing in a few hours. Maneuvering his ship away from her berth, the captain steered toward the open ocean. Upon gaining the harbor's protective breakwall, he gunned his ship's "twin Hall-Scott gas engines capable of making 25 knots"[7] dead into rough seas, high winds, and large swells. The captain steadily motored deeper into the channel until he could no longer deny that his chosen route was impassable. Unwilling to give up, he set a new course, boldly running his vessel parallel to Santa Cruz Island, where the large island's mass shielded his ship from much of the winds' brute force, but even so, ocean swells tied the *Yellowtail* "in knots."[8]

In Ventura and Santa Barbara Counties, terra-California disappears swiftly into the Pacific Ocean's Santa Barbara Channel. Three miles offshore, the bottom is six hundred feet below sea level, while mid-channel the floor is two thousand feet beneath the sea's surface. Winter water temperatures average fifty to sixty degrees Fahrenheit. In seas this cold, a man overboard could lose consciousness within an hour and die in the next five or six. Any boat attempting a November channel crossing must be prepared for cold waves sweeping over the bow carrying anything (or anyone) not tied down into the drink. Seamen learn to brace themselves with bended knees and fingers gripped tightly to fixed lines and railings while high winds and storm waves slam their ships, lifting them nearly clear of wave crests before heaving them deep into troughs. Swells come quickly this time of year, one after another, and in bad weather there's no predicting their direction. A haphazard crisscrossing of winds morph white caps into frothed milk before slicing through surging currents, the liquid equivalent of the spaghetti twist of lines incising rock where a ninety-foot-long road cut in Palmdale, California, bifurcates the San Andreas Fault. These were the seas that drove the *Yellowtail* back to port and turned Woodward and Hollenbach's faces green.

More than an hour before sunrise the next day, the archaeologists eagerly boarded the *Yellowtail* again. Ninety minutes later they were still marking time at the dock, amusing themselves by watching the inexperienced merchant marines run their ship aground in the channel, free it, and then jam the vessel against an oil dock from which they couldn't disengage. Imagine the chagrined expressions on those young men's faces as they stood on board while the ship was towed into port, an onshore audience in attendance.

It wasn't until the following day, four days later than planned, that the archaeologists finally stepped onto the pier at Bechers Bay to join their colleagues on Santa Rosa Island. Woodward delivered two letters from Comstock. The first, addressed to Harry "Bill" Fletcher, instructed the young man to assist the archaeological crew until such time as Couffer and Case arrived. When they did, the paleontologists would travel aboard the *Yellowtail* to Tecolote Canyon, where the first crew of paleontologists had reported remarkable fossil elephant remains. Of course, no one on the *Yellowtail* would know exactly where to deposit the young men, so Comstock sent maps for the captain's benefit. Comstock felt sure that these, together with the ranch superintendent's knowledge of the island, would land the young men in the right place. Wanting to ensure their safety and comfort, the curator of science made a number of suggestions that he expected young Fletcher to follow. "Take plenty of water" in "casks," he instructed. "Cache them somewhere near the beach" because "they will be too heavy to carry," "have some sort of bucket or water carrier" to fill when needed, and rely on Ken Stager's help to "estimate the right amount of food and supplies."[9] After spending two weeks at the dig site, the paleontologists were to move their dunnage and specimens to the beach in preparation for the *Yellowtail*'s arrival and their return to Bechers Bay—another perfectly constructed, intricate Comstock plan.

The second letter was addressed to Kenneth Stager. It filled him in on Harry Fletcher's assignment and asked Stager if he "could keep a fatherly eye on the archaeological camp, as [Comstock was] . . . a little concerned about the two girls working out near Skunk Point by themselves."[10] This request was not only in keeping with Comstock's benevolent nature, but it also proved prescient of future events.

Barbara Loomis and Marion Hollenbach were the "girls" Comstock referenced. After Woodward returned to the mainland and the paleontologists went off to dig up fossil elephants, the women would be alone at the archaeological site. Far from being a sexist remark, Comstock felt genuine apprehension about what might befall two young women out there by themselves. After having just spent time on that island himself, he knew conditions could be perilous—sprained ankles, broken limbs, sunstroke, steep cliffs, and swift currents, to name a few—but likely something else concerned him, too.

While Woodward was still on the island, the archaeologists worked together at the Skunk Point site and other locations, surface collecting chert arrowheads, drills, scrapers, tarred pebbles, broken and whole knife blades, and hand choppers. Twice in his journal Woodward noted the lack of shell hooks and shell blanks at Skunk Point, and their absence mystified him. "I am at loss to explain this," he puzzled, stating, "they did have shell hooks on this i[slan]d."[11] Though this absence piqued his curiosity, it wasn't enough to goad him into returning to Santa Rosa Island to investigate.

Loomis continued journaling throughout her time on Santa Rosa. Her entries are often mini-vignettes, some lighthearted and warm. She writes delightedly about the "foxes so thick they skitter along just ahead of me, bouncing in the grass,"[12] and briefly lists animal sightings: seals and sea lions, deer, crows, and the glossy-coated, black and white spotted skunk. She also recorded sighting three bald eagles. Willett observed the national bird frequently, too, and one of his sightings included a nest in a Torrey pine tree.

On Woodward's last day on the island, Barbara and Marion—or Marioneta[13] as he calls her in his journal—remained in camp, Marion recovering from the flu and Barbara otherwise busying herself. Undeterred by this lack of company, Woodward struck out with camera, journal, writing implement, and probably some kind of collecting bag in tow. In between photo-documenting Nidever's cave (where the sea captain and his men battled an unlicensed British vessel's crew of otter-hunting Pacific Northwest Indians)[14] and the Santa Rosa and Santa Cruz Island landscapes, he collected and wrote. While he walked through Old Ranch Canyon, which runs diagonally across the eastern tip of the island, he noted the hills beyond covered by thousands of white snow geese. The abundant presence of this large, opulently feathered, pink-beaked fowl that left white breast feathers all over those hills got Woodward thinking. He wondered if in centuries past these birds used this island as a winter stopover for their migrations. He wondered if the Indians ate them. He thought that possibly "the bones should appear in the debris."[15]

In fact, the people who lived on Santa Rosa Island did eat birds. More than five thousand bird bones have been found in just five sites on this island. Canada goose, snow goose, cormorant, and albatross dominate the avian remains upon which the Santa Rosa Chumash feasted.[16] While he walked and wondered about this, it is possible that Woodward picked up a point or a crescent, items that someone may have used to hunt fowl. The inspirational area Woodward walked through was near an island Chumash village located at the mouth of Old Ranch Canyon, aptly named Qshiwqshiw, which translates to "bird droppings" and which was probably one of the larger villages on Santa Rosa Island.[17] Woodward was right about people hunting and eating the snow goose, but he did not document his theory, or even his speculation. He left the work of proving it to future scholars.

When the California Fish and Game Commission's cruiser N. B. Scofield docked at Santa Rosa's pier the evening of November 28, the Willetts, Richard Case, and young Jack Couffer disembarked. The next day, Woodward boarded the ship, ceding the remaining investigation of Santa Rosa Island's archaeological treasures to his two female colleagues.

While the men and women of the thirteenth expedition camped on Santa Rosa Island, the board of governors discussed the future of the

CIBS. McKinney bluntly asked if the survey work should "be abandoned" until such time as "additional personnel" would allow the work to continue "as originally planned."[18] What had happened? Just two months earlier, McKinney had pushed hard on Comstock to utilize student and volunteer help to keep the CIBS in the field. In a previous meeting, the board of governors had spoken of the importance of the survey's continuation. What had prompted this reversal in McKinney's thinking? Regardless of the reason, the governors were in no mood to make another quick course correction and referred the matter to the science committee with instructions to report back in December. With the conclusion of that month's board meeting, the survey withstood the winds of one storm, but a funnel cloud still hung low near the survey's western horizon.

Chapter Twenty-Three

UNLUCKY THIRTEEN

"Japs Open War on U.S. with Bombing of Hawaii: Fleet Speeds Out to Battle Invader: Tokyo Claims Battleship Sunk and Another Set Afire with Hundreds Killed on Island; Singapore Attacked and Thailand Force Landed." Japan assaulted every main United States and British possession in the Central and Western Pacific and invaded Thailand today (Monday) in a hasty but evidently shrewdly-planned prosecution of a war she began Sunday without warning. Her formal declaration of war against both the United States and Britain came 2 hours and 55 minutes after Japanese planes spread death and terrific destruction in Honolulu and Pearl Harbor at 7:35 a.m., Hawaiian time (10:05 a.m., P.S.T.) Sunday.

—*Los Angeles Times*, December 8, 1941

In late November, Couffer joined his friend, Fletch (Harry Fletcher), on the island and the pair teamed up to work the archaeological site with Hollenbach and Loomis. Together they dug at Skunk Point, unearthing dog and fish jawbones, bone awls, mussels, key hole limpets, and a possible whalebone hut, none of which the "boys" seemed to find particularly remarkable. Even so, their exposure to archaeology proved memorable, ruminating within their minds while they slept beneath a canvas tent in a horse corral that was "separated from the other scientists by the whole [of the] island."[1]

These boys hoped to find something wonderful, something important and meaningful to science. They knew it was likely right in front of them, lying in the dirt beneath their feet or in the rocks they would chip at with pick-axes. Like Meadows, Comstock, Woodward, and von Bloeker, they yearned to make a contribution, their dreams the same ones that whispered to John Muir, Joseph Grinnell, and Charles Darwin. These boys, they had dreams.

On December 1, the Stagers boarded the *Santa Cruz* before breakfast, leaving the Willetts, Loomis, Hollenbach, and the three paleontologists in charge of their respective fields for the next two weeks. Shortly thereafter, Couffer, Fletcher, and Case departed Bechers Bay as well, their horses loaded down with water, food, digging equipment, tents, and sleeping bags. Fletcher returned to camp at four o'clock—he'd left behind two weeks' worth of bread and it cost him a half day's journey or more.

At Bechers Bay, Loomis and Hollenbach worked diligently on their whalebone structure, hoping to get it out of the earth before the eastern skies delivered its promise of winds and rain. Archaeology is hot, sweaty work, and the girls wanted to clean off and swim, even if the beaches were infested with dead shrimp. Hundreds had washed ashore the week before, covering the surf line "inches deep with live and dead creatures"[2] that the ravens and gulls feasted upon, but none of this dissuaded the women from entering the sea to wash off and cool down.

Rain arrived as predicted. Water seeped through their tents, the cold, damp air giving Loomis a sinus infection. Trying her best to ignore it, she and Hollenbach searched the area for new sites using ridgelines and creek beds to guide their explorations. One day, following a trickle of water, they found themselves in a narrow, rocky ravine. At its end stood four elk and some deer, animals the Vail and Vickers had imported as part of their big game hunting enterprise. With darkness approaching, they looked toward the sky as they walked, the last of the day's light providing just enough illumination for them to see the "heads of deer in twos and threes"[3] sketched against every skyline. As night closed in, they scrambled out of the canyon. From there, in the gathering darkness, they followed a ridge to the "sea, easier said than done,"[4] Loomis wryly remarked. Both women must have been glad when the moon came up at six o'clock and they could get their bearings. It was only then that they realized they were still a long way from camp.

The lush *Cañada Verde* stretches toward the far northwestern horizon of Santa Rosa Island as the young paleontological crew makes their way to their campsite. Courtesy of Jack Couffer.

Back at Bechers Bay, George Willett fretted over the girls' whereabouts. He considered rounding up a crew of cowboys to search for them,
but before mounting a rescue party the pair dragged themselves into
camp "terribly stiff and tired."[5] The Willetts were "anxious and angry,"
but "George soon forgave"[6] them. Ora, however, annoyed that they had
worried her husband, served the women a meal of chili and beans in "stiff
silence."[7]

On Saturday, December 6, the young women dug at their Skunk
Point site again, and by three o'clock they were sweating and covered in
dust. An ocean swim beckoned them, but before taking their dip they
noticed a vaquero lounging on his pony on a ridge above them as he
guarded a small herd of cattle. For what seemed like an hour, the girls
waited for him to leave, but when he didn't they headed to a spot out of
sight of the trail. Believing they were safe from scrutiny, they stripped off
their filthy clothes and "Marion, dusty and ecstatic," wearing "nothing at
all," started "dancing on the sand."[8] Suddenly, Hollenback let out a yelp.
"Barby! There's a cow puncher!"[9] she hollered.

Immediately both women raced for the safety of a cave in the nearby
cliff, where they quickly clothed themselves in the privacy of their make-
shift dressing room. Once fully attired, Loomis ran outside to look for
their transgressors, one of whom must have been the "head traveling
along the bluff above our cave."[10] Hell-bent on affixing responsibility for
this dirty trick, Hollenbach joined Loomis on the sand, ably scrambling
up the cliff to address the voyeurs directly. On the bluff just north of
where she and Loomis were dancing naked on the beach a few minutes
before, they found three mounted cowboys. The rest of the ranch hands
were also nearby. "Marion inquired sarcastically if they had lost their
cattle."[11]

"They had lost some,"[12] one of the cowboys replied.

Another "asked if . . . [we] wanted a ride home."[13]

"No Thanks,"[14] Marion said.

"Were [we] coming to the dance,"[15] one of the cowboys questioned.

"What dance?"[16] Marion challenged.

The dance "at the Ranch house—tonight."[17]

"We'll see,"[18] Marion said, and then she and Loomis followed the
cattle home. As they arrived in camp, the cowboys inquired about the
dance again, but the women ignored them.

That evening, ranch superintendent George Haise and his wife made a neighborly call on the researchers, their visit giving Loomis and Hollenbach a clue "that the 'dance'" the cowboys spoke about "was bogus."[19] Haise told the group that "they had lost two calves on the bluffs that afternoon," and then he mumbled something about "sea baths," which made Loomis suspect that he had seen them naked that afternoon. Later, they learned that he told Willett he "threw a rock to scare" them "off before the rest got there."[20] "We did not see any rock,"[21] Loomis complained indignantly in her field journal.

Comstock had previously voiced his concern about these two archaeologists, both unmarried and on the island unaccompanied by a man, which he felt made them vulnerable. While there could have been many reasons for his concern, it was likely the fact that it was 1941 and they were on a working cattle ranch located on an island in the Pacific Ocean primarily inhabited by a lot of men who didn't get to the mainland very often. As it turned out, his premonitions had been accurate, right down to the location of Skunk Point, Santa Rosa Island.

Today, this incident could be prosecuted as sexual harassment. Back then, however, Loomis and Hollenbach apparently chalked the event up to peeping tomfoolery, since no official documentation appears either in the museum archives or in letters or journals outside of Barbara Loomis's unpublished fieldnotes.

Approximately seventy years after bunking on Santa Rosa Island, Jack Couffer places their basecamp on a hillock near the mouth of a canyon where Vail and Vickers's cowboys left them with three horses confined in a cattle paddock adjacent to a stream filled with good, clean drinking water. A single photograph exists of their romantically rustic camp. In it the boys pose smiling next to the clean white canvas tent they staked and rigged in front of a wood railing. Behind them a hillside covered by what must be seasonal green growth, rises. A fence line marches up the hill's side, disappearing into the sky above. On the slope, deep, dry, spider vein-like ravines are etched into the earth, dug by water rivulets cascading down from the hill's crest to the flatland their camp occupied. To one side of their tent canned goods, a camp stove, and a large pot lay spread on a low table, and before them, atop a lush blanket of grass, their sleeping bags lay stretched out and ready to climb into at the end of a long

Couffer and Fletcher's Elephant Camp at Tecolote Canyon, December 1941. Courtesy of Jack Couffer.

day. Years later, when looking at that picture, Couffer said he thought they were camped at Arlington Canyon, but contemporary researchers disagree, believing that Fletcher and Case were camped at Cañada Tecolote, just where Comstock intended them to be.

The paleontologists quickly assessed the state of the fossil remains their compatriots—Richey, Fletcher, and Stock—had located just two weeks prior. Tasked with jacketing these valuable fossils in plaster casts to protect the bones on the long journey back to the museum, their hearts must have sunk when they found their quarry. The fossil treasures they hoped to collect had been pulverized by hundreds of cattle hooves, the bits and pieces unsalvageable. Undeterred, the boys poked around. "The first thing" they "found was this wonderful complete lower jaw" in a cliff,[22] a perfectly intact Columbian mammoth jawbone. It probably took more than some casual looking around to find this specimen, however, sited as it was on a steep cliff face at least six feet below the arroyo tableland. To work on it, the boys needed to plant their feet securely and hold on dearly lest a misstep or loose stone send them tumbling a long distance downward over jagged rocks. If they managed to survive that horrifying fall, they could be sure their bones would be broken in as many pieces as the fossils the cows had trampled at their original site.

Today, scientists in the field often try to extract fossils by keeping as much soil and rock matrix around them as possible. This protects them during their removal as well as throughout the jacketing and transportation processes. Couffer's photographs show a different preparation, however. The lower jawbones he and Fletcher excavated are pristine, the bones gleaming white and free from rock and dirt debris.

Working in this dangerous spot made removing their treasure arduous and time consuming, but each day they made progress. On Couffer's seventeenth birthday, the paleontologists decided the fossil could be extracted from the hill, so they intended to spend December 7, 1941, getting the treasure ready to take home. Removing it would make Couffer's birthday most memorable, and both boys were eager to complete the job. When they began working a heavy mist hung in the air, the moisture so thick it dampened the sound of hooves approaching on the arroyo. Startled by the clomping sounds they finally heard, they looked up from their work to see "the shapes of two riders materializ[ing]"[23] in the form of "classic cowboys" wearing "Mexican chaps and wide-brimmed hats dripping with fog."[24] One of them said, "Pearl Harbor's been bombed. You guys pack up. We 'gotta gitcha outta' here. We 'gotta gitcha back. . . . We don't know how you're going to get back to the mainland because all the harbors have been closed."[25] Confused, the birthday boy—who hadn't paid much attention to politics or high school geography—asked, "Where's Pearl Harbor?"[26]

Harry Fletcher working on the Columbian mammoth jawbones on a cliffside in Teco-lote Canyon, Santa Rosa Island, December 1941. Courtesy of Jack Couffer.

Crestfallen over the cowboy's rendition of the bombing of American soil and knowing they needed to act fast if they hoped to do anything worthwhile with "their" fossil, they came up with a plan. Years later, Couffer recalled their thought process: "we figured we'd done all that work,"[27] so "we just put a heavy plaster cast on it where it was figuring

On the day of Pearl Harbor, Jack Couffer took this picture of his buddy, Harry Fletcher, working on mammoth jawbones lying in a cliff in Tecolote Canyon. Courtesy of Jack Couffer.

that sometime in the future somebody else, or maybe even us, would come back and get it out."[28]

After doing exactly that, they hurriedly broke camp, but they couldn't leave yet—they had something else to do. Their archaeological work at Skunk Point had made an impression on them and they "had archaeology in [their] . . . heads,"[29] Couffer explained. Having found something "incredible," they needed to document it before leaving the northwest side of Santa Rosa Island. That season's torrential rains caused landslides to wash human bones out of the cliff faces and hillsides. "It was incredible how many graves were" exposed, Couffer remembered.[30] "We wanted to document the fact that Arlington Canyon was this rich archaeological site."[31]

Decades later Couffer covers a small photograph—taken the day after Pearl Harbor—with his hand and says, "[I] hesitate to show you this picture because it makes us look rather insensitive . . . but we weren't at all."[32] Slowly, he pushes the black and white photograph across the wooden table toward a group of rapt scholars surrounding him at the Santa Barbara Museum of Natural History (SBMNH). It depicts a nineteen-year-old man standing atop an arroyo, legs planted solidly on the ground, his horse standing patiently by his side with its reins dangling loosely onto the ground. Behind him, high clouds float above a coastal landscape of hills and cliffs, and below him, at the mouth of a large canyon, a sandy beach awash with ocean froth. Fletch, wearing a sweatshirt and a cowboy hat, is mugging for the camera, eyes alight. He's holding more than a dozen femurs, and ten skulls are piled like bowling balls near his feet.

"This was after we got our orders to leave. . . . The skulls eroded out of the embankment. . . . We picked up as many femurs as we could just as an example. I took this picture as a record of the wealth of material that was Arlington Canyon."[33] They weren't pothunters, Jack Couffer explains, "we weren't at all."[34] They meant no disrespect. The young men just wanted to document this site so they could show the evidence to more experienced archaeologists who might know what to do with this information.

The boys had no way of guessing that eighteen years later, Phil Orr of the SBMNH would bring back a femur he found at Arlington Canyon, Santa Rosa Island, and radiocarbon date it. Orr's was a momentous discovery of the oldest human remains ever found in North America, and the record stands today. Jack Couffer knew none of this in 1941, but he knew all about it seventy years later when he showed visitors at the SBMNH the snapshot of Fletcher holding those bones. "We discovered it!" he said with pride, believing that he and Harry Fletcher had first found the site where the oldest human remains in North America would later be documented.

If this were true, it would be another example of a brush the CIBS had with scientific immortality. But, this is not the case. Couffer and Fletcher were not in Arlington Canyon—Arlington Springs and Arlington Canyon are behind them in that photo. The boys did not discover the site where the oldest human remains in North America were later found; however, they did not fail to discover something new.

Another photo Couffer shared with scholars features clam ornaments with punctate decorations, tapering stem knives, and projectile points he collected near the site where Fletcher is photographed atop the arroyo. The artifacts are similar to those excavated by Phil Orr at Cañada Verde, which were radiocarbon dated to around four thousand years ago. Seeing these two photos, one well-known Channel Island researcher stated, "what Jack's dig demonstrates is that there were two contemporaneous villages existing at that time at these locations."[35] This alone, represents significant new information. No, they did not fail.

In the early 1900s, Phillip Mills Jones explored the arroyo on which Fletch stood on December 8, 1941. Today it is known as SRI-5 and it is part of a complex series of sites located along a bluff on the west side of Arlington Canyon. The site that Couffer mistakenly thought he and his buddy had "found" was actually located nearly two decades later in a place far different than SRI-5.[36]

In 1959, Phil Orr, a keen-eyed archaeologist, spotted some bones jutting out from a sidewall of Arlington Canyon. The bones lay buried by thirty-two feet of sediment. As was the case when Couffer and Fletch were on the island, erosion played a big role in Orr's discovery—as it often does in archaeology (and certainly on the northwest coast of Santa Rosa Island). Recognizing a bone of contention when he saw one, the SBMNH archaeologist took precautions before removing the three bones and a large chunk of earth encasing them. He named the remains Arlington Canyon Man after the canyon in which they were

This beautifully composed and executed photograph of the mouth of Tecolote Canyon exemplifies the artful, photographic eye that future cinematographer Jack Couffer would utilize in his professional career. The white specks in the photo appear to be a flock of gulls. December 1941. Courtesy of Jack Couffer.

found. Using the most current technology available to him, Orr dated them to ten thousand years old. No one else had found remains this old anywhere in North America. (Woodward was retired from LACM when Orr made his startling discovery. Nonetheless, the pair must have shared some long chats over Orr's consequential find, along with some good, or not-so-good, hooch.)

But this is not the end of the Arlington Canyon Man discovery. Over the years, scientists debated about whether the bones were male or female, changing their name to Arlington Canyon Woman before later reverting back to Arlington Canyon Man. Furthermore, forty-three years after Phil Orr dated "his" remains, Dr. John Johnson, Orr's successor at SBMNH, thought about those bones lying in a crate in a museum store-room and decided to date them again. More sophisticated technologies might yield new information, he reasoned. When Johnson finished his work, he and his colleagues reported that Arlington Man was not ten but thirteen thousand years old, indisputably the remains of the oldest human ever found in North America.[37]

Prior to this point in time, it was widely believed that hunting societies followed mammoths through Beringia, when lower sea levels meant a land bridge connected Russia to the Americas. The human journey was made possible when the ice sheets began to melt and an "ice-free" corridor offered access to what is now Alaska, Canada, and the lower United States. People used this route to travel southward into areas like present-day Clovis, New Mexico. Artifacts they left behind date their occupancy to approximately thirteen thousand years ago. This theory, variously called the ice-free corridor migration or Clovis first theory, held that people spread to coastal areas as resources diminished within the interior and only then did they develop maritime capabilities. Such a migration and the necessary technological advances that would have allowed people to populate the Channel Islands would have taken thousands of years. Yet, Arlington Man is as old as the Clovis culture. How could that be if the Clovis culture came first?

Combining the insights learned from Arlington Man, Daisy Cave, and Monte Verde in Chili (where the oldest evidence of human occupation in the Americas was found), a growing number of scientists today believe that people arrived on the West Coast of North America before they ever reached the interior of the United States on foot. They arrived by sea in boats, possessing a sophisticated maritime culture capable of readily utilizing ocean resources. This theory, first advanced in the 1970s, is called the Pacific coastal migration model. Recent geological evidence shows that the ice-free corridor did not become sufficiently ice-free to allow human foot traffic until 13,000 years ago, whereas "a linear migration route, essentially unobstructed and entirely at sea level, from northeast Asia into the Americas," was available to mariners about 16,000 years ago.[38] Shoring up the Pacific coastal migration theory are the nonskeletal artifacts found in Chile, Oregon, Texas, and the Channel Islands—especially the northern Channel Islands, where more than ninety-two[39] sites dating from 13,000 to 8,000 years ago[40] have been found. Taken all together, many researchers believe that human occupation of North and South America may have initially occurred between 18,500 and 14,500 years ago.[41]

An ecological corollary to the Pacific coast migration model is the kelp highway hypothesis, which proposes that kelp played an important role in man's migration to the Americas. Today, rich kelp beds nearly continuously fringe the coasts of Japan, Siberia, the Bering Strait, Alaska's shoreline, and the West Coast of North America. The kelp beds could have not only provided mariners with ample high-protein food, such as shellfish and fish, but also dampened Pacific Ocean swells and supplied safe moorings for their boats. Additionally, the many mainland and island coastal kelp habitats offered abundant spots to haul out to rest and seek freshwater sources and food, especially plants.

Thus, Phil Orr's 1959 discovery began the long, slow death of the Clovis first theory. Ushered in its stead by a new generation of archaeologists—whose ideas ignited controversy, heated debates, and late night discussions—is the Pacific coast migration and kelp highway theories of the peopling of the Americas.

If Couffer had been right about "their" site being the future location where the Arlington Man would one day be discovered, if the LACM had followed up on the boys' lead, or if Woodward had heeded ranch superintendent Mr. Smith's wise advice or reconsidered the nine words he himself had scrawled into his own journal—"He says Arlington cañon site has not been touched"[42]—perhaps it might have been Arthur Albert Woodward who discovered Arlington Man. And, if he had dated the finds and published a scholarly article about them, then maybe he and the LACM, along with the CIBS, would have been forever linked with this exciting discovery. It is what Couffer and Fletch had hoped to discover, the same dream that Woodward, von Bloeker, Comstock, and Meadows had pursued.

But Art Woodward did none of those things. He failed those boys and he failed the archaeologists who came after him. He did not publish Smith's recommendation. If he had, might history have changed? Or was Orr's discovery serendipitous, too? Did years of rain and erosion contribute to his discovery? Would Woodward have even had a chance of finding those remarkable bones? Would Orr have found more, or none at all, if erosion hadn't played its part? Speculation carries no weight. History did not unfold this way.

Across the island at Bechers Bay, Loomis and Hollenbach took Sunday, December 7, off as a day of rest. It was also the day the ranch hands had set aside to dehorn, brand, and castrate their young cattle. The women watched as the "punchers" (cowpunchers) sheared the hair around the cattle's horns in preparation for dehorning. This task completed, the young women naively asked the vaqueros what activity came next. The cowboys, probably smirking beneath their wide-brimmed hats, responded evasively. All the girls heard was some muttering about mountain oysters, a term that baffled them but which became clear when the cowboys "started roping claves and turning the little bulls into little steers."[43] Loomis noted rather delightedly that some of the roped calves had already been castrated, a fact that prompted one of the vaqueros to "caper" around the corral "yelling 'No *tiene huevos*, No *tiene huevos*'" (he has no eggs).[44]

Back at camp, the researchers turned on the radio. "News came in that Japan had bombed . . . Pearl Harbor on Oahu. . . . Congress convened by plane."[45] What everyone hoped would not happen had. The U.S. had entered into World War II.

The next day, radio news brought accounts of the men dying at Pearl Harbor, but Loomis and Hollenbach, perhaps seeking refuge from these gloomy reports, resumed their work in the field. They walked to Carrington Point, north of Bechers Bay, and worked past noon. It was a place where they could be alone with their thoughts, immersed in the remains of an ancient culture.

But once back in camp, war was all anyone could talk about. It consumed Loomis's journals: George Haise ordered to discontinue using the radiotelephone; California Fish and Game boats reportedly all taken over by the government; West Coast radio stations shut down; San Pedro blacked out; San Francisco blacked out; all western Canada blacked out. The researchers could not communicate with the museum, and no boats were allowed to sail to the islands. No one knew when they would be allowed to go home or if their island might be attacked next. "We suppose we will get transportation out—but we do not know,"[46] Loomis wrote.

When the vaqueros came to visit camp, Marion and Barbara joined them, their naked escapades of a few days before forgotten, or at least rendered insignificant compared to more recent events. One of the fellas, Joe, "was very nice," Loomis remarked, noting that he joked "about putting" the researchers "on as punchers and all of . . . [them] living on the tame and wild meat if . . . [they did] not get off the island right away."[47] It may have been an off-the-cuff comment meant to amuse the girls, but the possibility that Joe could be right surely weighed heavily upon them all.

More radio reports filtered in. Canada, Australia, and most of the American republics declared war on Japan. Cuba declared war on Germany, Italy, and Japan. False reports circulated and they were scary: the planes that attacked Pearl Harbor were painted with both the German swastika and Japan's rising sun; German pilots had carried out the attack.

In her journal entry on December 8, Loomis records that she went to the ranch barn. She does not specify why she was there, or with whom. Her entry is truncated and emotionless, yet its brevity exposes her forlornness and confusion: "We looked at the radio telephone . . . installed . . . in a big solid whale boat—the ship's radio station certificate on the wall behind it."[48] What was it about the boat, the phone, the certificate that commanded her to write those few sentences? Could it be that the phone—capable of connecting them to family, friends, associates, doctors—symbolized the change in their lives? This trusty device could no longer connect them to their "real" world. Perhaps Barbara felt a need to document, if only for herself, the reality she found herself in. Maybe when she looked at the phone and the whale boat—the boat, itself, a symbol of strength and man's conquest over nature—she felt vulnerable. They were stranded on this island, disconnected from the mainland. Modern technology had abandoned them. A phone could not get them off Santa

Rosa Island, and more importantly, what would happen with the war? They were marooned out there regardless of the heft of a whaling vessel or the brilliance of the modern technology it housed.

On the ninth, the archaeologists arose, prepared to work Skunk Point again, but rain kept them in camp. When it subsided, they headed toward the northern part of the island and Lobos Canyon. From there they "looked west down a valley between green sloping hills and a ... green flat bench at the bottom ... with a stream deep cut and winding down the center."[49] It was Cañon Verde (Green Canyon), an "unearthly" sight, Loomis recorded. Her observations and word choices are very different from the day before. Her tone evokes a sense of melancholy. She must have wondered if she would be forced to stay on the island. And, if so, for how long? Would this place become her home? As the women stood gazing at the canyon, a rider leading a packhorse appeared at the far end of the valley. Three more riders, another packhorse, and a loose horse followed. The girls shouted using their "wildest yelps"[50] to capture the riders' attentions. It was the boys, brought home safely from Tecolote Canyon, but they were too far away to hear their calls.

When they realized they wouldn't be noticed, the girls changed course, riding down Lobo Canyon to the beach on the north side of the island. As they rode, Loomis spied a "good looking flint" and a "large fine spear head" that lay next to another smaller one. Marion found two more points and "a great deal more chipped flint."[51] In a deep cut, they found exposed human remains and more masses of chipped stone flint. Though they seemed pleased with their finds, they continued onwards, more eager to catch up with the young men than to collect artifacts.

At camp that evening, the young men gushed about their finds, delivering reports of a "tremendous cemetery with skeletons buried flexed on right side with left hand over left side of face."[52] They carried on about the "many Pleistocene elephant deposits, ... some mixed into ... Miocene deposits," and "a new horse in the bank."[53] Everyone seemed excited to see the boys safe back at camp. Dinner must have been abuzz with an exchange of news.

Rain kept the entire group in camp on December 10. There was still no word from the museum, but they readied themselves for departure nonetheless. George Willett skinned his specimens, Ora packed food, and the rest of them readied as many extraneous items as they could.

The radio broadcasted continuous war news: Japanese planes had flown over San Francisco the night before, but dropped no bombs; the entire West Coast was blacked out: two British battleships, the *Prince of Wales* and *Repulse*, were sunk off the coast of Malaysia; fighting continued over Manila and the Philippines.

George Haise's visit to camp provided much-needed respite from the somber news. Talk turned to dehorning and Haise's efforts to poison the ravens that sometimes pecked the eyes right out of his calves, eating them alive. "They're the coyotiest birds to poison,"[54] he complained. The researchers chatted with him, but did not turn off the radio. Battles raged over Hawaii. Announcers broadcasted blackouts, then contradicted themselves. Newsmen gave instructions for complying with those blackouts, telling listeners that when "a 2 minute fluctuating siren and" a clear and "steady 2 minute whistle" sounded, civilians would know it was time to cover their windows with heavy curtains, turn off all electricity, and rely on candles and flashlights.[55] Loomis's journal records Italy's declaration of war against the United States and that of the United States against Italy and Germany. To escape the broadcasts, she and Hollenbach enlisted the boys to help them at their dig only to release them to their own devices a short time later—they were kids, after all. Happy to have their freedom, the pair bolted, indentured servants set loose.

The women continued to work at various spots before cutting across Old Ranch Canyon, which diagonally bifurcates the eastern tip of the island. From a distance they noticed the gully tops capped by snow geese and sat down to enjoy the view. These must have been the same birds Woodward noticed during his visit earlier in the expedition. The white of the birds' feathers against the green hills must have made for a memorable sight. In the quiet of the afternoon, the tableau would have surely exuded a sense of calm that gave the young women time to contemplate what future, if they could envision one, lay ahead.

Couffer and Fletcher saw these same birds, too. They noticed how thickly the fowl congregated, their feathers flocking the hill like snow or cotton candy, and the sight tempted the two young men to do more than just sit and admire. Stealthily the pair crawled up the hillside, careful to avoid being seen by the birds. As they reached the crest, the flock became audible to them. Years later, when recounting the scene at his kitchen table, Couffer recalled that they "could hear them talking.

Gabble. Gabble. Gabble.[56] His fingers moved quickly in imitation of the geese's bills, his tone growing solemn with the memory.

Reaching the top of the rise, the friends glanced at each other. "Ok, let's have a look," Couffer whispered to Fletch. Together they peeked their heads up over the hill. Before them at eye level, thousands of birds sat, squawked, and waddled, but the boys' quick movements startled the flock. The fowl rose as one great beast in a clatter of beating wings and monosyllabic *whouks* and *heenks*. The noise ascended as the birds climbed high into the sky and as a single unit, the white mass crossed the canyon, settling like snowflakes on another ridge. "It was an incredibly moving thing. God, I'll never forget how thrilling it was,"[57] Couffer recalled.

From their perch on top of an adjacent gully, Loomis and Hollenback saw the geese startle. They watched the flock rise up into the sky and spied what had spooked the birds: two thrill-seeking boys whose heads suddenly appeared where all those geese sat moments before.

Loomis and Hollenbach stayed in the field well past dusk, where they could breath in clean salt air, smell wild scents, and photograph statuesque elk and pigs darting wildly out of bushes. They must have reluctantly returned to camp and more war news.

Comstock's original plan called for a California Fish and Game cruiser to pick up the researchers in Bechers Bay, but with the imposition of radio silence, no communication between the researchers and the museum occurred. Still, the CIBS staffers were confident that Comstock would not abandon them on an island in the Pacific Ocean. On the morning of the thirteenth expedition's scheduled departure (coincidentally also the thirteenth of December), they scanned the horizon for a vessel sent to fetch them. Shortly before noon, two masts appeared in the distance. The boys, pegging it as fishing boat that would do them no good, made bets with the others about their hunch. Barbara and Marion laid odds against them, both sure the vessel had come for them.

By noon, anchored in Bechers Bay to deliver them home was Edwin Stanton's schooner, the *Santa Cruz*. Comstock had not let them down. The staff was ready to pack up and go, but Woodward strode off the ship and into camp to deliver the sobering news that they would have to spend a last night on the island. Port Hueneme closed at dark, and there was no time to load the ship and make the voyage back before then.

The next day, when the researchers moved their gear and specimens onto the *Santa Cruz,* missing from their cache was the fossil mammoth jawbone Couffer and Fletch had carefully jacketed in plaster and left on a hillside, awaiting future safe passage to the LACM. The boys felt certain they would eventually return for this treasure, but it was not to be.

McKinney did not welcome the researchers home with any apparent fanfare, at least according to the lack of media notifications, press releases, memorandums, or newspaper clippings in NHM's archives. Only a single sentence in the LACM weekly newsletter gives evidence of their return. It is unknown whether or not McKinney left his office to welcome the marooned employees back to work, but so mundane was their rescue that just four days after their safe return to the mainland the director-in-charge made no mention of it during his presentation at the board of governors meeting.

Instead, McKinney once again focused on his reorganization plans, which the board tabled after lengthy debate. However, unfortunately this was not the end of discussions pertaining to the Departments of Science and History, as some board members complained that during the recent reorganization Arthur Woodward had "conducted himself in a manner that no longer could be ignored."[58] The board was too savvy to detail the misbehavior in official minutes, and therefore the particulars will never be known, but they discussed the matter of Woodward at some length, concluding that "the Director and the Board had been lenient to a fault and that ... action should be taken to correct the matter."[59] But, unable to reach a consensus about how to appropriately discipline the archaeologist, the board passed a motion instructing the chairman of the history committee (Dr. Owen C. McCoy) and the president of the board (Dr. von KleinSmid) to inform Woodward that "a change in his attitude"[60] was desired. This was how McKinney welcomed his people back to the marble and cork-floored hallways of the LACM.

It is interesting that with all the modifications and uncertainties of the many complicated itineraries Comstock and von Bloeker created, less than a week after the United States entered into the Second World War (and just one day later than their carefully constructed original plans specified), Comstock succeeded in orchestrating the rescue of his CIBS staff from an island in the Pacific Ocean. But even a feat this satisfying

The Los Angeles County Channel Islands Biological Survey crew aboard the *Velero III*, August 1939. Back row, left to right: Arthur Woodward, George Kanakoff, Lloyd Martin, Meryl Dunkle, Don Meadows, and Jack von Bloeker. Front row, left to right: Russell Sprong, John Adams Comstock, and Jewel Lewis. Courtesy of Department of Anthropology, NHM.

had to have been bittersweet for the curator of science as well as the researchers, for when they boarded the *Santa Cruz* to leave Santa Rosa Island, they must have known that their safe passage presaged the end of the CIBS, two years too early with goals unmet. An ungodly war had sabotaged their efforts to collect, catalogue, chart, and map North America's Galapagos, and there was not a single thing they could do about it. McKinney could not have orchestrated a more definitive end. The Channel Islands Biological Survey was over.

In retrospect, the abrupt end to the survey was a sign: the world was changing, science was changing, and the museum was changing. The kind of work the CIBS had engaged in would soon give way to DNA and genetics, photo cataloguing, and three-dimensional imaging. Collecting would always have a place in museums and science—it is vital—but it would no longer be the primary focus.

One man, however, never gave up on his deeply held belief that the work they had started held value. Though he grasped the improbability of resurrecting the survey, he struggled with its incomplete state. Less than nine weeks after the war's end, John Adams Comstock contacted Sergeant Jack C. von Bloeker Jr., stationed in Lowry Field, Colorado. "Personally," Comstock wrote, "I wish we had all of the old gang back on the job and could take up the Channel Island Survey where we left off. There is still much to do."[61]

EPILOGUE

"EXTRA! IT'S PEACE: Complete Surrender by the Japanese."
President Truman announced at 7 p.m. today that the Japanese have accepted the Allied surrender terms.

—*Honolulu Star-Bulletin*, August 14, 1945

Even with all the external strife and internal LACM management turmoil, the CIBS had a good run. At least forty-two scientific articles were published, many in the *Bulletin of the Southern California Academy of Sciences*. And despite the rancor within the museum during the CIBS years, for the researchers it all fell away like sand from a dog's fur once they got out onto those islands. What became of all these flawed and tragic, yet good and wonderful people?

In 1941, after being rescued from Santa Rosa Island, Marion Hollenbach made a comment in the LACM's weekly newsletter that scientists are still talking and writing about. She said the Indians on Santa Rosa Island chose for their village sites "prominent bluffs along the coastline, usually at the mouth of one of the numerous canyons were water was available."[1] This comment might not seem like much, but over the past two decades well-known archaeological scholars such as Mike Glassow from the University of California–Santa Barbara, Jon Erlandson from the University of Oregon, Jennifer Perry from California State University–Channel Islands,

Amy Gusick from the LACM, Torben Rick from the Smithsonian, and others have been writing about the importance of water and viewshed for Channel Island native people's village site selections. Marion Hollenbach was one of a group of early female archaeologists whose works are called out in a book written in 2013 by David L. Browman.

Hollenbach held a bachelor's degree from the University of New Mexico. In 1938 she accepted a job with the LACM as curator of pre-Columbian art and the Pacific Islands. After writing her thesis entitled, "Dogs in Native American Culture," she earned her master's degree from the University of Southern California in 1940. During the war she served as a WAVE officer (in the naval women's reserve) and taught at an officer training school at Smith College, where she met her future husband, Allan Saunders of the University of Hawaii. In 1945 she left the LACM and moved to Hawaii the following year, where she filled her time with civic and educational pursuits. Hollenbach finished a second master's degree at age fifty-two (1960), founded the League of Women Voters of Honolulu, and ran for the state board of education in 1974, on which she served for six years. A building at the University of Hawaii, Saunders Hall, is dedicated to the service of the husband and wife team. She, along with Barbara Loomis, are believed to be the first trained female archaeologists to have worked on the Channel Islands. Marion accomplished much during her ninety years on earth.

George "Uncle George" Kanakoff was known as a jokester, teacher, scientific collector, chonchologist, theater performer, and newspaper editor. After the CIBS ended, Kanakoff continued working at the museum, escaping from the education division in 1948 when he was appointed curator of invertebrate paleontology. He was so happy to be back in the science department that he remained in that post until his retirement in 1966. But even in retirement he frequented the museum—there were just so many projects to keep working on. Only his death in 1973, at the age of seventy-six, prevented his return to the lab. In his obituary, a former student spoke on behalf of the many he taught at the museum, writing that Kanakoff was their "beloved 'Uncle George'" and they "were his devoted 'slaves,' collecting and sorting fossils with an eagerness and interest he instilled in [them]."[2] He collected so prodigiously that some of his collections probably still need sorting today.

George Willett was forty-seven when he came to work at the LACM in 1927. He became the head of the Department of Ornithology and Mammalogy the following year, but his talents weren't limited to these fields. For example, there are forty-one species and eight subspecies of mollusks—gastropods, pelecypods, and chitons—that bear his name as describer. He began collecting birds on the Channel Islands in 1905, a practice that ended with the last CIBS expedition. He added 450 Channel Islands birds to the museum's collections and grew the mammal collection from 926 specimens to over 8,000 by the time of his death in 1945.

In late 1941, Kenneth Stager (Ken or Kenny) replaced Jack von Bloeker Jr. when Jack jumped ship in favor of the Hancock Foundation. At the time of his hire, Stager held a bachelor's degree in zoology, but over the following twenty-two years he earned his master's and doctorate degrees, the latter at age forty-seven. Like the man whom he replaced at the LACM, Stager was a collector, with many of the specimens he amassed having particular importance today since they came from areas that have dramatically changed ecologically and thus represent an irreplaceable snapshot into the past. Stager retired from the LACM in 1976, but he remained active as a volunteer until health problems limited his mobility in the early 2000s. When he died in 2009 at the age of ninety-four, the *Los Angeles Times* devoted half of a page to his obituary in recognition of his contributions to ornithology.

Meryl B. Dunkle was principal of the Santa Catalina Island School in Avalon from 1923–1932. After his stint with the CIBS ended, the gentle botanist and quiet PhD continued to teach high school in Long Beach, California, and collect plants. In 1964, he published a book of poems entitled *Songs of the Trail* that he dedicated to his wife, his inspiration and the woman who "trod the trails of life" with him.[3] Two well-known and respected Channel Islands researchers, Charles Drost and Steve Junak, credit Dunkle's botanical leadership of the CIBS, specifically on Santa Barbara Island, as being "particularly important" because it culminated in "the first comprehensive floristic list for Santa Barbara Island."[4] The list to which they refer is found in Dunkle's 1950 paper entitled "Plant Ecology of the Channel Islands of California." It is appropriate that Drost and Junak applaud this particular piece, as it appears to be Dunkle's last published scientific work. Dr. Dunkle died at eighty-eight years of age in 1969.

Don Meadows published a half dozen or so articles related to Channel Islands Lepidoptera. Fifty percent of these were written prior to the CIBS's launch. He participated in seven of the thirteen expeditions and is remembered as the "Father of the Channel Islands Biological Survey." At some point after the CIBS was aborted, he sold or donated his micro moth and butterfly collection to the LACM, and in 1950 he bequeathed his large moth collection to the Smithsonian,[5] thus completing his metamorphosis from lepidopterist to respected Orange County, California, historian as thoroughly as any caterpillar emerging from its cocoon as a butterfly. Meadows taught high school for the rest of his career and wrote and lectured on California and Baja history, focusing on Orange County and the Spanish mission era. Between 1951 and 1980, he authored about fifty articles and books and reviewed thirty-one books on history and travel in the Southwest.[6] He was, according to Jerry Powell, a Berkeley lepidopterist, "acclaimed as an historian and researcher, bibliophile, outstanding teacher, professional writer and a friend, confidant, critic, and mentor to a diverse group of admirers, none of whom had any appreciation of his contributions as a lepidopterist."[7]

Meadows never earned his doctorate degree, never taught at Santa Ana Junior College, and never attained the level of scientific immortality to which he seemed to aspire. Still, he lived a life he loved. He lived several lives, it seems: devoted husband, father, and friend; schoolteacher; lepidopterist; and historian. In essence, he was a butterfly in life, enjoying a variety of passions that sparked various interests within him. In any regard, no matter the turmoil that may have existed between the Long Beach professor and the museum staff, John Adams Comstock—Meadows's colleague and friend—never ceased to think well of him. In an article published in 1942, Comstock acknowledged Meadows's donation of the first specimen of a new subspecies of painted tiger moth by naming it *Arachnis picta meadowsi*. More personally, in 1965, Comstock wrote his old friend, by then a well-established Orange County historian, to "express . . . pleasure over . . . [Meadows's] accomplishments" and "over the good deed ... [he] did in prompting ... [Comstock] to take up the Biological Survey of the Channel Islands."[8]

Don Meadows died a beloved ninety-eight-year-old man in 1994.

Ten months after Arthur Albert Woodward stepped off the *Santa Cruz* and onto Santa Rosa Island, his presence signaling to the CIBS staff marooned there that they were going home, the Office of Strategic Services (a precursor to today's CIA) recruited him to open a field office in Hollywood. His assignment was to analyze and report on certain areas in the South Pacific by scrutinizing photographs and movie frames depicting South Pacific island locations. He was also instructed to study the indigenous population's attitude toward foreign occupation. Nine months after it opened, the OSS closed, but Woodward was asked to join Admiral Richard Byrd aboard his ship as the naval explorer sailed through the South Pacific islands searching for prospective air bases. It was an assignment right up Woodward's alley.

Per LACM employment records, Woodward returned to the museum in 1944 as curator of history. In 1947, he married Barbara Loomis and she became his third wife and lifelong companion. At the museum, Woodward resumed his role as a well-respected expert in Indian trade goods and Navajo silver, the subjects he wrote most about throughout his career. Some sources credit him with authoring or editing at least eighteen books and two hundred articles on these and other topics, including at least four articles about the Channel Islands.

Woodward was a consummate collector of maps, books, old manuscripts, and diaries. He took meticulous notes and recreated drawings for his own collections that he unearthed in the National Archives in Washington, DC, and elsewhere. When he retired from the LACM in 1953 and moved with Barbara to Tucson, Arizona, he brought with him his collection that eventually numbered over twenty thousand titles. Once in Tucson, he branched out into museum consulting, helping to design exhibits for the Arizona Pioneers' Historical Society and the Tubac Presidio State Historic Park. In 1964, he began teaching at the University of Arizona and was granted an honorary PhD. In the late 1960s, he volunteered for the Amon Carter Museum of Western Art in Fort Worth, where he was tasked with traveling throughout the United States to look for complementary pieces of art for the museum's collection. In the early 1980s, he was bereft when his beloved Barbie preceded him in death; he followed her four years later, dying in 1986 at the age of eighty-eight. A friend remembered Woodward as "open and warm, yet blunt, straightforward, not devious or even diplomatic. He drank... but didn't make trouble."[9] In classic Art fashion, always getting the best of everyone, before he died he bought the local bars dry, requiring them to avoid serving liquor to mourners seeking solace on his death day.

While Art Woodward did not achieve scientific immortality from his work on the Channel Islands, he also did not actively pursue it like Meadows and von Bloeker did—perhaps such an undertaking was just too conformist for the likes of him. Nonetheless, Woodward is recognized as having moved the field of archaeology forward by some of today's most well-respected Channel Islands scholars. René L. Vellanoweth includes Woodward in his short list of twentieth-century San Nicolas Island archaeologists who broke the mold of the antiquarians who came before them. According to Vellanoweth, they did this by attempting to build cultural histories "based on the chronological distribution of artifacts and features." As a "culture historian," Vellanoweth explains, Woodward was part of "national trends in archaeology that focused on understanding technological development through time by ordering artifacts from simple to complex and comparing human-made objects across broad geographical regions." "In short," Woodward and his early twentieth-century colleagues "were true archaeologists who, far from seeing ... artifacts as treasure pieces, tried to understand their place in Californian, American, and world culture history."[10] The authors of *California Maritime Archaeology: A San Clemente Island Perspective* echo these sentiments, writing that while Woodward's style had much in common with earlier nineteenth-century archaeologists, there was "a rigor in Woodward's excavation techniques and record-keeping that was far superior to any nineteenth-century account of San Clemente Island." These are legacies of which Art Woodward could certainly be proud.

Throughout his life, John Adams Comstock—a generous, kind, Renaissance man—helped others with gifts of cash, housing, encouragement, and humor. In addition to publishing extensively, during his twenty years at the museum Comstock inspired many youngsters' interest in science, a few of whom participated in the survey. Lloyd Martin was one of them. Martin recalled meeting Comstock in 1927 when he was still a kid living in a home for boys. He credited "Doc" for "sav[ing] . . . his life, adopting him like a son and teaching him all he knew."[11] Martin came to work at the museum in 1933 at the age of twenty-three and spent thirty-three years there, retiring as curator of Lepidoptera. Reid Moran was another survey participant whom Comstock mentored. Moran's interest in science grew to the point that he earned his PhD after his service in the U.S. Army Air Corps during World War II. In 1957, he became curator of botany at the San Diego Natural History Museum, where he remained until his retirement twenty-five years later.

Comstock must have been genuinely disturbed by McKinney's reorganization, yet he never publicly complained about it except in that 1941 letter (included in Chapter 21) to his boss, Roland McKinney, in which he aired his feelings. When in 1944 the museum elevated his salary 9 percent (the first pay raise he had received since joining the museum sixteen years earlier) and changed his title to chief curator of science, he must have felt some modicum of satisfaction. It wasn't enough to entice him to stick around for long, however, because just four years later Dr. John Adams Comstock and his wife retired to Del Mar, California (near San Diego), where he began the last decades of his productive life.

In San Diego, Comstock became active in civic affairs, helping to establish Torrey Pines State Park and preserve a lagoon for birds, not boats. He also variously served as associate curator, research associate, and member of the San Diego Natural History Museum's board of directors.[12] He and his wife traveled extensively and were often gone from home for four to six months at a time. While their travels frequently took them to Arizona, they also collected in Puerto Vallarta (Mexico), American Samoa, and Central America, the latter accomplished through a road trip to the Guatemalan border. The gentleman scientist never stopped documenting his scientific discoveries, either. His last paper was published within twelve months of his passing in 1970 at age eighty-seven.

Jack Couffer, the youngest member of the CIBS, grew up quickly after being stranded on Santa Rosa Island. During his last year in high school, he continued to work at the museum as a student assistant, but as soon as he could he followed his mentor, Jack C. von Bloeker Jr., into the army. While there he attached himself to the special project von Bloeker had been enlisted to assist with: building the bat bomb. Together with Harry Fletcher (another CIBS staffer) and a crew of batty guys, the team built a bomb that would save the world. In the end, it burned down a brand new, secret U.S. military base, which is to say that it may have been highly effective in Japan's paper and thatch-roofed cities. The U.S. brass made other plans, however, ditching the bat bomb in favor of the atomic bomb. Couffer, von Bloeker, and Fletcher might have been sorry that their project was canned, but surely none of them would have traded the adventures that led up to the discovery of millions of bats in Texas caves, their companionship with an adult tiger that slept with Fletcher in his tent, or the burning of a U.S. military base. Yes, they had a "helluva" time trying to make it work. Young Jack Couffer would eventually write a book on his World War II exploits entitled *Bat Bomb: World War II's Other Secret Weapon.*

When the war ended, Couffer attended the University of Southern California intending to major in zoology, but before long he switched to cinema and launched a successful career as a writer, director, and cinematographer. He worked frequently for Disney and received an Academy Award nomination for his camera work on *Jonathon Livingston Seagull.* After spending a lifetime chasing down stories to film and write about, Couffer retired to his family home in Corona del Mar, California, where he continues to write books and scripts. The mammoth jawbones he and Fletcher left at Tecolote Canyon have never been recovered by either park personnel, the SBMNH, the LACM, or any of the many researchers working on the islands today. They are a treasure lost, but not for lack of Couffer's and Fletcher's trying.

Jack C. von Bloeker Jr. left the LACM in the fall of 1941, shortly before World War II aborted the ongoing efforts of the CIBS. Still, von Bloeker retained his aspirations and never forgot the urgings of Joseph Grinnell and E. Raymond Hall, who encouraged him to expand upon the compilation of Channel Islands mammals that he began in the late 1920s. It took von Bloeker nearly a quarter century to publish *Land Mammals of the Southern California Islands,* but he did. And to be fair, a lot happened during the twenty-four years he worked on the project after the CIBS disbanded.

When von Bloeker accepted the position at the Allan Hancock Foundation in the fall of 1941, his motivations not only included a desire to remain working in a scientific capacity while exiting the stifling environment McKinney had created for the museum's scientists across the street, but he also wanted to take advantage of the opportunity to pursue his dream of earning his doctorate in philosophy, likely in vertebrate zoology or a related field. One year later, when he was recruited by the U.S. Army Air Force to work on the secret bat bomb project, he put both his employment and academics on hold. After the bat bomb project was canceled, von Bloeker hoped to enter Officer Candidate School, but that fell through, too, prompting him to write to his longtime friend, mentor, and former professor at Los Angeles City College, A. W. Bell. In that letter, von Bloeker lamented that he had been "born under an unlucky star."[13] Certainly, bad fortune had befallen him: his mother's abandonment and early death; his unemployment during the Great Depression; the mugging he had suffered at the hands of three thugs who taped his mouth shut, tied his hands and legs with piano wire, knocked him out with the butt of a pistol, and left him in the bushes; two failed marriages, though he and Ona, his third wife, remained together for the rest of their lives; the aborted bat bomb project; and then his inability to get an appointment in Officer Candidate School. For a man with a burning desire to succeed, he had it tough and no one can say he didn't give it his all. His mentor Bell assured him that his time would come.

And it did. His star brightened after he was honorably discharged in December 1948. Within nine months he accepted a one-year position with the Hancock Foundation. Though the job was only twenty hours per week, it paid nearly what he had received at the museum for full-time work and allowed him time to resume his PhD. While working at the Hancock Foundation, he also secured a permanent teaching position at Los Angeles City College, a post he held until 1970.

In line with his plan, in 1949 von Bloeker submitted a draft doctoral thesis entitled, "A Preliminary Study of the Recent Mammal Fauna of the Channel Islands Area of Southern California." By the spring of 1950, he was jubilantly looking forward to taking his German and French scientific reading examinations, followed by daily written and oral preliminary doctoral examinations in the fall. Barring any issues with his exams, he expected to finish his thesis and take his final examinations in May 1951. He could then claim his doctorate of philosophy some twenty years after setting this goal for himself. But something must have intervened that prevented von Bloeker from earning that degree. No explanation has been recorded, but those three little letters, PhD, were never appended to his name.

Today, more than a half century after *Land Mammals of the Southern California Islands* was published, this work is still cited (sixty times on Google Scholar) and referred to by scientists who consider it a benchmark piece about terrestrial mammals on the Channel Islands. Jack C. von Bloeker Jr. published nearly 170 articles (some of which were meeting notes for scientific organizations) and was a member—either charter member, life member, editor, vice president, president, or board of director—of dozens of scientific organizations. Von Bloeker's works contributed to the knowledge scientists and conservation managers have today about the Channel Islands. He is remembered at the Museum of Vertebrate Zoology in Berkeley, at the Santa Barbara Museum of Natural History, at the Natural History Museum of Los Angeles County (his alma mater), and by many, many others. *Land Mammals* was the first—and to date, only—complete compilation of information on the mammal fauna of the Channel Islands.

Von Bloeker moved to Green Valley, Arizona, with his wife, Ona, in 1969. He applied for a position at Pima Community College, but it is not clear whether he was hired and the college could not confirm his employment. Notices in local papers advertised the frequent lectures he gave on wildlife, plants, geology, and ecology at Coronado National Forest.

On January 26, 1991, Jack's unlucky star returned. At eight o'clock on a winter Saturday evening, von Bloeker drove his station wagon down a hill near his home. A seventeen-year-old boy, clothed in dark attire, was skateboarding along the same route, and von Bloeker's car struck him. The boy died. Jack's son said there was a trial, but it's possible it was just an investigation as no local newspaper accounts followed such a trial and the *Arizona Daily Star* ran only a single article covering the accident. Whatever ensued, the tragedy deeply affected the bat scientist. Two months after it occurred, Jack C. von Bloeker Jr. was dead. He left a house full of bird and animal collections, scarab beetles, swizzle sticks, and stamps.

Jim Dines of the Los Angeles County Natural History Museum (NHM) states that von Bloeker's "lasting contribution was as a field collector and preparer at which he excelled."[14] The fruits of his work can be found in museum storerooms across the country. In California, his specimens are located at the NHM, the Museum of Vertebrate Zoology at Berkeley, the Santa Barbara Natural Museum of History, and the Western Foundation of Vertebrate Zoology in Camarillo. The Smithsonian also houses some of his specimens. Scientists and students remember von Bloeker for the collections of animals he amassed, which are still available for their use. Thus, while he might not have earned his PhD, Jack C. von Bloeker Jr. is remembered more, perhaps, than any of his other CIBS colleagues. Furthermore, as a result of *Land Mammals of the Southern California Islands*, his seminal work that no one has updated or replicated, he earned a modicum of scientific immortality.

Roland J. McKinney was director of the LACM from May 1939–January 1946, after which he established himself as a consultant to Walt Disney Studios in New York City. Later positions he held include: directorship of the Pepsi Cola annual art competition, consultant to the Department of American Art at the Metropolitan Museum of Art in New York City, and chairman of jurors for the Corcoran Gallery of Art's 23rd biennial in 1953. During his life, he published several books about art, including at least one for children. The Baltimore Museum of Art states he died in 1971. In retrospect, McKinney's strong support of art proved predictive of a major event in LACM's future, while on a larger scale the attention he placed on education, exhibitry, and school children foretold a trend that museums worldwide embrace today.

Since the CIBS ended, much has happened at the LACM. After the budget constraints of the war years eased, the 1940s and 1950s saw the museum's expansion in education, science, and history. In 1958, the facility enlarged beyond Exposition Park when it opened silent film star William S. Hart's twenty-two-room Spanish colonial revival mansion. This satellite museum, which is free of charge per Hart's request, includes outbuildings and a surrounding park that exhibited his extensive collections of artwork. During this same time period, the art division—aided by the powerful, art-favoring museum associates—began making plans to withdraw from the LACM. In support of this goal, the Los Angeles County Board of Supervisors allowed associates use of a portion of the County's La Brea Tar Pits property in exchange for their agreement to build a new art museum and fund art acquisitions. Fronting Wilshire Boulevard's famed Miracle Mile, the Los Angeles County Museum of Art opened in 1965. The private fundraising void left by the museum associates' departure was filled by the Natural History Museum of Los Angeles County Foundation, which to this day supports the science and history missions of the original LACM.

During the next decade, a multimillion-dollar gift from George C. Page allowed the NHM to realize its long-envisioned goal of developing a museum at the La Brea Tar Pits. The Page Museum, which opened in 1977, incorporates an active ice age fossil dig site in its exhibits and extensively uses experiential learning to teach visitors about the extinct animals that once lived in Los Angeles. The museum also features an exhibit officially known as the *Fossil Lab* (unofficially, the "fish bowl"), which was purportedly the first exhibit in the world to process and clean fossils in the public's full view. Its importance goes beyond the real-life science it displays, as this exhibit began the internal process of the NHM refocusing its attention outward rather than inward, thereby establishing a trend now emulated by museums the world over.

Notwithstanding the popularity of the La Brea Tar Pits, during the last decades of the twentieth century the museum functioned primarily as a research institution that struggled to find its place in the Los Angeles community. Attendance flagged, budget woes left some exhibits broken and others stale, management indiscretions dampened staff morale, a blacktop parking lot and other additions detracted from the once-beautiful Beaux Arts building, and a location near the center of the 1965 Watts and 1992 Rodney King riots negatively affected the museum's desirability as a family destination. As a result, during the 1990s the museum undertook a series of actions designed to stabilize finances, strengthen the board, and strategically enhance staffing. Essential to the successful implementation of this strategy was the county's agreement to match the museum foundation's annual operating support. This guarantee enabled museum leadership to assure private sector donors that capital projects could be sustained because county money now stood behind the museum's programming and maintenance expenditures for the long term. Once these tasks were accomplished, a small group of governors, trustees, and museum staff quietly entertained discussions about what lay ahead for the museum, including the possibility of building a new facility that could capitalize on synergies between visitors, members, and donors. As the oldest anchor institution in Exposition Park, however, leaving its long-time home was not necessarily an attractive—or cost-effective—alternative. After eighteen months, NHM leadership and the board concluded that the museum would remain in Exposition Park. The benefits included retention of a historic structure, a freeway-accessible site that would be gaining rail transit services in the future, and the positive spillover effect of the neighboring university's campus infrastructure upgrades (at USC). Moreover, since 1913 the museum had functioned as a resource to the generally underserved neighborhood in which it stood: south central Los Angeles. Serving this—and all of Los Angeles's communities—by enriching lives and meeting stakeholder needs would be a far greater accomplishment than building a new facade.

At this point, the museum developed a new vision statement: to inspire wonder, discovery, and responsibility for our natural and cultural worlds. This mission, together with the decision to remain in Exposition Park, profoundly inspired the ways in which the museum began to formulate its programming and future course. The director tasked with implementing the new plan described the museum's assets as including "incredibly distinguished research ... fabulous collections [that date back 4.5 million years and consist of 35 million specimens, second in size nationally only to the Smithsonian] and probably the largest public education program of any natural history museum in the country."[15] The museum focused on ways to better utilize these assets to not only demonstrate current and future relevance, but also to engage Los Angelinos and the world at large in meaningful conversations. Following the lead of the Page Museum's successful "fish bowl" *Fossil Lab* exhibit, NHM increasingly began looking outwards, toward the people it served. In essence, it was not the museum's physical structure or its employees that were paramount, but its visitors. This important philosophical change of focus began before other nationally recognized natural history museums adopted similar intentions, and it drove the museum's mission and vision forward into the twenty-first century.

Thus began a ten-year program that included restoring and renovating the historic 1913 building and its galleries to tell larger, more futuristic, and more integrated science and history stories, constructing the nature garden that surrounds a portion of the building in Exposition Park, and adding multimedia exhibits that utilize collections in ways that allow

Leaving San Miguel Island, August 1939. From left to right: Meryl B. Dunkle, Jewel Lewis, Russel Sprong, Jack von Bloeker, Lloyd Martin, Donald Meadows, and George Kanakoff.

visitors to experience science rather than merely receive messages and information. Taking advantage of its location within a global biodiversity hotspot, NHM also began developing programs that study life within the landscapes around Los Angeles County. Consequently, the museum has become a leader in urban biodiversity and citizen science. These physical and internal transformations took the institution from an ivory tower culture to one with a public face that brings the community and their perspectives into the museum's conversations.

As the museum moves forward into the next phase of its history, it is pushing this vision further and deeper into its DNA, literally.[16] However, though much of the science being conducted at NHM is cutting edge, a key concept inherent in all of NHM's programs is asking people to look around in order to experience—and to really see—their environment, because "making observations is the basis of science."[17] Additionally, and most importantly, the museum is purposefully reaching out and listening to a diverse audience when creating its programming.[18] All of these philosophies together have contributed to soaring attendance and the attainment of an impressively diverse visitorship: 40 percent of onsite visitors are non-Anglo, the highest index of all of Los Angeles's largest cultural institutions. These days, the museum's greatest assets—its collections and the science they inspire—fortify its greatest strength, namely its commitment to and ability to engage the public.[19]

The Channel Islands Biological Survey is an essential part of the museum's history. Much more than a journey never before attempted, and more than an ambitious undertaking that did not realize its stated objectives, the CIBS laid a foundation for the future. The survey marked "a crucial transition from the collecting expedition in vogue during the Victorian era to more modern, problem-oriented scientific research."[20] Furthermore, through its use of both museum staff and community scientists—schoolteachers, cooks, immigrants, science-hungry teenagers, and women—the CIBS looked to its own backyard and embraced the full range of scientific disciplines with the explicit hope of enhancing not only science but also the public's understanding of the world around them. As a result, the CIBS created its own scientific immortality, one that lives on both through the collections it amassed and in the philosophy of community involvement and collaboration that it championed.

APPENDIX

Channel Islands Biological Survey Itineary, Participants, and Dates

	Exp #	John A. Comstock	Jack von Bloeker, Jr	George Kanakoff	Ona B. von Bloeker	Arthur Woodward	Chris Henne	George Willett	Ora A. Willett	Lloyd Martin
	245	23	184	179	110	113	83	84	81	85
EXPEDITION #1: 2/17/39—2/19/39 (3 days)										
San Clemente	1									
	1	2/17/39 3						2/17/39 3		
	1	2/19/39						2/19/39		
EXPEDITION #2: 4/1/39—4/8/39 (8 days)										
Camp Chinigchinich										
San Clemente	2									
	2		4/1/39 8			4/1/39 8				4/1/39 8
	2		4/8/39			4/8/39				4/8/39
EXPEDITION #3: 5/27/39—5/30/39 (4 days)										
Santa Barbara	3									
Campo de los Conejos (rabbits)	3		5/27/39 4							5/27/39 4
	3		5/30/39							5/30/39
EXPEDITION #4: 7/21/39—8/19/39 (33 days)										
San Nicolas	4.1									
El campo de la Juana Maria	4.1		7/21/39 7	7/21/39 7		7/21/39 7				7/21/39 7
	4.1		7/28/39	7/28/39		7/28/39				7/28/39
San Miguel	4.2									
El Campo del Cabrillo	4.2		7/28/39 7	7/28/39 7		7/28/39 7				7/28/39 7
	4.2		8/4/39	8/4/39		8/4/39				8/4/39
Santa Rosa	4.3									
Camp Nidever	4.3		8/4/39 7	8/4/39 7		8/4/39 7				8/4/39 7
	4.3		8/11/39	8/11/39		8/11/39				8/11/39
Santa Cruz	4.4									
	4.4	8/11/39 9	8/11/39 9	8/11/39 9		8/11/39 9				8/11/39 9
	4.4	8/19/39	8/19/39	8/19/39		8/19/39				8/19/39
EXPEDITION #5: 11/7/39—12/7/39 (31 days)										
San Clemente	5									
El Campo de las Chollas	5		11/7/39 31	11/7/39 31		11/7/39 31		11/7/39 31	11/7/39 31	
	5		12/7/39	12/7/39		12/7/39		12/7/39	12/7/39	
EXPEDITION #6: 11/23/39—11/26/39 (4 days)										
San Clemente	6									
El Campo de las Mosquitoes	6									11/23/39 4
	6									11/26/39
EXPEDITION #7: 3/16/40—3/23/40 (8 days)										
Santa Barbara	7									
El Campo de los Gatos	7			3/16/40 8						3/16/40 8
	7			3/23/40						3/23/40
Catalina	7									
Arrive	7		3/16/40 1							
Depart	7		3/16/40							

Channel Islands Biological Survey Itinerary, Participants, and Dates (*cont'd*)	Exp #	John A. Comstock	Jack von Bloeker, Jr	George Kanakoff	Ona B. von Bloeker	Arthur Woodward	Chris Henne	George Willett	Ora A. Willett	Lloyd Martin
	245	23	184	179	110	113	83	84	81	85
EXPEDITION #8: 4/10/40—4/28/40 (19 days)										
San Nicolas	8									
El Campo de los Boregos	8	4/10/40 3	4/10/40 19	4/10/40 19	4/10/40 19	4/10/40 19	4/10/40 19			
	8	4/12/40	4/28/40	4/28/40	4/28/40	4/28/40	4/28/40			
EXPEDITION #9: 8/15/40—8/30/40 (16 days)										
Anacapa	9									
	9		8/15/40 16	8/15/40 16	8/15/40 16		8/15/40 16			
	9		8/30/40	8/30/40	8/30/40		8/30/40			
EXPEDITION #10: 11/23/40—12/12/40 (20 days)										
San Nicolas	10									
Dutch Harbor	10		11/23/40 20	11/23/40 20	11/23/40 20	11/23/40 20	11/23/40 20			
	10		12/12/40	12/12/40	12/12/40	12/12/40	12/12/40			
EXPEDITION #11: 1/20/41—1/27/41 (8 days)										
Santa Catalina	11									
	11							1/20/41 8	1/20/41 8	
	11							1/27/41	1/27/41	
EXPEDITION #12: 2/14/41—4/9/41 (54 days)										
San Clemente	12.1									
	12.1		2/14/41 8	2/14/41 8	2/14/41 8		2/14/41 9	2/14/41 8	2/14/41 8	
	12.1		2/22/41	2/22/41	2/22/41		2/22/41	2/22/41	2/22/41	
Santa Catalina	12.2									
	12.2		2/22/41 21	2/22/41 21	2/22/41 21			2/22/41 9	2/22/41 9	2/22/41 22
	12.2		3/15/41	3/15/41	3/15/41			3/2/41	3/2/41	3/15/41
Anacapa	12.3									
	12.3		3/15/41 7	3/15/41 7	3/15/41 7		3/15/41 7	3/15/41 8	3/15/41 8	3/15/41 1
	12.3		3/22/41	3/22/41	3/22/41		3/22/41	3/22/41	3/22/41	3/16/41
Santa Cruz	12.4									
	12.4		3/22/41 7	3/22/41 7	3/22/41 7					3/22/41 8
	12.4		3/29/41	3/29/41	3/29/41					3/29/41
Santa Rosa	12.5									
	12.5		3/29/41 12	3/29/41 12	3/29/41 12		3/29/41 12			
	12.5		4/9/41	4/9/41	4/9/41		4/9/41			
EXPEDITION #13: 11/8/41—12/14/41 (37 days)										
Santa Rosa	13									
	13	11/8/41 8				11/25/41 5		11/28/41 17	11/28/41 17	
	13	11/15/41				11/29/41		12/14/41	12/14/41	

Channel Islands Biological Survey Itineary, Participants, and Dates (cont'd)

	Exp # 245	John Shrader 75	Don C. Meadows 67	M.B. Dunkle 70	Russel Sprong 54	Marion G. Hollenbach 40	Theodore Reddick 16	-----One Trip Ponies----- James DeLong, E.C. Williams, Howard Keller, Jack H. Nordheim, Harry Geiger, Leo Kartmann, Barker Woodward, Richard Case, Jack C. Couffer, Harry Fletcher, King A. Richey, Ken Stager, Carol Stager, John C. Stock, Barbara Loomis, Reid Moran, Jewel Lewis 334	Total Expedition # Days 1,598
EXPEDITION #1: 2/17/39—2/19/39 (3 days)									
San Clemente	1								
	1		2/17/39 3						
	1		2/19/39						
EXPEDITION #2: 4/1/39—4/8/39 (8 days)									
Camp Chinigchinich San Clemente	2								
	2		4/1/39 8	4/1/39 8	4/1/39 8		4/1/39 8		
	2		4/8/39	4/8/39	4/8/39		4/8/39		
EXPEDITION #3: 5/27/39—5/30/39 (4 days)									
Santa Barbara	3								
Campo de los Conejos (rabbits)	3		5/27/39 4	5/27/39 4	5/27/39 4		5/27/39 4	James DeLong 4 5/27/1939	
	3		5/30/39	5/30/39	5/30/39		5/30/39	5/30/39	
EXPEDITION #4: 7/21/39—8/19/39 (33 days)									
San Nicolas	4.1								
El campo de la Juana Maria	4.1		7/21/39 7	7/21/39 7	7/21/39 7			Jewel Lewis: 7/21/1939 7	
	4.1		7/28/39	7/28/39	7/28/39			7/28/39	
San Miguel	4.2								
El Campo del Cabrillo	4.2		7/28/39 7	7/28/39 7	7/28/39 7			Jewel Lewis: 7/28/1939 7	
	4.2		8/4/39	8/4/39	8/4/39			8/4/39	
Santa Rosa	4.3								
Camp Nidever	4.3		8/4/39 7	8/4/39 7	8/4/39 7			Jewel Lewis: 8/4/1939 7	
	4.3		8/11/39	8/11/39	8/11/39			8/11/39	
Santa Cruz	4.4								
	4.4		8/11/39 9	8/11/39 9	8/11/39 9			Jewel Lewis: 8/11/1939 9	
	4.4		8/19/39	8/19/39	8/19/39			8/19/39	
EXPEDITION #5: 11/7/39—12/7/39 (31 days)									
San Clemente	5								
El Campo de las Chollas	5							Barker Woodward: 31 11/7/1939	
	5							12/7/39	

Channel Islands Biological Survey Itineary, Participants, and Dates (cont'd)

	Exp #	John Shrader	Don C. Meadows	M.B. Dunkle	Russel Sprong	Marion G. Hollenbach	Theodore Reddick	-----One Trip Ponies----- James DeLong, E.C. Williams, Howard Keller, Jack H. Nordheim, Harry Geiger, Leo Kartmann, Barker Woodward, Richard Case, Jack C. Couffer, Harry Fletcher, King A. Richey, Ken Stager, Carol Stager, John C. Stock, Barbara Loomis, Reid Moran, Jewel Lewis	Total Expedition # Days
	245	75	67	70	54	40	16	334	1,598
EXPEDITION #6: 11/23/39—11/26/39 (4 days)									
San Clemente	6								
El Campo de las Mosquitoes	6		11/23/39 4	11/23/39 4	11/23/39 4		11/23/39 4	E.C. Williams 4 11/23/1939	
	6		11/26/39	11/26/39	11/26/39		11/26/39	11/26/39	
EXPEDITION #7: 3/16/40—3/23/40 (8 days)									
Santa Barbara	7								
El Campo de los Gatos	7		3/16/40 8	3/16/40 8	3/16/40 8				
	7		3/23/40	3/23/40	3/23/40				
Catalina	7								
Arrive	7								
Depart	7								
EXPEDITION #8: 4/10/40—4/28/40 (19 days)									
San Nicolas	8								
El Campo de los Boregos	8		sched-uled, did not	sched-uled, did not				Harry Geiger, Leo 19 Kartman: 4/10/1940	
	8		partici-pate	partici-pate				4/28/40	
EXPEDITION #9: 8/15/40—8/30/40 (16 days)									
Anacapa	9								
	9		8/15/40 10	8/15/40 16				Jack H. Nordheim: 16 8/15/1940	
	9		8/24/40	8/30/40				8/30/40	
EXPEDITION #10: 11/23/40—12/12/40 (20 days)									
San Nicolas	10								
Dutch Harbor	10	11/23/40 20				11/23/40 20		Howard Keller: 20 11/23/1940	
	10	12/12/40				12/12/40		12/12/40	
EXPEDITION #11: 1/20/41—1/27/41 (8 days)									
Santa Catalina	11								
	11								
	11								

Channel Islands Biological Survey Itineary, Participants, and Dates (*cont'd*)

	Exp # 245	John Shrader 75	Don C. Meadows 67	M.B. Dunkle 70	Russel Sprong 54	Marion G. Hollenbach 40	Theodore Reddick 16	-----**One Trip Ponies**----- James DeLong, E.C. Williams, Howard Keller, Jack H. Nordheim, Harry Geiger, Leo Kartmann, Barker Woodward, Richard Case, Jack C. Couffer, Harry Fletcher, King A. Richey, Ken Stager, Carol Stager, John C. Stock, Barbara Loomis, Reid Moran, Jewel Lewis 334	Total Expedition # Days 1,598
EXPEDITION #12: 2/14/41—4/9/41 (54 days)									
San Clemente	12.1								
	12.1	2/14/41 8	scheduled, did not	scheduled, did not				Redi Moran: 2/14/1941 8	
	12.1	2/22/41	participate	participate				2/22/41	
Santa Catalina	12.2								
	12.2	2/22/41 21	scheduled, did not	scheduled, did not				Reid Moran: 2/22/1941 21	
	12.2	3/15/41	participate	participate				3/15/41	
Anacapa	12.3								
	12.3	3/15/41 7	scheduled, did not	scheduled, did not				Reid Moran: 3/15/1941 7	
	12.3	3/22/41	participate	participate				3/22/41	
Santa Cruz	12.4								
	12.4	3/22/41 7	scheduled, did not	scheduled, did not				Redi Moran: 3/22/1941 7	
	12.4	3/29/41	participate	participate				3/29/41	
Santa Rosa	12.5								
	12.5	3/29/41 12	scheduled, did not	scheduled, did not				Redi Moran: 3/29/1941 12	
	12.5	4/9/41	participate	participate				4/9/41	

Channel Islands Biological Survey Itineary, Participants, and Dates (*cont'd*)

	Exp #	John Shrader	Don C. Meadows	M.B. Dunkle	Russel Sprong	Marion G. Hollenbach	Theodore Reddick	-----One Trip Ponies----- James DeLong, E.C. Williams, Howard Keller, Jack H. Nordheim, Harry Geiger, Leo Kartmann, Barker Woodward, Richard Case, Jack C. Couffer, Harry Fletcher, King A. Richey, Ken Stager, Carol Stager, John C. Stock, Barbara Loomis, Reid Moran, Jewel Lewis	Total Expedition # Days
	245	75	67	70	54	40	16	334	1,598
EXPEDITION #13: 11/8/41—12/14/41 (37 days)									
Santa Rosa	13								
	13					11/25/41 20		Kennneth Stager: 24 11/8/41—12/1/41	
	13					12/14/41		Carol Stager: 24 11/8/41—12/1/41	
								King A. Richey: 8 11/8/41—11/15/41	
								Harry Fletcher: 37 11/8/41—12/14/41	
								John C. Stock: 8 11/8/41—11/15/41	
								Barbara Loomis: 20 11/25/41—12/14/41	
								Richard Case: 17 11/28/41—12/14/41	
								Jack C. Couffer: 17 11/28/41—12/14/41	
								****Where Expeditions spanned multiple Islands, the first day of the island stay is used to calc # of days on the island, but the last is not, until the return trip home, except where someone joined trip for only 1 island, then all days are counted for # of days total	

NOTES

INTRODUCTION

1. The California Channel Islands are continental islands, or islands that are connected to a continent by the continental shelf, whereas the Galapagos Islands are oceanic islands, which have never been connected to a continent. Greenland, Sicily, and the California Channel Islands are examples of continental islands, whereas Iceland, the Hawaiian Islands, and the Galapagos Islands are examples of oceanic islands.

2. Department of the Interior, Information Service, "National Park Service," March 14, 1940, Natural History Museum, Los Angeles County Archives.

3. Personal email communication with Raymond Ingersoll, professor emeritus of geology and tectonics at the University of California, Los Angeles, September 2, 2018.

4. Leslie Reeder Myers et al., "Sea Level, Paleogeography, and Archeology on California's Northern Channel Islands," *Quaternary Research* 83, no. 2 (2015): 265.

5. Ibid.

6. Larry D. Agenbroad et al., "Mammoths and Humans as Late Pleistocene Contemporaries on Santa Rosa Island," in *Proceedings of the Sixth California Islands Symposium*, edited by D. A. Garcelon and C. A. Schwemm (Arcata, California: Institute for Wildlife Studies, 2005), 6.

7. Daniel R. Muhs et al., "Late Quaternary Sea-Level History and the Antiquity of Mammoths (*Mammuthus exilis* and *Mammuthus columbi*), Channel Islands National Park, California, USA," *Quaternary Research* 83, no. 3 (2015): 515.

8. Exceptions to the rule include instances where the same species inhabiting different environments grows larger on one island but smaller on another. Biologists explain this seemingly contradictory occurrence by considering the ecological niches the species occupies and whether competitor species occupied the island earlier or later than the "conflicting" species. For instance, two species of rattlesnakes inhabiting both the mainland and an island off the coast of the Gulf of Mexico have switched relative sizes. On the island, the larger mainland predator shrunk to half its size, while the smaller mainland snake grew two times larger. This is explained by understanding that the small mainland snake migrated to the island earlier, and thus—as the theory would predict—grew in size. Then, by the time the bigger mainland snake arrived on the island, the "large rattlesnake" niche was taken, so it shrank in order to accommodate the "small rattlesnake" niche.

9. Clutch/litter size and frequency of birth is a benefit of large animal size, but it is not necessarily directly tied to Foster's Rule.

10. Larry D. Agenbroad, "Channel Islands (USA) Pygmy Mammoths (*Mammuthus exilis*) Compared and Contrasted with *M. columbi*, Their Continental Ancestral Stock," in *The World of Elephants—International Congress* (Rome, Italy: 2001), 474.

11. Ibid.
12. Agenbroad et al., "Mammoths and Humans as Late Pleistocene Contemporaries on Santa Rosa Island," in *Proceedings of the Sixth California Islands Symposium*, 3–7.
13. Some people may find within this book some archaic word choices, such as Indian, boy, or girl. They are not intended to offend, but to give the book the flavor of the time in which the story takes place.
14. Gina M. Semprebon et al., "Dietary Reconstruction of Pygmy Mammoths from Santa Rosa Island of California," *Quaternary International* 406 (2016): 1.
15. Torben Rick and Leslie Reeder-Meyers, "Deception Island: Archaeology of 'Anyapax, Anacapa Island, California," *Smithsonian Contributions to Anthropology* 52, (2018), 45.
16. Mark L. Raab et al., *California Maritime Archaeology: A San Clemente Island Perspective* (Plymouth, United Kingdom: AltaMira Press, 2009), 164–65.
17. Torben C. Rick et al., "Flightless Ducks, Giant Mice and Pygmy Mammoths: Late Quaternary Extinctions on California's Channel Islands," *World Archaeology* 44, no. 1 (2012): 4.
18. Todd J. Braje et al., "Finding the First Americans," *Science* 358, no. 6363 (2017): 593.
19. Frederic Caire Chiles, *California's Channel Islands: A History*, (Norman, Oklahoma: University of Oklahoma Press, 2015), 10.
20. The author is an All Eight member.
21. Todd J. Braje et al., *Channel Islands National Park Archaeological Overview and Assessment* (Ventura, California: Cultural Resource Division, Channel Islands National Park, 2010), 1.7.
22. Torben Rick, "Introduction: New Directions in Channel Islands Archaeology," *Pacific Coast Archaeological Society Quarterly* 37, no. 3 (Summer 2001): 1, http://www.pcas .org/assets/documents/introductionRick_000.pdf.

CHAPTER 1

1. Arthur Woodward, "Archaeological and Historical Fieldwork Conducted by Arthur Woodward during the Los Angeles Museum–Channel Islands Biological Survey of 1939–1941," unpublished manuscript, edited by Chris D. Coleman, Department of Anthropology, NHM, original journals in Arizona Historical Society, MS 1189, Arthur Woodward Papers, 1898–1986, 1860s–1980s (bulk 1920s–1960s), 52.
2. Ibid.
3. Ken Woodward, *Rubaboo: The Story of Arthur Woodward—Adventurer, Historian, Archaeologist—Who Was Driven by His Need to Know* (San Diego, California: Ken Woodward, 2014), 182.
4. Woodward, "Archaeological and Historical Fieldwork," 53.
5. Donald C. Meadows, "Progress Report of the Los Angeles Museum Channel Islands Biological Survey, San Clemente Island Expedition, April 1 to 8, 1939," Natural History Museum of Los Angeles County, 14.
6. Ibid.
7. The first inhabitants of North America today refer to themselves and their brethren in many different ways. Using their tribal names is the most accurate when describing their own heritage, but it can be difficult when many different tribes are discussed. Other frequently used terms include First Nation, native, Native American,

American Indian, Aboriginal, indigenous, and even Indian. Some tribal people find the term Indian to be derogative, but it is used in this book because during the time of the CIBS it was a common term that the researchers and scientists in this book utilized with all due respect.

8. In this book, depending on context, the term *Chumash* is used to either designate mainland Chumash only, or more broadly to encompass mainland Chumash and island Chumash/Chumash islanders—these latter two terms used interchangeably to denote northern Channel Island people. *Gabrielino/Tongva* is used to designate mainland people, whereas *island Gabrielino, island Tongva,* or *southern Channel Island Tongva* are used for southern Channel Island people.

9. Woodward, "Archaeological and Historical Fieldwork," 54.

10. Ibid., 54–55.

11. Ibid., 55.

12. Ibid., 53.

13. Ibid., 41.

14. Ibid., 48.

15. Ibid., 33.

16. Andrew Yatkso, "Reassessing Archaeological Site Density at San Clement Island," *Proceedings of the Society for California Archaeology* 2 (1989): 189.

17. Woodward, "Archaeological and Historical Fieldwork," 33.

18. "About: What is Historical Archaeology?" Society for Historical Archaeology, https://sha.org/about-us/what-is-historical-archaeology/.

19. Sam Negri, "Historian Takes 'Shotgun Approach' to Life," *Arizona Republic* (Phoenix, Arizona), May 17, 1982.

20. Woodward, *Rubaboo,* 10.

21. Ibid., 144.

22. "The 'Grinnell' Method," The Museum of Vertebrate Zoology at Berkely, last modified 2015, http://mvz.berkeley.edu/Grinnell_Method.html.

23. "Joseph Grinnell (1877–1939)—MVZ;s First Director," The Museum of Vertebrate Zoology, last modified 2015, http://mvz.berkeley.edu/Grinnell.html.

24. Woodward, "Archaeological and Historical Fieldwork," 27.

25. Pothunters is a derogatory word describing relic seekers who defile and destroy archaeological sites for their personal collections or private financial gain.

26. Keith A. Dixon, "Early History of SWAA," reference found under section entitled "Purposes," *Southwestern Anthropological Association* 22 (2018). At the time of its founding, the SWAA was called the Southwestern Archaeological Federation, https://swaa-anthro.org/early-history-of-swaa/.

27. Woodward, *Rubaboo,* 47.

CHAPTER 2

1. Phyllis Van Doren, "Remembering Doc Comstock," *Environment Southwest,* color slides by Bob Van Doren (Winter 1983): 15, NHM Archives.

2. Pacific Slope Section of the Lepidopterists' Society 26th Annual Meeting, "John Adams Comstock Award," August 26, 1979, 1, University of California, NHM Archives.

3. Van Doren, "Remembering Doc Comstock," 19, NHM Archives.

4. John Adams Comstock to Don Meadows, November 5, 1965, Don Meadows Papers (MS-R001), UC Irvine, Special Collections & Archives.
5. Donald C. Meadows to John Adams Comstock, Los Angeles Museum, Exposition Park, Los Angeles, California, January 31,1938, Don Meadows Papers (MS-R001), UC Irvine, Special Collections & Archives.
6. Donald C. Meadows to Edwin L. Stanton, Long Beach, California, March 1, 1938, Don Meadows Papers (MS-R001), UC Irvine, Special Collections & Archives.
7. Nancy Moure, "The Struggle for a Los Angeles Art Museum, 1890–1940," *Southern California Quarterly* 74, no. 3 (1992): 265.
8. Rufus Bernhard von KleinSmid, "Eugenics and the State" (1913), 2.
9. Don Meadows, "Progress Report of the Los Angeles Museum—Channel Islands Biological Survey, San Clemente Island Expedition April 1 to 8, 1939," 3, 28–29, and 33–34, NHM Archives.
10. Don C. Meadows to the board of governors, Los Angeles Museum, December 20, 1938, NHM Archives.
11. Ibid.
12. E. I. White, "One of the Most Amazing Events in the Realm of Natural History in the Twentieth Century," *London Illustrated News*, March 11, 1939; quoted in Keith Stewart Thomson, *Living Fossil: the Story of the Coelacanth* (New York: WW Norton & Company, 1992), 37.
13. Keith Stewart Thomson, *Living Fossil: The Story of the Coelacanth* (New York: WW Norton & Company, 1992), 29.
14. Ibid., 36–38.
15. Ibid., 38. Thomson writes that Courtenay-Latimer's estimate was "surely exaggerated."

CHAPTER 3

1. Allan A. Schoenherr, C. Robert Feldmeth, and Michael J. Emerson, *Natural History of the Islands of California*, no. 61 (Berkeley and Los Angeles: University of California Press, 2003), 150, 266.
2. John Johnson, curator of anthropology at the Santa Barbara Museum of Natural History, interview by Corinne Heyning Laverty on April 26, 2016, Santa Barbara, CA.
3. Michael Glassow, professor emeritus at the Department of Anthropology, University of California, Santa Barbara, and John Johnson, curator of archaeology at the Santa Barbara Museum of Natural History, personal email communication with author, October 30, 2018.
4. Jennifer Perry, professor of anthropology at California State University Channel Islands, personal email communication with author, April 26, 2016.
5. Ibid.
6. Golla, Victor, "Linguistic Prehistory," in *California Prehistory Colonization, Culture, and Complexity*, edited by Terry L. Jones and Kathryn A. Klar (Lanham, New York: AltaMira Press, 2007), 54.
7. John Johnson, personal oral communication with author, May 30, 2019.
8. Arthur Woodward to Phil Orr, Santa Barbara Museum of Natural History, May 28, 1940, Arizona Historical Society, MS 1189 Woodward, Arthur, 1898–1986, Papers, 1860s–1980s (bulk 1920s–1960s).
9. Ibid.

10. Ibid.

11. Jennifer Perry, professor of anthropology, California State University Channel Islands, personal email communication with author, April 26, 2016.

12. Jennifer E. Perry, "The Archaeology of Ritual on the Channel Islands," in *California's Channel Islands: The Archaeology of Human-Environment Interactions*, edited by Christopher S. Jazwa and Jennifer E. Perry (Salt Lake City: University of Utah Press, 2013), 139.

13. L. Mark Raab, Jim Cassidy, Andrew Yatsko, and William J. Howard, *California Maritime Archaeology: A San Clemente Island Perspective* (Lanham, New York: AltaMira Press, 2009), 201.

14. Constance Cameron, "Animal Effigies from Coastal Southern California," *Pacific Coast Archaeological Society Quarterly* 36, no. 2 (2000): 48–9.

15. American Antiquities Act of 1906, 16 USC 431–33.

16. Rebecca Tsosie, "Indigenous Rights and Archaeology," in *Native Americans and Archaeologists: Stepping Stones to Common Ground*, edited by Nina Swidler, Kurt E. Dongoske, Roger Anyon, and Alan S. Downer (Walnut Creek: AltaMira Press, 1997), 68.

17. Ibid.

CHAPTER 4

1. A 1998 settlement between the National Parks Conservation Association, the National Park Service, and the Vail and Vickers family, former owners of Santa Rosa Island, terminated all cattle on Santa Rosa as of December 31, 1998, but allowed deer and elk to remain on the island until the end of 2011.

2. Todd J. Braje, *Shellfish for the Celestial Empire: The Rise and Fall of Commercial Abalone Fishing in California* (Salt Lake City: University of Utah Press, 2016), 174, 176.

3. "San Clemente Island," Santa Barbara Botanic Garden, last updated 2019, www.sbbg.org /conservation-research/channel-islands/san-clemente.

4. Allan A. Schoenherr, C. Robert Feldmeth, and Michael J. Emerson, *The Natural History of the Islands of California* (Los Angeles: University of California Press, 1999), 318.

5. "San Clemente Loggerhead Shrike, *Lanius ludovicianus mearnsi*; 5-Year Review: Summary and Evaluation" (Carlsbad: U.S. Fish and Wildlife Service, Carlsbad Fish and Wildlife Office, June 17, 2009), 5, https://www.fws.gov/carlsbad/SpeciesStatusList /5YR/20090617_5YR_SCLS.pdf.

6. Andrew Yatsko, "From Sheepherders to Cruise Missiles: A Short History of Archaeological Research at San Clemente Island," *Pacific Coast Archaeological Society Quarterly* 36, no. 1 (2000): 20.

7. "San Clemente Loggerhead Shrike; 5-Year Review," 15.

8. Donald C. Meadows, "Progress Report: The Los Angeles Museum Channel Islands Biological Survey, San Clemente Island Expedition, April 1 to 8, 1939," 25, NHM Archives.

9. Anonymous, undated, untitled memo filed with documents pertaining to the thirteenth expedition of the CIBS, NHM Archives.

10. Donald C. Meadows, "Progress Report," 10.

11. George Willett, memo to John A. Comstock, March 10, 1939, NHM Archives.

12. Ibid.

CHAPTER 5

1. Board of governors meeting minutes, February 2, 1939, 51, Natural History Museum of Los Angeles County.
2. Anonymous, "More Than 100 Proposed for McKinney Post," *The Baltimore Sun* (Baltimore, Maryland), January 16, 1938, 20.
3. Daniel Catton Rich to Preston Harrison, December 27, 1938, Roland Joseph McKinney papers, 1926–1955, Archives of American Art, Smithsonian Institution.
4. Ibid.
5. Archaeological investigations on the Channel Islands began as early "as the 1870's. The best known of these ... expeditions related to the *United States Geographical Surveys West of the One Hundredth Meridian* which were published in volume seven of the series regarding that survey." Arthur Woodward, "Archaeological and Historical Fieldwork Conducted by Arthur Woodward during the Los Angeles Museum—Channel Islands Biological Surveys of 1939–1941," unpublished manuscript, edited by Chris D. Coleman, 27. Additionally, Woodward's own notes reveal that he read Sebastián Juan Vizaíno's Spanish logs from the spring of 1769: Arthur Woodward Collection, box 65, folder 6, Arizona Historical Society, Tucson, Arizona, Department of Anthropology, Natural History Museum of Los Angeles County.
6. Anonymous, "Savants Will Explore Isles," *Los Angeles Times* (Los Angeles, California), March 16, 1939, ProQuest Historical Newspapers.
7. Anonymous, "Britain Gives Nazis Warning, Backed by 2,000,000 at Arms," *Los Angeles Times* (Los Angeles, California), April 1, 1939.
8. Ibid.
9. Arthur Woodward, "Archaeological and Historical Fieldwork Conducted by Arthur Woodward during the Los Angeles Museum–Channel Islands Biological Survey of 1939–1941," unpublished manuscript, edited by Chris D. Coleman, Department of Anthropology, NHM, original journals in Arizona Historical Society, MS 1189, Arthur Woodward Papers, 1898–1986, 1860s–1980s (bulk 1920s–1960s), 37.
10. Ibid.
11. Ibid.
12. Edward O. Wilson, "The 8 Million Species We Don't Know," *New York Times* (New York), March 3, 2018.
13. Courtney A. Hofman et al., "Tracking the Origins and Diet of an Endemic Island Canid (*Urocyon littoralis*) across 7,300 Years of Human Cultural and Environmental Change," *Quaternary Science Reviews* 146 (2016): 152.
14. Courtney A. Hofman et al., "Mitochondrial Genomes Suggest Rapid Evolution of Dwarf California Channel Islands Foxes (*Urocyon littoralis*)," *PLOS One* 10, no. 2 (2015): e0118240, 1.
15. Ibid.
16. DDT was banned in 1972, but the chemical is still in the sea floor and continues to rise up the food chain.
17. Timothy J. Coonan, Catherin A. Schwemm, and David K. Garcelon, *Decline and Recovery of the Island Fox: A Case Study for Population Recovery* (New York: Cambridge University Press, 2010), 80.
18. Arthur Woodward, "Archaeological and Historical Fieldwork," 38.

19. Ibid.
20. Charles V died in 1556 and in Spain he was known as Charles I, though it is unclear whether Woodward was aware of the discrepancy.
21. Theodore Reddick, notes on the Channel Islands Biological Survey, April 1–8, 1939, 2, courtesy of Don Meadows Papers (MS-R001), UC Irvine, Special Collections & Archives.
22. Meryl B. Dunkle, "Contributions from the Los Angeles Museum–Channel Islands Biological Survey 21: New Plants from the Channel Islands," *Bulletin of the Southern California Academy of Sciences* 39, part 2 (May–August 1940): 176.
23. Greg Pauly, associate curator of herpetology, Natural History Museum of Los Angeles County, email communication with author, November 3, 2018.

CHAPTER 6

1. Don Meadows's brief account states that DeLong was on both Santa Barbara Island trips (1939 and 1940). However, in a published note written by John A. Comstock for the *Bulletin of the Southern California Academy of Sciences* (vol. 45) entitled, "Contributions from the Los Angeles Museum–Channel Islands Biological Survey 33: Brief Notes on the Expeditions Conducted Between March 16, 1940 and December 14, 1941," DeLong is not included in the 1940 muster. Additionally, because Meadows's accounting of DeLong's participation in the 1940 crew was contained within a compiled list of the other participants (all of whom had gone on both trips), it is the author's belief that DeLong's inclusion by Meadows in 1940 staffing was in error. Further corroborating this is that in the unpublished "Geological Reconnaissance" report found within Meadows's files at the Langston Library at the University of California, Irvine, Delong states that he studied the island over the course of two days while a member of the CIBS—the third expedition lasted two days while the seventh was a week-long trip.
2. An introductory note written by John A. Comstock for the *Bulletin of the Southern California Academy of Sciences* (vol. 38, September–December, 1939) entitled, "Contributions from the Los Angeles Museum–Channel Islands Biological Survey," published February 10, 1940, includes Woodward in the third expedition's staff. However, in Don Meadows's preliminary statement entitled, "The Biology of Santa Barbara Island, California," which covers both the third and seventh expeditions, Woodward is not mentioned as a participant. Additionally, because Woodward's fieldnotes do not cover the Santa Barbara Island expeditions, the author assumes he did not participate on either Santa Barbara Island expedition during the CIBS.
3. The Xantus's murrelet was divided into two species, the Scripps's murrelet and Guadalupe murrelet, in recognition of the fact that these two species do not interbreed and have different physical characteristics, including bill shape, facial patterns, vocalizations, and genetics.
4. Donald C. Meadows, "The Biology of Santa Barbara Island, California: Preliminary Statement," unpublished, undated, Don Meadows Papers (MS-R001), UC Irvine, Special Collections & Archives. Information found approximately on page 4 (nonpaginated) under the heading "Historical Background" and subheading "Indians."
5. Ibid. Information found on the first page under the heading "Introduction."

6. A. W. Bell to Jack von Bloeker Jr., August 12, 1944, Santa Barbara Museum of Natural History, Vertebrate Zoology Department.

7. John "Jack" Christian von Bloeker III, interview with author, February 21, 2011.

8. Ibid.

9. Jack Couffer, *Bat Bomb: World War II's Other Secret Weapon* (Austin: University of Texas Press, 1992), 3.

10. Author interview with Paul Collins, curator of vertebrate zoology, Santa Barbara Museum of Natural History, November 1, 2018. Von Bloeker's collection was left to the museum and Collins helped move it out of von Bloeker's last residence in Arizona.

11. Jack von Bloeker Jr. to the scholarship committee, Los Angeles Junior College, January 10, 1933, Santa Barbara Museum of Natural History, Vertebrate Zoology Department.

12. Anonymous, "Thugs Kidnap, Rob U.C. Man," *Oakland Tribune* (Oakland, California), December 17, 1935.

13. Anonymous, untitled article, *Columbia Daily Spectator* (New York), December 2, 1936.

14. A. W. Bell to Jack von Bloeker Jr., October 8, 1936, Santa Barbara Museum of Natural History, Vertebrate Zoology Department.

15. Jack Couffer, interview with author, February 5, 2011.

16. Ibid.

17. Ibid.

18. Couffer, *Bat Bomb*, 3.

19. Ibid.

20. Jack von Bloeker Jr., unpublished, unnamed, undated, handwritten fieldnotes covering the third expedition, Santa Barbara Museum of Natural History, Vertebrate Zoology Department.

21. Ibid.

22. Lloyd F. Kiff, "Historical Changes in Resident Populations of California Islands Raptors," in *The California Islands: Proceedings of a Multi-disciplinary Symposium*, edited by Dennis Power (Santa Barbara: Santa Barbara Museum of Natural History, 1980), 663.

23. Meryl B. Dunkle, "The Byways of Life," in *Songs of the Trail* (New York: Exposition Press, 1964), 43.

24. Jack von Bloeker Jr., unpublished fieldnotes.

25. Meryl B. Dunkle, "Los Angeles Museum Channel Islands Biological Survey Santa Barbara Island Report: Botany," unpublished, undated draft, Don Meadows Papers (MS-R001), UC Irvine, Special Collections & Archives.

26. Ibid.

27. Ibid.

28. Ibid.

29. Ibid.

30. Ibid.

31. Ibid.

32. Ibid.

33. Anonymous, "Channel Island Yields Rarities to Museum," *Los Angeles Examiner* (Los Angeles, California), March 24, 1940.

34. A. J. Van Rossem, "A Survey of the Song Sparrows of the Santa Barbara Islands," *The Condor* 26, no. 6 (1924): 219.
35. Jack von Bloeker Jr., unpublished fieldnotes.
36. Donald Meadows to John Adams Comstock, June 7, 1939, Natural History Museum of Los Angeles County.
37. Bess Settle, "Scientists Leave Here for Islands," *Long Beach Press Telegram* (Long Beach, California), July 16, 1939, Don Meadows Papers (MS-R001), UC Irvine, Special Collections & Archives.
38. Ibid.

CHAPTER 7

1. John Adams Comstock to N. A. Vail, July 20, 1939, NHM Archives.
2. Arthur Woodward, "Archaeological and Historical Fieldwork Conducted by Arthur Woodward during the Los Angeles Museum–Channel Islands Biological Survey of 1939–1941," unpublished manuscript, edited by Chris D. Coleman, Department of Anthropology, NHM, original journals in Arizona Historical Society, MS 1189, Arthur Woodward Papers, 1898–1986, 1860s–1980s (bulk 1920s–1960s), 76.
3. Michael Glassow, personal email communication with author, March 8, 2018.
4. Patricia C. Martz, "Prehistoric Settlement and Subsistence on San Nicolas Island," in *Proceedings of the Sixth California Islands Symposium*, edited by Dave Garcelon and Catherin A. Schwemm (Arcata: Institute for Wildlife Studies, 2003), 76–77.
5. Ibid., 77.
6. Ivan H. Strudwick, "The Native Depopulation of Santa Catalina Island," in *California's Channel Islands: The Archaeology of Human-Environment Interactions*, edited by Christopher S. Jazwa and Jennifer E. Perry (Salt Lake City: University of Utah Press, 2013), 172.
7. The name of the sea captain who was sent to remove the Nicoleño people from San Nicolas Island has variously been suggested to be either Charles Hubbard or Isaac Sparks, http://calliope.cse.sc.edu/lonewoman/literary.
8. Accounts citing that the Lone Woman jumped overboard for her baby and was subsequently abandoned on San Nicolas Island may have begun through numerous newspaper accounts published as early as 1847 (*Boston Atlas*, "A Female Crusoe"). As explained by Sara L. Schwebel, editor of Scott O'Dell's *Island of the Blue Dolphins: The Complete Reader's Edition*, that account was circulated by more than twelve East Coast newspapers and repeated "for more than seventy years." Emma Chamberlain Hardacre further promulgated this account that Schwebel credits as influencing Scott O'Dell's rendition of the story, which he popularized in Chapter 7 of *The Island of the Blue Dolphins*; Hardacre, "Eighteen Years Alone: A Tale of the Pacific," *Scribner's Monthly* (1880, republished in booklet form in 1950 and again in the early 1960s). *Pieces of Eight Channel Islands: A Bibliographical Guide and Source Book* by Adelaide L. Doran also includes an entire chapter on the Lone Woman, including various sources of misinformation.
9. Steven J. Schwartz, "Seven Short Weeks: The Lone Woman's Time in Santa Barbara" (paper presented at the 9th California Island Symposium, Ventura, California, October 2016).

10. Scott O'Dell, *Island of the Blue Dolphins: The Complete Reader's Edition*, edited by Sara L. Schwebel (Oakland: University of California Press, 2016), 7, 19, 191–96

11. Marla Daily, "Nidever, George," Islapedia, entry last updated April 6, 2018, https://www .islapedia.com/index.php?title=NIDEVER,_George.

12. Steven J. Schwartz, "Seven Short Weeks."

13. O'Dell, *Island of the Blue Dolphins*, 15.

14. Ibid., 2.

15. There is no evidence that trees ever existed on San Nicolas Island; Patricia C. Martz, "Prehistoric Settlement and Subsistence," 66.

16. Allan A. Schoenherr, C. Robert Feldmeth, and Michael J. Emerson, *The Natural History of the Islands of California* (Los Angeles: University of California Press, 1999), 338.

17. Steven Schwartz, personal email communication with author, April 9, 2018.

18. Donald C. Meadows, "Progress Report of the Los Angeles Museum–Channel Islands Biological Survey, Fourth Expedition: San Nicolas, San Miguel, Santa Rosa, and Santa Cruz Islands, July 21 to August 19, 1939," 7, NHM Archives.

19. Woodward worked at the National Museum of the American Indian, sponsored by the Heye Foundation, from late 1925 to early 1928.

20. Ken Woodward, *Rubaboo: The Story of Arthur Woodward—Adventurer, Historian, Archaeologist—Who Was Driven by His Need to Know* (San Diego, California: Ken Woodward, 2014), 49.

21. Arthur Woodward (attributed), note on the back of a photograph in NHM Archives.

22. Michael A. Glassow, "The Occurrence of Red Abalone Shells in Northern Channel Island Archaeological Middens: Implications for Climatic Reconstruction," in *Third California Islands Symposium: Recent Advances in Research on the California Islands*, edited by F. G. Hochberg (Santa Barbara: Santa Barbara Museum of Natural History, 1993), 574.

23. Arthur Woodward, "Archaeological and Historical Fieldwork," 68–69.

CHAPTER 8

1. "Murray, E. F.," Islapedia, last edited on October 17, 2018, http://www.islapedia.com/ index.php?title=MURRAY,_E._F.

2. Dean Smith, email communication on October 17, 2018 with Bancroft Library. The library could not corroborate that F. Murray was employed by H. H. Bancroft; however, a search for William Henry Ellison's book, *The Life and Adventures of George Nidever*, 1802–1883 (Berkeley, University of California Press, 1937), came up with a Stanford Libraries SearchWorks catalog entry that lists Murray as a contributor to Ellison's book; "The Life and Adventures of George Nidever, 1802–1883" Stanford Libraries SearchWorks, https://searchworks.stanford.edu/view/1969069.

3. Photograph located in the NHM Archives.

4. Arthur Woodward, "Archaeological and Historical Fieldwork Conducted by Arthur Woodward during the Los Angeles Museum–Channel Islands Biological Survey of 1939–1941," unpublished manuscript, edited by Chris D. Coleman, Department of Anthropology, NHM, original journals in Arizona Historical Society, MS 1189, Arthur Woodward Papers, 1898–1986, 1860s–1980s (bulk 1920s–1960s), 72–73.

5. Ibid.

6. Ron Morgan, "An Account of the Discovery of a Whale-Bone House on San Nicolas Island," *Journal of California and Great Basin Anthropology* 1, no. 1 (1979): 173.
7. Arthur Woodward, "Archaeological and Historical Fieldwork," 77.
8. Ibid.
9. Ibid., 73.
10. Ibid.
11. Ibid., 77.
12. Ron Morgan, "An Account of the Discovery of a Whale-Bone House on San Nicolas Island," 173.
13. Newspaper clipping from unknown newspaper, no author, dated July 22, 1939 (Part II), courtesy of NHM Archives.
14. Steven J. Schwartz, "Some Observations on the Material Culture of the Nicoleno," in *Proceedings of the Sixth California Island Symposium Ventura, California, December 1–3*, edited by Dave Garcelon and Catherin A. Schwemm Arcata (Institute for Wildlife Studies, 2005), 84–85.
15. Jon M. Erlandson et al., "From the *Island of the Blue Dolphins*: A Unique Nineteenth-Century Cache Feature from San Nicolas Island, California," *The Journal of Island and Coastal Archaeology* 8, no. 1 (2013): 76.
16. Lisa D. Thomas, personal communication with author, February 7, 2017.
17. Louis Sahagun, "With Island Dig Halted, Lone Woman Still a Stinging Mystery," *Los Angeles Times*, March 25, 2015.
18. Andrew Yatsko, personal email communication with author, September 12, 2018.
19. Ibid.

CHAPTER 9

1. Donald C. Meadows to Mrs. Meadows and Donald Meadows from San Nicolas Island, July 26, 1939, Don Meadows Papers (MS-R001), UC Irvine, Special Collections & Archives.
2. Ibid.
3. Jack von Bloeker Jr. to John Comstock, July 27–28, 1939, NHM Archives.
4. Donald C. Meadows to Mrs. Meadows from San Miguel Island, July 30, 1939, Don Meadows Papers (MS-R001), UC Irvine, Special Collections & Archives.
5. Donald C. Meadows, "Progress Report of the Los Angeles Museum–Channel Islands Biological Survey, Fourth Expedition: San Nicolas, San Miguel, Santa Rosa, and Santa Cruz Islands, July 21–August 19, 1939," 13, 14, NHM Archives.
6. Charles Rozaire (1927–2016) was curator of archaeology at NHM from 1963–1990. He received his PhD from UCLA in 1957. "Rozaire, Charles," Islapedia, last edited April 7, 2019, https://www.islapedia.com/index.php?title=Welcome_to_Islapedia.
7. Jon M. Erlandson et al., "An Archaeological and Paleontological Chronology for Daisy Cave (CA-SMI-261), San Miguel Island, California," *Radiocarbon* 38, no. 2 (1996): 359.
8. Jon M. Erlandson et al., "Paleoindian Seafaring, Maritime Technologies, and Coastal Foraging on California's Channel Islands," *Science* 331, no. 6021 (2011): 1181.
9. Erlandson, et al., "Paleoindian Seafaring, Maritime Technologies," 1184.
10. Erlandson, et al., "An Archaeological and Paleontological Chronology," 370.
11. The buying and selling of San Miguel Island is a misnomer, as the island has been continually owned by the U.S. government since the Treaty of Guadalupe Hidalgo in

1848. Early transactions were more in the nature of occupations. The U.S. government granted the first official lease to Captain William G. Waters in 1911.

12. The diary Minnie Waters kept was published in 1990 by the Santa Cruz Island Foundation as "Mrs. Waters' Diary of Her Life on San Miguel Island, January 1–June 27, 1888," in occasional paper no. 4.

CHAPTER 10

1. Herbert S. Lester to John Adams Comstock, February 15, 1941, NHM Archives.
2. Betsy Lester Roberti, *San Miguel Island: My Childhood Memoir, 1930–1942* (Santa Barbara: Santa Cruz Island Foundation, 2008), 7, 9.
3. Arthur Woodward, "Archaeological and Historical Fieldwork Conducted by Arthur Woodward during the Los Angeles Museum–Channel Islands Biological Survey of 1939–1941," unpublished manuscript, edited by Chris D. Coleman, Department of Anthropology, NHM, original journals in Arizona Historical Society, MS 1189, Arthur Woodward Papers, 1898–1986, 1860s–1980s (bulk 1920s–1960s), 90.
4. A single reference of the word "Çiquimuym" is found in the surviving 1542 manuscript account chronicling Juan Cabrillo's voyage along the West Coast of North America; John Johnson, personal email communication with author, April 7, 2018.
5. Jon M. Erlandson et al., "The Cico Chert Source on San Miguel Island, California," *Journal of California and Great Basin Anthropology* (1997): 129.
6. Jon M. Erlandson, Torben C. Rick, and Nicholas P. Jew, "Wima Chert: 12,000 Years of Lithic Resource Use on California's Northern Channel Islands," *Journal of California and Great Basin Anthropology* (2012): 83.
7. Ken Woodward, *Rubaboo: The Story of Arthur Woodward—Adventurer, Historian, Archaeologist—Who Was Driven by His Need to Know* (San Diego, California: Ken Woodward, 2014), 17.
8. "Hoffmann, Ralph," Islapedia, last updated September 4, 2018, http://www.islapedia.com/index.php?title=HOFFMANN.
9. Donald C. Meadows to Mrs. Meadows, July 30, 1939, Don Meadows Papers (MS-R001), UC Irvine, Special Collections & Archives.
10. Ibid.
11. Unsigned, undated, two-page document written in von Bloeker's script and located in the Jack von Bloeker Jr. files at the Santa Barbara Museum of Natural History, Department of Vertebrate Zoology.
12. Arthur Woodward, "Archaeological and Historical Fieldwork," 91.
13. Donald C. Meadows, "Progress Report of the Los Angeles Museum–Channel Islands Biological Survey, Fourth Expedition: San Nicolas, San Miguel, Santa Rosa, and Santa Cruz Islands, July 21–August 19, 1939," 14, NHM Archives.
14. Elizabeth Sherman Lester, *The Legendary King of San Miguel: The Lesters at Rancho Rambouillet* (McNally & Loftin, West, originally published by W. T. Genns, 1974, first softcover edition, 1970), 57.
15. Donald C. Meadows to John Adams Comstock, July 30, 1939, Arizona Historical Society, MS 1189, Woodward, Arthur, 1898–1986, Papers, 1860s—1980s (bulk 1920s–1960s).
16. Donald C. Meadows to John Adams Comstock, August 3, 1939, Don Meadows Papers (MS-R001), UC Irvine, Special Collections & Archives.
17. John Clayton, "Nine Years in 'Solitary,'" *Los Angeles Times*, December 11, 1938.

CHAPTER 11

1. Torben C. Rick, "Household and Community Archaeology at the Chumash Village of Niaqla, Santa Rosa Island, California," *Journal of Field Archaeology* 32, no. 3 (2007): 259.
2. Arthur Woodward, "Archaeological and Historical Fieldwork Conducted by Arthur Woodward during the Los Angeles Museum–Channel Islands Biological Survey of 1939–1941," unpublished manuscript, edited by Chris D. Coleman, Department of Anthropology, NHM, original journals in Arizona Historical Society, MS 1189, Arthur Woodward Papers, 1898–1986, 1860s–1980s (bulk 1920s–1960s), 131.
3. Ibid.
4. Ibid., 115.
5. A. E. Gusick and J. M. Erlandson, "Paleocoastal Landscapes, Marginality, and Initial Settlement of California's Islands," in *An Archaeology of Abundance: Reevaluating the Marginality of California's Islands*, edited by K. Gill, J. Erlandson, and M. Fauvelle (University of Florida Press, Gainesville, forthcoming), found in the table, currently unpaginated.
6. Arthur Woodward, "Archaeological and Historical Fieldwork," 122.
7. Torben C. Rick et al., "Archaeological Survey, Paleogeography, and the Search for Late Pleistocene Paleocoastal Peoples of Santa Rosa Island, California," *Journal of Field Archaeology* 38, no. 4 (2013): 324, 328.
8. Donald C. Meadows, "Progress Report of the Los Angeles Museum–Channel Islands Biological Survey, Fourth Expedition: San Nicolas, San Miguel, Santa Rosa, and Santa Cruz Islands, July 21–August 19, 1939," 16, NHM Archives.
9. Woolley, Will, "Maritime Ranching on Santa Rosa Island," in *Island of the Cowboys: Santa Rosa Island*, edited by Kerry Blankenship Allen (Santa Barbara: Santa Cruz Island Foundation, 1996), 113.
10. Arthur Woodward, "Archaeological and Historical Fieldwork," 120.
11. Anonymous, "Perspiring Mammalogist Has Fox Hunt on the Museum Roof," *Los Angeles Times* (Los Angeles, California), September 16, 1939.
12. Donald C. Meadows to Mrs. Meadows, August 10, 1939, Don Meadows Papers (MS-R001), UC Irvine, Special Collections & Archives.
13. Arthur Woodward, "Archaeological and Historical Fieldwork," 133.

CHAPTER 12

1. Donald C. Meadows, "Progress Report of the Los Angeles Museum–Channel Islands Biological Survey, Fourth Expedition: San Nicolas, San Miguel, Santa Rosa, and Santa Cruz Islands, July 21–August 19, 1939," 20, NHM Archives.
2. Ibid.
3. Ibid.
4. Donald C. Meadows to "Dear Sweetness," (Mrs. Meadows), August 13, 1939, Don Meadows Papers (MS-R001), UC Irvine, Special Collections & Archives.
5. Donald C. Meadows, "Progress Report," 20.
6. Arthur Woodward, "Archaeological and Historical Fieldwork Conducted by Arthur Woodward during the Los Angeles Museum–Channel Islands Biological Survey of 1939–1941," unpublished manuscript, edited by Chris D. Coleman, Department

of Anthropology, NHM, original journals in Arizona Historical Society, MS 1189, Arthur Woodward Papers, 1898–1986, 1860s–1980s (bulk 1920s–1960s), 133.

7. Hipppocampus is the scientific name for seahorse.

8. Amy E. Gusick, "The Early Holocene Occupation of Santa Cruz Island," in *California's Channel Islands: The Archaeology of Human-Environment Interactions*, edited by Christopher S. Jazwa and Jennifer E. Perry (Salt Lake City: University of Utah Press, 2013), 50; Jon M. Erlandson et al., "Three Paleocoastal Lithic Sites on Santa Cruz Island, California," *PaleoAmerica* 2, no. 1 (2016): 3.

9. Douglas J. Kennett et al., "Historic Chumash Settlement on Eastern Santa Cruz Island, Southern California," *Journal of California and Great Basin Anthropology* (2000): 212.

10. Jennifer E. Perry and Michael A. Glassow, "Prehistoric Settlement in Island Interiors: Evidence from California's Santa Cruz Island," *Journal of Island and Coastal Archaeology* 10, no. 2 (2015): 201.

11. Jennifer E. Perry, "The Archaeology of Ritual on the Channel Islands," in *California's Channel Islands: The Archaeology of Human-Environment Interactions*, edited by Christopher S. Jazwa and Jennifer E. Perry (Salt Lake City: University of Utah Press, 2013), 142.

12. Ibid., 142–43.

13. Jennifer E. Perry, "Chumash Ritual and Sacred Geography on Santa Cruz Island, California," *Journal of California and Great Basin Anthropology* (2007): 121.

14. Ibid., 104.

15. Perry and Glassow, "Prehistoric Settlement in Island Interiors," 199.

16. Arthur Woodward, "Archaeological and Historical Fieldwork," 135.

17. Arthur Woodward, "Archaeology," included in Donald C. Meadows, "Progress Report," 36.

18. Perry and Glassow, "Prehistoric Settlement in Island Interiors," 202.

19. Frederic Caire Chiles, *Justinian Caire and Santa Cruz Island: The Rise and Fall of a California Dynasty* (Norman: The Arthur H. Clark Company, an imprint of the University of Oklahoma Press, 2011), 30.

20. Ibid., 39.

21. Ibid., 57.

22. Ibid., 83–84. Justinian Caire initiated a tree planting program on Santa Cruz Island that included groves of blue gum eucalyptus, Monterey and Italian stone pine, walnut, almond, peach, pear, fig, and other trees. Caire's daughter, Delphine, oversaw the program.

23. "Marla Daily," Islapedia, http://islapedia.com/index.php?title=DUFFIELD,_Henry _Cowie,_Jr.

24. Author's recollection of the Feast of the Holy Cross, May 3, 2016. Carey refers to Carey Stanton, Henry to Henry Duffield, and Glen to Eagles band member Glenn Frey, who died January 18, 2016.

25. Donald C. Meadows, "Progress Report," 20.

26. There never was a hotel at Prisoners Harbor, but one of the island's former owners, the Caire family, had a two-story house there. The reference to a hotel is from Jack von Bloeker Jr.'s "Land Mammals of the Southern California Island," published in the *1967 Proceedings of the Symposium on the Biology of the California Islands*, edited by Ralph Philbrick, 245–64.

27. Arthur Woodward, "Archaeological and Historical Fieldwork," 142.
28. M.B. Dunkle, "Botany," included in Donald C. Meadows, "Progress Report," 34.

CHAPTER 13

1. John A. Comstock to the commandant of the Eleventh Naval District, San Diego, California, October 26, 1939, NHM Archives.
2. Jack von Bloeker Jr., personal journal, under the heading "Aboard the Velero III, at dock, Terminal Island, Los Angeles, Co., California. November 7, 1939," unpaginated, Santa Barbara Museum of Natural History, Department of Vertebrate Zoology.
3. Ibid.
4. Ibid.
5. Ibid.
6. Arthur Woodward, "Archaeological and Historical Fieldwork Conducted by Arthur Woodward during the Los Angeles Museum–Channel Islands Biological Survey of 1939–1941," unpublished manuscript, edited by Chris D. Coleman, Department of Anthropology, NHM, original journals in Arizona Historical Society, MS 1189, Arthur Woodward Papers, 1898–1986, 1860s–1980s (bulk 1920s–1960s), 160.
7. Jack von Bloeker Jr., personal journal, under the heading "Horse Beach Cove, San Clemente Island. L.A. Co., Calif. November 7, 1939," unpaginated, Santa Barbara Museum of Natural History, Department of Vertebrate Zoology.
8. Ibid.
9. Hildegarde Howard, "George Willett: May 28, 1879–August 2, 1945," *The Condor*, no. 48 (1946): 61.
10. Ibid.
11. Arthur Woodward, "Archaeological and Historical Fieldwork," 191.
12. Ibid.
13. Ibid., 191–92.
14. Andrew Yatsko, personal communication with author, September 17 and September 26, 2018.
15. Arthur Woodward, "Archaeological and Historical Fieldwork," 181.
16. Ibid.
17. Ibid., 204.
18. Roy A. Salls was among the last archaeologists to excavate Big Dog Cave in 1985.
19. Board of governors meeting minutes, November 16, 1939, 73, NHM Archives.
20. Ibid.

CHAPTER 14

1. Board of governors meeting minutes, February 15, 1940, 86, NHM Archives.
2. Ibid.
3. Ibid.
4. Ibid.
5. Jack C. von Bloeker Jr. to Dr. Richard M. Bond, chief of the Regional Biology Division of the Soil Conservation Service, Department of Agriculture, May 28, 1940, NHM Archives.

6. Harry Geiger served as archaeological assistant and Leo Kartman served as botanist and assistant entomologist. Neither participated in any other expeditions.

7. John Comstock (attributed, found in Comstock's NHM file), letter to Jack von Bloeker Jr., March 27, 1940, NHM Archives.

8. Chris Coleman, Department of Anthropology, NHM, and Jim Dines, Department of Birds and Mammals, NHM, personal email communication with author, December 5, 2016. No record of the photograph or the dog bones are at the museum.

9. Arthur Woodward, "Archaeological and Historical Fieldwork Conducted by Arthur Woodward during the Los Angeles Museum–Channel Islands Biological Survey of 1939–1941," unpublished manuscript, edited by Chris D. Coleman, Department of Anthropology, NHM, original journals in Arizona Historical Society, MS 1189, Arthur Woodward Papers, 1898–1986, 1860s–1980s (bulk 1920s–1960s), 224.

10. Torben C. Rick et al., "Dogs, Humans and Island Ecosystems: the Distribution, Antiquity and Ecology of Domestic Dogs (*Canis familiaris*) on California's Channel Islands, USA," *The Holocene* 18, no. 7 (2008): 1078.

11. Rick et al., "Dogs, Humans and Island Ecosystems," 1083.

12. René L. Vellanoweth, "Archaeology, *Island of the Blue Dolphins*, and the Lone Woman of San Nicolas Island," in Scott O'Dell, *Island of the Blue Dolphins: The Complete Reader's Edition*, edited by Sara L. Schwebel (Oakland: University of California Press, 2016), 210.

13. Arthur Woodward, "Archaeological and Historical Fieldwork," 225.

14. Woodward's fieldnotes read: "So far Kroeber has been refuted on the following points. Basketry is definitely island material—mostly sea grass—cremation was practiced on this island and on San Clemente [Island] to a certain extent. It begins to appear that culturally these islands are more closely affiliated with the Canalino-Gabrielino group than with the Shoshonean groups further south. Aside from the sporadic traces of cremation which are definite the other culture traits are definitely allied to the Chumash-Gabrielino rather than the Shoshonean. Both surface and midden excavated data have yield evidences of these contacts." Arthur Woodward, "Archaeological and Historical Fieldwork," 238.

15. Ibid.

16. A. L. Kroeber, *Handbook of the Indians of California*, Bulletin 78 (Washington, D.C.: General Publishing Company, Ltd., Dover edition, Government Printing Office, 1976), 635.

17. Ibid.

18. Arthur Woodward to Phil Orr, Santa Barbara Museum of Natural History, May 28, 1940, Arizona Historical Society, MS 1189, Arthur Woodward Papers, 1898–1986, 1860s–1980s (bulk 1920s–1960s).

CHAPTER 15

1. Under Grinnell's tutelage while at the University of California, Berkeley, von Bloeker Jr. received his BA in 1937 and MA in 1938.

2. Jack C. von Bloeker Jr., "Contributions from the Los Angeles Museum–Channel Islands Biological Survey, 22: A New Subspecies of White-Footed Mouse from the Anacapa

Islands, California," *Bulletin of the Southern California Academy of Sciences* 40, part B (September–December 1941): 161.

3. Jack von Bloeker Jr., memorandum to John A. Comstock, April 30, 1940, NHM Archives.

4. Ibid.

5. Jack von Bloeker Jr. to Dr. Richard M. Bond, chief of the Regional Biology Division of the Soil Conservation Service, Department of Agriculture, May 28, 1940, NHM Archives.

6. Administrative council meeting minutes, June 27, 1940, NHM Archives.

7. Ibid.

8. Board of governors meeting minutes, August 15, 1940, 104, NHM Archives.

9. Board of governors meeting minutes, September 19, 1940, 107, NHM Archives.

10. "Department of History, Science, and Art," memorandum, September 1940, NHM Archives.

11. Michael A. Glassow, editor and compiler, *Channel Islands Archaeological Overview and Assessment* (National Park Service, December 2010), 5.2.

12. Charles Hillinger, *The California Islands* (Los Angeles: Academy Publishers, 1958), 105.

13. Marshall Bassford McKusick et al., *Introduction to Anacapa Island Archaeology (Los Angeles: Department of Anthropology*, University of California, 1959), 75, 78.

14. McKusick et al., *Introduction to Anacapa Island Archaeology*, 84.

15. Richard M. Bond to Jack von Bloeker Jr., May 22, 1940, NHM Archives.

16. Ibid.

17. Ibid.

18. Ibid.

19. Ibid.

20. Ibid.

21. Gregg R. Howald et al., "Eradication of Black Rats from Anacapa Island: Biological and Social Considerations," in *Proceedings of the Sixth California Islands Symposium*, edited by David K. Garcelon and Catherin A. Schwemm (Arcata: Institute for Wildlife Studies, 2005), 299–300.

22. Richard M. Bond to Jack von Bloeker Jr., June 3, 1940, NHM Archives.

23. Ibid.

24. Ibid.

25. Jack von Bloeker Jr. to Dr. Richard M. Bond, June 6, 1940, NHM Archives.

26. Ibid.

27. D. L. Whitworth, H. R. Carter, and D. M. Mazurkiewicz, "Scripps's Murrelet Nest Monitoring at Anacapa Island, California in 2014: Continued Recovery 12 Years after Eradication of Black Rats," unpublished report, California Institute of Environmental Studies, Davis, California, 2015 (prepared for the American Trader Trustee Council, National Fish and Wildlife Foundation, and Channel Islands National Park), 11, https://training.fws.gov/resources/course-resources/pesticides/IPM/Whitworth-et -al.-ATTC-AnacapaIslandScripps-Murrelet-Nest-Monitoring2014Final.pdf

28. Torben C. Rick, "A 5,000-Year Record of Coastal Settlement on Anacapa Island, California," *Journal of California and Great Basin Anthropology* (2006): 70.

29. Todd J. Braje et al., *Channel Islands National Park Archaeological Overview and Assessment* (Ventura: Cultural Resource Division, Channel Islands National Park, 2010), 5.1.

30. Leslie A. Reeder and Torben C. Rick, "New Perspectives on the Archaeology of Anacapa Island, California: Preliminary Research at ANI-2," *Proceedings of the Society for California Archaeology* 21 (2009): 121.

31. Torben C. Rick, "Historic Period Chumash Occupation of 'Anayapax, Anacapa Island, Alta California," *California Archaeology* 3, no. 2 (2011): 274.

32. Reeder and Rick, "New Perspectives on the Archaeology of Anacapa Island," 122.

33. Torben C. Rick and Leslie Reeder-Meyers, "Deception Island: Archaeology of 'Anyapax, Anacapa Island, California," *Smithsonian Contributions to Anthropology* 52 (2018): 66, 73, 80, 86, 92.

34. Weekly newsletter, Los Angeles County Museum, July 17, 1940, NHM Archives.

35. Weekly newsletter, Los Angeles County Museum, July 24, 1940, NHM Archives.

36. Jack C. von Bloeker Jr. to Richard M. Bond, January 15, 1941, NHM Archives.

37. W. Dwight Pierce, "Contributions from the Los Angeles Museum–Channel Islands Biological Survey, 18: A Strepsipterous Parasite of a Leaf Hopper, With Descriptions of Related Species from the Same Host Genus," *Bulletin of the Southern California Academy of Sciences* 40, part 1 (Jan–April 1941): 6.

38. W. Dwight Pierce, "Contributions from the Los Angeles Museum–Channel Islands Biological Survey, 9: A Rare Myriapod From Anacapa Island, Compared with Two Texas Species," *Bulletin of the Southern California Academy of Sciences* 39, part 2 (May–August 1940): 164.

39. Ibid., 158.

40. Jack C. von Bloeker Jr., "Contributions from the Los Angeles Museum–Channel Islands Biological Survey," 161.

41. Jack C. von Bloeker Jr., "A New Subspecies of White-Footed Mouse from the Anacapa Islands," 162.

CHAPTER 16

1. Weekly newsletter, Los Angeles County Museum, September 4, 1940, NHM Archives.

2. Donald C. Meadows to John Adams Comstock, September 3, 1940, NHM Archives.

3. Ibid.

4. Ibid.

5. Ibid.

6. Ibid.

7. Ibid.

8. Ibid.

9. Ibid.

10. Ibid.

11. John Adams Comstock to Donald C. Meadows, July 26, 1939, NHM Archives.

12. Meadows to Comstock, September 3, 1940.

13. Arthur Woodward to Dorr, September 6, 1940, NHM Archives.

14. Ibid.

15. Ibid.

16. Comstock to Meadows, September 10, 1940.

17. Ibid.
18. Ibid.
19. Ibid.
20. Ibid.
21. Donald C. Meadows to the commanding officer of the U.S. Coast Guard, San Francisco, September 4, 1940, Don Meadows Papers (MS-R001), UC Irvine, Special Collections & Archives.
22. Ibid.
23. Woodward simply refers to them as "mussels," but they are likely California mussels that are native to the West Coast of North America.
24. Arthur Woodward, "Archaeological and Historical Fieldwork Conducted by Arthur Woodward during the Los Angeles Museum–Channel Islands Biological Survey of 1939–1941," unpublished manuscript, edited by Chris D. Coleman, Department of Anthropology, NHM, original journals in Arizona Historical Society, MS 1189, Arthur Woodward Papers, 1898–1986, 1860s–1980s (bulk 1920s–1960s), 244.
25. Ibid., 247.
26. Ibid., 255.
27. Anonymous, "Island Yields Ancient Finds," *Los Angeles Times* (Los Angeles, California), December 13, 1940, NHM Archives.
28. Arthur Woodward, "Archaeological and Historical Fieldwork," 255.
29. Ibid., 257.
30. Ibid., 243.
31. Ibid., 257.

CHAPTER 17

1. Howard Robertson, secretary for the board of governors, board of governors meeting minutes, January 16, 1941, 116, NHM Archives.
2. Ibid.
3. Ibid.
4. Frederic Caire Chiles, *California's Channel Islands: A History* (Norman: University of Oklahoma Press, 2015), 235.
5. Allan A. Schoenherr, C. Robert Feldmeth, and Michael J. Emerson, *Natural History of the Islands of California*, vol. 61 (Berkeley and Los Angeles: University of California Press, 2003), 147.
6. Linda Marsa, "Reinterpreting an Ancient Island," *American Archaeology* 17, no. 4 (Winter 2013–2014): 20.
7. Desireé R. Martinez, Wendy G. Teeter, and Karimah O. Kennedy-Richardson, "Returning the *tataayiyam honuuka'* (Ancestors) to the Correct Home: The Importance of Background Investigations for NAGPRA Claims," *Curator: The Museum Journal* 57, no. 2 (2014): 203.
8. Wendy G. Teeter, Desireé Reneé Martinez, and Karimah O. Kennedy-Richardson, "Cultural Landscapes of Santa Catalina Island," in *California's Channel Islands: The Archaeology of Human-Environment Interactions*, edited by Christopher S. Jazwa and Jennifer E. Perry (Salt Lake City: University of Utah Press, 2013), 159.
9. Martinez, Teeter, and Kennedy-Richardson, "Returning the tataayiyam honuuka' (Ancestors) to the Correct Home," 201.

10. John Shrader, student archaeologist, to Mr. Woodward, undated letter, NHM Archives.

11. Marsa, "Reinterpreting an Ancient Island," 20.

12. Michael Glassow, email communication with author, July 11, 2017.

13. Torben Rick, email communication with author, June 21, 2017, and March 20, 2018.

14. Torben C. Rick et al., "From Pleistocene Mariners to Complex Hunter-Gatherers: The Archaeology of the California Channel Islands," *Journal of World Prehistory* 19, no. 3 (2005): 195.

15. Marsa, "Reinterpreting an Ancient Island," 20.

16. Teeter, Martinez, and Kennedy-Richardson, "Cultural Landscapes of Santa Catalina Island," 158.

17. Ivan H. Strudwick, "The Native Depopulation of Santa Catalina Island," in *California's Channel Islands: The Archaeology of Human-Environment Interactions*, edited by Christopher S. Jazwa and Jennifer E. Perry (Salt Lake City: University of Utah Press, 2013), 183.

18. Schoenherr, Feldmeth, and Emerson, *Natural History of the Islands of California*, 154.

19. Marsa, "Reinterpreting an Ancient Island," 22.

20. Teeter, Martinez, and Kennedy-Richardson, "Cultural Landscapes of Santa Catalina Island," 158.

21. Strudwick, "The Native Depopulation of Santa Catalina Island," 184, 186.

22. Chiles, *California's Channel Islands: A History*, 218.

CHAPTER 18

1. John A. Comstock to Meryl Dunkle, February 14, 1941, NHM Archives.

2. John A. Comstock to N. R. Vail, February 4, 1941, NHM Archives.

3. G. L. Woodruff, lieutenant commander, U.S. Navy, to John A. Comstock, February 27, 1941, NHM Archives.

4. G. M. Ravenscroft, captain, Eleventh Naval District, to John A. Comstock, March 11, 1941, NHM Archives.

5. Ibid.

6. Ibid.

7. John A. Comstock, "Contributions from the Los Angeles Museum–Channel Islands Biological Survey, 33: Brief Notes on the Expeditions Conducted between March 16, 1940 and December 14, 1941," *Bulletin of the Southern California Academy of Sciences* 45, part 2 (May–August 1946): 102.

8. John A. Comstock, "Contributions from the Los Angeles Museum–Channel Islands Biological Survey, 26: A New Race of Arachnis Picta from Santa Catalina Island," *Bulletin of the Southern California Academy of Sciences* 41, part 2 (May–August, 1942): 83.

9. Ibid.

10. Comstock, "Brief Notes on the Expeditions Conducted between March 16, 1940 and December 14, 1941," 102.

11. C. Meighan, "Rock Art on the Channel Islands of California," *Pacific Coast Archaeological Society Quarterly* 36, no. 2 (2000): 17.

12. Wendy G. Teeter, Desireé Reneé Martinez, and Karimah O. Kennedy-Richardson, "Cultural Landscapes of Santa Catalina Island," in *California's Channel Islands:*

The Archaeology of Human-Environment Interactions, edited by Christopher S. Jazwa and Jennifer E. Perry (Salt Lake City: University of Utah Press, 2013), 166.
13. John Shrader to Mr. Woodward, undated letter, NHM Archives.
14. Ibid.
15. Meighan, "Rock Art on the Channel Islands of California," 23.
16. Jennifer E. Perry, "The Archaeology of Ritual on the Channel Islands," in *California's Channel Islands: The Archaeology of Human-Environment Interactions*, edited by Christopher S. Jazwa and Jennifer E. Perry (Salt Lake City: University of Utah Press, 2013), 145.
17. Meighan, "Rock Art on the Channel Islands of California," 27.
18. John A. Comstock to Jack von Bloeker Jr., March 7, 1941, NHM Archives; John Shrader to Mr. Woodward, undated letter, NHM Archives.
19. [George Willett], "Anacapa Island, March 15 to 22, 1941," report, NHM Archives.
20. John A. Comstock to Jack von Bloeker Jr., March 21, 1941, NHM Archives.
21. Board of governors meeting minutes, March 20, 1941, 119, NHM Archives.
22. Board of governors meeting minutes, January 29, 1942, 156, NHM Archives, referring to "Statement of Proposed Policy for the Science Division Los Angeles County Museum," March 20, 1941, 156, NHM Archives.
23. Board of governors meeting minutes, January 29, 1942, 156, NHM Archives.
24. Ibid.
25. Board of governors meeting minutes, March 20, 1941, 120, NHM Archives.
26. Ibid.
27. Arthur Woodward to John Shrader, March 27, 1941, Arizona Historical Society, MS 1189, Arthur Woodward Papers, 1898–1986, 1860s–1980s (bulk 1920s–1960s).
28. Ibid.
29. Anonymous, "Island Lookout Post Proposed, Army May Establish Station on Santa Rosa 35 Miles Off Coast," *Los Angeles Times* (Los Angeles, California), February 23, 1941, NHM Archives.
30. John A. Comstock, "Weekly Newsletter, Los Angeles County Museum, Exposition Park," Department of Science, Channel Islands Biological Survey, April 16, 1941, NHM Archives.
31. Ibid.

CHAPTER 19

1. Board of governors meeting minutes, April 17, 1941, 121, NHM Archives.
2. Ibid.
3. Ibid.
4. Ibid.
5. Ibid.
6. Ibid.
7. Ibid.
8. Jack C. von Bloeker Jr. to E. Raymond Hall, curator of mammals, Museum of Vertebrate Zoology, April 24, 1941, Museum of Vertebrate Zoology historical correspondence, MVZA.MSS.0117, Museum of Vertebrate Zoology Archives, University of California, Berkeley.

9. Jack C. von Bloeker Jr., "Contributions from the Los Angeles Museum–Channel Islands Biological Survey, 22: A New Shrew from Santa Catalina Island, California," *Bulletin of the Southern California Academy of Sciences* 40, part 3 (September–December, 1941): 163.

10. Ibid.

11. Ibid.

12. Ibid.

13. Ibid.

14. Board of governors meeting minutes, April 25, 1941, 124, NHM Archives.

15. Ibid.

16. John Adams Comstock to U.S. Civil Service Commission, Washington, DC, May 6, 1941, board of governors meeting minutes, April 25, 1941, 124, NHM Archives.

17. Jack C. von Bloeker Jr. to Professor Alden H. Miller, director, Museum of Vertebrate Zoology, May 13, 1941, Museum of Vertebrate Zoology historical correspondence, MVZA.MSS.0117, Museum of Vertebrate Zoology Archives, University of California, Berkeley.

18. John Adams Comstock to U.S. Civil Service Commission, Washington, DC, May 6, 1941, NHM Archives.

19. Raymond E. Hall to Jack C. von Bloeker Jr., May 15, 1941, Museum of Vertebrate Zoology historical correspondence, MVZA.MSS.0117, Museum of Vertebrate Zoology Archives, University of California, Berkeley.

20. Alden H. Miller to Jack C. von Bloeker Jr., May 15, 1941, Museum of Vertebrate Zoology historical correspondence, MVZA.MSS.0117, Museum of Vertebrate Zoology Archives, University of California, Berkeley.

21. Ibid.

22. Ibid.

23. Jack C. von Bloeker Jr. to Alden H. Miller, May 20, 1941, Museum of Vertebrate Zoology historical correspondence, MVZA.MSS.0117, Museum of Vertebrate Zoology Archives, University of California, Berkeley.

24. Alden H. Miller to Dr. Alexander Wetmore, 26 May 1941, U.S. National Museum, Washington D.C. MVZA.MSS.0117, Museum of Vertebrate Zoology Archives, University of California, Berkeley.

CHAPTER 20

1. Reid Moran to the Los Angeles County Board of Supervisors, May 11, 1941, Los Angeles County records, Kenneth Hahn Hall of Administration, Customer Service Center.

2. A. W. Bell, chairman, Department of Life Sciences, Los Angeles City College, to the board of supervisors, May 8, 1941, Los Angeles County records, Kenneth Hahn Hall of Administration, Customer Service Center.

3. Ibid.

4. Matt Weinstock, "Town Talk," *Los Angeles Daily News* (Los Angeles, California), August 11, 1941, NHM Archives.

5. These quotes all come from a variety of letters housed in four boxes pertaining to the LACM, held at the Kenneth Hahn Hall of Administration, Customer Service Center, third floor, room 383.

6. Matt Weinstock, "Town Talk," *Los Angeles Daily News*, April 11, 1941, text of article included in Roland J. McKinney to the chairman of the board of governors, August 21, 1941, NHM Archives.
7. Ibid.
8. Roland J. McKinney to the chairman of the board of governors, August 21, 1941, NHM Archives.
9. Ibid.
10. Ibid.
11. Ibid.
12. A. W. Bell, "Reorganization at the Los Angeles Museum," *Science* 94 (1941): 255–56.

CHAPTER 21

1. Science division meeting minutes, September 23, 1941, 1, NHM Archives.
2. Ibid.
3. Ibid.
4. Ibid.
5. Ibid.
6. Ibid.
8. Ibid.
9. Science division meeting minutes, September 23, 1941, 1–2, NHM Archives.
10. John Adams Comstock to Roland McKinney, October 25, 1941, NHM Archives.
11. Ibid.
12. Science division meeting minutes, September 23, 1941, 2, NHM Archives.
13. Ibid.
14. Ibid.
15. Ibid.
16. Ibid., 3.
17. Ibid., 2.
18. Ibid., 6.
19. Ibid.
20. Ibid.
21. John Adams Comstock to N. R. Vail, September 26, 1941, NHM Archives.
22. Kenneth E. Stager to Roland J. McKinney, October 5, 1941, NHM Archives.
23. John Adams Comstock to Roland McKinney, October 25, 1941, NHM Archives.
24. Ibid.
25. Ibid.
26. Ibid.
27. Ibid.

CHAPTER 22

1. John Adams Comstock, "Contributions from the Los Angeles Museum–Channel Islands Biological Survey 33: Brief Notes on the Expeditions Conducted between March 16, 1940 and December 14, 1941." *Bulletin of the Southern California Academy of Sciences* 45, part 2 (1946): 105.

2. Barbara Loomis, "Santa Rosa Island, November–December 1941: Tuesday, November 25," unpublished fieldnotes, original journals in Arizona Historical Society, MS 1189, Arthur Woodward Papers, 1898–1986, 1860s–1980s (bulk 1920s–1960s).

3. Unsigned, undated, typewritten memo included in the archives of the thirteenth expedition at NHM.

4. Anonymous, "Women Explore Island: Feminine Archaeologists to Seek Elephant Fossils," *Port Hueneme Harbor Express* (California) vol. 1, November 27, 1941, NHM Archives.

5. The informal survey consisted of Michael Glassow, Amy Gusick, and Chris Coleman, who agree that Hollenbach and Loomis were possibly the first women archaeologists on the Channel Islands; email correspondence with author, October 30, 2018.

6. Arthur Woodward, "Archaeological and Historical Fieldwork Conducted by Arthur Woodward during the Los Angeles Museum–Channel Islands Biological Survey of 1939–1941," unpublished manuscript, edited by Chris D. Coleman, Department of Anthropology, NHM, original journals in Arizona Historical Society, MS 1189, Arthur Woodward Papers, 1898–1986, 1860s–1980s (bulk 1920s–1960s), 258.

7. Ibid., 36.

8. Barbara Loomis, "Santa Rosa Island, November–December 1941: Sunday, November 23," unpublished journal entry, original journals in Arizona Historical Society, MS 1189, Arthur Woodward Papers, 1898–1986, 1860s–1980s (bulk 1920s–1960s).

9. John Adams Comstock to Bill Fletcher, November 21, 1941, NHM Archives.

10. John Adams Comstock to Kenneth Stager, November 21, 1941, NHM Archives.

11. Arthur Woodward, "Archaeological and Historical Fieldwork," 261.

12. Barbara Loomis, "Santa Rosa Island, November–December 1941: Tuesday, November 25," unpublished journal entry, original journals in Arizona Historical Society, MS 1189, Arthur Woodward Papers, 1898–1986, 1860s–1980s (bulk 1920s–1960s).

13. Marioneta could be a mistranscription of *Marionita*, where the Spanish feminine suffix "-ita" is used as a diminutive to transform a noun into a term of endearment.

14. "George Nidever's Santa Rosa Island Story," National Park Service: Channel Islands National Park, California, last updated June 10, 2016, https://www.nps.gov/chis/learn/historyculture/nidever.htm.

15. Arthur Woodward, "Archaeological and Historical Fieldwork," 263.

16. Jon M. Erlandson et al., "Paleoindian Seafaring, Maritime Technologies, and Coastal Foraging on California's Channel Islands," *Science* 331, no. 6021 (2011): 1182–83.

17. Torben C. Rick, "8000 Years of Human Settlement and Land Use in Old Ranch Canyon, Santa Rosa Island, California," in *Proceedings of the Seventh California Islands Symposium*, edited by C. C. Damiani and K. K. Garcelon (Arcata: Institute for Wildlife Studies, 2009), 28.

18. Board of governors meeting minutes, November 26, 1941, 148, NHM Archives.

CHAPTER 23

1. Jack Couffer, personal interview with author, February 5, 2011, 4.

2. Arthur Woodward, "Archaeological and Historical Fieldwork Conducted by Arthur Woodward during the Los Angeles Museum–Channel Islands Biological Survey of 1939–1941," unpublished manuscript, edited by Chris D. Coleman, Department

of Anthropology, NHM, original journals in Arizona Historical Society, MS 1189, Arthur Woodward Papers, 1898–1986, 1860s–1980s (bulk 1920s–1960s), 263.

3. Barbara Loomis, "Santa Rosa Island, November–December 1941: Thursday, December 4," unpublished journal entry, original journals in Arizona Historical Society, MS 1189, Arthur Woodward Papers, 1898–1986, 1860s–1980s (bulk 1920s–1960s).

4. Ibid.
5. Ibid.
6. Ibid.
7. Ibid.
8. Ibid., "December 6, 1941."
9. Ibid.
10. Ibid.
11. Ibid.
12. Ibid.
13. Ibid.
14. Ibid.
15. Ibid.
16. Ibid
17. Ibid.
18. Ibid.
19. Ibid.
20. Ibid.
21. Ibid.
22. Couffer, interview with author, 5.
23. Jack Couffer, *Bat Bomb: World War II's Other Secret Weapon* (Austin: University of Texas Press, 1992), 1.
24. Ibid.
25. Jack Couffer, group interview at the Santa Barbara Museum of Natural History, February 21, 2011, 13.
26. Couffer, *Bat Bomb*, 2.
27. Couffer, group interview, 14.
28. Ibid.
29. Couffer, interview with author, 5.
30. Couffer, group interview, 14.
31. Ibid.
32. Ibid.
33. Ibid., 14–15.
34. Couffer, interview with author, 5.
35. John Johnson, email communication with author, March 25, 2011.
36. Ibid.
37. Leslie A. Reeder, Torben C. Rick, and Jon M. Erlandson, "Forty Years Later: What Have We Learned about the Earliest Human Occupations of Santa Rosa Island, California?," *North American Archaeologist* 29, no. 1 (2008): 42. Orr's estimate, when calibrated to adjust radiocarbon years to calendar years before present, would make his dates significantly older (one or two thousand years or more) than reported. Calibration was not a research protocol during Orr's professional career.

38. Jon M. Erlandson et al., "The Kelp Highway Hypothesis: Marine Ecology, the Coastal Migration Theory, and the Peopling of the Americas," *The Journal of Island and Coastal Archaeology* 2, no. 2 (2007): 162.

39. Amy E. Gusick, and Jon M. Erlandson, "Paleocoastal Landscapes, Marginality, and Initial Settlement of California's Islands," in *An Archaeology of Abundance: Reevaluating the Marginality of California's Islands*, edited by Kristina M. Gill, Mikael Fauvelle, and Jon M. Erlandson, (Gainesville: University Press of Florida, 2019).

40. Jon M. Erlandson, Torben C. Rick, and Todd J. Braje, "Fishing up the Food Web?: 12,000 Years of Maritime Subsistence and Adaptive Adjustments on California's Channel Islands," *Pacific Science* 63, no. 4 (2009): 712.

41. Tom D. Dillehay et al., "New Archaeological Evidence for an Early Human Presence at Monte Verde, Chile," *PLOS One* 10, no. 11 (2015): e0141923.

42. Arthur Woodward, "Archaeological and Historical Fieldwork," 133.

43. Barbara Loomis, "Santa Rosa Island, November–December 1941: Sunday, December 7, 1941."

44. Ibid.

45. Ibid.

46. Ibid., "December 8, 1941."

47. Ibid.

48. Ibid.

49. Ibid., "December 9, 1941."

50. Ibid.

51. Ibid.

52. Ibid.

53. Ibid.

54. Ibid., "December 10, 1941."

55. Ibid.

56. Couffer, interview with author, 7.

57. Ibid.

58. Board of governors meeting minutes, December 18, 1941, 150, NHM Archives.

59. Ibid., 151.

60. Ibid.

61. John A. Comstock to Sergeant Jack C. von Bloeker Jr., Lowry Field, Denver, Colorado, November 8, 1945, NHM Archives.

EPILOGUE

1. LACM weekly newsletter, science division, "Santa Rosa Island Party Returns," December 18, 1941, NHM Archives.

2. Louie Marincovich, "Obituary, George Paul Kanakoff, 1897–1973," *Malacological Review* 7 (1974): 64.

3. Meryl B. Dunkle, "The Byways of Life," in *Songs of the Trail* (New York: Exposition Press, 1964), dedication page.

4. Charles A. Drost and Steven A. Junak, "Colonizers, Waifs, and Stowaways: Arrival of New Plant Species on Santa Barbara Island over a 30-Year Period," in *Proceedings of the Seventh California Islands Symposium*, edited by C. C. Damiani and D. K. Garcelon, (Arcata: Institute for Wildlife Studies 2009), 217.

5. Jerry A. Powell, "Don Meadows, Nearly Forgotten as a Lepidopterist," *Journal of the Lepidopterists Society* 6, no. 1 (2007): 50, 52.

6. Ibid., 53.

7. Ibid.

8. John Adams Comstock to Don Meadows, November 5, 1965, Don Meadows Papers (MS-R001), UC Irvine, Special Collections & Archives.

9. Bob Cunningham, "Art Woodward: Maverick Southwesterner," *The Journal of Arizona History* 33, no. 3 (1992): 301, NHM Archives.

10. René L. Vellanoweth, "Archaeology, *Island of the Blue Dolphins*, and the Lone Woman of San Nicolas Island," in Scott O'Dell, *Island of the Blue Dolphins: The Complete Reader's Edition*, edited by Sara L. Schwebel (Oakland, University of California Press, 2016), 205.

11. Phyllis Van Doren, "Remembering Doc Comstock," 19, NHM Archives.

12. Ibid.

13. A. W. Bell to Jack von Bloeker Jr., August 12, 1944, Santa Barbara Museum of Natural History, Vertebrate Zoology Department.

14. Jim Dines, email communication with author, March 29, 2017.

15. Diane Haithman, "Chief Named for Museums," *Los Angeles Times* (Los Angeles, California), September 6, 2001, 42.

16. DISCO (Diversity Initiative for the Southern California Ocean) is a joint effort between several museum departments, the Smithsonian, and community scientists that will result in barcoded DNA samples of thousands of ocean creatures. This project hopes to understand biodiversity in the ocean simply by taking water samples and then sorting out the DNA found within them.

17. Lori Bettison-Varga, president and director of the NHM, interview with author, March 23, 2018.

18. Examples include the recent tattoo exhibit, which collaborated with local Los Angeles tattoo artists in order to integrate modern tattoo practices, art, and social culture with ancient traditions, artifacts, and photographs evidencing the past. This exhibit succeeded in introducing a whole new community of people to the museum who may not otherwise have visited. Another example is a project initiated because parents in underserved areas wanted to keep their children engaged throughout the summer months. NHM heard about this need and responded by collaborating with the Los Angeles Department of Parks and Recreation to help teachers develop science-based programs. The result was ESTEAM, a program that creates esteem within children by teaching them about science, technology, engineering, arts, and math.

19. Jane Pisano, former president and director of the NHM, interview with author, April 27, 2018.

20. L. Mark Raab et al., *California Maritime Archaeology: A San Clemente Island Perspective* (Lanham, Maryland: AltaMira Press, 2009), 45.

SELECT BIBLIOGRAPHY

Agenbroad, Larry D. "Channel Islands (USA) Pygmy Mammoths (*Mammuthus exilis*) Compared and Contrasted with *M. Columbi*, Their Continental Ancestral Stock." In *The World of Elephants—International Congress*, 473–75. Rome, 2001.

Agenbroad, Larry D., John R. Johnson, Don Morris, and Thomas W. Stafford Jr. "Mammoths and Humans as Late Pleistocene Contemporaries on Santa Rosa Island." In *Proceedings of the Sixth California Islands Symposium*, edited by D. A. Garcelon and C. A. Schwemm, 3–7. Arcata: Institute for Wildlife Studies, 2005.

Bell, A. W. "Reorganization at the Los Angeles Museum." *Science* 94, no. 2437 (1941): 255—56.

Braje, Todd J. *Shellfish for the Celestial Empire: The Rise and Fall of Commercial Abalone Fishing in California*. Salt Lake City: University of Utah Press, 2016.

Braje, Todd J., Tom D. Dillehay, Jon M. Erlandson, Richard G. Klein, and Torben C. Rick. "Finding the First Americans." *Science* 358, no. 6363 (2017): 592–94.

Braje, Todd J., Julia G. Costello, Jon M. Erlandson, Michael A. Glassow, John R. Johnson, Don P. Morris, Jennifer E. Perry, and Torben C. Rick. *Channel Islands National Park Archaeological Overview and Assessment*. Ventura: Cultural Resource Division, Channel Islands National Park, 2010.

Brown, Kaitlin. "Crafting Identity: Acquisition, Production, Use, and Recycling of Soapstone during the Mission Period in Alta California." *American Antiquity* 82, no. 2 (2018): 244–62.

Cameron, Constance. "Animal Effigies from Coastal Southern California." *Pacific Coast Archaeological Society Quarterly* 36, no. 2 (2000): 30–52.

Chiles, Frederic Caire. *California's Channel Islands: A History*. Norman: University of Oklahoma Press, 2015.

———. *Justinian Caire and Santa Cruz Island: The Rise and Fall of a California Dynasty*. Norman, Oklahoma: The Arthur H. Clark Company, an imprint of the University of Oklahoma Press, 2011.

Clayton, John. "Nine Years in 'Solitary.'" *Los Angeles Times*, December 11, 1938.

Comstock, John A. "Contributions from the Los Angeles Museum–Channel Islands Biological Survey, 33: Brief Notes on the Expeditions Conducted between March 16, 1940 and December 14, 1941." *Bulletin of the Southern California Academy of Sciences* 45, part 2 (1946): 94–107.

———. "Contributions from the Los Angeles Museum–Channel Islands Biological Survey, 26: A New Race of Arachnis Picta from Santa Catalina Island." *Bulletin of the Southern California Academy of Sciences* 41, part 2 (May–August 1942): 83–85.

Coonan, Timothy J., Catherin A. Schwemm, and David K. Garcelon. *Decline and Recovery of the Island Fox: A Case Study for Population Recovery*. Cambridge: Cambridge University Press, 2010.

Couffer, Jack. *Bat Bomb: World War II's Other Secret Weapon*. Austin: University of Texas Press, 1992.

Cunningham, Bob. "Art Woodward: Maverick Southwesterner." *Journal of Arizona History* 33, no. 3 (1992): 295–310.

Dillehay, Tom D., Carlos Ocampo, José Saavedra, Andre Oliveira Sawakuchi, Rodrigo M. Vega, Mario Pino, Michael B. Collins, et al. "New Archaeological Evidence for an Early Human Presence at Monte Verde, Chile." *PLOS One* 10, no. 11 (2015): e0141923.

Dixon, Keith A. "Early History of SWAA." Reference found under section entitled "Purposes." *Southwestern Anthropological Association* 22 (2018): 1–5. https://swaa-anthro.org/early-history-of-swaa/.

Drost, Charles A., and Steven A. Junak. "Colonizers, Waifs, and Stowaways: Arrival of New Plant Species on Santa Barbara Island over a 30-Year Period." In *Proceedings of the Seventh California Islands Symposium*, edited by C. C. Damiani and D. K. Garcelon, 215–28. Arcata: Institute for Wildlife Studies, 2009.

Dunkle, Meryl B. "Contributions from the Los Angeles Museum–Channel Islands Biological Survey, 21: New Plants from the Channel Islands." *Bulletin of the Southern California: Academy of Sciences* 39, part 2 (May–August 1940): 175–78.

———. "The Byways of Life." In *Songs of the Trail*. New York: Exposition Press, 1964.

Erlandson, Jon M., Douglas J. Kennett, B. Lynn Ingram, Daniel A. Guthrie, Don P. Morris, Mark A. Tveskov, G. James West, and Phillip L. Walker. "An Archaeological and Paleontological Chronology for Daisy Cave (CA-SMI-261), San Miguel Island, California." *Radiocarbon* 38, no. 2 (1996): 355–73.

Erlandson, Jon M., Torben C. Rick, Todd J. Braje, Molly Casperson, Brendan Culleton, Brian Fulfrost, Tracy Garcia, et al. "Paleoindian Seafaring, Maritime Technologies, and Coastal Foraging on California's Channel Islands." *Science* 331, no. 6021 (2011): 1181–85.

Erlandson, Jon M., Douglas J. Kennett, Richard J. Behl, and Ian Hough. "The Cico Chert Source on San Miguel Island, California." *Journal of California and Great Basin Anthropology* (1997): 124–30.

Erlandson, Jon M., Kristina M. Gill, Michael A. Glassow, and Amy E. Gusick. "Three Paleocoastal Lithic Sites on Santa Cruz Island, California." *PaleoAmerica* 2, no. 1 (2016): 52–55.

Erlandson, Jon M., Lisa Thomas-Barnett, René L. Vellanoweth, Steven J. Schwartz, and Daniel R. Muhs. "From the *Island of the Blue Dolphins*: A Unique Nineteenth-Century Cache Feature from San Nicolas Island, California." *Journal of Island and Coastal Archaeology* 8, no. 1 (2013): 66–78.

Erlandson, Jon M., Michael H. Graham, Bruce J. Bourque, Debra Corbett, James A. Estes, and Robert S. Steneck. "The Kelp Highway Hypothesis: Marine Ecology, the Coastal Migration Theory, and the Peopling of the Americas." *Journal of Island and Coastal Archaeology* 2, no. 2 (2007): 161–74.

Erlandson, Jon M., Torben C. Rick, and Nicholas P. Jew. "Wima Chert: 12,000 Years of Lithic Resource Use on California's Northern Channel Islands." *Journal of California and Great Basin Anthropology* (2012): 76–85.

Erlandson, Jon M., Torben C. Rick, and Todd J. Braje. "Fishing up the Food Web?: 12,000 Years of Maritime Subsistence and Adaptive Adjustments on California's Channel Islands." *Pacific Science* 63, no. 4 (2009): 711–24.

Glassow, Michael A. "The Occurrence of Red Abalone Shells in Northern Channel Island Archaeological Middens: Implications for Climatic Reconstruction." In *Third California Islands Symposium: Recent Advances in Research on the California Islands*, edited by F. G. Hochberg, 567–76. Santa Barbara: Santa Barbara Museum of Natural History, 1993.

Golla, Victor. "Linguistic Prehistory." In *California Prehistory Colonization, Culture, and Complexity*, edited by Terry L. Jones and Kathryn A. Klar. Lanham, New York: AltaMira Press, 54.

Gusick, Amy E., and Jon M. Erlandson. "Paleocoastal Landscapes, Marginality, and Initial Settlement of California's Islands." In *An Archaeology of Abundance: Reevaluating the Marginality of California's Islands*, edited by Kristina M. Gill, Mikael Fauvelle, and Jon M. Erlandson, 59–97. Gainesville: University of Florida Press, 2019.

Gusick, Amy E. "The Early Holocene Occupation of Santa Cruz Island." In *California's Channel Islands: The Archaeology of Human-Environment Interactions*, edited by Christopher S. Jazwa and Jennifer E. Perry, 40–59. Salt Lake City: University of Utah Press, 2013.

Charles Hillinger. *The California Islands*. Los Angeles: Academy Publishers, 1958.

Hofman, Courtney A., Torben C. Rick, Jesús E. Maldonado, Paul W. Collins, Jon M. Erlandson, Robert C. Fleischer, Chelsea Smith, et al. "Tracking the Origins and Diet of an Endemic Island Canid (*Urocyon littoralis*) across 7,300 Years of Human Cultural and Environmental Change." *Quaternary Science Reviews* 146 (2016): 147–60.

Hofman, Courtney A., Torben C. Rick, Melissa T. R. Hawkins, W. Chris Funk, Katherine Ralls, Christina L. Boser, Paul W. Collins, et al. "Mitochondrial Genomes Suggest Rapid Evolution of Dwarf California Channel Islands Foxes (*Urocyon littoralis*)." *PLOS One* 10, no. 2 (2015): e0118240.

Howald, Gregg R., Kate R. Faulkner, Bernie Tershy, Bradford Keitt, Holly Gellerman, Creel, Eileen M., Matthew Grinnell, Steven T. Ortega, and Donald A. Croll. "Eradication of Black Rats from Anacapa Island Biological and Social Considerations." In *Proceedings of the Sixth California Channel Islands Symposium*, edited by David K. Garcelon and Catherin A. Schwemm, 299–312. Arcata: Institute for Wildlife Studies, 2005.

Howard, Hildegarde. "George Willett: May 28, 1879–August 2, 1945." *Condor* 48 (1946): 49–71.

Kennett, Douglas J., John R. Johnson, Torben C. Rick, Don P. Morris, and Juliet Christy. "Historic Chumash Settlement on Eastern Santa Cruz Island, Southern California." *Journal of California and Great Basin Anthropology* (2000): 212–22.

Kiff, Lloyd F. "Historical Changes in Resident Populations of California Islands Raptors." In *The California Islands: Proceedings of a Multidisciplinary Symposium*, edited by Dennis Power, 651–74. Santa Barbara: Santa Barbara Museum of Natural History, 1980.

Kroeber, A. L., *Handbook of the Indians of California*. New York: Dover Publications, Inc., 1976, originally published by Government Printing Office in Washington, DC, Bulletin 78, 1925.

Lester, Elizabeth Sherman. *The Legendary King of San Miguel: The Lesters at Rancho Rambouillet*. Santa Barbara: W. T. Genns, 1974.

Marincovich, Louie. "Obituary, George Paul Kanakoff, 1897–1973." *Malacological Review* 7 (1974): 63–64.

Marsa, Linda. "Reinterpreting an Ancient Island." *American Archaeology* 17, no. 4 (Winter 2013–2014): 19–23.

Martinez, Desireé R., Wendy G. Teeter, and Karimah Kennedy-Richardson. "Returning the *tataayiyam honuuka'* (Ancestors) to the Correct Home: The Importance of Background Investigations for NAGPRA Claims." *Curator: The Museum Journal* 57, no. 2 (2014): 199–211.

Martz, Patricia C. "Prehistoric Settlement and Subsistence on San Nicolas Island." In *Proceedings of the Sixth California Islands Symposium, Ventura, California, December 1–3, 2003*, edited by Dave Garcelon and Catherin A. Schwemm, 65–82. Arcata: Institute for Wildlife Studies, 2003.

McKusick, Marshall Bassford, Richard Van Valkenburg, Charles E. Rozaire, and B. K. Swartz. *Introduction to Anacapa Island Archaeology*. Los Angeles: University of California, Los Angeles, Department of Anthropology-Sociology, 1959.

Meighan, C. "Rock Art on the Channel Islands of California." *Pacific Coast Archaeological Society Quarterly* 36, no. 2 (2000): 15–29.

Morgan, Ron. "An Account of the Discovery of a Whale-Bone House on San Nicolas Island." *Journal of California and Great Basin Anthropology* 1, no. 1 (1979): 171–77.

Moure, Nancy. "The Struggle for a Los Angeles Art Museum, 1890–1940." *Southern California Quarterly* 74, no. 3 (1992): 247–75. doi:10.2307/41171631.

Myers, Leslie Reeder, Jon Erlandson, Daniel R. Muhs, and Torben Rick. "Sea Level, Paleogeography, and Archeology on California's Northern Channel Islands." *Quaternary Research* 83, no. 2 (2015): 263–72.

O'Dell, Scott. *Island of the Blue Dolphins: The Complete Reader's Edition*, edited by Sara L. Schwebel. Oakland: University of California Press, 2016.

Pacific Slope Section of the Lepidopterists' Society. "John Adams Comstock Award." 26th Annual Meeting. Davis: University of California: August 26, 1979.

Perry, Jennifer E. "Chumash Ritual and Sacred Geography on Santa Cruz Island, California." *Journal of California and Great Basin Anthropology* (2007): 103–24.

———. "The Archaeology of Ritual on the Channel Islands." In *California's Channel Islands: The Archaeology of Human-Environment Interactions*, edited by Christopher S. Jazwa and Jennifer E. Perry, 137–55. Salt Lake City: University of Utah Press, 2013.

Perry, Jennifer E., and Michael A. Glassow. "Prehistoric Settlement in Island Interiors: Evidence from California's Santa Cruz Island." *Journal of Island and Coastal Archaeology* 10, no. 2 (2015): 184–206.

Pierce, Dwight D. "Contributions from the Los Angeles Museum–Channel Islands Biological Survey, 9: A Rare Myriapod from Anacapa Island, Compared with Two Texas Species." *Bulletin of the Southern California Academy of Sciences* 39, part 2 (May–August 1940): 158–71.

———. "Contributions from the Los Angeles Museum–Channel Islands Biological Survey, 18: A Strepsipterous Parasite of a Leaf Hopper, with Descriptions of Related Species from the Same Host Genus." *Bulletin of the Southern California Academy of Sciences* 40, part 1 (January–April 1941): 1–12.

Powell, Jerry A. "Don Meadows, Nearly Forgotten as a Lepidopterist." *Journal of the Lepidopterists Society* 61, no. 1 (2007): 50–54.

Raab, L. Mark, Jim Cassidy, Andrew Yatsko, and William J. Howard. *California Maritime Archaeology: A San Clemente Island Perspective*. Plymouth, United Kindgom: AltaMira Press, 2009.

Reeder, Leslie A., and Torben C. Rick. "New Perspectives on the Archaeology of Anacapa Island, California: Preliminary Research at ANI-2." *Proceedings of the Society for California Archaeology* 21 (2009): 119–23.

Rick, Torben C. "8,000 Years of Human Settlement and Land Use in Old Ranch Canyon, Santa Rosa Island, California." In *Proceedings of the Seventh California Islands Symposium*, edited by C. C. Damiani and D. K. Garcelon, 21–31. Arcata: Institute for Wildlife Studies, 2009.

———. "A 5,000-Year Record of Coastal Settlement on Anacapa Island, California." *Journal of California and Great Basin Anthropology* (2006): 65–72.

———. "Historic Period Chumash Occupation of 'Anayapax, Anacapa Island, Alta California." *California Archaeology* 3, no. 2 (2011): 273–84.

———. "Household and Community Archaeology at the Chumash Village of Niaqla, Santa Rosa Island, California." *Journal of Field Archaeology* 32, no. 3 (2007): 243–63.

———. "Introduction: New Directions in Channel Islands Archaeology." *Pacific Coast Archaeological Society Quarterly* 37, no. 3 (Summer 2001): 1–9.

Rick, Torben C., Courtney A. Hofman, Todd J. Braje, Jesús E. Maldonado, T. Scott Sillett, Kevin Danchisko, and Jon M. Erlandson. "Flightless Ducks, Giant Mice and Pygmy Mammoths: Late Quaternary Extinctions on California's Channel Islands." *World Archaeology* 44, no. 1 (2012): 3–20.

Rick, Torben C., Jon M. Erlandson, Nicholas P. Jew, and Leslie A. Reeder-Myers. "Archaeological Survey, Paleogeography, and the Search for Late Pleistocene Paleocoastal Peoples of Santa Rosa Island, California." *Journal of Field Archaeology* 38, no. 4 (2013): 324–31.

Rick, Torben C., Jon M. Erlandson, René L. Vellanoweth, and Todd J. Braje. "From Pleistocene Mariners to Complex Hunter-Gatherers: The Archaeology of the California Channel Islands." *Journal of World Prehistory* 19, no. 3 (2005): 169–228.

Rick, Torben C., Phillip L. Walker, Lauren M. Willis, Anna C. Noah, Jon M. Erlandson, René L. Vellanoweth, Todd J. Braje, and Douglas J. Kennett. "Dogs, Humans and Island Ecosystems: The Distribution, Antiquity and Ecology of Domestic Dogs (*Canis familiaris*) on California's Channel Islands, USA." *Holocene* 18, no. 7 (2008): 1077–87.

Rick, Torben C., and Leslie Reeder-Myers. "Deception Island: Archaeology of 'Anyapax, Anacapa Island, California." *Smithsonian Contributions to Anthropology* 52. Smithsonian Scholarly Press, Washington, DC, 2018.

Roberti, Betsy Lester. *San Miguel Island: My Childhood Memoir, 1930–1942.* Santa Barbara: Santa Cruz Island Foundation, 2008.

"San Clemente Loggerhead Shrike *Lanius ludovicianus mearnsi*; 5-Year Review: Summary and Evaluation." Carlsbad: U.S. Fish and Wildlife Service Carlsbad Fish and Wildlife Office, June 17, 2009. https://www.fws.gov/carlsbad/SpeciesStatusList/5YR/20090617_5YR_SCLS.pdf

Schoenherr, Allan A., C. Robert Feldmeth, and Michael J. Emerson. *Natural History of the Islands of California.* Vol. 61. Berkeley and Los Angeles: University of California Press, 2003.

Schwartz, Steven J. "Seven Short Weeks: The Lone Woman's Time in Santa Barbara." Paper presented at the 9th California Island Symposium, Ventura, California, October 2016.

Schwartz, Steven J. "Some Observations on the Material Culture of the Nicoleño." In *Proceedings of the Sixth California Islands Symposium, Ventura, California, December 1–3,*

2003, edited by Dave Garcelon and Catherin A. Schwemm, 83–91. Arcata: Institute for Wildlife Studies, 2005.

Semprebon, Gina M., Florent Rivals, Julia M. Fahlke, William J. Sanders, Adrian M. Lister, and Ursula B. Göhlich. "Dietary Reconstruction of Pygmy Mammoths from Santa Rosa Island of California." *Quaternary International* 406 (2016): 123–36.

Strudwick, Ivan H. "The Native Depopulation of Santa Catalina Island." In *California's Channel Islands: The Archaeology of Human-Environment Interactions*, edited by Christopher S. Jazwa and Jennifer E. Perry, 172–89. Salt Lake City: University of Utah Press, 2013.

Teeter, Wendy G., Desireé Reneé Martinez, and Karimah O. Kennedy-Richardson. "Cultural Landscapes of Santa Catalina Island." In *California's Channel Islands: The Archaeology of Human-Environment Interactions*, edited by Christopher S. Jazwa and Jennifer E. Perry, 156–71. Salt Lake City: University of Utah Press, 2013.

Thomson, Keith Stewart. *Living Fossil: The Story of the Coelacanth*. New York: WW Norton & Company, 1992.

Tsosie, Rebecca. "Indigenous Rights and Archaeology." In *Native Americans and Archaeologists: Stepping Stones to Common Ground*, edited by Nina Swidler, Kurt E. Donogoske, Roger Anyon, and Alan S. Downer, 67–76. Walnut Cree: AltaMira Press, 1997.

Van Rossem, A. J. "A Survey of the Song Sparrows of the Santa Barbara Islands." *Condor* 26, no. 6 (1924): 217–20.

Vellanoweth, René L. "Archaeology, *Island of the Blue Dolphins*, and the Lone Woman of San Nicolas Island." In Scott O'Dell, *Island of the Blue Dolphins: The Complete Reader's Edition*, edited by Sara L. Schwebel. Oakland: University of California Press, 2016.

von Bloeker, Jack C., Jr. "Contributions from the Los Angeles Museum–Channel Islands Biological Survey, 22: A New Subspecies of White-Footed Mouse from the Anacapa Islands, California." *Bulletin of the Southern California Academy of Sciences* 40, part 3 (September–December 1941): 161–62.

———. "Contributions from the Los Angeles Museum–Channel Islands Biological Survey, 23: A New Shrew from Santa Catalina Island, California." *Bulletin of the Southern California Academy of Sciences* 40, part 3 (September–December, 1941): 163–64.

Waters, Minnie. "Mrs. Waters' Diary of Her Life on San Miguel Island January 1–June 27, 1888." Santa Barbara: Santa Cruz Island Foundation, occasional paper no. 4, 1990 (1995).

von Kleinsmid, Rufus Bernhard. "Eugenics and the State." Indiana Reformatory Printing Trade School, 1913.

White, E. I., "One of the Most Amazing Events in the Realm of Natural History in the Twentieth Century." *London Illustrated News*, March 11, 1939. Quoted in Keith Stewart Thomson, *Living Fossil: The Story of the Coelacanth*. New York: WW Norton & Company, 1992.

Whitworth, D. L., H. R. Carter and D. M. Mazurkiewicz. "Scripps's Murrelet Nest Monitoring at Anacapa Island, California in 2014: Continued Recovery 12 Years after Eradication of Black Rats." Unpublished report, California Institute of Environmental Studies, Davis, California (prepared for the American Trader Trustee Council, National Fish and Wildlife Foundation, and Channel Islands National Park), 2015.

Woodward, Ken. *Rubaboo: The Story of Arthur Woodward—Adventurer, Historian, Archaeologist—Who Was Driven by His Need to Know*. San Diego, California: Ken Woodward, 2014.

Woolley, Will. "Maritime Ranching on Santa Rosa Island." In *Island of the Cowboys: Santa Rosa Island*, edited by Kerry Blankenship Allen, 107–13. Santa Barbara: Santa Cruz Island Foundation, 1996, printed by Kimberly Press, Inc., Goleta, California.

Yatsko, Andrew. "From Sheepherders to Cruise Missiles: A Short History of Archaeological Research at San Clemente Island." *Pacific Coast Archaeological Society Quarterly* 36, no. 1 (2000): 18–24.

———. "Reassessing Archaeological Site Density at San Clemente Island." *Proceedings of the Society for California Archaeology* 2 (1989): 187–204.

INDEX

Page numbers printed in *italics* refer to figures, maps, or photographs.

Los Angeles County Museum of History,
Science, and Art (LACM): approval
of CIBS by board of governors, 50;
Comstock's office at, 40–41; direction of after end of CIBS, 331–35; and
funding of second CIBS expedition,
75–76; McKinney's arrival at, 111;
media and public response to reorganization of, 277–82; meeting on
future of CIBS after reorganization
of, 283–89; Napoleon exhibit in 1940
and World War II, 226; newspaper
coverage of in 1939, 191; and ownership of specimens collected by CIBS,
115, 116; reorganization of, 46–49, 205,
206–7, 217–18, 220, 246–47, 268–69,
271–76, 318; von Bloeker's career at,
102; and Woodward as director of
history and anthropology, 24. See also
Channel Islands Biological Survey
Los Angeles Examiner, 114
Los Angeles Herald Express, 243
Los Angeles Illustrated Daily News, 278,
280
Los Angeles Times, 44, 76, 77, 169, 191, 243
lupine (Lupinus moranii), 261

MacArthur, Robert, 7
mammals, and ecology of Santa Catalina Island, 254. See also bats; bison;
cat(s); cattle; Channel Islands fox;
Channel Islands spotted skunks;
deer mice; dogs; elk; goats; mammoths; mule deer; rabbits; racoons;
sea mammals; sheep; shrews; white-
footed mouse
mammoths, and Channel Islands, 5–11,
171, 293, 305
Martin, Lloyd, 16, 22–24, 77, 79, 92–93, 81,
94, 116, 117, 124, 125, 186, 189, 202, 261,
319, 327, 334
material culture, and Kroeber's influence
on archaeology, 34
McKinney, Roland J., 112: career of after
end of CIBS, 331; Comstock and
management of LACM, 111, 114;
and future of CIBS after LACM

reorganization, 283, 285–89, 298;
LACM's decision to hire, 75–76; and
proposals to reduce science department of LACM, 246–47, 268–69; and
publicity for LACM in 1939, 191, 205;
and reorganization of LACM, 205,
206–7, 217–18, 220, 265, 271–76, 280,
318
Meadows, Donald C., 81, 94, 186, 189,
319, 334: and All Eight Club, 16; and
CIBS expedition to Anacapa Island,
227, 231; and CIBS expeditions to San
Clemente Island, 22–23, 24, 25, 70, 71,
73, 77, 93, 202; and CIBS expedition
to San Miguel Island, 145, 154–55,
156, 157; and CIBS expeditions to San
Nicolas Island, 116, 117–18, 124, 127,
140–41, 209; and CIBS expedition to
Santa Barbara Island, 96, 99, 100–101;
and CIBS expedition to Santa Cruz
Island, 173; and CIBS expedition to
Santa Rosa Island, 166; early life of,
44–45; letters to Comstock at end of
1940 field year, 232–40; life and career
of after end of CIBS, 324–25; and
origins of CIBS, 15, 39, 45–46, 49, 50,
52; personal collection of, 115–16; and
planning of future CIBS expeditions
in fall of 1939, 111, 113–14; and position as LACM staff, 226;
Mexico, and history of Channel Islands,
13–14, 181, 256. See also Guadalupe
Hidalgo, Treaty of; Spain
middens: and San Clemente Island,
89–90; and San Nicolas Island, 132,
133; and Santa Barbara Island, 99; and
Santa Cruz Island, 187
Middle Ranch (Santa Catalina Island),
265
military. See Coast Guard; Navy
Miller, Alden, 275–76
Millikan, Robert A., 48
missions (Spanish), removal of Channel
Islands indigenous peoples to, 56, 58,
118, 120, 176
mobile settlement strategy, of Chumash
on Santa Cruz Island, 177

internment camps for Japanese-Americans, 193; and military use of San Nicolas Island, 124; Pearl Harbor and awareness of by CIBS participants, 313–16; and tourism to Santa Catalina Island, 256; von Bloeker and Couffer's involvement in bat bomb project during, 105, 328
Wrigley, Philip, 256

Wrigley, William, Jr., 14–15, 255

Xaxas (Chumash village), and Santa Cruz Island, 179, 180, 181

Yellowtail (ship), 76, 77, 78, 227, 294–95

Zoological Society of San Diego, 70